THE OTHER RUSSIA

THE OTHER RUSSIA

MICHAEL GLENNY
AND NORMAN STONE

VIKING

VIKING
Published by the Penguin Group
Viking Penguin, a division of Penguin Books USA Inc.,
375 Hudson Street, New York, New York 10014, U.S.A.
Penguin Books Ltd, 27 Wrights Lane,
London W8 5TZ, England
Penguin Books Australia Ltd, Ringwood,
Victoria, Australia
Penguin Books Canada Ltd, 2801 John Street,
Markham, Ontario, Canada L3R 1B4
Penguin Books (N.Z.) Ltd, 182–190 Wairau Road,
Auckland 10, New Zealand

Penguin Books Ltd, Registered Offices:
Harmondsworth, Middlesex, England

First American Edition
Published in 1991 by Viking Penguin,
a division of Penguin Books USA Inc.

10 9 8 7 6 5 4 3 2 1

LIBRARY OF CONGRESS CATALOGING IN PUBLICATION DATA
Glenny, Michael.
The other Russia: the experience of exile/Michael Glenny and
Norman Stone.
p.   cm.
Includes biographical references (p.   ) and index.
ISBN 0-670-83593-5
1. Russians—Foreign countries—Biography.   2. Russian S.F.S.R.—
Exiles—Biography   3. Soviet Union—Exiles—Biography.
4. Refugees. Political—Soviet Union—Biography.   I. Stone, Norman.
II. Title.
DK35.5.G53   1991
909′.049171082—dc20   90–50409

Printed in the United States of America
Set in Times Roman
Map by Capricorn Design

This book is dedicated to all those who once lived in Russia and patiently told us the stories of their lives.

Contents

Acknowledgements

For reasons of space and editorial exigency it has been possible to include only approximately one-third of the contributions so willingly provided by our informants. The authors wish to thank *all* those who told us the stories of their lives; even if they were not incorporated into the final published text, every contribution without exception was of the greatest value in enabling us to build a total picture of Russian emigration since 1917. Without this, it would have been impossible to write this book.

The authors' special thanks are due to the Markish family: Madame Esther Markish, Dr Simon Markish and Mr David Markish, whose generous help in enabling the authors to meet a large number of their informants greatly assisted the gathering of material for this book.

The authors are grateful to Christine Stone, whose idea this was and who has been extremely helpful with the long job of editing; Louise Pim, who helped to shape a very difficult manuscript; Brenda Thomson, who after heroic labours put the manuscript into its final form; Richard Davies of the Leeds Russian Archive; Professor Marc Raeff; Sir Isaiah and Lady Berlin; Dr Harold Shukman; Dr Michael Heller; Mr and Mrs Kirill Fitzlyon; Professor and Mrs Lionel Kochan; and the staffs of the Bodleian Library, Oxford, and the School of Slavonic and East European Studies, University of London.

Norman Stone
Michael Glenny
October 1989

A R C T I

SPITSBERGEN

Norwegian Sea

NORWAY

Oslo

DENMARK

SWEDEN

Barents Sea

NOVAYA ZEMLYA

Kara Sea

WEST GERMANY

Copenhagen

Stockholm

Kuusamo

Murmansk

EAST GERMANY

Berlin

Baltic Sea

FINLAND

Prague

Gdansk (Danzig)

Ventspils

Liepāja

Helsinki

Imatra

POLAND

LITHUANIA

Riga

Tallinn

Vyborg

L. Ladoga

CZECHOSLOVAKIA

Warsaw

Vilnius

LATVIA

ESTONIA

Kronstadt

Leningrad (St Petersburg)

Arkhangel

Lublin

Brest

Luga

Novogorod

HUNGARY

Lvov

Dubno

Minsk

BYELORUSSIA

R Dnieper

Kamenets-Polodsky

Zhitomir

Gomel

River Ob

ROMANIA

Chernovtsy

Vinnitsa

Bershad

Kiev

Chernigov

Moscow

Zagorsk

Kirov

River Volga

U   R   A   L   S

S   I   B   E   R   I   A

Bucharest

MOLDAVIA

Kishinev

Smela

Ryazan

Gorky

Orël

Perm

Constanta

Odessa

Poltava

Kursk

River Don

MORDOVIA

Kazan

Sverdlovsk (Ekaterinburg)

Kherson

Kharkov

Tambov

Saransk

Ufa

Istanbul (Constantinople)

Simferopol

Sevastopol

Yalta

CRIMEA

Donetsk

DONBASS

Sea of Azov

Saratov

Ulyanovsk

River Irtysh

Rostov-on-Don

R. Don

River Volga

Volgograd (Stalingrad)

Orenburg

Magnitogorsk

Chelyabinsk

Omsk

Black Sea

Novorossiysk

KUBAN

Kropotkin

Astrakhan

Novosibirsk

TURKEY

Armavir

GEORGIA

Kislovodsk

Batum

ARMENIA

Tbilisi

AZERBAYDZHAN

Derbent

Caspian Sea

KAZAKHSTAN

Aral Sea

Semipalatinsk

R. Irtysh

IRAQ

Baku

TURKMENISTAN

UZBEKISTAN

Tehran

Ashkhabad

Tashkent

Frunze

Samarkand

KIRGHIZ

IRAN

TADZHIKISTAN

AFGHANISTAN

Kabul

PAKISTAN

KASHMIR

O C E A N

East Siberian Sea

Bering Strait

Bering Sea

Laptev Sea

River Lena

S I B E R I A

Sea of Okhotsk

River Lena

R. Amur

• Krasnoyarsk

Lake Baykal

River Amur

Birobidzhan

• Khabarovsk

Blagoveshchensk

Irkutsk •

R. Sungari

Harbin

Vladivostok

• Ulan Baatar

Tokyo •

Sea of Japan

J A P A N

MONGOLIA

Beijing (Peking) •

Yellow Sea

C H I N A

Shanghai

East China Sea

Introduction

The poetess Anna Akhmatova remarked that life in the Soviet Union went in alternating periods: there would be a moment of vegetarianism, and then you would be back in the mincing machine. She had long experience of that machine, which took her husband and her son. She herself had the chance to live in the West, but she lived on in the Soviet Union, a literary lady in rather squalid circumstances. She did not like it: she would still be saying of people when she was quite old, 'that is a Soviet man'; and it would not be a term of endearment. On the contrary, 'Soviet' just meant tyranny, inefficiency, starvation, as well as, at the official level, torrents of lies. This was not the Russia which enlightened, educated people in St Petersburg before 1914 had expected to come about. Still, it was Russia, and patriotism kept many people living there (or returning) who might otherwise have emigrated – as, in the vegetarian periods, you could, with difficulty, manage to do.

The emigration of Russians has been one of the major population movements of modern times. The numbers cannot easily be established, since many of the states to which the emigrants went had only rudimentary equipment for counting people and many of the people involved had rather unrevealing travel documents – a Nansen passport, issued to refugees by agencies of the League of Nations; or perhaps the nationality of one or other of the independent republics which emerged from the territory of Tsarist Russia between 1918 and 1939–40. Estimates of the numbers of these emigrants, from 1917 to the present, are not less than three million.

Strangely enough, in the nineteenth century Russians had not made up an important part of the great wave of European emigration over the Atlantic. Jews, Baltic nationalities, Armenians, and Ukrainians from the Habsburg Empire had gone in great numbers; and there had always been an important movement of political exile, although the numbers involved were not very high. Russians (and Ukrainians) moved around the Tsarist Empire a great deal, but not, in large numbers, abroad. In part, this no doubt happened because bureaucrats got in the way – Russia and Turkey were the only countries before 1914 which required passports; more important was the comparative lack of railways to transport you to the nearest port; more important still was lack of money. The cheapest form of Atlantic cross-travel took about a month's wages in England, where wages were much higher than in Russia, and a peasant of Ryazan, even if he had wanted to go, could not have found the fare for the much longer journey. Russia did not have an emigrant culture. Germans or Scots might think of emigration as second nature and be prepared to adapt at once to the ways of 'abroad'; they prospered across the Atlantic, and produced several leading figures of late-nineteenth-century (and twentieth-century) industry. There have, of course, been highly successful Russian emigrants, but the emigration, by and large, laid stress on its Russianness, not on its adaptability.

The great emigration just after the Revolution consisted disproportionately of the educated classes. There were simple soldiers, peasants and Cossacks, but in the – perhaps – two million people who left in the first wave of 1917–21 was a high proportion of people on whom the early Communists declared war – 'former people', as they were called, who had their houses requisitioned, were given the lowest class of rations, were sometimes forced to sell matches in the street to survive, and who were under constant threat of being imprisoned or shot. Officers who fought on the White side in the Civil War of 1918–21 were evacuated in chaotic circumstances from Novorossiysk in March 1920 and then from the Crimea in February 1921.

The International Labour Office calculated – the figure is no doubt not to be trusted – that roughly one million Russians had emigrated to continental Europe: 400,000 to France, which took them in because wartime losses had led to an unusually high demand for labour; 150,000 to Germany, where inflation of the Mark meant that exiles (who included Vladimir Nabokov's family) could survive in decent style; 90,000 to Poland; 40,000 to Latvia; 35,000 to Yugoslavia; and the rest to Bulgaria or Czechoslovakia.

In some of these cases, religious associations or the need of a new state for educated personnel gave the emigrants a reasonable status. In

Czechoslovakia, for instance, President Masaryk gave them a good welcome, and helped to establish both a University Law Faculty and the Russian Foreign Archive, a very valuable collection of documents which was returned to Moscow in 1946. In Bulgaria, Yugoslavia and to some extent in Romania, Orthodoxy helped; the King of the new Yugoslavia (then called the Kingdom of the Serbs, Croats and Slovenes) was violently anti-Communist. But in Western Europe, refugees were treated incomparably more harshly than they are nowadays and, some very rich people apart, many of these Russians had an extremely hard time. Initially, only three thousand made their way to Great Britain (although, of course, there had been a fairly large migration of Jews from the western provinces earlier on).

Right up to the present day, the emigration has continued. A second wave coincided with the end of the Second World War, when people took any opportunity to escape from Stalin's tyranny. A great many of them, this time round, were Ukrainians who had seen the murder by starvation of countless millions of peasants in the famine of 1933 or in the purges that followed in the cities. Their movement is now most active in Canada, and they cannot be straightforwardly classed with the first wave of emigration. A third wave came as the Soviet Union relaxed its treatment of would-be emigrant Jews, and throughout the 1970s and, with interruptions, the 1980s, there has been a notable migration of these Jews – some to Israel, but a large number to the United States, where a 'Little Odessa' joins the 'Little Italy' of New York. The result has been, altogether, a movement of perhaps three million people to countries all over the world: from the aged ladies whom you can still see, aristocratic Edwardian ways and all, at the Russian churches in Emperor's Gate in London or the rue Daru in Paris, to the heavily accented taxi-drivers of Brooklyn who will play the semi-dissident pop-musician Vysotsky on the car tape.

One very striking feature of all three waves – inevitably, of the first more than the others – is the way in which the emigrants have kept together. There is now a kind of émigré international that will look after you in any city in the non-Communist world, and even in some cities of the Communist states in Eastern and Central Europe where some of the emigrants of the 1920s managed to survive. A main reason for this is, of course, that the educated element was strong: there was, from the start, a large infrastructure of book publishing, Russian newspapers, Russian clubs (such as the Pushkin Club in London) and charitable organizations. This has been extended by later emigrants who managed to escape from Stalin or the harsh 'period of stagnation' in the 1970s. It is striking that a very high proportion of the best Soviet writers have had to leave the country: Solzhenitsyn above all, but also Brodsky, Sinyavsky (at the Sorbonne), Maximov, Aksyonov, and Viktor Nekrassov (who decided to go when the police raided his flat, taking away five sacks of 'material', three of them containing back numbers of *Paris Match*). The emigration of so many of the country's most distinguished intellectuals has marked the whole movement from the beginning: Merezhkovsky, Bunin, Berdyayev, Kandinsky, Bely, Tsvetayeva, Prokofiev (although he, like Bely, returned eventually). Sometimes these writers faced a life of greater hardship in the West than, by conforming, they would have had at home: Gaito Gazdanov, for instance, drove a taxi at night in Paris and wrote during the day in a tiny flat.

To write a history of Russian emigration would be a task so complex as to involve a whole team, although we can hope that one day it will be done. The purpose of this present book is different: to illustrate what life was like for some of those emigrants, at various times and in various places, including, where possible, their memories of life in Russia before 1917 or in the Soviet Union afterwards. We have interviewed a great number of people, and others have kindly given us manuscripts of their memoirs so that we could rescue this all-important source from oblivion. 'Oral history' now amounts – rightly – to something of an industry, and tapes of interviews have been built up at various points in the West; below we indicate where these may be found. In this book we cannot present more than a small sample of what such sources can yield. Still, Russian emigrations have been such a story of disaster and resilience that they deserve at least the beginnings of a record.

The sources used for this book are of three types: recorded interviews, manuscripts in personal possession and articles printed in hitherto little-known places.

Of these, the recorded interviews form easily the largest item. They were conducted either by Michael Glenny, in Russian, or by interviewers working under his direction, including Anatole Lieven; the interviews took place in England, France, Israel, Switzerland and the United States. There were over 160 such interviews, but considerations of space have prevented us from using more than one-third of them; and those that are used are themselves severely truncated (in most cases). Transcripts of these interviews have been preserved, and are deposited at the School of Slavonic and East European Studies, University of London, with copies to the Russian Archive, Brotherton Library, University of Leeds. In editing the recorded interviews, all the questions have been omitted. Sometimes, for the sake of continuity in the text, part of an answer has been summarized; this is indicated by square brackets around the summary. Major omissions in the texts are indicated by a row of dots.

The oral history of the Russian emigration has been advanced in a number of places. In England, the Bradford Heritage Recording Unit, Central Library, Bradford, may be consulted; in the United States, the State Department's Soviet Interview Project has resulted in a considerable collection, for which the Library of Congress, Washington, and the Russian Research Center, Harvard University, may be consulted. The Hoover Institution at Stanford, and the Bakhmetev Archive at Columbia University, New York, contain a great amount of manuscript material. A considerable further amount of manuscript material – part of it already sent to the Leeds Russian Archive – may also be found at Nicholas House, 27 Blenheim Road, London W4 1ET, a hostel for refugees established by Mrs April Fitzlyon (Zinoviev). The Bibliothèque Nationale in Paris contains a number of Russian political archives, although many of the French collections appear to have been purloined in 1940, in the period of German occupation and Nazi–Soviet collaboration. In Paris in the early 1970s there was a television recording series on Russian emigrants, the *Archives du 20e siècle*, of which Professor Georges Niva, at the University of Geneva, was historical adviser. A final source, of great importance for the history of the emigration, would be the *Russky zagranichny arkhiv*, now somewhere in Moscow. This archive used to be at the Clementinum, the library of the Charles University of Prague, and contained a formidable amount of manuscripts and documents pertaining to political and military history (I have heard, though cannot guarantee, that the Tsarist and later Red Army General A. A. Brusilov left a second volume of his memoirs in it, one far more critical of the Soviet State than the first, well-known, volume). In 1945 the archive was taken to Moscow, and has not surfaced since.

A bibliography of the Russian emigration would necessarily be enormous, but the subject is now attracting serious work and study of the emigrations is becoming much easier. An authoritative book by Marc Raeff, *Russia Abroad. Cultural History of the Russian Emigration 1919–1939* (Oxford University Press), is appearing in January 1990; and the same author has master-minded a volume of great usefulness: *L'émigration russe. Revues et recueils 1920–1980. Index général des articles* (Paris, Institut d'Études Slaves, 1988). Recent books, with good indications to where further work can be done, are: Robert H. Johnson, *'New Mecca, New Babylon'. Paris and the Russian Exiles 1920–1945* (McGill Queens University Press, 1989); and Lazar Fleischmann, *Russky Berlin 1921–1924* (YMCA Press, Paris, 1984). An excellent account of emigration is to be found in Nina Berbrova, *C'est moi qui souligne* (Actes Sud, 1989). Harold Shukman (ed.), *The Blackwell Encyclopaedia of the Russian Revolution* (Blackwell, 1988), is the most convenient book for points of reference.

It seems more than likely that the Soviet side will open up on the subject of emigrants and returned emigrants. The press, where strongly affected by the current wave of *glasnost*, now publishes again and again on these subjects.

I

Escape in the Ocean

SLAVA KURILOV

*We begin these memoirs with a remarkable story of escape. Slava Kuri-
lov, born in 1936, was a distinguished oceanographer, a one-time
research engineer in the Academy of Sciences in Moscow – a first-rate
worker, as his survival in this minor odyssey shows. He defected in 1975
by jumping ship, and now lives in the United States.*

It happened one unforgettable night several years ago in the Pacific
Ocean near the Philippines.

The deck was no longer under my feet. For several moments I flew
through the air, until I felt the waves parting, gently welcoming me
into their embrace. Coming up to the surface I looked around – and
froze in terror. Beside me, an arm's length away, was the huge hull of
the liner and its gigantic turning propellor. I desperately summoned up
my strength to swim out of reach, but I was held in the dense mass
of stationary water that was coupled to the screw in a mortal grip.
It felt as if the liner had suddenly stopped, yet only a few seconds
ago it had been doing eighteen knots. The terrifying vibrations of
the hellish noise went through my body; the screw seemed to be
alive: it had a maliciously smiling face and held me tight with invisible
arms.

Suddenly something flung me to one side, a whirlwind pounced on
me and I was flying into a yawning abyss . . .

It became very quiet. After the clanking of metal and sickening
vibrations of the ship's hull, the noise of the waves breaking and the
wind howling seemed to me the gentlest of sounds.

Night. A stormy ocean. Where was land? . . . The lights of the liner
moved further and further away. At last I became fully aware that I
was alone in the ocean. There was no one and nothing there to help

me, and my chances of reaching land alive were very slim. Yet at that moment my mind noted philosophically, 'You are now absolutely free!'

I remember a street in a little provincial town, a house and a room where I usually sat at a table unwillingly doing my homework. On the other side of the street was a tall grey fence. I could always see it when my mind wandered from my books and I raised my head. It was like a symbol of what stood between me and my daydreams. Sometimes, with an effort of will, I could wipe it away. I would imagine to myself huge ocean waves rolling over the fence until they gradually wore it down to the ground. Faraway visions opened up before me – white lagoons on a tropical island, palm trees on the shore, a lone sailing ship on the far horizon and the unbounded space of the ocean . . . But when I tired of dreaming and came to myself, that merciless fence was still there.

My patience came to an end on the day when my application for a visa to work on long-distance oceanographic vessels was turned down for the umpteenth time. Usually it was rejected without any reason being given, but this time a note passing sentence on me was attached to my dossier: 'We consider it inexpedient for Comrade Kurilov to visit capitalist states.'

There was only one way out: to flee. Anywhere at all, just to flee. I was living in a state where all the people were shackled to one gigantic, unseen Purpose, by a kind of ideology that was like the curse of an evil sorcerer. I could see fear in the people – in their eyes, in their stance, in their manner of talking, listening and glancing behind.

It was dreadful to see millions of healthy, strong men oppressed by constant fear – and it was terrible to live among them. It is a strange feeling, fear. When fear grips you, you notice with horror how you stop being a human being. All your good qualities are torn away, like autumn leaves, by gusts of fear. I was ripe for the craziest of actions. I was a captive in this country and only a saint can love his prison. Only one possibility remained – to wait for a convenient opportunity and to escape.

The opportunity soon presented itself.

One sad, drizzly day I read by chance in a newspaper that a large passenger liner would be sailing to the Equator with tourists on board. No visas would be needed: the liner would be on the open seas for twenty days without calling in at any foreign port. The cruise was called 'From Winter to Summer' and the passengers were to embark at Vladivostok.

The day of my flight to Vladivostok was in November 1974. Our plane made short stops in Irkutsk, Krasnoyarsk and Khabarovsk. There was a piercingly cold wind and forty degrees of frost. Everything around looked lifeless and dejected, as if on an abandoned planet. In Vladivostok it was noticeably warmer. We arrived a little late – there were already more than a thousand tourists on board. Due to depart on 7 December, the passenger liner *Soviet Union* was anchored in a bay with the romantic name of the Golden Horn.

The SS *Soviet Union* was built in Germany in the 1930s. During the Second World War she sank, and after the war Soviet salvage experts raised her from the sea-bed and refitted her to carry freight and passengers. At that time she was the largest freight–passenger vessel in the country, making coastal runs between the ports of the Soviet Far East. The ship was not at all suited to an escape – she was like a well-designed high-security prison. The side did not go straight down from the deck, as with other vessels, but bulged outwards in a smooth curve. If anyone were to fall overboard, they would not fall into the water but into this curving side. All the portholes hinged on a horizontal axis which divided the round opening into two parts. On most ships it is easy to climb through the portholes, but only a baby could get through these semi-circular apertures. Just below the waterline, metal anti-roll fins more than a metre wide were welded on from bow to stern. To jump overboard and reach the water, avoiding the bulging hull and those metal fins, one would have to run along the deck and do a swallow dive. It would be difficult to make such a dive from the upper decks (where there was room for a run-up) as they were over twenty metres above sea-level. Only Tarzan could do such a dive while the ship was actually moving.

When I examined the stern of the liner thoroughly with the eye of a potential fugitive, I realized that a jump would be feasible in only two narrow places – between the tips of the gigantic screw and the ends of the underwater fins, at the point where the wake was thrown off from the hull. It was possible that there might be no passengers at the end of the main deck, as there were large refuse-containers on the sides of the ship there; the distance to the water here was about fourteen metres, not including the gunwale.

Standing on the quay by the stern of the liner I measured this distance with my eyes. It made me hesitate for a moment – but not for long, and I took my decision to jump.

Before we set sail we had only a general idea of our route: the liner would leave Vladivostok and would then cut across the Sea of Japan; she would make a short stop in the Straits of Tsushima, where a wreath would be dropped at the place where the Russian fleet was destroyed in 1905. Then she would head south into the Pacific and would make for the Equator. In accordance with tradition, those who were crossing the Equator for the first time would have to undergo the 'crossing the line' ceremony presided over by the sea-god Neptune and his retinue. The whole route from Tsushima to the Equator was kept secret from the passengers, but we were all well aware that the *Soviet Union* would not approach foreign shores too closely. The holidaymakers were enthusiastically informed that they could spend the whole journey tanning themselves under a tropical sun, bathing in the pools and admiring the colourful panorama of the ocean – well, even that is a lot for Soviet people.

Special lecturers had been invited, to inform passengers about the politics and economics of the nearby countries; there was even an oceanographer to add to our knowledge of the geography of the Pacific.

On the day when our group of thirteen people from Leningrad went on board, we ran straight into a heated argument over berths in the cabins. It turned out that there were no single cabins at all – the first-class ones were for two people, the second-class cabins for four and the third-class for six or more. All passengers had been assigned bunks in advance, as if they were on a warship. The cabins were not identical and people soon discovered that, for the same price, others were getting better accommodation; in addition, people didn't want to share with unknown shipmates, preferring quite naturally to be with their friends.

The problem seemed insoluble; arguments had been going on for three days already and the number of dissatisfied passengers increased by the number of new arrivals. A judgement worthy of Solomon was reached on the day before our embarkation: it was proposed that all those who were discontented could leave without any compensation whatsoever.

Cursing the Soviet regime (not aloud, of course) the passengers dispersed to their cabins. Our group was 'lucky'; having arrived later than all the rest, we had not yet had time to discover all the inconveniences and so to get upset. Only a few hours were left until the liner sailed and we gathered in our cabin to celebrate the ship's departure and the beginning of our holiday.

At the very height of the party we heard the Captain's order over the loudspeakers: 'Prepare for the ship's departure. Everyone to your stations!' Orders rang out. Mooring-ropes, like snakes, crawled along the deck. The water swirled around the screw. Strips of water appeared between the quay and the side of the liner.

The cruise organizers tried to control all the passengers' free time. To this end groups of twenty-five to thirty were formed, taking no account of what people actually wanted; a commissar was appointed to each group and everybody was given a coloured scarf as a distinguishing mark. Each group had to sit together in the restaurant, to go to lectures and the cinema together and, worst of all, to participate in various idiotic games under the leadership of the organizers.

The girls were the first to revolt. It turned out that some groups consisted of women only, and they resolutely demanded to be 'diluted' by a suitable number of men. The women in the other groups did not want to give up their men – there were few enough as it was. Regrouping went on for several days, but it ended with even more discontent. Then the cruise organizers made some concessions, and proposed retaining the groups only at the dinner table. The boldest and most independent passengers immediately lost their scarves.

At first they woke us in the mornings and tried to drive us to the lectures, but soon they realized that to fulfil this task they would have to tie up the tourists and carry them into the lecture hall on stretchers, locking the door of the auditorium before the lecture began. In the end the organizers of the trip gave up and left people to their own devices.

What do you think would happen if several hundred healthy, active young men were made the close neighbours of a still larger number of young women? And for only twenty days? One only had to go down the stairs to the cabin decks to hear immediately an unceasing buzz of voices and smell the aroma of alcohol and perfume wafting through the air. From behind the door of each cabin came the sound of music, singing, dancing, laughter and female squeals, unremitting quarrels, drunken cries, lovers' groans, endless toasts and clattering dishes.

The passengers gave themselves up to merry-making, beginning at lunchtime and going on till the morning on each precious day of their holiday. Relatively few people turned up for breakfast – most were still sound asleep. Almost everyone appeared at lunchtime. At suppertime envoys from various partying groups ran up to grab some sandwiches from the tables and disappear back down to the cabin quarters as quickly as possible. It looked as if many revellers could not even find time to go on deck to glance at the ocean and breathe some sea air.

As soon as darkness fell, dancing began. Music and songs were broadcast through loudspeakers from morning to midnight.

In planning my 'dirty deed' I was faced by a very difficult task: to determine the exact location of the vessel. I had a small-scale map of the Pacific, a constellation map of both hemispheres and a pair of binoculars. I planned to deduce the ship's route by dead reckoning and from the piecemeal information I could pick up in the chart room. I did not want to draw attention to myself and so I did not go into the chart room unless it was absolutely necessary; instead I stood for many long hours on the top deck with my binoculars, trying to see land on the horizon. I wanted to know, even if only approximately, how our route lay: would we always be in the open ocean or would we sometimes pass near land?

At last the mysterious course of our cruise was revealed: in one of the liner's halls we caught sight of a chart of the western Pacific with a line showing the route of the ship to the Equator and back, with even the dates indicated. For me this chart was a heaven-sent gift . . .

The ship was to cross the East China Sea within sight of the island of Taiwan and would then follow the eastern shores of the Philippines, turning into the Celebes Sea and reaching the Equator between the islands of Borneo and Celebes [modern Sulawesi]. During the days our route went closer to the coast, while at nights it moved further away.

Of course, this was only an approximate scheme of our course, and it was not totally reliable. It was likely, however, that in order to shorten the journey the Captain might have to come quite close to the shore near the little island of Siargao and again at the southern tip of Mindanao. After I had analysed the route carefully, I realized that it would be possible to leave the liner only at these two places.

We crossed the Tropic of Cancer in sight of Taiwan. Passengers poured upstairs and filled all the liner's decks. The sun appeared from behind the clouds but it was quite chilly; a strong gale was blowing. Little Chinese junks were spread over the water up to the shores of the island; sometimes they seemed to disappear into the waves so that only their masts were visible. The island was still quite a long way off – its mountains looked blue in the distance and even with binoculars it was hard to make out any details.

Later, near the island of Luzon, the Captain suddenly changed course and we came so close to the shore – some five or six miles away – that we could see palm trees. It was impossible to get to the side of the ship: all the passengers and crew, it seemed, had gone on deck to catch even a glimpse of a foreign land.

The next day, before dawn, I went on deck. I was embraced by a warm, caressing trade wind, huge cumulus clouds were floating across the sky and all around, as far as the eye could see, was a boundless phosphorescent ocean of extraordinary beauty.

At midday we again approached land. Little coral islands beckoned to us with their bays and snow-white breakers. Palms crowded right to the water's edge and enticed us from afar with their green branches. Sometimes large waves rolled right up to their feet before breaking.

After an hour or two we moved away towards the open sea again, but those shores remained in my memory like a dream, like a mirage . . .

After that, right up to the island of Siargao, we saw land only on the horizon. I felt like a wild animal, born in captivity, then let out on a chain to have a look at its native jungle for the first time. One little jump separated me from this seductive beauty and freedom. But there could be no question of jumping in broad daylight, of leaving the ship in full view of hundreds of eyes – a lifeboat would instantly be lowered. Night is the fugitive's time.

And then, almost unnoticed, the day stole up: 13 December. The thirteenth is not the best of dates for risky adventures, but if you have very little choice then you must forget superstitious fears.

In the morning I asked a girl I had got to know, who was keen on astronomy, to go with me to the chart room – it was easier to go there with her. Only the First Mate and a sailor at the wheel were there. While the girl chatted to the Mate, I went up to the navigation chart. The liner was still a long way from the north of Siargao but her course would be along its coast at a distance of about ten nautical miles. I managed to observe that the island was mountainous and so might be visible from afar. Its length was nineteen nautical miles in all: that meant that it would take us only one hour to sail past its shores. At

20.00 hours ship's time the liner should be about halfway along the coast of the island.

Yes – the last opportunity was that night. Then or never.

I did not go in to breakfast. I was present at lunch, but ate nothing. I knew from experience that the stomach must be completely empty before a long swim. In the morning I did some yoga cleansing-exercises: I drank two litres of water and passed it through my bowels not my bladder, followed by other complicated flushing routines and breathing exercises.

Only then did I really comprehend that this would be my last day on the liner. I could not think about the future. I had no future. At the appointed time I would pick up my swimming things, go to the stern of the ship, take a jump into the darkness and . . . The rest was completely unknown. I could not think about my past – that had no importance whatsoever in these last hours. My attention was held only by the present. I was aware of my every step, every feeling, every transitory movement of my spirits; conscious of everything going on around me, I noticed a multitude of tiny details in the atmosphere, in people's behaviour, in the environment. I became extraordinarily astute. At first I was afraid that others were bound to notice my changed condition, but their glances were so superficial, passing so quickly from one thing to the next, that they were not aware of themselves let alone of me. I felt as if I could read people's minds and feelings, yet my eyes never once met any shrewdness in anyone else's look. I suddenly began to understand Japanese kamikaze, Roman gladiators, smugglers, and all those who had ever waited for a duel or for the appointed hour of an escape. I prepared myself through a 'ceremony of self-awareness' for a kind of mystical initiation into the secrets of life and death. In such circumstances it is best to be alone.

The sunset was magnificent, triumphant, flooding the sky with all the shades of the rainbow. Night fell, dark and starless. The liner drew close to the northern end of Siargao. I went on deck. A strong south wind was blowing and there was a heavy swell. Black storm clouds were approaching from the west and there were occasional flashes of lightning.

I went up to the topmost deck but I could see nothing, even with binoculars. Where the island should have been there was not even one light. I went forward to the navigator's bridge and asked the sailor on watch there about shore lights. He clearly found my question trivial, glanced to the south-west, and replied that there were no lights on the island. I could see that without his help.

What if the Captain had changed course and we were further from the coast than I supposed?

It was already about seven o'clock. I had a last look in the direction where the island should have lain. Impenetrable gloom. The sky was covered with storm clouds. Lightning flashed almost continuously at different points on the horizon.

'There's a storm blowing,' I rejoiced inwardly. 'The Captain won't risk sending a boat to search for me at night because he won't take chances with his crew. I shall have the whole night ahead of me!'

I went into the restaurant towards the end of supper – just to show myself. All the Leningrad group were there together and were having a spirited conversation. I silently looked at them. I did not want to say anything false at such an important moment.

'I shan't be back for a while,' I said softly but clearly, and went to the door without waiting for any questions.

I went up to the top deck again and began to scan the horizon to the west. There were still no lights. There was no moon, no stars. And I did not even have a compass. 'No matter,' I thought. 'The die is cast.'

I returned to my cabin to make my last preparations. I put on a short vest, swimming trunks and several pairs of socks; I wound a scarf round my neck – it could come in useful as a bandage.

I sat for several minutes making up my mind. From this moment I was consciously and voluntarily issuing a challenge to the Soviet State. I had never before reached such a point of crisis in my life.

In my hand I had a bag with flippers, mask and snorkel. I carefully placed a towel over my swimming gear, then slowly set off along the corridor. It was about a hundred metres from the for'ard cabin, which had been mine, to the companionway leading up to the deck, and from there I had to go about the same distance – in the open – to the stern. I felt as if I were walking a tightrope above an abyss.

Dancing had begun on the boat-deck, near the stern, where I had to pass. I could hear one of my favourite songs: 'When I sailed afar from my native port . . . '

Making my way between the dancing couples, I felt no fear – I had become a little boy running away from his grandmother into the enticing forest with its wild beasts.

I went down the steps to the stern of the main deck. There was a camp-bed with three sailors sitting on it. I walked to the ship's rail and stood there for several moments. I could not risk jumping right in front of their eyes. I imagined them immediately picking up the telephone which hung above their heads and informing the bridge. The 'Man Overboard' signal would be given at once and searchlights would start looking for me without delay.

I went up to the boat-deck again and took stock of the situation. There was very little time left. In half an hour, by my calculations, the liner would have passed the island.

I went down again. Two of the sailors had disappeared, and the third had made up his bed and turned his back to me.

I lent one hand on the rail, vaulted overboard and kicked against the side as hard as I could . . .

My flight over the water seemed endless. I was well aware that I had not only crossed the frontier of the State; I had also gone over some psychological barrier and would come out on the other side a completely different person.

I had calculated my flight trajectory well. Once overboard, I turned my body with a sharp movement so that my feet were towards the stern of the ship and my back towards the water. For some time I seemed to fly in this horizontal position away from the stern; then I felt the force of inertia becoming weaker and I was falling almost vertically with my back downwards. At that moment I began smoothly to turn my body so that I could enter the water with my legs at a slight angle. I realized that I would not be able to cancel inertia completely, but I knew that it would be disastrous to end up in a vertical position with my legs first – I would be tipped over and hit my face and stomach against the water.

I flew those fifteen metres in darkness as I had expected. I successfully went into the sea with my legs at an acute angle and without losing hold of the bag with my swimming things – an accident which I dreaded. A strong stream of water swirled me round, but at the last moment I managed to clutch the bag tight to my stomach.

Holding my breath, I tried to stay underwater until the large pools of light from the stern-lamps went past. It was totally dark for a while and then I was lit by a bright beam. I was sure I had been noticed in the strong glare. But it soon grew quite dark again. I threw away the towel, which no longer had any purpose for me, put on my mask and snorkel and took some deep breaths. The water was quite warm: it would be possible to swim for a long time in such a temperature. I put on the flippers and gloves with webbed fingers. The bag was not necessary any more. My watch with its luminous face said 20.15 ship's time.

I was alone in the ocean at night – there was nothing around me but black overhanging clouds, with not a light to be seen anywhere. I filled my lungs with air and kicked with the flippers so that I could push myself out of the water up to the waist. All that I could see were the tops of enormous waves and the night sky. The liner had disappeared. This puzzled me so much that I did not know what to think. Again and again I peered into the darkness in the hope of discovering the ship. If I glimpsed its side-lights, I reckoned, that meant that they had turned round and were looking for me; if its stern-lights, then my absence had not been noticed immediately, or indeed had not yet been noticed at all. At last I found myself at the height of a particularly large wave and managed to make out the stern-lights at a distance of about one nautical mile. I heaved a sigh of relief. Even if the 'Man Overboard' alarm were now given, the liner would still move on quite a lot further through inertia. I feared the ship's return more than all the other dangers put together. To me, a return to the liner meant something worse than death.

Once again I searched the horizon from the crest of one of the huge waves. In the west, where there should have been an island, was not the remotest sign of a light. For another half-hour I still waited in dread lest I should see the side-lights of the ship, but my fears were needless. Nobody could have noticed anything.

At first I orientated myself from the lights of the departing ship, of which I occasionally caught sight . . . I dragged myself from billow to billow, feeling a bit as if I were crawling among dunes in the desert. Almost all the rollers had luminous crests which broke noisily. Sometimes gusts of wind blew spray so hard that I felt I was being whipped with sharp needles. It was very hard to breathe. The waves often broke over my head, so I had to clear my snorkel before each breath. I took great care with my breathing: I inhaled lightly and tentatively, then, after breathing out energetically, I breathed in deeply and held my breath until I felt another breath was essential (not less than a minute). I felt I would not be able to survive on the surface of the water with such infrequent breathing. From experience, I knew only too well that if no more than a couple of drops of water got into my lungs I would not be able to recover my breath.

I constantly lost my sense of direction. I would swim among the hills of water for several minutes in what I believed was the right direction, until I was tossed to the top of an especially tall wave. Then I would find that the ship's lights were not to my left as I had expected, but to my right, or behind me, or even ahead of me. Again I would turn towards the west and remain in a trough for a while. Sometimes reaching a crest would reveal no lights and I would have to wait for the next wave.

After this had happened ten times I realized that I would not be able to go on in this way for much longer – the liner would soon disappear from view altogether. What should I do then? The horizon was darker to the south-east than in other directions. There was constant lightning in the west and large storm clouds were heading towards me from there. It would be foolish to orientate myself by the direction of the wind, for that could so easily alter. Only one more or less reliable factor remained: the disposition of the clouds.

When the liner had finally vanished over the horizon, I began to comprehend that I was absolutely alone in the stormy night sea. Soon the rain clouds were right over my head and there was a downpour. The cloud formation changed so much that I began to doubt my course. I could look at the sky only if I held my breath, which disturbed my breathing rhythm so that for a while afterwards I had to concentrate on my snorkel, ignoring all else.

I kept changing direction; first I thought I had to swim one way, then another. I could keep going while my possible error was only ninety degrees, but when I became uncertain whether I should go one way or in completely the opposite direction I stopped and looked at the night sky. The cloud cover was very thick. There was not a single star to be seen. Had I not had to pay so much attention to my breathing, I should probably have been able to hold my course until the morning by watching the movements of the clouds on the horizon. But most of my time was spent low down and I had only a few seconds in all at the top of the highest waves. I could only really observe the clouds above my head.

I felt that it was not even midnight yet and that I had no hope at all of finding my way in this terrible nighttime ocean. I began to feel afraid. Waves of fear rolled through me, starting from my hands and feet, attacking my heart and then passing through my neck to my head. Fear began to smother me. My breathing became more frequent and I felt I was choking. As before, waves broke over me and water went into my snorkel. I realized I would not be able to last even half an hour in such a condition.

I believe it is possible to die of fear. I started remembering stories about sailors who had perished, for no particular reason, in the first few days after a shipwreck. It is as if you stimulate your own fear – one wave of panic gives rise to another, even stronger. I felt as if cramp were gripping my throat and I wanted to scream. Another few minutes and I would suffocate.

At that moment, however, the thought flashed into my mind that I was still in a far from hopeless situation and that I was hastening my own end. With a great effort of will, I 'looked fear in the face'. I had learnt how to do this a long time ago, when I used to walk in the local graveyard at night to practise being brave. I was only seven or eight then. I felt that that was the only place for me to develop fearlessness. It is a very simple trick once you master it. If you 'look away' for a moment, terror can attack you again with all its former strength. You have to keep your concentration for some time to stop the waves of panic entirely.

My fear passed. Once again I was able to breathe deeply and evenly. There was nothing else I could do in my position but keep on the surface of the water and wait for morning. I realized that I could not find my way without stars.

I had been so preoccupied with the first stage of my flight that I had rather lost sight of the second: to get to land alive. If only I had a compass! For some reason I had imagined the tropics very differently: calm sails, a scorching sun, warm, humid nights with stars bright as emeralds, a full moon gently slipping between the occasional little clouds . . .

Several exhausting hours passed. I tried simply to stay on the surface of the water and save my strength. A large, black cloud stole up on me unnoticed and rain started to pour over me. I managed to swallow a little, while holding my breath, having first moved my snorkel to one side. I did not feel thirsty, but how long might I have to last without anything to drink?

The wind seemed to be dying down slightly. Waves were breaking over me less often. The clouds thinned and one or two stars smiled through.

Suddenly I noticed a very bright star in the gap between the clouds. It could only be the planet Jupiter. I tried to memorize the disposition of the clouds in case the planet vanished again, and then I started moving with assurance towards the west. Jupiter disappeared just as suddenly as it had appeared, but now I could at least swim confidently for a couple of hours. A little later there was an even bigger gap in the clouds and I made out Orion's belt in the south-east. I could now swim in a straight line, hardly diverging from my course at all. Sometimes I simply turned over on to my back to get a better view of the clouds and continued to move westwards without stopping.

I noticed a light in the west. Soon it doubled. Both lights became brighter and nearer. At the same time a big dark cloud moved overhead, covering a large part of the sky. Although I was very reluctant to steer by a couple of unidentified lights – they could belong to a moving ship which I might follow goodness knows where – I really had no choice and I started swimming towards the lights. The waves had become gigantic again and I found myself in the 'valleys' between the 'sand dunes' most of the time. Then it began to drizzle; the wind blew the black clouds to the south-east but higher cloud still covered the sky and Jupiter did not show itself again. Sometimes I did see individual stars, but I could not distinguish the constellation they belonged to. Soon even the mysterious lights disappeared. Once more I had to stop and wait.

I remembered the far-off days of my childhood when I had not yet learned to swim. At that time I was living in the town of Semipalatinsk, which only later was to receive its sad notoriety as a nuclear firing-ground where numerous atomic and nuclear bombs are tested, sometimes several a day. When I lived there the subterranean firing-ground was still being built and for some reason we used to call this area 'the moon'.

Semipalatinsk is situated on the banks of the large Siberian river, the Irtysh. In the summer I often used to go bathing and fishing with the other children. I was only seven or eight and could not swim, so my mother gave me permission to go only on condition that I kept away from the water. She reassured herself by making me promise on my word of honour, and she never forgot to do this on any occasion.

I used to sit on the bank and longingly watch my contemporaries swimming and diving – nobody else had such a strict mother. They used to laugh at me, trying to persuade me to join them, and would call me the worst name I could imagine: 'Mummy's boy'. But I never once broke the promise I had given.

Once my parents sent me to a Pioneer camp for the whole summer and my mother forgot to extract the usual promise from me. It was my only chance to learn to swim and I was not going to let it pass. The Pioneer camp was set in a pine wood, and about a kilometre away was a deep lake with steep, overgrown banks and white water-lilies. Nobody used to swim there; it had a bad reputation and superstitious people used to say that a water-sprite lived in it. Every night, when everybody else was asleep, I ran to this lake alone and taught myself to swim. It was not easy, of course – in general I was a dreadful coward.

Two years later, in summer, I announced to the other kids on our street that I intended to swim across the Irtysh and I invited anyone who was interested to join me. The Irtysh is a large, navigable river with steep banks, many whirlpools and a strong current. It is more than half a kilometre wide at Semipalatinsk. The inhabitants of the town usually liked to swim in one of its narrow, safe channels, which had flat sandy banks and a gentle current. None of the other boys or even the older youths wanted to swim across the main river with me and they, of course, were right. To get across to the other side in a suitable place meant swimming against the current for three or four kilometres, possibly even five – I had no idea then of how far the current would take me.

One clear sunny day I left the house accompanied by two friends. The time had come to carry out my plan.

On the other side of the Irtysh was a small village called Zhana-Semey, while about ten to fifteen kilometres south of that was the future nuclear firing-ground – I knew the area well. The river was spanned by a railway bridge which was strongly guarded against 'American spies'. Only steamers could pass under the bridge; anyone attempting to swim past or sail in a small boat would be shot without warning by the security guards, and we were all aware of this. I had to manage to swim across the river above the bridge because beyond it was a port where swimming was completely forbidden.

At first I swam across the Semipalatinka – a channel of the Irtysh about a hundred metres wide – and landed on an island. It was the beginning of summer and the temporary pontoon bridge had not yet been put in position. This island was very beautiful in summer: grass grew higher than a man's head and the whole island was covered in huge trees and thick bushes. At that time of the year it was more or less impenetrable. It took me some hours to push my way across the thicket to the opposite side and then I spent just as long walking along the shore against the current to the very end of the island. I met no one on my way. When I got to my destination I measured the distance with my eyes and was seized by fear: the bridge was hardly visible downstream.

It was, however, too late to retreat. I got into the water and resolutely set off for the opposite bank.

I had reached about the middle of the river when I noticed a large steamer coming upstream. At first I decided to wait and let it go past, but, after about twenty minutes, I realized that I would not have time to get to the opposite bank – the railway bridge was already clearly silhouetted against the sky. I was pretty tired but kept on swimming ahead, although I was cutting across the steamer's path.

I was colourfully sworn at; I came right under the very bows of the steamer and almost got caught up in its thrashing paddle-wheel.

Another hour or more passed, and at last I reached the opposite bank, right at the wire fences marking the prohibited zone of the bridge.

My feelings of achievement and pride soon gave way to pangs of guilt towards my mother. The sun was already going down towards the horizon and I still had the whole return journey to cover – I had to walk about five kilometres upstream, barefoot, on stones, so that I could swim across the river to the island, push through it again and swim across the Semipalatinka. I could not phone – there were no telephones in the town – nor could I get on a train to return to the town. I had neither clothes (I had hidden them on the island) nor money, and ticket inspectors on Soviet trains are merciless. I swam across the Irtysh in the sunset and the Semipalatinka when it was already completely dark. There was no time to search for my clothes on the island and I walked home in my swimming trunks.

The clouds thinned again and in places stars came out, at first singly and then in whole groups. I did not know the night sky well enough to be able to recognize constellations from individual stars, but at last I managed to make out Gemini and then Orion's belt once more and the very bright star, Sirius, to which it points. Again I could confidently swim due west.

My unlimited, immoderate love for the sea has been the cause of all my failures in life. This passion began from the first moment I can remember and has remained with me always. My nearest relatives and all their ancestors were hopelessly land-bound people, and indeed you will not find anywhere on the globe that is further from the sea than my hometown of Semipalatinsk in Kazakhstan, in the very heart of Asia. I read all the stories I could find about the sea, but not even they could satisfy me. My parents believed that I would grow out of all this nonsense, as many boys do; they wanted me to take a degree in engineering.

I alone knew perfectly well that I would never grow out of it, never mind become an engineer. At fifteen, as sea-worshippers have done since time immemorial, I ran away from home (to Leningrad) and tried to get work on a ship sailing far away; but, alas, I had been born in the wrong time and the wrong place. I could not go to sea for three reasons: I had no visa, I had no residence permit for Leningrad and I was not yet sixteen. Much later I was to return to Leningrad and enter the Institute of Oceanography, but I never managed to get a visa for a long-distance voyage.

I forced myself to return to reality. Many hours had already gone by and it had probably turned midnight. Orion had passed its zenith and was now to be seen in the south-west, directly in front of me, in all its brilliance. Then dawn came and put out all my stars and I felt my solitude more keenly. I swam more slowly, steering by the clouds.

The sky was grey at first, then blue–violet shades appeared. In a few minutes the colours became brighter, with dark red strips cutting across the sky; the clouds seemed to be adorning themselves in yellow. The rising sun came up over the ocean. I was surrounded by a swell of large waves. The clouds turned pink and swept across the sky in all directions. It was a windy day. How odd to remember that a week ago I had been wearing winter clothing and there had been a severe frost.

In the west, on the very line of the horizon, I could see puffs of cumulus clouds, but however hard I stared I could not make out anything else there. There was no land visible. I grew alarmed. Had I made a mistake in my calculations? Perhaps the current had carried me a long way off course during the night? Perhaps the Captain had changed direction and the liner had been sailing much further from the coast of the island than I thought? Perhaps the liner had not yet reached the island or had already passed it when I jumped? Any of these was possible. The ocean was absolutely empty. There was nothing to be seen but sea and sky.

Fear attacked my heart again. A real danger was imminent: my illusory island had vanished. Land should have been not too far away, somewhere to the west. Mindanao was about a hundred miles away.

I suddenly thought of another, no less terrible, danger: by now they had probably discovered my absence on the ship. She might return; it would not be difficult to find me, and I would be dragged out of the water like a kitten, by the scruff of my neck.

'No,' I suddenly shivered. 'Anything but that. I'd rather be in this position. I prefer the company of sharks. Better to die a free man in the ocean.'

It was this that urged me on. I had to survive in order to encourage other fugitives or shipwrecked victims. I had to keep heading to the west for as long as my strength lasted. And I continued swimming . . .

Before my escape I did not just sit at a window dreaming of journeys and adventures. I trained a great deal and in a variety of ways. I devoted one year to practising fasting and, for about one-third of that year, I ate nothing and drank only one glass of water a day. I began with a ten-day fast. Then, after a month's 'rest', I stopped eating again and this time held out for twenty-one days. I was convinced that I could live for much longer without food. I wanted to fast for the classic period of forty-two days, but I had to drop this experiment after thirty. After two training fasts of twelve and fourteen days respectively, I again set off on a long 'journey' without food. On the thirty-sixth day I had to stop; a sickly-sweet saliva was appearing in my mouth and the taste was enough to make me shudder in revulsion. I could not sleep for three nights and became very weak. At this time I was living alone in a forest and, when by chance I met someone out walking, I noticed horror in his eyes at my emaciation. On the last day of my fast I went to the market in Yalta and stood in a queue for two hours for a bunch of radishes. The assistant at the counter enquired understandingly, 'You've got a stomach ulcer?' For a year after this experiment I could not eat any food containing sugar.

*

I came round again. All about me was a completely deserted ocean – there were neither dolphins nor birds nor flying fish. Sometimes I would peer into the depths but I could see nothing but blue–violet tones and shadows, perhaps of sharks, perhaps of some large sea-monsters. I preferred not to think about sharks: fear always followed close on the heels of such thoughts.

Soon clouds filled the sky and the sun went in. A light rain started falling again. After midday, when the sun had passed its zenith, I noticed a faint, unmoving contour on the horizon among the white clouds. I waited for another big wave to lift me high enough to determine whether it was land or merely a mirage. The wind had dropped. The clouds were no longer scudding across the sky as they had done earlier, but were moving at an even, leisurely pace from south-west to north-east. Only in the west did they hang motionless, like whipped cream. Hopes arose in me that perhaps the island was somewhere near. It was impossible that clouds would hang so steadily in one place over water.

From experience I knew that cumulus cloud always gathers over mountains, and Siargao was a mountainous island. The sun began to shine out from behind the clouds straight into my face. It was about two o'clock. I again noticed some barely discernible mountain peaks in the west. They began somewhere further south and disappeared into the dense, towering clouds. Sometimes I seemed to make out faint, motionless outlines further to the north where the clouds were thinner.

An hour passed, perhaps two. Now I could distinguish a fixed, craggy contour from any position – I didn't have to wait for a large wave.

'Land!!!' I could not deny myself the pleasure of shouting the magic word aloud and of hearing my own voice.

Perhaps it was my ghostly island of Siargao? I almost felt I had succeeded – now at least I had hope.

The sun looked out for the last time, as if it were saying goodbye to me, and hid itself away again. In a few minutes the sky filled with all the colours of the rainbow, the bright shades changing and merging as I watched. At first the clouds became deep red and then their edges turned bright orange. A little later they became yellow with glorious, pink-tinged centres. A while afterwards, the clouds turned lilac and dark violet. Darkness fell swiftly. My second lonely night in the ocean began.

The stars came out unnoticed. In the west, where my mysterious island had disappeared from view, I could now see many lights. They were wandering about the hillsides and ran along the line of the horizon. It was very dark and a deathly silence descended on to the surface of the water. The ocean's even breathing was very soothing and I felt almost safe. On the first night the breaking rollers had lit up the whole surface of the water but, now that the sea was quiet, my every movement seemed to be accompanied by a bluish tongue of flame and it looked as if I were burning in a slow fire of phosphorescence.

Of course, I was terribly conspicuous to anything in the deep. I had read somewhere that on just such starry nights monsters swim up to the surface: sea-snakes, gigantic squid, enormous skate – and sharks go out on nighttime hunts . . . I waited for them with horror and curiosity. From time to time I thought I heard sounds resembling the babble of a woodland stream, or voices calling my name. I caught more distinct sounds of music and song, as if a pleasant female choir were singing. At times it was so silent it was eerie. I tried to make as little noise as possible but I could not avoid the phosphorescence from the water. It stopped only when I did not move at all, yet I simply had to swim . . . I was calmed by the gentle, peaceful splashing of the waves; like chords of music they broke the sinister silence so harmoniously that I could have been sitting on the banks of the lake with its waves lapping quietly on the shore at my feet. I imagined a sea-nymph coming up out of the depths, waving her tail coquettishly and laughing seductively. Then the most remarkable creatures appeared: nereids and tritons on the backs of sea-turtles. I was constantly aware of a presence beside me. Often heavy breathing, laughter and groans sounded behind my back. I could see flashing lights under the water, an inexplicable luminescence and the phosphorescent tracks of unseen sea-creatures. I was afraid to look into the depths for too long: God knows what I might see!

But alas – nobody appeared and nothing disturbed the silence of the ocean. In the end I ventured to lift my mask on to my forehead, moved my snorkel to one side and breathed through my nose. Deep, rhythmical breathing dispersed my fears. Throughout the journey I tried, as far as possible, to keep calm – let the sharks think that I lived there too! That was my only weapon.

For the last few hours I had been drawing noticeably closer to the island. It occurred to me that I might even reach it at night, or at the latest in the morning.

My legs were beginning to get tired; I was swimming more slowly, trying to bring other muscles into use, but that improved things only for a short while. I dreamt of meeting a dolphin or a turtle and asking it to help me but, for some reason, there did not seem to be any around. (Sometimes they would help; I had read about this.) I could not permit myself to lose concentration even for a moment: I had to keep my breathing under control. I took very deep breaths but, with such a slow rhythm, it would be easy to get drops of water into the lungs and have a coughing fit; this had happened to me several times before both on and under water. I knew only too well how hard it was to swim in such a condition.

I was not in the slightest bit hungry or thirsty – I had prepared myself for all sorts of unforeseen circumstances. I felt that I could easily live without water for two weeks, and for no less than two months without food with a small quantity of sea-water. What then? Something would turn up . . . Something always turns up . . .

A little light haze appeared in the air and the whole island looked pale blue, almost transparent, in the distance. It was almost indistinguishable from the colour of the sky, but its clearly visible contour-line allowed me to feel confident that it wasn't a mirage.

Several more hours passed. I noticed with satisfaction that the island's southern tip, particularly on the horizon, was becoming a little darker, which suggested it was closer. I changed course and headed for the south-west. As it later turned out, this was an unforgivable mistake.

Before noon the sun was covered by clouds but later I fell under its scorching rays. Now that it had passed its height and was shining into my face from above, my shoulders, arms, chest and part of my back were exposed and began to burn unbearably. But, fortunately, white cumulus clouds appeared once more and hid me in their shadow.

After midday I caught sight of a black object fairly close to me. At first I thought it was the bottom of a capsized boat. I had glimpsed the thing only from the crest of a big wave and I seemed unable to get any nearer to it. Then it suddenly vanished. It could have been a solitary little rock or a reef or something else – who could tell?

At about this time I got caught up in a strong coastal current and was carried to the south – but I discovered this only later. My attention had been distracted by a boat which I noticed to the south of me. I first saw tall masts above the horizon but it took a long time for the hull of the vessel to appear. When it did at last show itself, I could easily recognize a small fishing trawler of about 500–600 tons. According to my calculations, I was in the three-mile coastal zone and there was no sense in avoiding it. It was heading straight for me and I even stopped swimming. But, after less than quarter of an hour, it suddenly changed course and passed about 100–200 metres to the north between me and the island. There was nobody on deck and, wave as I might, call as I might, nobody noticed me. And I had been so convinced that it had been sent by God! When it had gone past me, I felt a deep disappointment, bordering on despair.

Evening was approaching. The ocean around me was full of life; large fish often leapt out of the water and big birds flew right above my head. I could see the island distinctly now. It had a fairytale beauty. A line of dancing palms stretched the length of its shore. Straight in front of me I could make out steep hanging cliffs, covered with dense greenery, and the entrance of a picturesque bay. The sides of the mountains were covered in many different shades of green, and only here and there did small white spots suggest the presence of naked rock. Puffs of snow-white cloud hung motionless, covering the bare peaks of the bluish mountains.

The island seemed to be uninhabited. I could see no clear signs of life, of houses or smoke or any buildings.

An hour passed, perhaps more. It was extraordinarily quiet. Then suddenly, to my horror, I discovered my mistake: my island had noticeably begun to move to the north and was drifting further and further in that direction right before my eyes.

Before I had worked out what was happening and could sharply change my course towards the north, the southern tip of the island had appeared in front of me and, beyond that, open ocean stretched to the very horizon. I was totally at the mercy of the current and realized to my alarm that it was slowly carrying me past land. However much I tried to swim more energetically, however hard I tried to squeeze out the strength that was left in my tired muscles, the distance between myself and the island grew no less.

Now I was swimming due north. I still had hopes of a miracle, but gradually the coast moved further away and I realized I had no chance of reaching this bewitched island.

I was desperately tired and drooped in the water without moving. It began to get dark. Large, surging waves gently raised and lowered me in the water. When I had rested a little, I slowly started swimming north – there was nowhere else to head. The island of Mindanao was too far away.

My third night in the ocean crept up unnoticed . . . It was completely dark. After some time I saw two lights to the north-east – perhaps in the sea, perhaps on the shore. The lights were close together and flashed with an irregular frequency. It was probably, I thought, a boat using lights to attract fish. The lights seemed very far away but I had no choice but to swim towards them. I had to swim somewhere.

My legs suddenly stopped obeying me and hung helplessly; I propelled my body with my arms alone. I had the sensation that my legs were not there any more; only by reaching down to touch them could I convince myself that they were still there. When they 'came back' I tried to get them working. Gradually they started 'going away' more and more frequently.

My face, neck and chest were very painful from sunburn. I was feverish and felt drowsier and drowsier. Sometimes I even lost consciousness for a few moments. As I was afraid for my breathing I put my mask on again and put the mouthpiece of the snorkel into my mouth.

Eventually my legs would serve me no longer and just hung lifelessly. My lungs, however, were working as rhythmically as they had at the beginning of my swim, thanks to my lengthy training in breathing on the principles of yoga, and I still had plenty of strength left in my arms.

I was attacked by violent shivering. I lost consciousness more frequently, and whenever I came round I would discover that I was not swimming towards the lights but away from them.

Soon I completely lost any sense of time and felt as if I had been swimming for a very long time – a whole eternity. It seemed I was starting to suffer from hallucinations. I had only to lose concentration for a moment as some thought-picture flashed across my mind and that picture would take on a tangible form.

On my first and second nights, phosphorescence on the water surface had been caused only by my swimming movements. Now it was constantly present – it settled on me. Because of my own light it became hard for me to see what was a few metres away.

The twin lights came no closer. They could have been from some ship that was moving away from me. Thoughts of death came. It seemed senseless to prolong my life for another few agonizing hours. I had no hope of seeing another dawn. This third night in the ocean was very dark, much darker than the two previous ones. I tried to look around but could see nothing but those two winking lights.

I decided to die. It was difficult to carry out this decision in my position. (I very much regretted not having brought a knife with me.) I could think of only two methods. The first was to throw away all my breathing equipment and swallow a lot of water; the second was to go underwater and hold my breath until shortage of oxygen finished me. The latter way seemed less painful and more reliable.

I was not afraid of death. I had died many times in my vivid dreams: I had been stabbed in the stomach; I had been shot by all types of firearms; I had been sentenced to death by hanging; I had twice had my head chopped off by guillotine; and another couple of times I had been drowned.

I was suddenly aware of a quiet voice: 'Swim to the sound of the breakers.' Indeed there had been a distant rumbling for some time, although I had paid no attention to it. Now I started listening and I thought it sounded like the characteristic noise of jet aeroplanes constantly landing and taking off. The voice inside kept insisting that I should swim towards this thunder of waves – they were somewhere to the left of me and I was still making for the lights which were visible a long way ahead.

At last I obeyed, changed course and began swimming towards the breakers. From that moment I lost any feeling of time and swam in a state of trance.

Each time that I became conscious among those high waves I felt I was coming to a deep spiritual turning-point, as if some irreversible phenomenon were taking place in my psyche and in my body. I experienced the loss of something that was priceless and wonderful. I was surprised to discover myself in the night ocean and slowly tried to remember all that had happened to me. I could hardly feel my body but went on making swimming movements with my arms. The vast, luminous mass of moving water rolled tirelessly all around me. Some dim snatches of memories came to me but I could not connect them into any whole. I could clearly remember only one scene: stormy waves were lifting me up beside a huge ship with bright lights and then the ship moved away and I was left alone in the ocean. I could remember nothing else at all.

An endless time passed. Suddenly something shook me violently and

I began to fall helplessly into some abyss. I can distinctly remember my first thought: 'I am still alive. I am on the reef.' The wave retreated and I found myself in foamy, swirling water, but the roar of the breakers had moved away to the side. I was fully conscious at last and was beginning to decide what I should do, when again I heard an approaching rumble.

The phosphorescence of the sea beside me gave an impression of total darkness all around – you can get just the same effect when you sit by a blazing campfire at night. What I then suddenly saw at a distance of about thirty or forty metres has imprinted itself on my memory for ever.

It was a gigantic wave with steep, very slowly falling crests. Never in my life had I seen such an enormous wave – it even seemed to be touching the sky. The crest was surrounded by a glowing aureole and the entire wave was flooded with a bluish radiance, from bottom to top.

This wave, of course, was no bigger than any of those which arise on the outer side of a reef at a time of heavy ocean swell, but I was at the very foot of the wave where an observer rarely finds himself. From my point of view this wave seemed gigantic, as though in a fairy tale. It moved very slowly and was fantastically beautiful. I watched it from a little way to the side, totally absorbed in contemplating it, without yet comprehending its danger. Its curving shape was so perfect that it seemed alive, and created by some inspired hand.

The wave seemed to be standing still and was as if woven out of blue radiance and liberally sprinkled with glittering spray. The enchanting curve of the crest, like a swan's neck, continued to hold its perfect form – the water poured over freely, smoothly flowing in a cascade of light and dancing tongues of flame.

Suddenly I heard a muffled thundering to my right. I turned my head and froze in amazement – at once I felt my end had come.

A water mountain – there could be no other name for it – was now clearly discernible in the darkness and was moving straight for me, but so slowly that for several seconds I could watch it in horror, as if bewitched. The wave did not break over me as I assumed it would. An irresistible force dragged me up its steep slope right to the very foot of the falling crest. Instinctively I clutched my mask and snorkel and managed to take a deep breath. The crest started to break over me and then pulled me under it. For a moment I found myself still in the air, under the crest, as if in a cave. Then my body was in a swirling current of water; the inner power of the wave turned me round like a screw, threw me head over heels several times, twisted me in all directions before it tired. I started to push up to the surface without any concept of how deep under the water I might be. I just managed to be relieved that I hadn't been smashed against the reef and that I still had my mask and snorkel. I moved my legs – the flippers were still there.

I had sufficient breath to get up to the surface, although, by my reckoning, it took me quite a time to get there. I gulped in fresh air hungrily through the snorkel and at last got my breath. Meanwhile I had caught sight of another massive wave quite close to me in an aureole of light and bluish flame.

'Where is the reef and how many more waves will I be able to stand?' I wondered.

This wave approached very slowly, majestically, triumphantly. I started breathing in and out deeply, trying to fill my lungs with as much oxygen as possible. This time the wave seemed like a huge snake to me; it had curved its neck elegantly and was poised to attack me at any second. The very next moment this wave-snake swallowed me. I had barely enough breath to get to the surface – I was already breathing without any precautions, like a drowning man – but even so I had time to come to myself before I noticed that there was already a third wave hanging over me.

At first I made my farewells to life, but then I realized that I had to try to keep my body on the crest and I quickly took up a horizontal position, turning my back to the front of the wave as I had done years before in the Black Sea. But there the waves had been mere dwarfs compared with those I was now facing, in the Pacific Ocean, on the windward side of a reef. This time the wave quickly grabbed me and carried me at great speed for quite a long distance on its crest, at first forward and then back as it retreated.

I got up to the surface easily and swam, without wasting time, in the direction the waves were heading. 'Somewhere there, beyond the reef, there should be a lagoon,' I hoped.

The next wave seemed to be a very long time appearing, for some reason, but at last I saw it. It was not a mountain, simply a very large wave with a steeply falling crest. I quickly took up my horizontal position on its crest and it carried me a long way forward, leaving me almost on the surface of the water, so that it was quite easy to catch my breath and prepare for the next wave. Now I was swimming all the time in the waves' direction of flow; several times they neatly lifted me up and bore me forward, further and further away from the overgrown giants on the seaward side of the reef.

Suddenly I felt something hard under my feet. I could stand up to my chest in water. Around me I could see random currents of water, splashes of foam and phosphorescent spray all swirling about. Before I fully came to my senses, another large wave approached and carried me some distance further. I was up to my waist in water, then a new wave picked me up, taking me several metres forward. Now the depth of the water was only up to my knees. I had enough time to take a few tentative steps, to catch my breath and look around.

A dark night sky. Boundless ocean. Not one light on the horizon.

A large wave crept up unnoticed and I was moving again. When it ebbed I tried to stand, but this time I could not touch the bottom. I realized that I had been borne into the lagoon – the reef was now behind me.

It was quiet all about me; there was a muffled rumbling of the ocean somewhere behind. It seemed that I was on the waters of a calm bay. It was pitch dark. There was nothing all around: but somewhere in the centre of the lagoon, I reasoned, there should be an island – every schoolboy knows that from geography lessons.

I tried to swim by keeping the roar of the waves behind me but after half an hour or so this became hard to do – the rumbling seemed to come first from the right, then from the left, then from all directions at once. So I decided to swim so that the noise of the waves would be getting fainter all the time. I changed my course many times, always heading for 'silence' and, so I supposed, my illusory island.

In the end I reached a point where the waves could be heard only from one direction. I turned my back to the sound and swam straight ahead without stopping.

My every movement was accompanied by flashes of bluish flame and from the side I must have looked like an unextinguishable, blazing bonfire. I noticed, moreover, that my own light was growing brighter and brighter and was substantially hindering me from observing the water ahead and around me.

I had been swimming for more than an hour in the lagoon. It was somehow strange to swim in this unaccustomed silence and on a surface as smooth as a lake. Whenever I made a careless movement and water splashed, the noise seemed too loud, like discords shattering the sweet melody of silence. At last I could lift my mask to my forehead again, move my snorkel to the side and have a better look around.

I remembered about sharks again. First I examined all the uncovered parts of my skin. I could easily distinguish every drop of water and even the light fluff on my arms and legs. Although I could feel no pain, I knew from experience that in water even a deep wound sometimes fails to cause any sensation of pain. Indeed, I could see droplets of blood under the water, rolling from some wound; in the depths they were blackish, on the surface dark red; then they spread into muddy little clouds – and all without the slightest pain. I could see blood on grazed knees and bound them with my scarf. It had undoubtedly happened on the reef when I had been clambering on its sharp coral ledges.

I knew that there could be more sharks in the lagoon than on the windward side of the reef, and I still had no idea of how much further I should have to swim to the island. Blood occasionally attracts those sharks which do not usually attack people. I had read somewhere that sharks in lagoons do not normally touch local people but more frequently attack unknown newcomers – just like country dogs.

Suddenly a strangely puzzling thought occurred to me: 'What if the sharks are simply afraid of me? I must look like some incomprehensible, glowing monster.' Lots of deep-sea creatures have their own 'haloes'. Again I put on my mask, took my snorkel into my mouth and looked down. The depth of the water was no more than ten to twelve metres here, and all the sea-bed below me was lit by a mass of lights: it was as if I were flying very low over a town at night. It was obviously a living coral reef. I had read so much about this, had dreamed of seeing one, even with one eye, and here it was in front of me, unexpectedly, in all its beauty in the middle of the night.

The rumble of the waves was a long way off and resembled rolls of thunder. I was swimming with great difficulty; apart from general weariness, I felt that my breathing was becoming more rapid: it seemed that interrupting my breathing on the reef had taken its toll. I tried to keep on swimming with the noise of the waves to my back.

At last I saw a group of lights a little to my left. They twinkled welcomingly and didn't seem to be very far away. My breathing was growing worse and worse – every fifteen minutes I tried just to float in the water, but this didn't help any more. I simply hadn't enough air. I hungrily caught it in my mouth and began wheezing. The water here was little more than five metres deep.

Suddenly I noticed, to my right and in front of me, the tops of palm trees silhouetted against the dark sky. They were much closer than those lights by which I had been guiding myself and I headed towards them – I had lost all my faith in lights. The bright luminescence of my body simply blinded me; I could not see the surface of the water for more than an arm's length in front. Unexpectedly, I began to feel afraid of the darkness, which happens to me only very rarely.

Several hours had already passed since I had left the reef. I felt dreadful and had to rely on my strength of will. It seemed I would spend the rest of my life swimming into the unknown and that those palms outlined against the sky were merely a mirage, like the lights to my left.

At last, when I was beginning to lose consciousness and was slowly suffocating, I tested the bottom for the final time – and my foot landed on something hard. I was standing up to my waist in water and could hardly believe my own senses . . . In front of me, as far as I could see, was the dark water of the lagoon. It was very shallow and I walked up to my chest in water for a long time, then swam a bit, then walked waist-deep in water. At this moment I was afraid of sharks more than anything else on earth. 'What if I'm eaten by sharks now?' I shuddered at the thought. 'It would be a terrible pity!'

I emerged on to coral sand at the foot of very tall palm trees. I left a trail of luminous water and my body glittered like some princess's ball-gown. Only now did I feel completely safe. The ocean was behind me and with it all my past . . .

Leaves rustled somewhere high above my head. Bright stars could be seen between occasional clouds. To left and right, along the shore as far as the eye could see, were rows of tall palm trees, their tops clearly silhouetted against the night sky. Somewhere out there on the other side of the lagoon was a rumble of breakers.

I felt uncontrollably tired and immediately fell asleep on the sand beneath the palms.

I did not sleep for long, being woken by the bites of ants and mosquitoes. My body was still phosphorescent, particularly my damp clothes, and I had only to move my hand to any small object that I wanted to have a look at and I could see it sufficiently clearly in my own light. The luminescence of my body faded extremely slowly – it was useful in the dark night. I decided to go deeper into the island. I was shivering violently, as often happens with sunburn, and I felt it would be warmer in the forest than on the edge of the lagoon.

Palm trees were growing only along the beach; soon I came into banana groves and walked through them for a long time. Then I started coming across all sorts of unknown trees and shrubs entwined with climbing stems and hanging lianas; I saw many rotting trunks, large branches and big leaves. The undergrowth grew denser so that the thicket was impassable; water was squelching underfoot and the soil seemed to be giving way under my feet; it was as if I had wandered into a swamp. I decided to return to the shore of the lagoon.

I was in a happily imperturbable condition. The world had become new for me, mysterious and wonderful. I was not suffering in the slightest from the homesickness I had feared. It was as if I had lost nothing and left nothing in my own country – and yet I had loved it very much. Later I often used to contemplate this miracle. All this had happened not gradually, but at once; I had crossed the psychological barrier that night.

The wind rushed through the tops of the trees and the banana leaves rustled. I breathed in the smell of the sea and of water-plants. I emerged on to the beach in a different place and unexpectedly stumbled across a native canoe. It was made out of one long tree-trunk, hollowed out inside in several places with very thick partitions between them. One of the hollowed-out compartments was large enough for me to stretch out in to my full length. The boat was dry; I threw fresh banana leaves inside and decided to sleep a little. Walking had warmed me up and my clothes had partially dried. I 'lit up' the sides and bottom of the boat with my hands to make sure there were no ants or other biting insects there, then lay down inside and instantly fell asleep.

I woke up after about an hour: too much skin had been exposed to tiresome mosquitoes and their bites were very painful. I climbed out of the boat and set off at random along the beach. Scooping up sea-water in my hands, I several times poured phosphorescent plankton on my clothing and my body: the night was not over yet and light might still come in useful. The luminescence glowed with all its former strength and I could see and chase off mosquitoes before they could bite me. Later, I thought, when this luminescence wears off, I shall be able to use the light of glow-worms. A gentle sea-breeze pleasantly refreshed my skin. It was very quiet. Stars shimmered in the still waters of the lagoon. The sand was coarse and clean; it was a pleasure to walk on it.

I decided to wait for morning and then find some sheltered spot and dry off in the sun. In my path I came across coconuts; I held them in my hands for the first time in my life and examined them carefully. I broke several nuts open between two stones but there was no milk inside. I remembered reading that milk is only found in green nuts, but for those I would have to climb to the top of a palm. 'I'll do that tomorrow,' I decided.

I put pieces of white coconut flesh in my flippers. I could not eat – all the inside of my mouth was inflamed from sea-water and from the mouthpiece of the snorkel. I had not the slightest desire to eat; I was thirsty, but very far from the condition where people die of thirst.

I imagined myself as Robinson Crusoe and immediately fell in love with my island. It had everything one could dream of: high mountains, rich tropical greenery and, all around, a warm ocean right up to the horizon. I would be able to make fire – I felt sure of that. I had done so several times in the forests of my northern country. I was confident that I would be able to find all the food I could want in the jungle and in the waters of the lagoon; as for clothing, I had no need of that – savages live out their lives without clothes . . .

'First I'll find a secluded place and then I'll build a hut – there should be bamboo on the island and it's the easiest building material of all. Banana and palm leaves will make a perfect roof. Then I'll begin to explore the island – every mile of the shore, every little cove . . . '

I lost myself completely in daydreams. I felt I was the master of a fairytale tropical island. I walked along the edge of the lagoon and imagined that I was the happy discoverer of this island. I desperately wanted to dance a wild Greek dance and started to do so on the sand below the palms.

Suddenly I saw a group of natives . . .

They had, apparently, just arrived. They stopped and stood rooted to the spot. Nearest stood a short, dark-skinned man in a white shirt and light trousers. He cried out in fright and took a jump back. There was a long pause . . .

At that moment I realized I would have to do something to convince these people of my peaceful intentions. I threw down my flippers and mask and raised my hand with fingers outstretched – I had read somewhere that this gesture is used by some tribes to show they have no weapons. Then I gestured towards the ocean and made several swimming movements with my arms.

There were two or three minutes of silent, tense apprehension before one of the natives slowly began to approach me. A little later I appreciated the cause of this alarmed disbelief: all my body was still phosphorescent in the darkness and these people had at first taken me for a dancing dervish.

The tension soon relaxed and I was quickly surrounded by children; they are always braver than adults.

It was one large family – father and children. At first they all came up and touched me in turn, then they started talking all at once in some incomprehensible language. I managed to pick out only one word: 'American'.

I stood in a circle of children and smiled foolishly. One of them noticed my flippers, snorkel and mask on the sand. The children threw themselves on these and began examining them with curiosity. A little girl of about twelve asked me in Spanish and English who I was and where I came from. I could speak a little English and we began to understand one another better.

Numerous questions were flung at me. For some reason they decided that there must have been a shipwreck somewhere not too far out to sea and that I was a surviving member of the crew. I was repeatedly asked, 'Where are the other people?' I tried to explain that my ship was whole and unharmed and that I alone had jumped into the ocean. They couldn't understand this at all. An innocent but, for me, philosophically very difficult question followed:

'But why?'

It seemed funny even to me when I looked at myself from the outside. What could I answer? Why indeed had I done it? It was almost as if they had asked me why I was living on this earth . . .

We walked for an hour, or perhaps more, until we came to their home. We climbed up to the high porch and went inside. There was no electric light in the house and one of the adults lit a kerosene lamp.

An elderly woman, the mistress of the bungalow, offered me some local hot drink, and as soon as I had taken several sips I realized how thirsty I was. When I had drunk everything there was in the kettle, the housewife, surprised at nothing, put a whole bucket of water on the fire. I carried on drinking glass after glass but I firmly refused food: my mouth was badly inflamed.

They told me that I was in a village called General Luna on the island of Siargao. 'That means I wasn't too far out in my calculations,' I thought. 'The Captain must have changed course and passed further away from the island so that I had to swim much farther than I expected.'

It was long after midnight. I was put to sleep in a bed with a mosquito net. I was so exhausted that I didn't even object. I fell asleep as soon as my head touched the pillow.

When I awoke I could not understand where I was. It was quite light; bright sunbeams were shining through slits in the window and the half-open door. The housewife helped me to wash with a jug and brought me a glass of the same drink.

'Why have they woken me so early?' I wondered. I began to be aware of an inexplicable flurry of movement in the house. The husband offered me a shirt and some linen trousers, which I did not need at all, but it would have been awkward to refuse and I thanked him.

Some sixth sense told me that I ought to go out on to the porch. Below, under the palms, I could see a large crowd of dark-skinned people. There were more than two hundred of them and they all clapped when I appeared and started shouting something in Spanish. Then – my eyes fell on what could only make me shudder with all my being . . .

'Lord, why am I so stupid and naive? And to think I could have escaped into the jungle this very night!' Behind the crowd I had seen a green jeep and several people in obviously military uniform with machine guns over their shoulders. A narrow corridor formed in the crowd of local people and two of the armed men, an officer and a soldier, came over to me.

Before getting into the jeep I looked round at my surroundings and cast a last loving look at those blue mountains which had been so near.

Farewell, my mysterious island! I had let the unique moment of opportunity escape . . .

Fate was kind to me. Although I was a captive in the Philippines for six months and even spent a month and a half in prison, this was only a continuation of my adventures. Hadn't I dreamt of something like this long ago when I stared at that implacable grey fence?

PART ONE

The End of the Old Order
1900–1921

1917 the Provisional Government had lost control of the countryside, the Army and finance. In an atmosphere of constant strikes and strato-spheric inflation combined with agrarian outrage and military mutiny, only the Bolsheviks offered a coherent programme backed by sufficient force. On the night of 7 November 1917 Bolshevik forces arrested what was left of the Government in the Winter Palace.

It was difficult to emigrate from the capital in the winter of 1917–18, but the harshness of initial Bolshevik rule (and the extreme privations it brought) caused many middle-class people to flee. They did so towards the south, where rival centres of power were being set up. A Volunteer Army, under former Tsarist generals, came into existence in much of the north Caucasus, under Cossack protection, and later spread to the northern shores of the Black Sea, under the guns of British warships and with the collaboration of the French. For a brief period in 1918 there was also a German occupation of the Ukraine, which was governed by a 'collaborationist' regime under Hetman Skoro-padsky. He, a one-time Tsarist general who now supported the cause of an independent Ukraine, welcomed former associates, and Kiev in particular became crowded with Russians from the stricken cities of the north (the atmosphere is brilliantly described in Mikhail Bulgakov's novel, *The White Guard*, a book long suppressed in the Soviet Union, but since 1986 obtainable). Further centres of resistance to Bolshevik rule were established, again with patronage from foreign powers, in the Far East, where Admiral Kolchak became 'Supreme Ruler', and in the north. In the Baltic states, which became independent in 1918, groups of Russians, and Baltic Germans, set up military forces, and reconstituted Poland also went to war with the Bolsheviks in 1919–20.

The Bolsheviks survived this multifarious attack, the last White forces being evacuated from the Crimea in February 1921. Peace treaties with the new states in the West followed, recognizing new frontiers which detached from the Soviet Union considerable amounts of once-Tsarist territory. Gingerly, acknowledgement of the new Soviet State followed, and Lenin proclaimed, with the New Economic Policy, a general relax-ation of controls which enabled something like normal life to start again. Until Stalin re-imposed harsh political controls, emigration by legal means was still possible; Leonid Krasin, an engineer who had been well known in St Petersburg before the war and was now Commissar for Foreign Trade, seems frequently to have helped his old friends to emigrate. After 1926, legal emigration became virtually impossible.

2

The Death of Stolypin

GALINA NIKOLAYEVNA VON MECK

Galina Nikolayevna von Meck was born in 1891 into an aristocratic Moscow family and died in London in 1985. In 1911 she was witness to one of the crucial events of Russian history: the assassination of the Prime Minister, Stolypin.

I come from a very large family, so large that I personally never knew many of them. My father, too, knew very few of his von Meck relatives. But then some of the Mecks remained very German; and some of my old aunts only ever spoke German, and never learned a word of Russian.[1] They lived in Riga and ended their days there . . .

[My father was born in 1862, in Moscow, and was married in 1883; I was born in Moscow too, in 1891.] I still have many memories of the last century; my recollections of the first ten years of my life are very clear. I still remember everything that happened at home, such as the day in 1897 when my father installed the new electric light[2] . . .

My father graduated from the School of Law but never practised as a lawyer nor went into the civil service.[3] He went straight into the family firm, the Moscow–Kazan Railway Company.[4] The greater part of the line was built by my grandfather. My father began as what would nowadays be called a 'management trainee'. Later, when he had proved his ability, he was elected Chairman of the Board of Directors, to which he was re-elected again and again, every three years, because he was such an able, energetic and far-seeing man . . .

My mother's maiden name was Anna L'vovna Davydova. She belonged to the famous Davydov family.[5] My mother's mother was Alexandra Tchaikovskaya, the composer's sister – 'Sashenka Davydova', as she was known. Tchaikovsky corresponded with her frequently, and often used to visit her at our estate, Kamenka.

My father was very broad-minded, but he was not a liberal. He considered it one's duty to serve the Tsar. At the same time, he did everything possible to help the workers. Everything he did on the railway was done for the good of the railwaymen, and they used to call him 'Our Old Man', because they felt he was one of them and on their side. They looked on him as a father and adored him, to such an extent that when he was arrested after the Revolution, they all protested. On the first occasion that he was arrested I personally collected forty thousand signatures to a petition demanding his release.[6] He was arrested altogether six times, and on the last occasion, in 1928, he was shot. For all that time after the Revolution he stayed in Russia and never attempted to emigrate. He was offered the chance of leaving the country, but he refused to go. He declared that he would not leave Russia and would stay at work for as long as he was able. And he did; even when he was in prison, he kept on working at his job – the railway.

Unlike many families, we never stayed in one house for very long, but changed homes rather often. Each of us had our own room, and it was very comfortable. Perhaps one of our nicest houses was the one in Denezhny Street in Moscow. It was one of the most typical residential streets, with private houses belonging to the nobility surrounding us on either side.

It was in the Arbat district.[7] Across the Arbat was the main road leading out of Moscow, and all around it were many *pereulki* [side-streets], small streets lined with private houses. The people who lived there were predominantly the Moscow nobility, and they mostly lived in a very old-fashioned style; they simply refused to accept that times had changed and they wouldn't accept the new way of life, which we Mecks accepted with enthusiasm. So we stood out as rather separate from the general run of Moscow nobility, and many of them regarded my father as a bit of an upstart, because he was never wholly 'one of them' and his German surname made him somewhat alien. We, on the other hand, although we didn't give ourself airs, slightly despised all these gentry because they were so terribly old-fashioned in their attitudes.[8]

The house that Gorky lived in is in that district. It is a most striking, remarkable house, built in the art nouveau style. If I'm not mistaken, it was originally built by Ryabushinsky, a merchant. In general, the

Moscow merchant class, the famous and successful ones, were highly educated people who supported the arts and generally held aloft the torch of culture – much more than our dear old nobility ever did. One of the richest Moscow industrialists of that time was Savva Morozov, who gave a great deal of money, for instance, to the Moscow Arts Theatre. My father and I knew the Morozov children; we danced together at balls and were constantly meeting at parties and so on. Apart from Savva Morozov, one of the most interesting men who patronized the arts was Sergei Shchusev.[9] He made a remarkable collection of French art, and founded a gallery for paintings by the French Impressionists.

We had quite a large [domestic] staff. My father had a manservant, part of whose job was to be on duty in the front hall, letting people in and out and helping them with their coats. Then there was a male cook – or rather, the chef. And where do you think he worked after the Revolution? In the Kremlin! They employed him because he had been the von Mecks' cook.

When I grew older, there were governesses in the household. There was a French woman and an English woman; later there was a Scottish woman and tutors as well. [The Scots girl, Miss Scott – 'Scottie', as we called her –] is mentioned in that book written about British governesses called *When Miss Emmy Was In Russia*[10] . . . she was more of a companion to my sisters than a governess.

I began learning English when I was still practically a baby. I was talking English almost before I could walk, because my cousin had an English tutor, and I picked it up from him extremely quickly.

Apart from the house in Moscow, there was an estate in the country, near Kiev. It was very big, with a lot of land. We sold wheat to England. We had a large herd of cattle [five hundred dairy cows], and made butter which was sold in Kiev – every week 720 lb of our butter was carted to the city. The journey took a long time, it being a considerable distance to cover by cart, but the butter was so good it was never spoiled. As soon as it reached Kiev, queues would form for the Meck butter. The greatest irony of all was after the Revolution when I went into a shop in Kiev to buy butter and they asked me, 'Do you want the ordinary sort – or Meck butter?' Even though it wasn't Meck butter any longer, the expression was still used to mean the first quality.

When we were still young we went to the country at the end of April. We would then spend the whole summer there, until October. The moment we arrived it was off with our shoes and stockings and from then on we went barefoot; I always wore boys' clothes, because I had lessons with my brothers and cousins and played all their games. Apart from the cows there was every kind of animal. We had our own stud farm, which bred remounts for the Army.

My parents later bought a small estate near Moscow. Small though it was, it had a beautiful old eighteenth-century house, dating from the reign of Catherine the Great, with thick walls and a classical arch over the front door – a historic building. There my father bred every variety of central Russian cattle. All summer the place was always full of guests; friends and relatives would come from Moscow and Petersburg, even from abroad. Then musicians would come and stay with us, and we often used to have musical evenings; there was a special 'music pavilion' in the garden, in which there were three grand pianos: two Bechsteins, and an Hérard which had belonged to my grandmother, a most beautiful instrument. All of them were confiscated by the Bolsheviks; I only hope they looked after them and made good use of them.

We had concerts in Moscow too, and from a musical point of view they were often the most interesting, because so many good musicians would be back in Moscow for the autumn and winter after spending the summer in various parts of the country. Our Moscow concerts were held every Wednesday, usually from October till May. To each one we invited some famous musician, and often one or more of the outstanding students about to graduate from the Conservatoire.

When the 1905 Revolution happened I was at boarding school, fairly insulated from events, but even so we were somewhat affected by the uprising in Moscow. One night at school there was panic in the dormitories. A furniture factory, owned by a German called Schmidt, was set on fire. From the school we could see it blazing. The headmistress decided to evacuate most of the girls. All of us whose parents lived near enough to fetch us were sent home. I was one of them. Father walked all the way to the school through side-streets, backyards, and even over fences and barricades to bring me home.

The back of our house was quite near the famous Presnya district,[11] where the revolutionaries had barricaded themselves. There was real fighting there. We children thought it was all very exciting, and at first we were secretly on the side of the revolutionaries. But in the end our sympathies turned against them, because two of our local traffic policemen were shot from behind, and someone took a shot at Father when he went out to help a woman and her small children.

My sister Kira was married during all this upheaval. She was going to spend her honeymoon in Petersburg, but had to come back because of the general strike. Railway strikes also hit our railway, the Moscow—Kazan line. The Government insisted that Father should give them the names of the ringleaders. He refused point-blank, but dismissed the men, who were mostly mechanics and engine drivers. When things returned to normal he took them all back.

But despite the Japanese War [1904–5] and the Revolution, it was also a time of great brilliance in the arts. Besides concerts, which we never missed if we could help it, I must say that we loved opera and ballet more than the theatre. After all, we were related to Tchaikovsky! The intelligentsia in particular was utterly absorbed by Stanislavsky's Moscow Arts Theatre, until the appearance of Tairov and his theatre of 'Expressive Gesture'. I personally was never attracted to Stanislavsky's naturalism. It was good, but a little too good. Of course, Chekhov reigned supreme, especially at the MAT, but in my personal opinion (I know many people will disagree with me) Chekhov's plays distorted the idea of what Russians were like in the first decade of this century. Even now I meet people in England who are quite convinced that Russians, however educated, are all 'Chekhovian' – weaklings swayed by their emotions, spineless creatures who wallow in life's complications without facing up to them. There were lots of quite different people in Russia, you know – people who worked, achieved, created; people who 'got to Moscow' if they wanted to, unlike those wretched Three Sisters! I never could understand why they didn't just buy a railway ticket and *go* to Moscow! My father, of course, was an exceptional, outstanding figure. But there were plenty like him . . .

It was my fondness for opera that made me a witness to one of the most tragic events in Russian history. In 1911 we went to Kiev. The Tsar was going there to unveil a memorial to one of his ancestors [to Alexander III, the Tsar's father] and to go to the races; being President of the Kiev Horse-Racing Society, my father had to be there as the Tsar's official host at the racecourse. He took me with him, and we stayed with my uncle Dmitry Davydov. We attended the unveiling of the memorial. The Tsar himself gave the command. He was not a big man, but his voice could be heard in every corner of that vast square.

Next day the Tsar, three of his daughters and the Tsarevich, the heir, little Alexei, were my father's guests at the racecourse. I was to have presented a bouquet to the Empress, but unfortunately she didn't come; she hated crowds and horse-racing bored her. I was left clutching my useless bouquet, so I decided to make use of it to get a better look at the little boy, and I handed it to him. I remember his frightened stare before he ran away to join his father, and my own feeling of annoyance that my appearance seemed to upset him so much. Years later I learned that because of his haemophilia he was schooled to avoid any sudden contact, in case he fell over and started an internal haemorrhage, and so his natural shyness was made worse, turning him into a pathetically timid little creature . . .

Then a crowd surged around the Imperial box, trying to get as near as possible. They were kept back by police and soldiers. I didn't want to get caught up in all that crush, so I kept to one side and just watched. With my camera I took a perfect snapshot of Stolypin, the Prime Minister.[12] I was surprised to see him quite alone, not even guarded by a single policeman. He was a splendid-looking man, tall and very imposing in his white summer uniform. I remember wondering what he was thinking about.

Father left for Moscow next morning, and I was supposed to go with him, but I so much wanted to see the gala performance of Rimsky-Korsakov's *Tsar Saltan* at the Kiev Opera House that evening that I persuaded Uncle Dmitry to take me. We sat in a box in the first tier. When act I came to an end, people left their seats and boxes to walk around, chat and fan themselves (it was very hot that evening). As the doyen of the Kiev nobility, my uncle had to be 'in attendance' at the Imperial box, so I was left alone in our box. I amused myself by watching what was going on in the stalls.

I watched Stolypin standing in the space between the front row of the stalls and the orchestra pit, talking to a group of people around him. I also noticed Professor Chernov, a famous paediatric surgeon, on the other side of the centre aisle. Then I noticed a man in a black suit pushing his way through the crowd towards the Prime Minister's party. Suddenly I saw him raise his arm – and a moment later came two revolver shots! There was a hush, and everyone turned to stare at the row where the man in black was jumping over the seats, making for the exit to the left of the stage. Stolypin remained standing for a while, blood slowly seeping through his uniform. Professor Chernov hurried over. The Prime Minister collapsed into his seat, but before he was hidden from me I saw him look over to his left at the Imperial box. The Tsar, who was talking to my uncle in the corridor behind the box, came back to see what had happened. The usual version of the story is that when the Tsar appeared at the edge of the box, Stolypin made the sign of the Cross, blessing the Emperor, but that is not true: I was watching him intently, and what Stolypin did, although badly wounded in the stomach, was to raise his left arm and twice wave to the Tsar to go back into the box and keep out of sight – a sensible gesture, absolutely in keeping with Stolypin's character, a mixture of courage and sound common sense.

Some officers caught the assassin as he was jumping over the last few seats near the exit. They would have lynched him if the police hadn't stopped them and arrested the man. Supported by several friends, Stolypin managed to walk out of the theatre – an act of amazing courage and will-power, which earned him an ovation. The whole audience began to sing 'God Save the Tsar', the curtain went up and the cast joined in, kneeling on the stage. The Tsar stood at the front of his box, obviously distressed but showing no fear.

As Uncle Dmitry and I were crossing the street behind the theatre, two ambulance-men came out of the stage door carrying a stretcher. On it was a man in bloodstained evening dress, a member of the orchestra whose place was directly under the Tsar's box. We wondered if the killer, having shot Stolypin, had also made an attempt to shoot the Tsar, missed him, and wounded this wretched musician instead. On the other hand, he could have been hit by a bullet that passed through Stolypin's body; I don't suppose we shall ever know.

Within five days Stolypin was dead. If (as a rule I think 'ifs' in history are a waste of time, but I know many people agree with me on this point) – if Stolypin had lived, Russian history would have taken a very different course . . .

3

On the Estate

PROFESSOR ELIZABETH KUTAISSOVA

Elizabeth Kutaissova was born into a land-owning family and her father became Governor of Volhynia, a province of the Ukraine. When the Revolution began in 1917, they were among the first émigrés.

My mother's family were the Rehbinders. They had an estate in Kursk. They were the opposite of *Cherry Orchard* types. Alexander Rehbinder was an agronomist, and their estate had a sugar factory, a brickworks, spirits distillery, leather factory and so on. They farmed their own land and even rented land from the peasants – which was most unusual; most of the landowners rented their land to the peasants – because they were expanding so fast. Their estate was called Shebekino, which is now a small town. They even opened a small agricultural college.

My mother's estate had been leased to a tenant and allowed to run down. When Father retired from the Government service in 1912, he took it over and grew vast amounts of cabbage and cucumbers and shipped it out by rail – we were only three versts [approx. three kilometres] from the station. The station master was terribly proud because once in one day he sent off a record thirty-five wagonloads of cucumbers!

The estate next door was owned by a picturesque and determined old lady called Alexeyeva (sister of the Mayor of Moscow, who was assassinated in 1905). She had even introduced electricity to her estate. After the Revolution her estate and ours were combined to make an early *sovkhoz*.[1] She was married to a young German called Huppert who had come out as an apprentice. He was also an improver, and used to ride round on a big white horse inspecting things. They built a new house and his wife wanted the Bishop to come and bless it. But a Bishop needed a closed carriage, which was hired for the occasion. I will always remember as a child watching the coachman washing the horses' hooves for the Bishop's visit!

After Father decided to go into agriculture we spent most of the year on our estate in Kursk. The winter we spent in Petersburg. So for us there was a choice of boarding school – an *institut* – or governesses. Father employed a charming girl student from a priest's family. The priests were very poor, so this girl had to earn her living. In her first year at university – you can imagine what it was like for a girl from the country, from a very restricted, poor background – she came under the influence of the left-wingers. I remember her having a great fight with my grandmother (whose late husband had been the Russian naval attaché in London) over the origins of man. This girl explained to her that man was descended from the monkeys 'as Darwin said'. Grandmother replied that she'd read the *Origin of Species* in England when it was first published in London in the 1860s and Darwin didn't actually say that. The girl was astonished! The students, you see, used to regard the land-owning gentry as hopelessly ignorant and backward. She confessed afterwards to Father that she had come to us intending to enlighten our darkness! Left-wing ideas, you see, had been so exciting for her, coming from that sort of background.

On Boxing Day the children of the estate used to come to the house. I remember preparing little presents for them – kerchiefs and scarves, filled with nuts and sweets. There were ninety children on the estate, the children of servants, coachmen, stokers in the brickworks and so on: not of the peasants. My brother had a Cossack to teach him to ride and he in turn taught him to play football. Our peasants were different from others – they were near to the railway and so, effectively, to Moscow. They used to go off and work elsewhere – they were really turning into workers. For the harvest we hired groups of women from Kaluga, a very poor province. There would be groups of twenty or thirty with two as cooks. In Russia the harvest has to be got in very quickly, because the summer is so short. The agent would ride round the villages looking for girls to help – these would only be the unmarried ones who were looking for money for their dowries. We were really a capitalist enterprise, using hired labour, milkmaids and so on, all the year round. My grandmother's estates were more normal: one was rented out, another was managed for her because she really lived abroad.

My father was Governor of Volhynia. (He resigned because of

Government pressure over the elections to the Fourth *Duma*[2] – they wanted him to rig them.) That time was very dull for us children. He had a difficult job because of the mixture of populations. The majority is now called Ukrainian – then, they were regarded as Russians. The towns were Jewish. One Russian tried to open a shop in Zhitomir, and was forced out. The landowners were Polish. There were also a large number of Czech and German immigrants. The difficulty for us was that the Poles, of course, were very anti-Russian. Normally the children of the Governor would have been friends with the children of local landowners, but the class divisions were strict as regards the governors of provinces, so this was obviously impossible for us, because they were Poles. Jewish friends were out of the question, of course. But at least Zhitomir was a garrison town, so we had a few friends among the children of the military.

Father noticed that where a German village and a Russian village were side by side, the Germans would be clean, tidy and prosperous, while the Russian one would be dirty and disorganized. Catherine the Great had hoped that the Russian peasants would imitate the German example, but they didn't. Also, the Germans kept to themselves. They were very well off, and many of their houses had hard tennis courts. My father was very suspicious of them – he thought they might be intended as artillery emplacements for the German Army!

My father was a strong supporter of Stolypin and backed him over the western *zemstvo* question.[3] I think he was in the theatre in Kiev when Stolypin was murdered.

My father told his chief of police that he wouldn't tolerate any pogroms. One festival day he told this man that he should take special precautions. The police chief replied that this was his men's day off, and why should he deprive them of it just to protect the Jews? I think this was a typical attitude – certainly not deliberate organization by the Government. Pogroms were known in Volhynia as 'tearing up pillows'. They were carried out by hooligans. Only rarely were people killed. Kishinev, of course, was an exception.[4]

My mother was then only in her early thirties. She had many new responsibilities as the Governor's wife. On one occasion she invited both the Orthodox and the Catholic Bishops to dinner. Our Orthodox Bishop was Khapavitsky, who already had a reputation for scholarship and for holding strong opinions. The Catholic Bishop was, of course, a Pole, and my mother expected them to speak French to each other.

But Khapavitsky couldn't speak French, and the Pole pretended he couldn't speak Russian, so they started to speak Latin to each other, which annoyed my mother very much. Fortunately, the German pastor was there too, and he could speak all three.

A household of servants followed us around. Here you find them through agencies, there it was through relations: 'my cousin has a maid who has a sister . . .'. There is nothing worse than the *bonne à tout faire* living apart from the family. In Russia the household was a community.

The servants were bewildered by the Revolution. Our Polish maid went to the revolutionary meetings; she couldn't understand a word, but she was absolutely fascinated. When we left, one servant brought his family to the flat hoping that in the reallocation of accommodation he would be able to protect our belongings.

We were on the estate in 1917. The previous owner had wanted to build his house like a mosque, with minarets, and on a mound. Only one minaret had been put up and that was visible for miles around. An agitator from Moscow came and convinced the people of the railway-station village that Father had mounted machine guns in this minaret on the hill. They went to destroy the minaret, and Father just had time to get the butler to empty all the wine bottles in our house so that they wouldn't get drunk – but in fact they didn't try to break into the cellar. After that Father decided to leave.

We were in Petersburg during the February/March Revolution. Father had expected something of the sort to happen, but he said, 'If the war is won, Nicholas II will go down in history as a great monarch. He has given a constitution and – quite fortuitously – Russia is getting very prosperous and well educated.' Father and Mother themselves used to be great patrons of the local schools.

No one before 1917 knew who Lenin was. My uncle (who was later murdered by the Bolsheviks) went to listen to Lenin speaking from the Kseshinskaya Balcony[5] as a curiosity. We didn't see any shooting. My father was more worried about what would happen to the land – the Provisional Government was discussing repartition. He was determined to hang on – it was his life.

We left Russia in September 1917, through Finland to Stockholm. There were very few others coming out at that stage – the first people we met were all in the embassies – but immediately after October they began to leave. My father was very excited when Alexinsky, the SR

[Socialist Revolutionary Party] leader, came out. 'If even *that* man is leaving . . . !'[6]

From Sweden we moved to Denmark, where we stayed until the Civil War was over. In 1919 there was a great moment of hope when the White troops of General Yudenich reached the outskirts of Petrograd.[7] A friend of ours, Count Benningsen, left his family and went back to Riga by boat. But we knew very little of what was going on in Russia.

There were enough Russians in Denmark for us to set up a little school – there were so many professors and teachers coming out. The embassy obtained permission from Denikin or Kolchak[8] to grant certificates, and on the basis of this I got into a Swiss university. My father wanted me to become a doctor: 'White or Red, they'll need doctors.' But I was a great friend of one of the daughters of Hetman Skoropadsky:[9] she was studying medicine; she was already in the year when you dissect corpses and she took me in to see them. I was so horrified that I switched to chemistry instead. What else could I study? Law? We weren't going to stay in Switzerland: we thought we were going back to Russia. Humanities? We wouldn't get a job. Another friend studied agriculture. We wanted useful jobs when we got back to Russia. The Bolsheviks had slaughtered the best people: we felt we had to help our country. My parents would never have believed, when they left, that it was the last time they would ever see Russia.

My father only had administrative skills, so we had to spin out the money we had brought out with us by selling jewellery. Very few people had much. Those who did were mainly those who had had villas abroad. The Cantacuzenes turned their villa into a boarding house. It's much easier to be poor when everybody's poor; there was little envy. I knew [a woman who had] been a very wealthy hostess in St Petersburg, and had kept a diplomatic salon which Paléologue, the French Ambassador, used to attend. She went to Paris hoping that her French friends would help her to be part of the French élite, but she was cold-shouldered – she couldn't return the hospitality.

None of the Russians became millionaires. Some became academics, some did very interesting work . . . but when it came to money most of them were hopeless!

On the whole, people remained within their old circles of acquaintanceship and family – regiment, occupation, political allegiance.

4

A Russian Moderate

SOFIA SERGEYEVNA KOULOMZINA

Sofia Sergeyevna Koulomzina (née Shidlovskaya) was born in 1904 in St Petersburg. Her father, S. I. Shidlovsky (1861–1922) was a landowner who became a middle-of-the-road liberal conservative in the Duma. The family emigrated in 1922.

My father was educated at the Lycée.[1] (Ours was a Lycée family for several generations. Both my grandfathers were there, as were my father and my uncle.) In those days, people with a higher education had to do only three months' compulsory military service;[2] after that [my father] went on a sort of Grand Tour, which included visits to Turkey, Egypt and so on.

During his last three years at the Lycée – from nineteen to twenty-one – he studied at university level, and a good deal of the time was devoted to studying law. When he graduated he took up the life of a country landowner, but he also worked in the Peasant Bank. The function of this bank was to buy up landlord-owned estates and then to resell the land on credit terms to peasants. It was one of the results of the Stolypin reforms.[3] Father was a great admirer of Stolypin. But it wasn't always an easy job; I remember him telling my grandfather how impossible it was to persuade the *obshchina* [commune] peasants to buy land, even from the best-run estates which had modern machinery and had used good fertilizers and so on; whereas the so-called *khutoryane* [peasants who had bought themselves out of the commune and set up as independent freeholders] always showed great interest in acquiring more land. You could always tell the difference between 'peasant' [i.e. communally held] land and 'freeholder' land: the latter was invariably better worked and far more productive.

My father always criticized the Slavophiles' sentimental, woolly-headed adoration of the peasant commune, the *mir* or *obshchina*; he thought it was pernicious nonsense, and that the commune completely killed initiative.

Looking back, though, I now see that my father's greatest qualities were objectivity and cool sobriety in his judgements – qualities that are comparatively rare in Russians. It was quite extraordinary, for instance, the degree to which the peasants on our estate respected him and turned to him for advice. He would never permit his attitude to be distorted by that kind of saccharine sentimentality about the peasantry that characterized the attitude of so many people – including that of my maternal grandfather, Saburov. Both Grandfather and Grandmother Saburov believed that they simply lived for their peasants and did everything for them (and they *did* do a lot for them), yet they were hopeless landowners. They ran their estate hopelessly badly and the peasants never came to them for advice; whereas the peasants' relations with my father were always conducted in serious, businesslike but friendly talks in which there was never a trace of condescension or patronizing on my father's part. I saw this. Yet at the same time, he always refused to look upon his estate as some kind of charity. This was characteristic of him. In his political life, he was incapable of idealizing the revolutionary movement; many educated, cultured Russians of that time undoubtedly did harbour a kind of revolutionary idealism, but my father never did. He greatly liked and respected Stolypin, certainly, but even in the Stolypin era he was a fairly confirmed pessimist about the future of Russia after a revolution. He was, for instance, a member of the so-called 'Provisional Committee of the *Duma*' at the time of the February Revolution in 1917, and he was offered a post in the Provisional Government – but he refused it.

He didn't believe that the Provisional Government could succeed. I remember meeting Kerensky at the time;[4] he knew I was my father's daughter, and he said to me, 'How I regret that your father hasn't joined us. We need him so badly; we tried so hard to persuade him.' My father simply didn't believe in Kerensky's ability as a statesman; he didn't believe that Kerensky had it in him to achieve anything that was politically constructive or sound. Broadly speaking, I think he was right. But remember, I was only fourteen at the time, and my father died when I was seventeen, and those are the years in which every adolescent is striving, consciously or not, to break away from their parents or to reject them.

And then my father also had a failing that is characteristic of Russians: a certain passivity. If he wasn't absolutely convinced that some course of action was absolutely correct and certain of success, he would back off and stay aloof. This extended to family matters too. He was, of course, a believing Christian, but he didn't share a certain streak of mystical exaltation that was a part of my mother's attitude to religion, and especially where my brothers were concerned he undoubtedly felt that there was something wrong in the way she brought them up. But he never once intervened or spoke out about this, he never interfered, and he never *gave* himself to us as a father. That is something, I think, with which I can legitimately reproach him – his constant emotional withdrawal . . . I suspect that he also showed the same characteristic in his social and political life . . .

He became the leader of the Progressive Bloc[5] in the Third and Fourth *Dumy* and became an active politician. He made speeches, he wrote his memoirs and so on – even so, he never rid himself of a certain scepticism, an unwillingness to fight for an issue if he wasn't absolutely certain that his viewpoint would prevail. I believe this trait was, in fact, characteristic of those Russians in public life at the time who were what we would call 'decent' people – an epithet that was very strong and meant a great deal in those days. The fact is, he wasn't a fighter.

Nevertheless, in the world of Russian pre-Revolutionary politics – the '*Duma* Decade' – he went very far and was very close to the centres of power. I've often wondered exactly what it was about him that caused people to respect and value him so highly. I've read the memoirs of Shulgin, Kerensky, Rodzyanko[6] and my father's own memoirs, and I think it was that he inspired trust and confidence, thanks to his ability to make objective, dispassionate judgements. Take Rodzyanko, for example, also a thoroughly decent man, but at the same time incredibly self-assured and somehow always wanting to prove himself, to show off . . . in everything Rodzyanko did or wrote there was always an attempt to convince you: 'Look what a splendid fellow I am! . . . How I foiled Rasputin, how I did this or that, what I said to the Tsar, and so on . . . ' My father, I think, lacked any trace of that kind of mettlesome spirit.

5

Things Fall Apart

PYOTR PETROVICH SHILOVSKY

Pyotr Petrovich Shilovsky was born in 1883 in St Petersburg. Under the Tsar he was a Provincial Governor and owned an estate at Ryazan. With the Revolution of February 1917, he watched the beginning of the end of his entire way of life.

I remember that I had my first tangible premonition of the impending catastrophe when I returned, at the end of February 1917, with Countess O. F. Heyden from a Red Cross meeting at Gatchina. When we left the train at Petersburg railway station, a Court footman who had come to meet my companion said, raising his cocked hat, 'Things are in a bad way in the capital . . . ' The carriage, with the Court coachman and footman up, moved quietly along Zagorodny Avenue, which was crowded with people who hastened to make way, showing outward respect . . . But that was the last time that a Court carriage drove through the streets of Petersburg. The Winter Palace was already surrounded by an excited crowd. Countess Heyden had to spend the night at the home of a humble, devoted acquaintance of hers, on Vasilevsky Island.

In the days that followed, the streets in the centre of Petersburg presented an interesting spectacle. They were filled with an extremely mixed crowd, which was made up of innumerable small groups, each gathered round a political speaker who had appeared from Heaven knows where. The things those speakers talked about – about finishing off the Germans in spite of the 'German party' in Russia's highest circles; about whether or not we needed to seize Constantinople; about how 'we' would set an example to Europe; about how to equalize property-ownership. And so on. The well-known progressive priest Petrov, whom I encountered somewhere, was filled with terror at this word 'we', a word that one heard buzzing in railway carriages and stations and in eating-houses and inns.

A sort of mass ecstasy was felt at this time by almost all classes of Russia's vast population. Everyone seemed to see things in the same way. Six months later, we beheld a different scene – a gulf had opened up between the plebs, the proletariat, and those who had assumed their leadership on the one hand, and, on the other, the 'bourgeois' – a gulf teeming with mutual bitterness and hatred. Every person who washed and dressed more or less smartly was called a 'bourgeois'. I repeat: in the first months of the 'new order', this class antagonism was not particularly noticeable. When they called on some privileged families on our English Embankment, the armed members of unofficial committees who were 'collecting weapons from the citizens' behaved very respectfully, and went away satisfied with the assurances of these privileged bourgeois that they would not act against 'the people'. My brother-in-law, Admiral Nebolsin, was talking on the telephone when some of these people came to our flat and entered the study. 'Wait: you can see I'm busy,' said the Admiral, irritably. And they waited quietly.

I mention these trivial incidents because they serve to illustrate my point that the Revolution, when it began, gave no sign of the ferocious form into which it developed ten months later. The slogan of the first days of the Revolution was: 'Support the State *Duma* against the reactionary Ministers.' The question of abdication by the Tsar was not raised . . .

The unreadiness of the masses for political life and self-government showed itself clearly in the street meetings I have mentioned, and in their susceptibility to emotional appeals. An orator might be speaking about the Straits, about how Russia must have Constantinople. The crowd listens attentively.

'From ancient times the Princes and Tsars of Russia', says the orator, raising his voice, 'cherished the idea of hanging Russia's shield for ever on the gates of Tsaregrad . . . '

'That's right, yes, that's true!' shouts the crowd.

'But what I tell you', comes from their midst, spoken by another man with something to say – a sharp, quick fellow, 'is that the common people don't need any Straits. What they need is to be given land, and not to be oppressed. If those gentlemen need the Straits, let them go and get them; but we won't go.'

'That's right, that's true!' is the reaction of the same crowd, with no less warmth than before.

It was 28 April 1917, the day when Milyukov, who had thought he could conduct the foreign policy of the new Russia with dignity, was obliged to leave the Ministry of Foreign Affairs.[1] A crowd of many thousands, consisting of all sorts, but mainly of soldiers, had gathered in front of the Maryinsky Palace . . . So far, everything was relatively calm and decorous. The Dean of the Anglican Church attached to the British Embassy, the Reverend Lombard, whom we knew, came up to us to voice his approval of everything that had happened and of the moderation of the revolutionaries. This was evidently the general opinion at the Embassy. But something was happening that was more serious than we thought.

Our butler, Albert, gave notice because his sons were opposed to his being in the service of 'capitalists'. Our staid cook, a respectable Lithuanian, began going off in the evenings to listen to the speakers at Kseshinskaya's house,[2] where Lenin had set up his headquarters, and reported the remarkable things he had learnt there with delight to our other servants. He, too, left us soon after. To crown everything, a telegram arrived from the excellent steward of my estate in Ryazan province, to say that, owing to difficulties with the peasants, he had been forced to leave the estate.

I decided to go down personally and find out what had happened. Since clearly nothing could be done without the co-operation of the provincial authorities, I resolved to call in at Ryazan.

When I entered the flat of the Commander of the local regiment, the worthy Colonel greeted me politely, but on learning why I had come, he at once assumed an official tone, and said that such matters were now being dealt with by the 'Soviet' at Government House.[3] Government House, where my wife grew up, and where, only three years earlier, I had called on the elegant Prince Obolensky, now presented an incredible spectacle. The fine furniture, carpets and mirrors had disappeared, and the parquet flooring was bespattered with spittle and strewn with cigarette ends. A few ragged armchairs stood against the walls, together with some benches brought in from the garden. A large number of untidily dressed soldiers, with some strange civilians, were either sprawling on the seats or rushing about. A gallant front-line colonel entered the Governor's former waiting room, with uncertain step, looking all around him; his sleeve bore several wound stripes. Nobody paid the slightest attention to him. We looked at each other in silence.

It took me half an hour to find out who it was I had to see, but at last I arrived in a room where some soldiers and workers were sitting at a kitchen table. To my surprise I was received very politely, and the Chairman – apparently a semi-educated man – turned out to know who I was.

'The committee is aware that relations between the peasants and you were good. There are no complaints against you. We are sending an instructor to your estate, who –' The words of the Chairman were interrupted by a desperate shriek.

'You are ruining the Army! It's impossible! I'll never go along with this!' This was shouted, in a tone of fearful excitement, by a young officer who rushed in from the next room. He was in hysterics.

'Calm yourself, Comrade. I, as Commissar, am looking into the matter myself,' said a young Jew who came running after the officer, trying to soothe him. Through the door, I could see other excited, grimacing faces. Everybody was arguing noisily.

There was no point in my remaining there, and I walked off through what had been the dining room on my way out. In the dining room, I saw two or three good-looking Jewesses, carrying on a lively trade in cigarettes and sandwiches. In a corner of the room stood a stall laden with goods.

To my considerable (but concealed) surprise, at the local branch of the State Bank they handed me, without hesitation, a cheque for 20,000 roubles as payment for oats supplied to the War Department. That was the last income I was to receive from my estate. I am still describing the era before the Kerensky period;[4] it was, however, already quite clear to me that authority was simply disintegrating without anyone to defend it.

All the same, I decided to visit my estate and my brothers, who had not left their homes. Things were still all right with them, although they were worried about the future. There was a serious situation on my estate. My peasants had 'removed' the yearly hired workers, and all the cattle – the dairy cows, the pedigree bulls, the calves – had been for several days in the care of the old bookkeeper and a young worker who had stayed loyal to me. When I arrived, the 'village committee' came to see me at the estate office, with the local postmaster at their head. We talked very politely. The committee advised me to hand over the whole estate, its peasant members adding that they did not want to use force: 'We will not hurt you' – they no longer addressed me as 'Your Honour'.

I tried, obviously without success, to instil into them the theory of the inalienability of property rights, even in time of revolution. It was decided that I should talk with the village assembly that evening, at the priest's house. Sixty men were present. After greeting them, I said briefly that troubled and difficult times had come upon us, but that the main thing was to end the war victoriously. To my last, louder words, the assembly responded with a general 'Hurrah!' Evidently, the mood prevailing in Petersburg had not yet reached the province. I remember that I explained to the peasants that if anyone's right to property was encroached on at all, the practice of seizing other people's possessions would spread further and further. 'And you won't be masters in your own families,' I prophesied.

The peasants stood firm on their point of view. 'Give us the estate freely; we'll look after it; we don't want to use force.' The priest assured me that, when I left, the peasants' feeling towards me was very favourable. I went back to the manor house to discuss with the bookkeeper what to do. There were two German prisoners-of-war who were efficient workers, and next morning, after I had seen to whatever I could, I set off to my brothers' estates.

A surprise awaited me at the railway station. By order of the Soviet or Commissar of Ryazan, an Army unit had been sent to the station, commanded by a cavalry sergeant-major. The very pleasant and well-mannered student-commissar who accompanied them was greatly worried about how to quarter twenty men, with their horses, on my estate, how to set up stalls where the horses could spend the night, and so on. Carts and sleighs (it was the time of the thaw) were also needed for the commander's baggage . . .

I was glad to see that the provincial organs of the Provisional Government, the local democratic committees, were prepared to do what they could to maintain civil order in the country, or at least a semblance of it. What was bad, however, was that the modest apparatus of the local police authority had been annihilated, and in its place the parallel power of the Soviets, with their Bolshevik wing, had been established and was spreading unchecked. The representatives of this power – both

genuine and self-styled – travelled freely all over Russia, knew exactly
what the official Government was trying to do, and put their own
measures into effect. In certain places, they proclaimed themselves the
supreme ruling authority.

When we read the truthful picture of military breakdown given by
Polovtsev,[5] we find it hard to understand why the Provisional Government, knowing the situation, left that powerful trump card, 'Down with
the War', in the hands of the Bolsheviks.[6] Their stubborn continuation
of the war when everything was falling to pieces in the country, when
the front was breaking up and hundreds of thousands of deserters were
being given the warmest of welcomes by the Bolshevik Party, which
they naturally joined, seems amazing stupidity and an act of deliberate
suicide. But I remember the howl of indignation when the story got
about that the question of leaving the war had been raised at some
session of the Provisional Government. Seemingly, the prolongation of
the war was an expression of that quixotic sense of honour, characteristic of our intelligentsia . . .

My brothers were living quietly on their estates, though they could not
be sure what the morrow held for them . . . Of all the big estates in
the neighbourhood, only ours remained. We expected no unpleasantness from our peasants; the threat of danger came from the 'strolling
players', as my elder brother called them. Alas, we were soon convinced
of the reality of that danger.

I had cheerfully settled in with the younger of my two brothers in
his charming house, recently built in the 'Empire' style at Alexeyevka,
when I received news from my own estate that, the day before, people
armed with authority had come from Government House and briskly
made off with my pedigree dairy cattle, with a view to slaughtering
them at Ryazhsk. 'It shouldn't only be the peasants who have to give
cattle for the Army's needs; let the landlords suffer as well . . . '

I fled to Ryazhsk. Near the town I caught up with the 'commission'
which had taken my herd. The cattle were grazing under the supervision
of my two German prisoners-of-war. There were two *zemstvo* [county
council] vets in the commission. They were very embarrassed, but it
was obviously no joking matter to oppose the power which had ordered
them to take my cattle for slaughter. Under the old order, it struck
me, they would have made a fuss and threatened to resign. I started

to get heated, and when some worker joined in our conversation, I flared up, shouted at him that he was supporting robbery and thrust my fist under his nose. Fortunately for me, the man – he turned out to be a commissar from the local Soviet – was not very strong on insolence, and such opposition from a bourgeois stunned him. He turned round and went away, probably to fetch help. I sharply informed the stupefied commission that I would lodge a complaint against them in Ryazan.

When I looked at my watch, I realized that in half an hour there would be a train leaving for Ryazan and Moscow, and hurried to the station. The station was crowded. In the spacious restaurant, everything was normal: clean tablecloths, waiters. But the 'strolling players' were already in evidence. I remember there was a rather fierce-looking sailor who was expounding something inflammatory to a respectable sergeant-major. 'No, no, that's impossible,' the latter was saying, with a sort of earnest melancholy.

I somehow got involved in the conversation, and it was just like the meetings in Petersburg. Exactly what it was that I put to the sailor – something political, obviously – I don't recall; but he answered me in the same way as the crowds round the orators in the capital: 'That's right, that's true.' As we calmly exchanged ideas, even his face was transformed. He went so far as to observe, modestly, that things were difficult 'for us' – we can see that the Government is bad, yet we don't know what is actually needed. 'But the educated people are against us.' As he said that, anger again flashed in his eyes.

The whistle announcing that the train was about to depart interrupted our conversation. I did not go to Ryazan. It was clear to me that I must give the estate up for lost and must live on whatever other income I had and what wages I could get. After all, the situation might improve. Ah, what incorrigible optimists we were!

Imperial Russia entered into the period of Revolution with an enormous amount of fixed capital – enormous not only in quantity but also in quality. One cannot imagine any treatment of the country's economy more absurd and wasteful than the sort of thing that went on under the Provisional Government. Nobody did anything about repairing rolling-stock or trams, and both forms of transport were obliged to endure inadmissible overloading . . . Under pressure from the Soviets, the Provisional Government requisitioned all depots and storehouses of every kind. The amount of thieving that went on in that connection was appalling, and the damage done to goods and to the furniture and carpets seized from the bourgeoisie incredible. And yet shortages took a long time to make themselves felt. Moscow's store of manufactured goods proved to be phenomenal. It was possible to exist for years without producing, merely by drawing on reserves.

However, another and perhaps even more valuable form of capital was also inherited by the new Russia: namely, the intellectual capital of the old regime. An impartial historian in the future will testify to the huge numbers of Russian scholars and scientists, in all branches of learning, who were educated in pre-Revolutionary Russia, and likewise to the advanced factories and works that were springing up like mushrooms and were staffed by brilliant engineers – not to mention Russian medicine, the work of the *zemstvos* and our achievements in the arts.

I leave it to historians to describe the cowardly and stupid way in which the Provisional Government went about combatting the growing strength of Bolshevism. They will have the task of explaining how millions of the lower classes of our population, who had only recently been good-natured or indifferent in their attitude to the upper classes, their 'ruling class', were transformed into an embodiment of ferocious, boundless hatred. It would be idle to assert that the annihilation of the bourgeois was carried out by some small group made up exclusively of foreigners, while the people remained aloof. Somebody arrested the bourgeois and counter-revolutionaries, somebody put them in prison, somebody guarded the camps and forced the prisoners to work, and somebody shot the victims of Bolshevik disapproval.

Food cards and rationing played a part here, of course, but disinterested zeal was also important. Personally, I formed the impression that if the Bolshevik leaders had not noticed the animal fury which filled the soldiers and the scum of which the first Soviets consisted, they would not have resorted to the needless mass executions, labour camps and other measures which history has marked down to their eternal discredit. I say 'needless' because I saw how frightened ordinary people were. The Bolsheviks could have got by perfectly well without such measures.

And Bolshevism did not reveal its bloody profile straight away. The anarchy and chaos that prevailed under Kerensky were so universally repugnant that the manifestation of strength and vigour which was felt immediately after 7 November 1917 met with approval even from some bourgeois. Previously, nobody had taken any notice of the militia, but it was different now, as I myself saw, when a cart-driver in Nevsky Prospekt ignored a militia man's order to keep to the side of the street; the militia man cocked his revolver and took aim at the offender. 'That's right, that's what's needed,' people in the crowd remarked. 'You don't play the fool with the Bolsheviks.'

At the beginning of the Revolution there were about thirty thousand officers in Petersburg, but it was impossible to unite them all under one flag. The flag of restoration of the old regime was unacceptable. Ideas were fragmented. Whom to support? What cause would one be fighting for, if called upon to sacrifice one's life? For Lvov?[7] For Milyukov? For Kerensky? Trotsky reports in his memoirs a remarkably vivid story told by a certain colonel about the unit under his command: 'I was ordered to take my unit to a certain place. The company fell in . . . Perfect discipline. We marched off to fulfil the Government's orders and arrest the person indicated. By the time we were halfway to our destination, half of my men had disappeared. The company just melted away. When we got there, all that remained were the officers and the sergeant-major . . .' Polovtsev describes a similar scene. His Caucasian native units simply hid themselves in the mountains when the time came to defend the local authorities against the Bolsheviks.

Between five and seven thousand Kronstadt sailors,[8] welded into a single striking force and united by a few easily understood slogans – an end to the war, improvement of the living conditions of the proletariat, nationalization of the factories, the land to go to those who worked it, and so on – were able to smash the age-old Tsarist order. Lenin began his programme in a very restrained way, without any such slogans as 'steal what has been stolen', 'destroy the bourgeois and the Tsarist officers', 'burn the landlord' . . .

I remember how, one fine morning – it was either 6 or 7 November – we saw from our windows on the English Embankment, moored to the granite wall of the embankment, in front of our very door, the fine cruiser *Aurora*.[9] Handsome sailors were calmly moving about on deck. Our female servants, not excluding the English nursery-governess, lost no opportunity of getting to know the new neighbours. Either the newspapers had not arrived, or they had little to say on the subject; in any case, we learnt from the servants that the cruiser had come to get rid of Kerensky. Whether Kerensky was removed or not did not seem a matter of great concern to anyone. Soviet historians describe the siege and capture of the Winter Palace and the arrest of the Ministers there in triumphant style: 'The besieged were invited to surrender. They did not reply. The signal was given. The guns of the Peter-and-Paul Fortress opened fire on the Winter Palace. The guns of the cruiser *Aurora* blazed away . . . '

The reader will get a very poor impression of me, but I must say in all honesty that I did not hear the salvoes of the *Aurora*. I must have slept through them.

What about the guns of the Peter-and-Paul Fortress? Everyone knew that there was only one gun there. Each day, on the stroke of noon, it fired a blank shell. A number of gun-muzzles did indeed look out on the city from the walls and embrasures of the Fortress, but these were weapons dating from the time of Peter the Great.

The days just before the *coup d'état* were much more alarming. Rifle-fire had occasionally been heard in certain districts. Worrying rumours circulated everywhere. On the doctor's advice, my wife went away for a few days to a quiet part of the city. Petersburg was a huge city, with two million inhabitants, and the armed conflict – crackling of rifle-fire in areas where the enemy was thought to be – took place between, say, three thousand Kerenskyites and twelve thousand anti-Kerenskyites. When the sailors joined the latter, victory was theirs. The man in the street did not even grasp very clearly what the difference was between them . . .

Shilovsky's flat in St Petersburg was repossessed by the authorities and the family moved to more modest accommodation in Tsarskoye (later Detskoye) Selo; the town was renamed Pushkin in 1937.

Lenin's regime was eager to secure the co-operation of the Russian intelligentsia, especially in the field of technology, and as a result Shilovsky, although opposed to the Bolsheviks, won some measure of security. He had for years been developing a monorail project and in 1919 was invited to Moscow to demonstrate his model. His plans were accepted and he was commissioned to build a monorail from St Petersburg to Tsarskoye Selo.

Living conditions and the problems of bringing up children in the new Russia, however, led Shilovsky and his wife to emigrate. They were granted exit visas with little difficulty, and in 1922 left Russia. Shilovsky's story is continued in Chapter 41.

6

The Kiev Pogrom

ALEXANDRE DE GUNZBURG

Alexandre de Gunzburg belonged to a well-known Jewish banking family in St Petersburg with numerous children and ramifications all over Europe. The Gunzburgs took special pride in their descent from the famous Rabbi, Jehuda Loeb, of Prague. They first prospered in Russia under Tsar Nicholas I (1825–55), who entrusted them with the State spirit-monopoly south of Kamenets-Podolskiy, on the Dnieper.

Alexandre's father, Horace, had been given the title of Baron by the Grand Duke of Hessen-Darmstadt and the Gunzburgs were well known in St Petersburg society, where they counted many intellectual friends. They were particularly connected with 'the Jewish question in Russia', trying to improve the situation of the Jews with the help of the more liberal and fair-minded elements of the aristocracy, and denouncing the anti-Semitism which surfaced after the assassination of Alexander II with the pogrom of 1881. In this period, the War Ministry was dominated by liberals, such as Dmitry Milyutin, who encouraged integration of Jews, and young Alexandre, with his brother Alfred, obtained commissions in Russian regiments.

The Gunzburgs, and others like them who lived in the smarter part of towns, would normally have been exempt from pogroms, since these usually began in regions with a dense Jewish population. But by 1905 the temper of anti-Semitism in Kiev had risen so far that even the richest and best-connected Jews might not be safe. The Kiev pogrom spread from Podol, a poor quarter of the city, to the Kreshchatik, its most famous street, containing the palace of the Governor-General. Alexandre de Gunzburg happened to be caught at the house of his brother Volodya, who was married to a Brodsky, from a family of large-scale sugar refiners in Kiev. He describes below the scenes that he witnessed.

Alexandre, born in Paris in 1863, married Rosa Warburg of the Ham-

burg banking family, and himself was a banker in St Petersburg. He left Russia in 1918, having been almost miraculously freed from prison, where he had been taken as a reserve officer – he was released by the intervention of Feliks Dzierzyński, head of the Cheka, who told him that he had 'heard so much good of your father and his children that I must help you'. Alexandre then moved via Paris to Amsterdam, where he was able to found a small private bank, but in 1940, escaping from the Nazis, he left Holland for Basle, where he died in 1948.

The memoirs of his daughter appear in Chapter 7.

The lower part [of Kiev] was called Podol, on the banks of the Dnieper, and was open to Jews, whereas the upper town and especially the Kreshchatik, where stood the Imperial palaces, the State Bank, the Central Post Office, the palace of the Governor-General and that of the Governor, was considered to be the capital: only Jews with permission to reside in Great Russia might live there. Jews who were in the highest class of taxpayer resided there, almost exclusively sugar manufacturers and refiners. To go from Podol to the upper town there were two parallel streets, one called Alexandrovskaya, on which stood the [Imperial] palace, and the other, the Institutskaya, which passed round the State Bank and the palace of the Governor-General; the two streets were joined by Sadovaya . . . Volodya Gunzburg's house was on the corner of Sadovaya and Institutskaya.

In 1905, Grandmother Rosenberg had just died at Kiev and many members of the family were there . . . The town was very unruly, for strikes were more or less general and . . . the station had a military guard, with patrols in the streets. General Kleigels, whom we knew as *Gradonachalnik*[1] of St Petersburg, was Governor-General with special full powers, since the revolutionary movement had not completely calmed down. He had been dismissed two days before Grandmother's death because of disagreements with St Petersburg. Uncle Yury had come from Berlin, with, if I remember rightly, a commission from the *Vossische Zeitung*[2] to report on the revolutionary movement.

We took the coffin with great ceremony to the Jewish cemetery, followed by a long procession of open carriages belonging to the rich Jews of the town. As we returned through the popular quarters, I saw people on their doorsteps, shaking their fists at us, though I ascribed this to the fine horses and carriages of our upper-middle-class style rather than to the fact that the occupants were Semitic.

After our return home, Yury took me with him in a cab to send a long telegram to Berlin from the post office. Some way from it, the main road was occupied by a group of excited hooligans, who were more or less drunk and threw stones at us. Yury had a cut in the ear, and I was wounded in the cheek. The cabby did not want to canter through this crowd, and we were lucky enough to obtain access to the house of a Karaite tobacco-merchant,[3] whose name, I regret to say, now escapes me. He had the door closed, and bandaged us as well as he could . . . That evening, when the road was clear, we got back to the Kreshchatik.

Next morning, there were sinister rumours that Podol was being pillaged, and after some while it became possible that the pogrom might reach the upper town, which had never happened in previous pogroms: but the feeling was that the rich Jews were more to blame since they probably exploited the people more than the small tailors and shop-keepers of the lower town, and therefore did not deserve special police protection. At ten or eleven o'clock, Volodya, with whom I was staying, went off to take part in a deputation to ask the Governor to stop the pogrom . . .

Soon, we could see women and peasants, and even soldiers, carrying goods in their aprons, and under their arms. The town was under martial law, and patrols criss-crossed it everywhere, but rumour had it that the Jewish shopkeepers were attempting to defend their streets – that is, 'to molest people going about their business' – so troops had fired and there had already been a hundred casualties or so. Kleigels refused to intervene, on the excuse that he no longer had the power, and that was why the Governor was approached. Though he promised to look into it, nothing was done or could be done to stop the pillaging without firing.

To understand what followed, it is vital to bear in mind that the houses of the Brodsky and Zaitsev families, like Volodya's, stood in the same street as the Governor-General's palace and the State Bank, which were protected by troops, so that it was difficult to have neigh-bouring houses sacked without intervening. I noted how Volodya's coachman left the yard with his horses, and how the servants slipped off, one by one, presumably to avoid having to take part in any affray. There remained only an under-maid, Zhenya, a Polish girl just twenty, and another maid, an Englishwoman called Green. There was a noise in the street, and the Polish girl warned us that the pillagers were coming. Clara Gunzburg, with her maid, Uncle Yury and Ivan went up to the second floor and locked themselves into, I think, a servant's room. The English maid grabbed a broom and swore to defend herself to the death. But they were already in the forecourt and the girl begged me to go back to a safe place. At that decisive moment – a split second – I remembered that I owed my son an example and went out to meet the crowd. I shouted, 'Have you no fear of Christ?', expecting this to make an impression on these Christians. But they came on, brandishing clubs, and I grabbed hold of a window cushion to show – it was a futile gesture – that I too was armed, and I went forward, pushing them out of the house . . .

At that moment, Grigory Alexandrovich Brodsky, who lived with his parents opposite Volodya's house on Sadovaya, came to help us. He was a keen hunter, and had a rifle which he fired at my attackers. The two of us covered the ground floor and, when we saw it was clear, Grisha went back home. But soon the house was attacked again and there was another battle. I remember a man grabbing a heavy wooden chair and beating me over the head: one of the blows was so powerful that my head was almost driven into my shoulders, one of my front teeth split and my collar-stud burst off. I was drowned in blood, collapsed and passed out.

When I came to, I was on the threshold of the kitchen, and, on opening my eyes, saw that the chief of the *okolodny* [local town watch] was removing Grisha's rifle: this was just in front of the house entrance. At once, the hooligans attacked him and knocked him down, as they had done with me. I got up and went to help – with a strange reflex of proper behaviour, in that instinctively I folded the collar that was covered in blood back over my neck and, keeping it up with my hand – the stud had gone – I crossed the street. On the threshold of the Brodsky house I had a new fight, next to Grisha who had collapsed. Just then his younger brother opened the door of the house and fired a few revolver shots, though without hitting anyone.

Just then I saw, coming from Institutskaya, and led by officers, a dozen black-banded soldiers with their rifles at the ready (I heard later on that they were from the Kherson regiment). The hooligans made off, but I saw the officer aiming at me.

'Don't shoot at me – it's them!' I shouted, but made instinctively for cover behind a telegraph pole. The officer fired, and I felt a sharp burning pain in my calf. I thought, 'The brute has broken my leg,' but did not fall and, as the street was now clear, I saw the *okolodnik*, who, with the Brodsky servants, was taking Grisha back inside. I went back home exhausted, and still bleeding . . . opposite me was one of the mob, whom Brodsky had mortally wounded, on the ground and leaning against the wall.

I do not remember what happened exactly after that but it must have been around midday that we were warned to flee, because the crowd, together with the police, holding icons and holy banners and singing hymns, was just then coming up from Podol towards the Kreshchatik. The crowd was coming up Alexandrovskaya, because on Institutskaya there was a cordon of troops defending both sides of the State Bank. It must have been because of these measures that Lazar Brodsky's house, like one of the Zaitsev houses, was saved – for except for these there was not one Jewish house that was not pillaged. Later on, when we went to see Volodya's house, not a single piece of furniture seemed intact, and wreckage of all sorts littered the floor. I forget whether the damage was put at 100,000 or 200,000 roubles . . . In my own room, I found my Gladstone bag split from one end to the other. My few clothes had been taken away . . .

There was no question of going out into the street. Fortunately, Volodya's garden was divided by a wooden fence from that of the British Consulate and, through two planks which the Consul had had unfastened, we were all able to take advantage of his invitation to take refuge in his house. He had hoisted the British flag on his house, which looked on to Alexandrovskaya, and no one invaded it; in any case, no Christian house was touched. I was settled on a *chaise-longue*, to keep my leg quite immobile, and from there I saw the tops of the banners, with the Cross above them, carried by the mob, and I heard their hymn-singing. The Consul asked for an infantry squad to protect his house and so Yury and I, a day or two later, could be photographed in the garden with people who had no hatred of Jews like ourselves.

I forget how long we stayed with Mr Smit [*sic*] and do not know how the family was settled. I know only that I stayed on alone, and when the doctor allowed it, I headed for Semmering, where Mother and the children had spent the winter . . . To take me to the station, the Consul requested an escort of dragoons and so it was with four cavalry troopers round the carriage that we arrived at the station – a sensation it was, although the station was still under martial law.

*

I shall not leave this description of the pogrom without mentioning Grisha Brodsky. At the time he was doing his military service, and was arrested, accused of murder. He stayed for a fortnight in prison, but some lower court acquitted him on the grounds of self-defence. However, the Union of the Russian People (anti-Semitic nationalists known as 'Black Hundreds') did not agree and, with pressure in St Petersburg, had the Tsar annul this verdict so that, on the highest order, Grisha was again accused of killing a Christian. The young would-be reserve officer was put in solitary confinement, and after two months appeared before the Kiev Appeal Court. The Brodsky family invited me to Kiev as chief witness . . . Brodsky was again acquitted. After his military service he emigrated to England, where he rendered signal service as an inventor during the First World War. I heard that he converted to Christianity.

7

The Coming of Chaos

ANNA ALEXANDROVNA HALPERIN

The daughter of Alexandre de Gunzburg, whose recollections are given in Chapter 6, married into the Halperin family, whose fortune came from twelve sugar refineries in the Ukraine in the 1880s. Their house in Kiev is now the Institute of Marxism–Leninism.

The memoirs of Madame Halperin's son appear in Chapter 37.

I was born in 1892 in St Petersburg, in the reign of Alexander III. My father, whose name was Ginzburg,[1] was a banker at a private bank owned by my grandfather, but I think founded by my great-grandfather. Unfortunately, they went bankrupt: they paid off all the debts, but in doing so they lost their own considerable fortune. As a result, we had to change our way of life and to be a little more careful with our spending. For instance, the house: prior to my birth, I was told, we lived in rich extravagance, but by the time I was born we were already as it were 'sitting on bare benches' – but our prestige remained as high as before. Instead of his previous home, though (a beautiful luxury flat), my grandfather had to move to a more modest flat – which may seem large nowadays, but it didn't seem so to us.

The house that my father later acquired, in 1911, cost millions. My grandfather also had a large house which was sold after the troubles. It was a grand house overlooking the canal on Tenth Boulevard – now known as Manezhny Prospekt, I think [the street was later renamed Kirov Prospekt].

My mother came from Germany. She was a cousin of my father's. Her father was also a banker. We had a very large family, scattered all over the place. Both my grandmothers, as it happens, were born in Kiev. One got married to a second cousin who was a banker, and the other not to a cousin – but still a banker! A third sister also married a banker in Odessa – one Ashkenazy. So we were truly a family of bankers – and of course we were great friends with all the bankers in London, in Paris, and so on.

My father also had an estate. As you probably know, Jews had no right to own an estate in Russia. It was against the law. There were special zones, however: a Jew could own an estate in Bessarabia.[2] My grandfather had an estate there, as did his brother. And they also happened to know other Jewish families who owned estates there. In Bessarabia you could own landed property; but in general we were not allowed to have our own country houses, with large gardens . . . I think you could own a *dacha* [country house] – there were some who had *dacha*s.

In summer we did not stay in the city. Every other year we travelled abroad, and in between we rented a *dacha* – either in Tsarskoye Selo or another place in that area. I remember one of the things I used to love doing: we would set off in a carriage or on horseback to go and see some grand occasion which was being put on for the Tsar or some member of the upper aristocracy. You had to have a pass to gain entry into the estates where such events took place. My father had one. Of course we could not take part, but we used to go and watch from a distance. We used to enjoy watching the weddings . . .

Even before the 1905 Revolution there was chaos. When that priest, Father Gapon, led the crowds to the Palace Square,[3] we were with friends at a *dacha* in the country. It seems they were informed by telephone that there was some unrest – but still we decided to travel back to Petersburg. We went in a carriage to the station to travel home, and got as far as the Nikolayevsky Bridge in St Petersburg. They told us that there had been demonstrations that afternoon. We could see the bivouacs of the soldiers, with their weapons stacked at the ready. This was in January 1905 . . . I was thirteen years old.

And then there were the Jewish pogroms . . . My father was caught up in a pogrom in Kiev – the famous Kiev pogrom of 1905. He suffered because the hooligans tried to break into the house. My aunt, because she had forgotten something, had gone to a friend's house – that of the British Consul – so she was out. My uncle had gone to the police station to draw attention to their plight and ask for assistance. We did not realize at the time that it was the police who were behind these attacks . . . When all this happened, we children were abroad. I remember [my father] travelled out to join us and arrived with his head covered in cuts. Anyone would think he had been in a brawl!

On another occasion, my grandfather was arrested near the Winter Palace. In his time, he had been *Konsul* for Hessen-Braunschweig, one of the German states. He received his title – the German title of *Konsul* – and was recognized accordingly in Russia. [He was the only titled Jew in Russia] – but they did not allow him to sign his title in the Palace Books (there were special books to register such ranks). We were of the mercantile class and had the right to lay claim to a title of nobility recognized in Russia, but for us to wish to become one of the gentry – that could not be allowed under any circumstances! All the same, my grandfather earned a high reputation at Court. I remember once travelling to Switzerland with my brother, and Grandfather was seeing us off at the ferry. It was a small boat, but on this occasion it came right into St Petersburg, along the Neva, rather than putting in at one of the quays on the outskirts of the city to take on passengers, as was usual. My grandfather was standing on the quayside saying goodbye to us, when Princess Volkonskaya came up to him – she knew him very well and greatly admired him. The police immediately got terribly nervous. They did not know my grandfather: but it was explained that this was von Ginzburg . . .

I got married in 1915. The war had begun and I was already a nurse at a hospital in St Petersburg. [My husband] courted me there and then I became his bride. He was an only son, so at that time they did not call him up. Secondly, he was listed as Managing Director of a sugar factory. He was therefore registered as the manager of a large, highly valued concern, and so fulfilled his duty there. As well as this, both he and my brother were members of organizations that ran clubs and welfare facilities for the soldiers and God knows what. They were pseudo-military organizations – but very useful and successful.

Life was great fun – before the Revolution. Of course, when we were forced to become refugees because of our political views, as you must realize, we did undergo some unpleasantness. But somehow, we always managed to stand aside from it. We suffered from anti-Semitism when we were already refugees – it was horrible. We were still in Russia at the time. We had arranged to travel on a steamer which was due to arrive from Constantinople and they nearly refused to allow us on board, although we had an agreement. The boat was supposed to be bringing goods for trading. When it arrived, not only did they refuse permission for the merchants to trade, but also they refused to let the ship leave harbour. The ship remained in harbour, in Odessa. Then, when it became obvious that they would have to leave, there were only 250 places on that ship – while there were 1500 people on the quayside, waiting to board her . . . at the very last minute you could only feel, 'Don't forget! Don't forget us!' It turned out that our names were not on the list. We were a large family with servants – there were thirteen people. This was the end . . . [But we still had all the right connections and] by some uncanny luck they had to amend the lists by hand, using a feather quill and ink. With such a quill they swiftly added our names and called us on to the ship. Thank God!

8

Terror Comes to Smela

COUNT ALEXEI BOBRINSKOY

Alexei Bobrinskoy was born into a wealthy aristocratic family and spent part of his childhood on their estate near Smela in the Ukraine.

My father was a big landowner in the province of Kiev near the little town of Smela. The great majority of the population of this small town were Jews. There they had a synagogue and three or four Jewish schools. These people were chiefly tradesmen and their commerce was in timber, grain, 'Colonial goods', salted herrings, iron-ware, cement and building materials. Some were craftsmen, tailors, shoemakers, painters.

Abraham Kossoy was the grocer. As a small boy I simply loved to pay him an occasional visit. His shop was full of most mysterious smells: coffee, vanilla sticks, nutmeg in glass jars, cakes of soap wrapped up in bright coloured paper with highly tempting names such as 'Violette de Parme' or 'Rose de France' were placed on shelves for the local beauties. Perfumes in fancy little bottles with refreshing effects guaranteed, and pompous names of 'White Bear' or real eau-de-Cologne made in Kiev, completed the display. Indeed, Mr Abraham Kossoy was a great expert in all these luxuries and his wise advice was not to be sniffed at. Last but not least, Mr Kossoy had a large provision of sugar, both in lumps and granulated, which he got straight from my father's sugar mills situated near by, and which he sold at a profit of what would be the equivalent of a halfpenny a pound.

Three banks had their branches in Smela: the Kiev Bank for Trade and Industry, the Mutual Credit Bank, and the Azov-Don Bank. In fact, Smela was a prosperous little town, where everybody lived happily.

No motor cars existed in those days and hens, ducks and even geese could safely stroll along Smela's quiet boulevards and rest under their shady acacia trees. From time to time a peasant cart drawn by two lethargic, enormous white oxen and laden with watermelons would appear on the horizon and disappear again . . . All would be quiet once more.

Then came the 1904–5 Russo-Japanese War. Manchuria was far away, and people could not understand why this war was necessary. Did not Russia possess enough land as it was? Why this crazy expedition with only one single-track railroad to the Far East? . . .

Bad news came from the front: Russian troops were retreating. Chinese-sounding names of localities were mentioned in our daily paper, the *Kiev Thought*. Much as they thought about it, the poor Kievans could not understand the events and were full of apprehensions. Small 'revolutions' broke out here and there, trains were delayed, supplies became scarce, soldiers on leave sometimes refused to return to the front. The atmosphere was tense and unsettled. How long was this unpopular war going to last?

Prayers for the success of the Russian arms were said in all churches, but the endurance even of the Russian people has a limit. A scapegoat had to be found. So of course it was the Jew. Did he not try to avoid conscription? Did he not make money while the peasant-soldier bled to death on the fields of Manchuria?

Yes, it was the Jew who was responsible for all the misfortunes that befell Russia and the Jew had to be punished. It would perhaps be wrong to accuse the Russian Government of organizing pogroms, but it may be said that in the circumstances it did not take sufficiently effective measures to prevent them. It had to defend the throne and save its own authority from the rebellious soldiery and the discontented workmen. It is also true that the police force in Russia in those days was completely inadequate to cope with the immense task of protecting the population from the low elements, always eager to fish in troubled waters.

There is something uncannily incomprehensible in the outbreaks of the human beast when it gets out of control. The peaceful crofter becomes a robber and a thief; the police lose their nerve; horror and fear creep into the minds of all. The population is immediately and magnetically divided into two sections: the persecutor and the persecuted. Both parties accept their mission and their fate with an unquestionable resolve. There is something fatal, pre-ordained in the events that follow public disturbances. How these disturbances begin and how they end – nobody knows; human power seems to be unable to direct them or stop them. And so it happened in peaceful Smela.

Some people came, some people started the outrages and the looting of peaceful Jews. When these people had enough, and the human beast was satisfied, it retired and the culprits were nowhere to be found.

The well-known English writer Maurice Baring[1] was staying with us just before [the Smela pogrom] and describes the rumours of pogroms in a masterly way in his book *The Puppet Show of Memory*.

Fortunately the pogrom in Smela claimed no victims; as it happened no one was killed, only material damage was done to Jewish property. Crowds of people broke into their houses, overturned their furniture, slashed open the pillows and scattered the down and feathers into the street . . . the streets were covered with down like snow. Terrorized Jews fled from their houses; the contents of their shops were looted.

The pogrom lasted for two days and ended as suddenly as it began. Now, relief had to be organized; something had to be done to repair this ghastly evil.

One afternoon a deputation from the Jewish community appeared at our gates and wished to speak to my father. He immediately went to meet them. There was my old friend Abraham Kossoy the grocer, there was the chemist, the printer and the fishmonger. They were extremely upset, miserable and brow-beaten. Some were in tears. They all had a sad story to tell about the outrages committed and the losses they had suffered. Abraham Kossoy stepped forward and said to my father: 'Sir, we have no protection except you, we have lived peacefully with you and your father, and before your father with your grandfather. You have always been fair to us and we have always been your good and loyal neighbours. Do something for us now. We want you to be the Chairman of our Jewish Relief Committee. We trust you, we want your help.'

My father was a kind man but this offer embarrassed him to the highest degree. He sympathized with the Jews, but he was a private citizen and a non-Jew. Would his name help the Jews to raise the necessary funds? That was the question. How could this relief be organized and to whom was he to appeal for donations?

But the delegation insisted on having him as their Chairman and, of course, he could not say 'No.' He agreed and said, 'I shall try to help you in every way, I promise.'

At that the delegation departed and my father set himself thinking how to go about this business. It was no use appealing for funds locally. Sums raised in this way would be quite insignificant compared with the amount needed. My father thought of England, of France and America. Surely the civilized world would not remain deaf to his appeal if it were properly worded and properly addressed? But Jewish committees all over the world were probably flooded with similar demands from dozens of other places where much greater damage to Jewish property was done, from places where Jews had even been killed by the raging mob. It was Smela, his beloved Smela, which had to be helped; that was his first and foremost thought [and it] gave him sleepless nights.

My father's lifelong hobby was archaeology and many famous archaeologists of Europe were his old friends. The name of Solomon Reinach, Curator of the Louvre and author of many books on art and archaeology, came to his mind. 'I need your help, my good friend,' wrote my father. 'Cry it from all house-tops of Paris, put me in touch with all the Jewry of the world, our case cries aloud to Heaven.'

It was probably just because my father was not a Jew that his appeal resulted in such a success. In Paris, Solomon Reinach immediately passed my father's appeal to the proper quarters, to the Rothschilds, and also to the big bankers in America. Money started pouring in from all sides. In less than three months 50,000 roubles in gold (the equivalent of £5000) were received, which in those days was a very handsome sum of money indeed. Reconstruction of damaged Jewish property began at once.

Some months later, one afternoon as my father and all the family were sitting on the veranda of our house, a great crowd of Jews again appeared at our gates. Oh, but it was a different crowd this time – a joyful, a happy crowd.

As they entered the spacious courtyard I saw my friend Abraham Kossoy heading the delegation, together with the Rabbi carrying something shiny and glittering in his hands: two silver cylinders, mounted with little silver bells. He stepped forward and in a melodious voice said, 'You have helped us in the hour of tribulation. When the sons of Israel were in peril and distress, you have stretched out your hand in defence of the right cause. We have come to acknowledge our gratitude to you.' Quoting the beautiful words of the Psalm he went on, 'For the Lord's anger endureth but a moment, in his favour is life; weeping may endure for a night, but joy cometh in the morning.'

Abraham Kossoy was holding a document framed and draped with purple velvet. It was the expression of thanks written on a parchment in Hebrew and in Russian.

I could see my father's hand tremble with emotion when he rose from his chair and his eyes were filled with tears as he accepted these gifts. Only later did I learn the tremendous honour that had been bestowed upon him: the silver cylinders contained the sacred Torah itself.

Bobrinskoy's recollections of the Revolution are given in Chapter 11.

9

Prisoner of the Tsar

IVAN ALEXANDROVICH YUKHOTSKY

Ivan Alexandrovich Yukhotsky was born in 1869 and grew up in Vyshny Volochok. He trained as a hydraulic engineer and in March 1890 went to Odessa, where he found employment as a supervisor of building work at the port. He was arrested several times for underground political activity. He became involved with two Jewish Marxist activists, Nakhamkes and Tsiperovich, and in 1895 was arrested again.

My job was to organize the building workers, with whom I mixed most. I knew very well what I was letting myself in for and for that reason to begin with I trod very warily. My wife [Berta] of course knew what was going on and I told her that I might be arrested. She never tried to stop me in my political activities; in fact she helped.

At this time I was gathering a 'circle' of building workers and there were some comparative veterans amongst them, men of over forty years, who had been the People's Will propagandists of the 1880s and who used to work with Khalturin.[1] The most active of the veterans was Ivan Kondratievich Kamensky, known as 'Khokhlov'; he was a joiner. He too had gathered together a circle of building workers who sometimes met at our place, where they listened to talks from Nakhamkes and Tsiperovich. They enjoyed the talks but were not very satisfied with the propaganda literature, of which there was very little. They said it was boring, not like the 'crafty bit of goods' or 'chatty stories' of the old People's Will pamphlets, but Nakhamkes did not have any of them.

I said that 'sometimes' they came to our flat, but to do this too often was suspicious, because it was in the Government harbour and in a separate house, where no one lived except me, and empty places were easy to watch. Therefore the workers had to use a flat in town, and so only Ivan Kondratievich came to me to get literature and to chat occasionally; sometimes one of the workers came on his own, so as not to arouse suspicion.

In January 1894 there were a great many arrests in Odessa and Nakhamkes and Tsiperovich were arrested. [One night when] we had eaten and started to get ready for bed, suddenly there was a quiet knock on the door. I asked who it was.

'Open up, Ivan Alexandrovich,' said the watchman of the Government harbour, Yefim Ivanovich. I opened the door and two policemen seized me by the arms and a 'tail' started to search me. Behind them stood the head of the Secret Police, Colonel Piramidov, and the Assistant Prosecutor of the Law Courts, Pollan.

'We must search you,' announced Piramidov.

'Please do,' I replied.

They turned everything inside out; they looked in the attic and in the storeroom, they dug up the earthen floor with a spade but did not find anything. I had nothing whatsoever. Piramidov discussed something with Pollan and then they began to write a report about my arrest and gave it to me to sign (that the deposition had been explained to me) and then they left. They left two policemen, who told me to take my bedclothes, get dressed and go with them. I can only guess how long the search lasted by the fact that it started at eleven o'clock in the evening and I did not go off with the policemen until dawn. I met the watchman as I was leaving the house and I said, 'Goodbye, Yefim Ivanovich.' He answered me in a funereal voice: 'Farewell.'

It was already light when they brought me to the Boulevard Police Station. The Inspector, Panasik, was rude. He did another search and went through everything. They put me in a cell on my own, which was roomy but dirty, with a window high up above. Behind the door there was a constant coming and going, shouts and the cursing of drunkards, as new prisoners were brought in. The window in the door was not shut; it was about five inches square, enabling me to see everything that was happening in the corridor. I do not remember whether I fell asleep after that sleepless night but it seemed to me that I saw [one of our circle], Nivinsky, being brought along the corridor, past my window. I thought that someone had warned Nivinsky, but maybe they had not managed to do this and Nivinsky had been caught red-handed. After a bit, I clearly saw them lead Nivinsky from a cell into the courtyard. I jumped up on the bed, which was near the window, and

I saw him, accompanied by two policemen, being led off. I decided not to admit to anything.

After lunch they took me off for interrogation, and this is approximately what passed between Piramidov and myself:

'Now, Yukhotsky, confess. At Nivinsky's house we found a whole store of literature.'

'That was at his place, not at mine.'

'But you gave him that literature?'

'No, I did not.'

'Come on, admit it. Nivinsky was not holding it for himself.'

'It's nothing to do with me.'

'What do you mean, nothing to do with you? You must be joking! Nivinsky says that it is your literature.'

'And I tell you I know nothing.'

Then the Assistant Prosecutor interrupted: 'Yukhotsky wants to cool off in solitary confinement and then he'll be more talkative, we'll just wait another week. Let's send him to prison.'

Two policemen came in and took me back to the cell. They ordered me to take my things and led me out on to the street; we got in a cab and went along the streets, through the suburbs and outside the town to a recently built prison. I prayed to God for one thing as I went into the prison – that I would emerge from it as cheerful as I went in.

It did not take long to hand me over. I went into the interior of the cross (the prison in Odessa was built in the shape of a cross) with a policeman and I climbed up to the third floor. The policeman opened the cell No. 480, lit the paraffin lamp, which was supposed to burn the whole night long, let down the bed, which was secured to the wall by a lock, showed me the slop pail and said that today there would be no food, as the prisoners had already eaten, and he left. The lock clicked on the door and I was left alone.

The cell was clean, an arched vault four paces in length and about six feet wide. I was completely alone. I lay down on the bed and to the right and left of me something was tapping in the wall. I understood that it was the prisoners talking to each other. I remembered that in my childhood there had been a prison at home in Volochok for political prisoners. We were always amazed at the cleverness of the prisoners, who by tapping on the wall knew everything that was going on; but I did not know the alphabet.

I began tapping but I only disturbed the others; however, they realized that this was the new detainee. On the next day I did not get up from my bed, as while I had been at the police station I had caught cold from the draught (the panes had been knocked out of the window). They brought a medical orderly and after him a doctor appeared in the cell doorway, a general in a uniform greatcoat, with red badges and a medal at his neck. The orderly told him about it and he said, 'Give him quinine,' turned and left. This was the famous Dr Rozen, a Jew converted to Christianity and famous because he trained criminals to hang men. It was said about him that when he was present during a hanging, seeing how inept one of the hangmen was, he pushed him away and did the job himself. 'That's how you hang people,' he said.

For a day or two I lay around in bed and did not feel like getting up; however, I had to pull myself together and get used to the prison life. In the morning they came in and removed the slop pail, the gendarme locked the bed away on the wall, then came with a mug of boiled water and some bread, and so the prison round was finished; until dinner time, you could either walk up and down, or sit on a stool – there was nothing else to do. But the tapping on the wall went on all the time and I just hindered them.

At last I understood that they were knocking to me in alphabetical order; that is, if the letter was the twentieth, then there would be twenty knocks on the wall. I began to listen and count the knocks. It came out: 'What is your name?' I answered with the same alphabet. They went on knocking: 'Let down a thread to the second floor when it gets dark.' Where could I find a thread? I looked round everywhere and found one in my trouser seams. When evening came and everything quietened down, I let down the thread and waited. They tugged and I pulled and there was the prison alphabet on a scrap of paper with directions on how to use it.

First you had to tap out the column, then the line:

а	б	в	л	ъ
е	ж	з	и	к
д	м	н	о	п
р	с	т	ц	ф
х	у	ч	ш	щ
ы	ю	я		

I soon became accustomed to it, as, having endless time alone, I practised diligently.

I soon found out who was in which cell. Nivinsky was also on the
third floor, at the opposite end. A fellow called Bareisha, whom I did
not know, had sent me the note with the alphabet. On the first floor
was Vainstein, who, I had learnt, had betrayed me and Nivinsky. At
first I thought that he had confessed everything because he was scared,
being very young (he was only about sixteen), and by tapping on the
wall I asked him to retract his statement, but he answered that he had
told the 'whole truth' and was silent.

For about one and a half weeks I was not called for interrogation,
but finally they got round to me. Piramidov sat behind the table;
opposite me was another of our group, Okolsky, and in front of him
was a piece of paper, covered with writing.

'There you are, Yukhotsky,' said Piramidov, 'Okolsky has admitted
everything and that he worked with you.' Okolsky stared at me, expecting me to grass on him.

'I do not know this gentleman,' I said.

'Well, he knows you,' sneered Piramidov. Okolsky's hands began to
tremble. 'Okolsky, do you know Yukhotsky?'

Okolsky answered in a funereal voice, 'I do not know Yukhotsky.'

'How is it you wrote down in detail that you knew Yukhotsky and
what you did?'

'I wrote that dictated by you. You made me write this statement
under duress.'

'All right, write down that you don't know anyone called Yukhotsky.'
Okolsky did so and they led him off to his cell.

They asked me to sit down on the left of the table, near the wall.
Piramidov ordered Rosenblium to be brought in (his name was completely unknown to me). Piramidov questioned him, pointing to me
and saying, 'Who is this?'

'It looks like Yukhotsky.'

'Where did you have a meeting with him?'

'On the Kulikovo Field, in November or December.'

Now I asked the questions: 'At what time?'

'About eight o'clock in the evening.'

'Was the place well lit?'

'No, badly.'

'How can you be certain that it was me? Almost a year has gone by, the place was badly lit, it was eight o'clock in the evening in November or December and it was already dark.'

'I said it might be.' And they led Rosenblium off to his cell.

They ordered Vainstein to be brought in and forbade me to ask questions. Pointing to me, they asked, 'Who is that?'

'Yukhotsky.' Then they led him out.

They brought in Gorev, another acquaintance. Pointing to me, they asked him, 'Who is that?'

Gorev, embarrassed, said, 'Yukhotsky.' They led Gorev away.

'Now then, Yukhotsky, are you still going to persist in your silence?'

I did not deny that I knew Gorev. I had recommended him as a sub-contractor for joinery work.

'We are not talking about that. You gave Gorev illegal literature.'

'No I didn't.'

'But he insists that you gave it to him.'

'And I say I did not.'

Then Piramidov started to get angry and threatened, 'You will rot in prison if you don't talk.'

I said nothing. Then he started talking pleasantly, saying that I should have pity on my wife and child. I still said nothing. I could not add anything more; he had made me very angry.

'As you wish.' And they led me off to my cell.

In prison I was sent a French textbook called *Margot*. At one time I had attended courses in French without much success, and I gave it up after two months. I decided to take up *Margot* in prison and I read it continually for two whole months until I was sent some books on mathematics – analytical geometry (the Institute of Technology Course), differential calculus (a course from the Institute of Highways and Communications) and integral calculus (a university course by Posse); Davydov's *Elementary Algebra* I had received earlier with the French book. As things went on, I saw that I might have to go through a full university course in prison, lasting on average one and a half years and sometimes even more.

At first, I admit, I hoped, but not for long (only until the first interrogation), that they would release me soon – after all they had not found anything. But after that I saw that it was a vain hope and I resolved to keep my spirits up, not to get nervy, and to study mathematics seriously; this would stand me in good stead in Siberia. So every day from nine o'clock in the morning when they finished cleaning out the cell, until twelve o'clock in the morning, for sixteen months I studied mathematics in a systematic way. Even before the books on higher mathematics arrived, I revised algebra, because we had been through the book by Davydov at school. Then I started on analytical geometry, then differential calculus and in the end, integral calculus. It doesn't take long to describe something that went on for so many months!

Worst of all were the interrogations; you got all worked up and waited for the call, so that when they finished, after about two months, I heaved a sigh of relief. You were allowed books from home, you could go for a walk, have visits and parcels. We started talking through the open windows. Although the warders could follow our conversations, how could two policemen possibly keep a watch on fifty-six windows? Especially as those two men had other things to do in the office: taking in parcels, sitting in on visits. In effect, solitary confinement turned into a public meeting.

The prison authorities then decided to muzzle our windows; they rehung them on vertical hinges instead of horizontal and it was no longer possible to open both halves together and stick your head through. Our conversations came to an end and we had to go back to tapping, which the warders were powerless to prevent. I, in fact, did not use it much; I made a rule for myself not to speak to anyone until midday and I did not answer any calls, however many times they knocked.

By the winter all the windows had been rehung. It didn't matter; we could stand it during the cold weather. But when spring 1896 arrived, as the weather outside became better, there was no ventilation at all. The inmates started getting edgy; it was stuffy. One beautiful day, 16 May, the mood heightened – everyone was tapping. They decided to smash the windows. Suddenly someone went 'wham'. Like a madman I seized my metal mug and knocked out two panes, then the whole political wing began to hum and all at once there was a dead silence; only the guards, like cats, on tiptoe were stealing down the corridor. This went on for half an hour, or maybe less – time is meaningless in prison.

The cell door opened and a guard entered and said, 'Get dressed.' I put on my coat and hat and he took me off to the 'cooler' . . .

In January 1897 Yukhotsky was sentenced to five years' labour in eastern Siberia. His wife and daughter joined him in his exile. They were allowed to return to Russia in April 1903. Yukhotsky subsequently travelled to the east again, the Revolution overtaking him in Siberia, where he worked as a surveyor and engineer. His later memoirs appear in Chapter 28.

10

In the Shtetl

NADEZHDA ULANOVSKAYA

Nadezhda Ulanovskaya was born in 1904 in a Ukrainian Jewish hamlet, of a family with some prestige – one grandfather had been a rabbi – but only a modest existence, from cloth-trading. After a struggle for education, Nadezhda was in Odessa when the Revolution broke out, supported the Bolsheviks and fought the Whites. She met and married an anarchist thirteen years older than herself, Alexandr Ulanovsky, who had suffered exile in the far north, at one stage with Stalin (whom he disliked). Ulanovsky was given a job abroad in 1921, to foment trouble in Germany; in 1926 he was sent for similar purposes to China, where his wife eventually joined him. They were lucky, in that, having had a great deal of contact with foreigners, they were not arrested in the Great Purge of the later 1930s; during the war, Alexandr served at the front, while Nadezhda took care of foreign correspondents. However, when purges were started again after the war, the Ulanovskys suffered imprisonment in camps, in terrible conditions, until after Stalin's death. They formed a well-known centre for dissidence in Moscow thereafter. Alexandr died in 1971 and Nadezhda finally emigrated, with most of what remained of the family, to Israel in 1975.

I spent my childhood in the Ukraine, in Bershad, a small town or *shtetl* in the Kamenets-Podolsky *guberniya*.

The prosperous Jews lived in the two parallel main roads – my grandfather, the Rabbi's, two-storeyed house, the two hardware shops belonging to Meydanov, a shoe shop, a millinery workshop and my aunt Rukhele Kolker's haberdashery shop were all there. So was the house of the poor but learned Hebrew teacher, Bogomolny, who gave private lessons to the children of well-to-do families.

Even the main streets of the small town were unpaved: in spring and autumn the mud was impenetrable and came over the tops of even the highest rubber boots. No trees or flowers were to be seen. During the [spring] festival of Lag-ba-Omer, the Jews went for picnics in the countryside. We went past Dolina and Yerushalimka, wretchedly poor districts, past huts with earth floors but with geraniums on the window-sills and embroidered curtains. All along the huts were stone fences, behind which could be glimpsed the estate of the bankrupted Counts Potocki, to whom the town had once belonged. On the outskirts of the town was the newly built village school, together with the post office. The headmaster, postmaster, excise official, police chief and Cossack commander all lived there. They all spoke Russian and from my earliest childhood I thought it a very beautiful language because it was spoken by these elegant and educated people. Beyond the outskirts, the fields, forest and Ukrainian villages began – it was from there that the peasants would drive their carts into our town on market days.

I spent many days in my grandfather's spacious house. My parents found it hard to make ends meet, frequently moved from house to house, but wherever they were it was over-crowded and food was scarce. My father was an unsuccessful small merchant. He had come to Bershad from a small town in the Kiev region by the name of Monastyrishche, which was somewhat smaller than Bershad. He had inherited a textile shop from his father, but he turned out to be a poor businessman and the business had to be wound up. He was very good with his hands, but in our circles being a craftsman was thought to be *infra dig.* – my mother, the daughter of a rabbi, would never have been allowed to marry the son of an artisan. My father had to engage in all kinds of questionable business deals, become a commission agent and travel round various cities. He heaved a sigh of relief after the February Revolution, when we moved to Odessa, and the old ideas about what work was suitable for a Jew of good family no longer mattered. He gave up 'business' and took a job in a mill: now he handled sacks of flour and was happy, though he was paid very little – 5 roubles a week, out of which he had to keep a family of six. On the other hand, for the rest of my life I was able to put against the question about my social origins on application forms that I was the daughter of a worker and not of a businessman.

My happiest childhood memories are linked with my grandfather, the Rabbi. When later on I heard the word 'gentleman', it always invoked the image of my grandfather with his reserved manners, quiet voice and distinguished appearance. His beard was meticulously trimmed, his sidelocks tucked behind his ears and altogether he looked much more worldly than the religious folk here, in Jerusalem.

I imagined God, in whose existence I believed implicitly, to be like my grandfather, only more powerful. Before a business trip by my father to Kiev, on which the family had pinned great hopes, I prayed to God, 'Make this journey successful and I shall dedicate the whole of my life to Thee. If Thou dost not, I shall know that Thou art not just or noble, not like my grandfather.'

In my childish religiosity I went to extremes, as I was subsequently to do with all my convictions. Tolerance came to me only with old age. As a child, I zealously observed all the Jewish ritual commandments and even caught out Grandfather breaking them. For example, Jewish law forbids one to eat any chicken or duck with a flaw. I noticed that every time a child or servant brought him a doubtful fowl for adjudication, he first of all enquired who had sent it. When I asked him why he wanted to know that, he said, 'If the chicken is from a wealthy home, I shall declare it forbidden food but if it comes from a poor home, I shall declare it kosher.'

'But by letting the poor eat food that isn't kosher, you are sending them to Hell.'

'No, the sin will be on my head. Anyway, God is not all that harsh: he will understand that a rich Jew will not suffer much if he has to throw away a chicken, while it is better for a poor Jew to eat it and feed his children with it.' I fervently prayed at night that God might understand my grandfather's kindness and not punish him.

I think I owe my first ideas of justice to my grandfather. Here is an example. Grandfather and Grandmother had a servant. One day she came back from market very pleased with herself: a peasant had given her 20 kopeks too much change. Grandfather got very angry. 'If a Jew cheats a Jew, that's a private transgression; but if he cheats a Gentile, he casts a shadow over the entire Jewish people and that's a terrible sin.'

We had our own family legend. One of our ancestors had also been a rabbi and had even been regarded as a holy man. One day, he was called to court to testify against a Jew accused of theft. Now testifying against his co-religionist would result in arousing all the Russians' hostility towards the Jewish community; on the other hand, he could not lie and protect a thief, either. So he went home and died. He did not commit suicide: he just died together with his wife and daughter. Before his death, he made an agreement with God that none of his descendants would suffer from extreme poverty, though they would not be rich either. Also, that none of them would die a violent death for seven generations. And none of them did, until one who was killed during the war, of the eighth generation.

I greatly loved Grandfather and spent nearly all my time with him. Nobody was allowed in his room when he received petitioners to rule on disputed matters, not Grandmother nor my aunts, but I was small and nobody felt shy in front of me, so I was allowed in even when divorces were discussed. Once I was astonished to hear Grandfather say to a friend with whom he often spoke about philosophical matters, 'Of course, a god with a white beard, sitting on a throne in the heavens, does not exist; but some higher force does.'

I discovered early on that Jews were subjected to injustice and persecution. I was eight years old at the time of the Beylis trial.[1] I collected a number of girls and we acted out the court proceedings. I gave every one a part to play and, naturally, I took the part of counsel for the defence for myself. I remember we staged it on the balcony of a girlfriend's house and the old man who lived there later told my grandfather, 'You should have heard the speech she made in Russian! Like a real advocate! She'll probably grow up to be a great woman.'

In spite of their poverty, my parents – with the help of Grandfather – did everything to give me a good education. From the age of five I went to the Khaymovich private school, where we were taught to read and write Russian, the four rules of arithmetic and the rudiments of geography. As far as I can remember, there were no boys at the school. They all went to the Hebrew school. It was customary for girls to be taught the Old Testament and Grandfather engaged a private tutor for me. I was with him for about two months. I read and spoke Hebrew but got no further than the Book of Genesis – after that I never opened the Old Testament again.

When I had finished at Khaymovich's, I went to the village school, where the course was supposed to last six years. After that you could join the fourth form at the *gymnazia* [high school, to which Jews were admitted]. The school was supposed to be free but the parents of the four Jewish children sent the headmaster a cartload of firewood each, while he pocketed the money allocated for heating.

I went to school on Saturdays as well but did not desecrate the

Sabbath by writing. The teachers turned a blind eye to this. I first fasted on the Day of Atonement when I was eleven, although I was exempt from doing so because of my age. But not eating for twenty-four hours was so hard it was a real achievement. I fasted out of a sense of solidarity with my nearest and dearest – particularly my mother, whose lips had gone blue from hunger by the time she returned from synagogue.

At school I excelled in Russian language, literature and history. My grandmother was an educated woman, who knew Russian and German but read nothing save religious literature – there was no other reading matter in Grandfather's house. I took books out of the library which the father of my girlfriend, Bogomolny, the Hebrew teacher, had opened in his house. The first result of my reading was to be delighted with the heroes of Jack London. I wanted to be as strong and bold as they, so I adopted the Muller system of gymnastics and took to brushing my teeth. I made friends with Russian boys – Volodya, the postmaster's son, and Slava, the innkeeper's. The three of us went skating on the river in winter. We had three skates between us – one skate each. The other Jewish girls did not skate, nor did they make friends with Russian boys.

Mother was very upset that I was such an ugly duckling, lanky, very dark and with sharp elbows. When I was twelve, I got scarlet fever and my hair was shaved off. When I recovered, a new crop of hair grew and turned out to be shiny and wavy. At school they began to say I was pretty, but I cared very little about my looks. On the other hand, I was flattered that, though I was the youngest in the class, Volodya and Slava listened respectfully to my tales about Jack London's heroes.

In the library, I read all the children's books and began to read Turgenev and Tolstoy as a change from Conan Doyle. When I had read sixteen volumes of Conan Doyle, I told the librarian: this is the most important writer after Turgenev and Tolstoy. Turgenev's novels *On the Eve* and *Virgin Soil* overwhelmed me. I understood what I had to do: study, get into a university and from there there was a straight road to Siberia or the scaffold. The idea of sacrificing my life for some great cause had an extraordinary attraction for me.

I talked about the matters that stirred me not only with my girlfriends and with boys but also with my father. I shared with them my tremendous discovery: all the evil in the world stems from ignorance. People do not know how to live because they can't read. 'What do you think,' my father said sadly, 'isn't Purishkevich literate?'[2] It then entered my head that some grown-ups understand a few things better than I can even though they speak Russian badly and don't read my favourite books.

To begin with I concentrated on the injustices perpetrated against Jews. At the beginning of the First World War, our headmaster, Zakrevsky, made an insulting speech in class accusing the Jews of being reluctant to fight. I stood up and answered him. I talked about the Pale of Settlement,[3] about my father going to Kiev and being afraid of being arrested, about Jews not being admitted to university, not being given commissions, however brave they might be. 'So why should Jews rush to the front line? Why should they spill their blood?' The children listened attentively. The headmaster did not interrupt me but when I finished he said, choked with fury, 'If you were older, you'd find yourself in Siberia. Collect your books and get out of my school.'

On the way, I rehearsed my speech again, but when I got closer to home I realized with horror what had happened to me: I had been expelled from school. I had lost the only opportunity of getting any kind of education. And now I had to announce this to my parents! My parents never reproached me about anything but I knew that, as far as they were concerned, what had happened was a real disaster.

For several months, I did no studying. I had a great deal of free time: I did not have to go to school or do any homework. And there were a lot of books left in the library I had not read. My parents did not burden me with domestic chores. My only duty was to rock the baby. I lay on a sofa, read books and rocked the cradle with my foot. I think I probably read all the books that there were in Bershad. From somewhere I got hold of *Speeches of a Rebel* by Kropotkin[4] and now the anarchists were added to the list of my heroes.

I was taken on again at school thanks to Aunt Rukhele, the owner of the haberdashery shop. All the local notables, the Cossack commander, the excise officer, the headmaster, were regular customers of hers. The headmaster was given an extra cartload of firewood and the matter was overlooked.

In the years of my childhood, or at any rate during those I can remember, there were no pogroms. But the grown-ups retained a memory of one that raged in 1905 and they constantly had a fear of pogroms. Grandmother and my aunts used to tell me about how the Jews hid in the cellars and how only Grandfather was not scared. He went to the post office and sent off a telegram about the disorders and troops were sent to our town. The thought that the Jews hid from the pogroms in cowardly fashion gave me no rest. I decided that fighting and dying, as my beloved heroes from the books I had read would have done, was better than hiding in cellars.

Thanks to the books, an enormous world opened up before me. Our *shtetl* seemed to me worthless and the Jews ignoramuses who considered themselves the salt of the earth. It infuriated me when they said *a goyisher kop, a goyisher tam* (a Gentile brain, Gentile taste). The heroes of Turgenev and Tolstoy were *goyim*, Gentiles, and they were people of high sensibility and nobility, who lead fine lives, and they were supposed to be inferior to my Aunt Marochka. Much later I understood that this contempt for *goyim* was brought about by the need for national self-assertion and explained by the humiliating position in which the Jews found themselves.

I was also pained by the snobbery that prevailed in the *shtetl* and the importance that was attached to *yikhes*, distinction of birth. *Yikhes* was determined either by learning or by wealth. For example, my uncle's rich father-in-law would never have let his daughter marry into our family if my grandfather had not been a rabbi. We did not belong to the highest *yikhes*; above us there was a whole circle of rich Jews. In protest against this snobbery, I made friends with some silly and worthless girl only because of her 'low' origins.

Everything in our little town irritated and outraged me. My only positive impression, connected with Jewishness, was my meeting with some young Zionists who lodged with my aunt. 'They have a worthwhile cause,' I said to myself when I got to know them. But it was too fleeting a meeting and left no traces.

I wanted to fight for the Revolution, for the people. But 'the people' was to a considerable degree an abstract concept to me. The Jews round me were not 'the people'. They were an unattractive lot, though I loved some of them. Nor were the *muzhik*s [colloq., peasants] – who came into town on market days, got drunk, cursed each other and beat their wives – anything like the people I read about in books. True, the Jews in town were kinder than the Ukrainian peasants, did not beat their wives or swear obscenely, but the world of the Jews was one which repelled me. Nothing beautiful or interesting took place in our *shtetl*. People were concerned only with their daily bread. I was aware that actually there was not enough daily bread for them to eat, but I considered that it was necessary to fight for a better future and they did not give a thought to any kind of struggle. Sympathy for my co-religionists and appreciation of the injustices perpetrated against them remained in my heart, but in order to fight for the workers and peasants, for the abstract 'people' from my books, it was essential for me to break with my surroundings.

My first step in this direction was to break with religion. I suddenly stopped believing in God, soon after my grandfather's death. At my cousin's there were cultured young people 'with ideas', university and grammar-school students. They even subscribed to the paper *Russkoe Slovo*.[5] I asked my cousin why she did not fast on the Day of Atonement. She answered: 'Because there is no God.' Suddenly my faith collapsed.

I hurried to announce to Grandmother that there is no God. She was shattered. 'The next thing will be for you to be baptized,' but such a thing never occurred to me. I felt that that would be real treason. On top of that, people got baptized only for their personal advantage and not for the sake of the Revolution.

By February 1917, I was thirteen. A Jew who had some business dealings with my father came to see us. They talked about business and then he asked casually, 'Did you know there's been a revolution? The Tsar has abdicated.' Father, naturally, turned to me. 'Did you hear?'

'Rubbish,' I said, authoritatively. 'That's not how it works. Revolution means barricades and shooting.' In Bershad things had gone on as usual – nothing extraordinary had happened. However, a few days later the newspapers reached our little town and for the first time I came to doubt my superiority over those around me. Demonstrations started to take place in the *shtetl*. We all marched together, Ukrainians, Russians and Jews. For the first time, I saw the blue-and-white flag and heard the Zionist anthem, '*Hatikva*'.

Soon, in search of a living, our family moved to Odessa. I fell in with completely different circles and in six months everything connected with the *shtetl* was for a long time erased from my memory.

II

'Long Live the Provisional Government!'

COUNT ALEXEI BOBRINSKOY

One morning in February 1917 Alexei Bobrinskoy, whose childhood memoirs appear in Chapter 8, arrived in St Petersburg to find the city in turmoil.

In February 1917 I was an officer, a very young officer of the Imperial Russian Army. During a short leave I went on a small shooting expedition into the forests of Novgorod where game was very plentiful. At that time of the year, with snow covering the ground knee-deep, we went after a much-coveted animal – the lynx.

We succeeded in tracking one and a beat was organized. I was the only gun present and, as the beaters started moving through the ice-bound forest, I saw a lynx coming out of the dense, snow-covered shrubs and killed him with buckshot at a distance of about thirty yards. He was a beautiful specimen . . .

The next morning a horse-drawn sledge took me to the railway station, a long journey of some thirty miles over a perfectly smooth snow-covered road. The gamekeeper saw me off as I caught the fast night train to St Petersburg. The railway carriage was fairly empty, I had a compartment to myself, the dead lynx was left in the luggage van. After a comfortable night I awoke at the Nicholas railway station in St Petersburg at about 7 a.m.

It was a cold winter morning, the sun was up and shining, the sky was of a perfect blue. I hailed a porter and gave him my Purdey shotgun and my valise and fetched the bag containing the dead lynx from the van. All seemed perfectly normal and peaceful as I went out of the station accompanied by the porter. I hailed a horse-drawn sledge and asked the driver the usual question: 'No. 60 Galernaya Street – how much?' There are no taximeters on sledges and the fare has to be agreed upon beforehand by bargaining between the customer and the coachman. A most unexpected reply came: 'I will take you to the address you wish, but the price will be ten roubles.'

I gasped with surprise. 'What? Ten roubles? The usual fare is one rouble, not ten.'

'Well, Sir,' answered the cabman, 'I will not risk my life for less.'

'What do you mean, risk your life? Are you crazy?' said I.

'I am not crazy, Sir,' replied the cabman. 'Don't you know we have most unusual events here in the capital? People have gone mad. They shoot in the streets and nobody knows where the shots are coming from. Why, only yesterday I saw a policeman shot dead in the Nevsky Prospekt. Hooligans are parading up and down the streets, prisons have been flung open. God knows what all that means, Sir. One is afraid to live – you may be shot from behind a streetcorner and nobody will arrest the murderer – the policemen are hiding. Terrible events are afoot . . . '

I was flabbergasted. I agreed to pay my driver the ten roubles he asked and we started off at a gay trot. The city was not fully awake yet, the squares were empty and the shops not yet open. Nothing happened. I arrived safely at my destination and paid the exorbitant sum.

'Tell me, Yegor,' I asked our old manservant as he opened the front door to me, 'what is it all about? I had to pay the cabman ten roubles for bringing me home from the station! It is ten times the usual fare.'

'Indeed, Sir,' replied Yegor, 'I am surprised you found a cab at all. These days we have been living through very anxious times. Shots are being fired all over the town. I am at a loss to understand what it is. They say some hot-heads are going about the factories and the big works telling the workmen to strike – about a hundred and thirty thousand of them are already on strike. Who pays them if they strike? They don't know what they want; they just want to be rowdy, the fools. If I were a general I would send them all to the front, then they would soon stop their silly strikes . . . '

I took a hot bath and went down to breakfast with my father. He was very pessimistic. He said, 'The Tsar is at Mogilev, at the GHQ, and our best regiments are at the front. Their empty barracks are used for training young recruits fresh from their distant villages – I dare say good boys, but ignorant. They got out of hand almost at once and joined the workmen who are on strike. The situation may become worse unless something is done now. The Guards ought to be brought back to their barracks immediately or we shall be plunged into anarchy.'

I went out for a walk. The beautiful River Neva was still frozen solid. I met several lorries packed with soldiers and workmen, singing and waving frantically. Some had red ribbons in their buttonholes. I could not hear what they were shouting. I was struck by the absence of police. What had happened to them? The streets were fairly empty.

As I was going along the English Embankment I met our old friend, Mr Skirmunt, warmly dressed in a fur-lined overcoat with a beaver collar. He was a member of the Upper Chamber and represented the constituency of Poland in the Council of Empire. We spoke in French.

'All this is very frightening, my friend,' he said to me. 'This small revolt can degenerate into a real revolution unless the Government takes strong measures instead of waiting.' Even as he spoke, several shots rang out from the other side of the Neva. (Little did I think that Mr Skirmunt, six years later, would become the Polish Ambassador in London, after Poland regained her independence.)

As the strike spread we remained without newspapers and the uncertainty became quite unbearable. The next day (28 February, old style[1]) I again went out for a walk and decided to go as far as the *Duma*, which seemed to be the centre of events. It was a long way, and Yegor's fears had come true. No sledges were to be seen anywhere. However, whether by sledge or by foot, I simply had to get the latest news . . . so by foot it had to be. Arrived at last, I saw great crowds of excited people marching towards the beautiful building which in the eighteenth century had been the palace of Prince Potemkin, the great statesman of Catherine the Great . . . before I knew what was happening I found myself pushed inside [by the crowd] . . . Fantastic disorder prevailed everywhere . . .

Soon the group with whom I found myself flooded into a large hall, already packed with people. I saw a spacious tribune on which sat Mr Chkheidze, a left-wing deputy,[2] while another fellow in soldier's uniform was addressing the audience. In a hoarse voice he screamed: 'Comrades, I am an old convict! . . . Now Freedom has dawned on Russia. Down with the Romanovs! Hurray!'

'Hurray!' echoed dozens of voices.

The Chairman, Chkheidze, intervened and said [in his strong Georgian accent], 'Comrade, we are assembled here not to discuss the future government of Russia. The power is in the hands of the *Duma*. All power to the *Duma* – hurray!'

His statement was not very convincing and the speaker would not give in. 'No, Comrade, you are wrong. We are the common people, we are here to determine how Russia should be governed. Down with the Romanovs! The land must belong to the working people – "Land and Freedom" should be our motto.'

'Land and Freedom!' echoed dozens of voices.

Chkheidze tried to put these *desiderata* into some shape and form. 'Comrades,' he said, 'of course the working people must have the land, but first we must insist upon the abdication of the Tsar, then we shall organize elections to the Constituent Assembly and only this legal body will be entitled to discuss the future form of government.'

'No,' howled many voices. 'Down with the Romanovs! Long live the Republic! Land to the working people!'

'I agree, of course,' said Chkheidze again, 'but a government cannot cease to exist. Surely you do not want to plunge our country into chaos? First we will obtain the abdication, and the power will be vested in the hands of the Grand Duke Michael, the Tsar's brother. Then, after the elections, the Constituent Assembly will decide –'

His voice was drowned in a storm of protests and shouts from the standing throng. 'Down with your Michael, down with the Romanovs. Long live the Republic. Land and Freedom to the working people!'

Even the most inexperienced politician could see at once that no constructive programme could be discussed at such a meeting. It was disorderly to a degree; threats and strong words were exchanged freely and the situation was becoming more and more confused. I began to feel very uncomfortable. On what grounds was I there?

Chkheidze went on, 'Comrades, this is the first meeting of the Soviet of the Workmen's and Soldiers' Deputies, which we have just formed; we must not be so disorderly. Respect the electors who sent you here; let us discuss our programme in dignity and calm . . . ' I realized that at least some of those present had been elected by the St Petersburg workmen and that this meeting was supposed to be a legal one, in spite of its disorderly appearance and rowdy behaviour. Fortunately, so far nobody had attempted to verify the mandates; no documents were asked for, but I decided to slip away before this might take place.

Managing at last to push my way towards the doors I found myself in the corridor. The deputies of the *Duma* had just finished their conference in the next hall and the President, Rodzyanko,[3] a huge man of at least six foot two, was leaving the hall, surrounded by his colleagues.

'Long live the *Duma*! Long live Rodzyanko! Land and Freedom to the people,' shouted the crowd. Only later did I realize that *two* legislative bodies – the *Duma* and the self-styled Soviet were sitting simultaneously in the same building – and the Soviet was the stronger, as later events have proved.

I was very glad to be in the open again. I went home on foot. As I was passing the Moshkov Lane I saw a great crowd of people rushing backwards and forwards from the Neva Quay to Millionnaya Street (near the Hermitage Museum). I heard voices say: 'It was a jolly good thing we shot him – he was sniping at the crowd from his window.'

'Who was sniping at the crowd?' I asked.

'Ah, some general of the Tsar, but we finished him off!'

I took a few steps in the direction of the scene of the murder. To my horror, I realized that it was the house of a general, retired long ago, who was living there peacefully with his wife; and, as I learnt later, he had no firearms and did not shoot at anybody. It was all a mistake. Some shots had been fired in the distance by some drunken soldiers, and a woman cook had shouted, 'It was from this house that the shots came,' pointing at the general's house. Thereupon the crowd had burst into his house and had killed the old man in a most savage way. When they realized their mistake it was too late. His wife escaped by the back door. The house was looted and the furniture smashed. Chairs and tables were thrown into the street out of the open windows.

On 1 March the *Duma* declared itself the legal Government of Russia, with Kerensky as Minister of Justice; Guchkov[4] became the War Minister and Rodzyanko became Premier. On 3 March the new Government sent Guchkov and another deputy, Shulgin,[5] to Pskov and, after a short conference with the Tsar, who was returning from the GHQ to the capital, obtained his abdication. That Shulgin was a nondescript fellow – I remember him very well. He used to come and see my father quite often. We always made jokes about his thin, curly blond hair and his stiff, starched, ridiculously high collar. It is hard to believe that this nonentity was chosen to put an end to the Russian Empire.

Although the Tsar was out of touch with his brother Michael, to whom the supreme power now belonged, as stated in the act of abdication, hopes were high that the Grand Duke Michael would re-establish some kind of acceptable government; but he, like Chkheidze, was overwhelmed by events.

On 4 March I was walking down the Nevsky Prospekt when I met a beautiful black limousine slowly driving through the dense crowd. I could almost touch the magnificent car with my hand, as it passed slowly along beside the pavement. Then suddenly I stood to attention, my hand to my cap, for there in the car was seated none other than the Grand Duke Michael himself . . . As he returned my salute, I got an impression of large grey eyes tense with anxiety, in a face of extraordinary palor. That same evening, we learned that he too had signed his abdication in favour of the Constituent Assembly.

So ended the Russian Empire. One by one, the Romanovs were murdered and the supreme power was thrown to the crowds, while in every Russian church, instead of the set prayer 'Long live the Tsar!' the people prayed, paradoxically, 'Long live the Provisional Government!'

From March 1917 we had the official Provisional Government with the unofficial, but very powerful, body of elected or self-elected people who called themselves 'the Soviet of the Workmen's and Soldiers' Deputies' . . . It was in effect the government behind the scene.

My work at the Admiralty gradually resumed its normal course. The war went on, but the organization and discipline of the Army were rapidly dwindling away. One day I noticed that the portraits of the Emperors had disappeared from the hall, all except those of Catherine the Great and Peter the Great. On their frames, however, large red ribbons were pinned. The clerks probably thought that this addition would be more in keeping with the revolutionary atmosphere of the time.

The Provisional Government decided to allow all émigrés to return to Russia. Amongst these was Trotsky, whom the British had arrested as a German spy and held in a prison in Halifax [Nova Scotia]. Litvinov and Chicherin were in London.[6] Lenin was in Switzerland. To all these revolutionaries the Revolution came as a great surprise. The German General Staff, eager to exploit the Revolution for its own purposes, decided to use Lenin as an agent to spread 'peace' propaganda in the Russian Army. The Germans financed Lenin's journey from Switzerland in a sealed railway carriage to Sweden. On 12 April he arrived in Stockholm accompanied by a group of German staff officers. After a short conference in one of the big hotels, during which Lenin received exact instructions from the Germans, he was taken by train to Finland and reached St Petersburg on 15 April in the evening. Some workmen greeted him, but on the whole his arrival passed quite unnoticed.

A few days later I went to a tea party at Madame Rodzyanko's house. Her husband, a retired colonel, was the brother of the President of the *Duma*. Various items of news were discussed; some of the guests were making wild prophecies about future events. Somebody made a remark about Lenin's arrival. Madame Rodzyanko, a delightful hostess who, like so many others, had never heard Lenin's name before, asked her guest, *'Lenin? Qui est Lenin? Est-ce qu'il est gentil?'* ['Lenin? Who is Lenin? Is he nice?'] Probably she thought he was a person whom she might invite to one of her next parties. *'Non, Madame. C'est un de ces affreux révolutionnaires,'* replied the guest, and the conversation passed on to more important and interesting topics.

The inactivity of the Provisional Government was beyond comprehension. Kerensky pursued the policy of 'wait and see', while the extremists kept organizing themselves more and more. No serious measures were taken against the troublemakers.

On 20 April, at about 3 p.m., I heard some shouting and rioting going on near the Admiralty. As I went out to see what was the matter, I saw a fairly large crowd of people with placards bearing the slogans: 'DOWN WITH THE GOVERNMENT', 'ALL POWER TO THE SOVIETS', 'DOWN WITH THE WAR'. A reserve battalion of the Finland regiment was particularly disorderly – soldiers with their uniforms unbuttoned, dishevelled and untidy, were shouting and strolling up and down the streets. No officers were to be seen. Some officials arrived and tried to persuade the demonstrators to disperse. The next day the same demonstration paraded down the Nevsky Prospekt with placards bearing slogans: 'DOWN WITH CAPITALISM. THE SWORD AND THE MACHINE GUN WILL DESTROY THEE'. No police were to be seen anywhere.

Nobody bothered about the war with Germany. Communists were getting stronger and stronger. On 18 May my mother's brother, General Polovtsev, was appointed Commander in Chief of the St Petersburg region. Kerensky was Minister of War. My uncle was a very brave man and his presence gave hope for stronger measures, but Kerensky was 'flirting' with the extremists and measures to restore order proposed by the General were never carried out. When he sent his young ADC to arrest Trotsky, the young officer was, to his great surprise, confronted by Kerensky himself, who was in a secret conference with Trotsky. Of course the arrest was not carried out. Lenin got the wind up and fled to Terioki in Finland. When the officer who was sent there to arrest him arrived, the sly fox was gone, half an hour before.

Finland was so near to St Petersburg, and so quiet; the Revolution had not yet reached its sombre forests and quiet lakes. I took a country house near a place called Imatra and settled my wife and my mother-in-law there. Food was also fairly plentiful, especially fish, which we caught in the lake. Once my wife caught a salmon weighing 30 lb. It was great fun. I could visit my family only at the weekend, as I had to return to the Admiralty for my work.

On 18 June some units of the Russian Army advanced and achieved important successes on the Austrian front. The towns of Halicz and Kalusz were captured by the Russians.[7] This did not suit the plans of the Communists, who were constantly working against the [continuation of the] war and for the immediate conclusion of peace 'without annexations and reparations'. Lenin intensified his propaganda against the war. Again, Kerensky did not take any measures to consolidate his situation; he did more harm to the Provisional Government than good by adopting the Communists' proposals, such as the registration of firearms belonging even to officers on active service. This amazing measure created much confusion, but as it was a law, I also had to go to the local police station, now called the Commissariat of Militia, and declare my revolver and my sword, which were part of my uniform. I had to stand in a queue with some other officers, who were amazed and indignant. Such stupid measures made Kerensky very unpopular. With the permit to possess a revolver (delivered by the militia office of my district) I did not feel very much safer. On the contrary, when special patrols of soldiers parading up and down the streets stopped me and asked me to produce the permit, I felt insulted. Some officers who did not comply with this order and refused to register their firearms were molested by the controlling pickets, some officers were killed by the revolutionaries. How could a war minister of any country adopt such a derogatory measure against the officers of a department of which he was chief?

Fortunately, almost at the same time there came out an order allowing officers to wear civilian clothes. Many availed themselves of this permission and took off their uniforms for good. Many did not wish to rejoin their units at the front, because discipline among the soldiers was getting worse and worse; soldiers' committees discussed every order and very often simply refused to do anything at all.

It became more and more obvious that Russia was now out of the war. Deserters took trains by assault and forced the engine drivers to go as far as it suited the soldiers. This completely dislocated the railway organization and the timetable ceased to exist. Trains got stuck, and the supply system collapsed into anarchy. All these conditions suited the Communists, who were seriously preparing their coup with the intention of taking power entirely in their own hands.

On the morning of 4 July I intended to go to Imatra and spend my usual weekend with my family. All seemed quiet on that particular morning; the streets were rather empty as I hired a cab to take me from our house to the Finland railway station. I was wearing my usual uniform . . . As my cab was getting near the Liteyny Bridge, which we were to cross in order to get to the station, which is situated on the right bank of the Neva, I saw a considerable crowd marching from the Finland side towards the bridge. I also heard a few distant rifle shots. My driver did not like the situation at all and, turning towards me, said, 'Well, Sir, I shall drive no further. I have had enough trouble through all these demonstrations – I am not going to expose myself and my old horse to new dangers. People have gone quite crazy.'

There we stopped on the somewhat deserted Neva Quay. I saw a boatman and shouted to him, 'Hey, listen, young man, will you take me in your boat to the other side? How much for the trip?' 'Three roubles. I will not risk my life for less,' came the answer. I agreed. I paid the cabman and went down the granite steps of the quay towards the boat. It was a pleasant crossing. The sun was shining warmly, the day was perfect. It took us some fifteen minutes to cross the river . . . I paid the three roubles and proceeded on foot to the Finland railway station.

On my way I saw many excited workmen, some with rifles in their hands. They were going towards the Liteyny Bridge with the intention of marching against the Provisional Government. Three artillery salvoes thundered out as I was about to take the train for Imatra. As I learned afterwards, it was the Guards' Artillery Battery, under Lieutenant Rehbinder, which was loyal to Kerensky and which tried to disperse the Communist demonstration. The effect of these three salvoes was very great. Not only did they disperse the disorganized workmen on the Liteyny Bridge, but the sound of cannon-fire created a panic in the streets leading to the *Duma*, where other demonstrators were forming their processions. These three salvoes saved Kerensky and his Government from ruin.

Three days later I returned to St Petersburg and discovered that everything was calm again. Lenin postponed his offensive until a more appropriate time. Strikes went on; constantly we had cuts in electricity. In the evening we often sat with candles. The situation was becoming more and more unsettled. Food became scarce due to the chaos on the railways. Some of my friends left for abroad; some went to Sweden via Finland. I sometimes envied them but, as I was on active service and the war was still on, I could not follow their example. Life in St Petersburg became more and more unpleasant.

Kerensky issued an order to destroy all stocks of wine and alcoholic drinks, to prevent their being looted by the crowds. Those who were entrusted with this mission, usually some self-demobilized soldiers of the garrison, were only too glad to get into the cellars belonging to the bourgeoisie. Our house was also visited in connection with this. Poor Yegor was livid with fear and indignation when a group of about eight or nine soldiers proceeded to smash the bottles of twenty-five-year-old Château Yquem and Green Chartreuse which were stored in my father's cellar. These uncouth intruders, as Yegor called them, waded knee deep in a fragrant pool of most exquisite French wine. A number of bottles were simply stolen by these custodians of the law. In the cellars of the Winter Palace some three million bottles of wine were smashed. The pavement was red with the flowing stream of Medoc mixed with Mouthon Rothschild and Napoleon brandy.

It was distressing to see how rapidly the military discipline of the soldiers garrisoned in barracks both in the capital and in the immediate vicinity was dwindling away. The barracks were full of young soldiers whose training was slack, and the officers attached to these units were not sure of their powers and were afraid to enforce obedience and drill. Idle young soldiers loitered about, listening to agitators and to soapbox orators who discussed political theories. 'Freedom', so lavishly proclaimed, meant to so many just slackness and freedom from all obligations. Soldiers got drunk and rowdy. In the Imperial residence of Gatchina were many ponds well stocked with tame carp. Each had a ring bearing a date through its nose. They were trained to rise to the surface to the sound of a little bell and get their food at a certain hour of the day. Some of them were very old. These credulous contemporaries of Catherine the Great became an easy prey to the soldiers of the Revolution, who summoned them to rise to the silvery tinkling of the little bell. The game reserves of the Tsar were ruthlessly destroyed by soldiers. The herd of rare European bison was completely exterminated. Nobody dared to stop these self-demobilized poachers.

It was an open secret that the Communists were getting large sums of money from Germany through the Swedish banks. Kerensky did nothing to stop this. A Communist woman agent, Sumenson, acted as intermediary and was much embarrassed to explain this sudden enormous increase of turnover with Sweden when she was asked to do so by General Polovtsev (my uncle). The British military attaché, General Knox, protested to Polovtsev saying that he was not going to give any information to the Provisional Government about the German spies, because his information immediately became known to the Communists. There was endless evidence of connivance between the services headed by Kerensky and the Communist-controlled Soviet. It became more and more obvious that the days of the Provisional Government were numbered. Russia was plunged into a state of complete chaos.

One day as I took a walk along the Quay I saw a crowd of people listening to an orator. I came nearer: the orator was talking about capitalism and the common property of the masses. He rolled his 'R' in a very marked way.

'See this watchmaker's shop, Comrades,' he cried. 'Well, the watchmaker is a capitalist! He has looted this stock of his – it really belongs to the people. Private merchants should be exterminated; they are the enemies of the proletariat. Go and take his stock of watches. Loot what has been looted from the poor people!'

I enquired from my neighbour whether he knew who the speaker was. 'Why,' he said, 'this is Lenin himself . . . ' I rapidly retraced my steps and disappeared in the crowd.

On this very same day, General Polovtsev told us about the review of the Cossacks of the Guard which was organized for Kerensky. The General pointed out that Kerensky, as War Minister, had to appear on horseback. Kerensky protested and wished to review the assembled regiment from a motorcar; his kidneys were weak and he did not like riding on horseback. After much discussion, a very quiet grey mare was brought from the Imperial stables. (It turned out later that this was the Tsar's personal mount.) Kerensky climbed up and proceeded to review the rows of mounted Cossacks, all famous horsemen. One stable-boy ran in front of the mounted War Minister, indicating to him the direction he was to take; another stable-boy ran behind, probably to assist the Minister if he slipped down from the saddle. Needless to say, the impression made on the Cossacks was lamentable. They could hardly contain their laughter. After the parade, the Commandant entertained Kerensky to luncheon, at which my uncle was also present. The Commandant proudly showed them a toy rifle which the sentry took away from the Tsarevich, fearing that the unfortunate boy (who was under home arrest together with all the Imperial family) might start a counter-revolution. Even Kerensky was annoyed at such an excess of revolutionary zeal.

The recollections of Alexei Bobrinskoy's wife are given in Chapter 20.

12

Crossing the Frontier

IRINA YELENEVSKAYA

Irina Yelenevskaya was born in 1898. In 1917 she and her parents moved from St Petersburg to Vyborg in Finland for the sake of her father's health. When he died the following year, Irina and her mother returned to Russia, determined to try to resume their former life. The devastation that they found in post-Revolutionary Petrograd, however, quickly changed their minds and they decided to go back to Finland. But the border had been closed, and escape was the only route.

One day in late August [1919] as I was walking along the embankment I met my maternal grandfather, Professor Smirnov, who was returning home from the Public Library, where he was librarian-in-charge of the Oriental Section. We had not seen each other for a long time and my grandfather was delighted to see me. I told him that we had made everything ready for our escape; everything of value had been sold and the proceeds of the sale had been converted from money into jewels, which would be easier to take with us and which might appreciate in value, whereas the exchange rate of roubles could only fall. But we had still not been able to find a person who might get us across the Finnish frontier.

Having heard my story, Grandfather said, 'Move over and come to live in my place. Nina (his elder daughter, my mother's sister) and her son are also moving in with me, otherwise I will have a whole mob of sailors forcibly billeted on me. What's more, if the three of you keep on living in your uncle's flat when it is virtually stripped bare, this may arouse suspicion.'

When I told my mother and uncle of Grandfather's offer, they were delighted with it, even though they strongly disapproved of the fact that he was living in sin with a friend of his other daughter. She had arrived at the beginning of the war as a refugee from Grodno and had stayed in Grandfather's house, since Petersburg was overflowing with refugees and it was impossible to find a room. Grandfather had been a widower for several years and Nina Konstantinova Grozmani began to run the household for him out of gratitude for his hospitality. Despite his advanced age, my grandfather was still a very attractive man and enjoyed great success with the ladies, and so, imperceptibly to outsiders, they came ever closer together. His daughters criticized their father for not legalizing this union, since Nina Konstantinovna was from a good family and should not have had to endure such a compromising position.

The following Sunday we went to see Grandfather and he offered us two rooms: the dining room, in which my mother and I were to live, and my late grandmother's little sitting room, where my uncle would sleep. The big drawing room was already occupied by Aunt Nina and her ten-year-old son Nikolasha; she had been widowed six months previously and was finding it very hard to live in such loneliness.

We informed the House Committee that we were moving to my grandfather's apartment, and the move was fixed for 15 September.

On the eve of our departure, the flat was empty except for the three beds that we were taking with us to Grandfather's place and several suitcases. We went to bed early in view of our impending departure, but before the electricity was cut off for the night there came a sharp ring at the front door. Throwing a cloak over my shoulders, I went to open the door: two sailors and two girls were standing on the landing. One of the sailors showed us a search warrant, and I let this charming party in. After a glance into the dining room, where I was sleeping, and into the study, where my mother was in bed, they stopped in perplexity, seeing that all the rooms were completely empty. I hastened to explain to them that we were moving out next day.

'We know these "moves",' said one of the sailors rudely. 'There's something fishy going on here. Come on, girls, search the beds and the suitcases of these citizenesses, and we'll take care of the Comrade Bourgeois.' At that moment my uncle appeared from his bedroom, wearing his splendid dressing gown.

The girls started their search with great zeal, ripping open pillows and mattresses and turning out all our ready-packed suitcases. Apart from clothes and shoes, however, they found nothing. Nevertheless, the sailors wanted to march us off to the local commissar's office, but we were saved by Pashkov, the Chairman of the House Committee, who had come up the stairs, seen the open door and entered our flat during the search. He declared that we were all Soviet employees who were moving over to live with a relative, because our flat was needed for some sort of workers' club. The Communist quartet were thus obliged to withdraw empty handed.

Next day, having loaded a cart with our remaining store of firewood, the three beds and our suitcases, we left Uncle's flat with a sense of relief.

We settled in comfortably at Grandfather's apartment and arranged between us the hours at which we should do our respective spells of cooking: Grandfather and Nina Konstantinovna, Aunt Nina and Nikolasha, and we three all maintained separate little households, each according to its own supply of rations and any food we managed to acquire on the black market.

In the evenings, when Nikolasha had been put to bed, my aunt would join us in the dining room and we would begin endless conversations about our former life and make predictions about the future of Russia. It was pleasant to be amongst one's own, from whom we did not have to hide or suppress any thoughts for fear of informers.

When the cold weather began, we realized that we would have to move even closer together, because our escape was still an aspiration that belonged in the indefinite future. Through his work for the Port Authority, my uncle had managed to acquire half a square *sazhen* [170 cubic feet] of firewood, and this amount of fuel would probably have to last for the whole winter. My mother and I moved into the big drawing room together with Aunt Nina and Nikolasha. There was a very efficient stove in this room and we took it in turns on alternate days to keep it burning.

From October the electricity was switched on only from eight o'clock in the evening; the earlier evening hours had to be spent by the feeble light of little paraffin lamps, each of which gave out about as much light as a *veilleuse* in front of an icon. Only rarely was there electric current throughout the night; when there was, it was not a cause for joy, because it was a sign that house searches were in progress in our district. On such evenings we kept an especially wary eye on Marina, the cook, who no longer worked for Grandfather but had kept her room in his apartment and was now the Chairwoman of the House Committee. I never understood how Grandmother had been able to keep this enormous, gloomy woman as her cook – admittedly she was a first-class cook – who had always made an unpleasant impression on me.

After several days of misunderstandings and mishaps, our 'commune' settled down into a strictly ordered pattern of life. Apart from Grandfather and Nikolasha, we all left for work in the morning. I prepared breakfast. It invariably consisted of wheatmeal porridge boiled in water, 'coffee' of roasted oats, and thin slices of black bread. We had long since forgotten the existence of butter, but through my job I sometimes got a supply of Ukrainian *povidlo* [a sort of plum jam], which we spread on our bread. It was my job to deal out the bread ration and the *povidlo*, as Mother and Uncle trusted my 'powers of resistance', and generally I managed to justify their confidence. But twice I fell from grace, unable to withstand the 'temptations of Tantalus': when doling out a tablespoonful of *povidlo* to each person, I could not resist putting a whole spoonful of the sweet, jam-like purée into my mouth.

As time went on, the lack of sugar and fats in our diet made itself felt. My uncle's face started to swell badly and several times I fainted while standing in the queue at the public canteen for soup, which consisted of a brew of boiled fish in which floated a few miserable cabbage leaves.

As soon as I came back from work, I had to start cooking supper. I returned home a couple of hours before my mother and uncle, whose journey from their place of work at the Port Authority lasted nearly an hour and a half. Thus I had time to go down to the canteen and bring back an enamel can of soup, after which I would either make fishcakes or, if I were lucky, meatballs of horsemeat, and sometimes pancakes of minced potato peelings. Due to the lack of fats, these had to be fried directly on the hotplate.

My aunt's cookery was much more impressive, because she managed to acquire, by hook or by crook, foodstuffs such as milk, eggs, groats and so on for Nikolasha, who had caught a heavy cold, had been put to bed and did not get up again. He constantly ran a slight temperature and there was an unhealthy flush on his cheeks like that of a consumptive, and the doctor said that his organism was weakening and could not fight the bacilli. In order to acquire these foodstuffs, my aunt would set off every Sunday with a rucksack to bargain with peasants in the countryside. After her husband's death, she had been left with a huge quantity of men's underwear and shirts, and it was these that she bartered for food. The peasants would not sell anything for money.

No one knew what 'connections' Nina, my grandfather's mistress, had, but she somehow fed him in a positively pre-Revolutionary manner. She would fry onions in butter, followed by plump steaks – and not horsemeat steaks either, but real beefsteaks. She also used to cook scrambled eggs and *pelmeni* [Siberian meat dumplings], and we would try our best not to look at all these delicacies, in order to prevent the secretion of our gastric juices, since there was nothing in our stomachs for them to digest . . .

This pattern of life continued until the end of February, while we continued to lodge with my grandfather, having been still unable to find anyone who would help us to cross the border into Finland. At last, in the middle of March, a colleague of my uncle's put us in touch with a Finnish milkmaid who, in partnership with a number of White officers, was engaged in helping those who wanted to escape from the 'Soviet paradise' by crossing the frontier. She and I came to an agreement on terms and the day of our escape was set for 16 March. It would have been dangerous to have put off our escape any later than mid-March, because the thaw would have started by then and the ice on the River Sestra might have begun to break up and move downstream.

At last came the day of our long-planned escape to Finland – 16 March 1920. The weather was glorious – a bright sun shone upon the snow still piled in the Petersburg streets, it was just starting to thaw and streams of water were beginning to rush along the gutters, while every now and again huge icicles would break off from the eaves of houses and shatter on the pavement.

We got up as usual at 7 a.m., but after drinking our roasted-oats 'coffee' and eating our wheaten porridge and black bread we did not set off for work; havin packed rucksacks with underwear, washing things and extra shoes, we sat down to await the arrival of our guide. She was supposed to take us to a border village and there to hand us over to some Finnish smugglers who would escort us over the frontier and into Finland . . .

Around noon, already dressed in fur coats and with rucksacks over our shoulders, we went to say goodbye to my grandfather. As was his custom, he was seated in his velvet dressing gown at his desk in the drawing room, working on his translation of the works of some Turkish poet. A handsome old man with a shock of curly grey hair, very reserved by nature, Grandfather was visibly upset, and tears were glistening in his eyes as one by one he embraced and kissed my mother, my uncle and myself.

Having said farewell to Grandfather, we went into the kitchen where our guide was waiting for us – a pretty, ash-blonde Finnish girl. Marina [the cook] had been sent out shopping.

Although our train was not due to leave until 4 p.m., we left home three hours before its departure, because we had to go the whole way from the Petersburg side to the Vyborg side and to the Finland Station on foot, and in addition we had to go and collect another woman who was planning to escape with us. When, however, we knocked on her door and she opened it, we were horrified by the sight of her: her face was contorted with anguish and her eyes were rolling. 'Go without me,' she gasped, sobbing. 'I haven't the strength to go with you, I'm terrified . . . ' She could not finish her sentence, but we realized that she was thinking about the increasing number of people who had been shot in recent weeks after being caught trying to cross the border into Finland. We did not try to persuade her, and after a silent gesture of farewell we continued on our way.

En route to the station, in two places we passed the corpses of fallen horses – or rather their skeletons, because all the meat and internal organs had been removed by starving people. In that winter of 1920 the famine was particularly severe and people would stop at nothing to assuage their hunger. They were not even afraid to buy meat from Chinese pedlars who hawked it from door to door, even though there were sinister rumours that this was the flesh of people shot by the Bolsheviks.

After a long walk we reached the Finland Station . . .

Our train was already at the platform. The carriages were full of soldiers returning from leave to various frontier posts, Finnish women in headscarves who had brought potatoes and watered milk to sell in the city, and other half-starved, grey-looking passengers like ourselves.

We managed to get a seat at the end of the carriage, near the door. In case of a police check, we had passes issued at my uncle's office certifying that we were all employees of the Petersburg Port Authority and had been given permission to travel to Shuralovo in search of food.

After a prolonged delay, the engine gave a puff and a whistle and started off. Suburban houses and soot-stained factory walls moved past the windows, to be followed by little *dacha*s and thin coppices of birch and spruce.

Our carriage stank of home-grown tobacco, the steam from wet felt boots and unwashed bodies. We kept silent, lest the other passengers should notice our 'bourgeois' accents. We travelled slowly; the train stopped for a long time at every station and it was six o'clock when we reached Shuralovo. By then most of the passengers had got out, so that apart from us the only people to alight at Shuralovo were a few Finnish women and two or three soldiers.

The sun was low in the western sky and throwing long shadows on the snow-covered road. At a sign from our guide we allowed all our fellow-passengers to get well away from the station, and we were the last to start walking up the country road, avidly gulping down the clean, frosty air. When we were alone on the road, our guide explained that there was a mile to walk to her farm and that when we approached the house we must be silent, because Red Army soldiers were billeted in one wing and it was wise to slip into the house as unobtrusively as possible.

The dark-blue twilight of March was setting in as we entered the glassed-in porch and then the big living room of our guide's house. The pinewood table was laden with every kind of food: black bread, ham, milk, eggs, butter and much else. The supper before our nighttime dash to the frontier was included in the payment – 100,000 'Duma' roubles per person.[1]

Having eaten our fill we went into the next room, much of which was taken up by a wide bed; all three of us lay down on it to await the arrival of the 'boys', as our guide called them, who were due to come and fetch us at about eleven o'clock at night.

Despite our physical tiredness, we could not sleep – our nerves were too wound up. We lay listening to every sound that came from outside. After ten o'clock all was silent in the wing occupied by the Red Army soldiers . . .

The clock in the next room struck eleven, then half-past, then twelve. My uncle opened the door into the room in which our guide and her mother were sitting, and enquired in a whisper about our new guides. The mother asked us to wait in patience a little longer; it often happened that the 'boys' were late. But when the clock struck one we could restrain ourselves no longer, and all three of us got up and went into the next room. The expression on our guide's face was one of such distress and unhappiness that our suspicion that we had been led into a trap instantly vanished. Nevertheless, we insisted that she should take us out to meet the smugglers halfway. We could not stay and wait for them till dawn; the approach of daylight would mean mortal danger for us, because then the Red Army soldiers billeted at the farm would come into the house for food.

After a long discussion we finally persuaded her to do as we asked. It was already 3 a.m. when we left by the back door that led into the kitchen garden. Beyond the garden was a small clearing, and beyond that rose up the dark wall of the forest. The moon was shining brightly; as fast as possible we ran across the clearing into the depths of the forest. The deep ski-tracks had been well used, so that the snow was packed hard and easy to walk on.

About a mile into the forest we emerged into a clearing to see a grim sight: two pairs of skis and four broken ski-sticks lay scattered about, the snow was heavily trampled in places and it was stained red with patches of blood. It was obvious that a fight had taken place here not long before our arrival.

'The Red soldiers caught the boys,' said our guide, wringing her hands. 'That's why they never came to fetch you.'

'That's most unfortunate,' said my uncle. 'There's nothing for it now – *you* must take us to the frontier.'

Our guide nodded in silence and began looking around her, as though trying to remember something. Three paths led into the clearing. She set out along the path by which, judging from the ski-tracks, the smugglers had come.

The deeper we went into the forest, the harder the going became. Although we were wearing felt boots, the snow often gave way under us and we would sink into it above our knees, while the weight of our rucksacks tended to press us in deeper . . .

The eastern sky began to lighten, heralding the sunrise. Suddenly, not far away, we heard men's voices and the clink of weapons. Our guide signalled to us to lie down in the snow under some bushes. The voices drew nearer. I clearly heard one of them say, 'Well, Comrades, that's enough of blundering about in the forest. We obviously won't catch the bourgeois. It'll be light soon, and they're afraid of crossing the frontier in daylight.'

Evidently a Red Army ski-patrol was passing near us. We lay in the snow holding our breath and trying not to look at each other.

When the voices could be heard no longer, we got to our feet. 'It's not far to the border from here,' whispered our guide, and set off along the path. But she soon stopped, looking about her in perplexity. When we caught up with her we saw that the path simply petered out among the bushes. There was nothing but thick forest on all sides. 'I've brought you the wrong way,' she said despairingly.

After some discussion we decided to move in the opposite direction to the rising sun, as we knew that the frontier lay in a general westward direction.

The going now became even harder, as we were walking on virgin snow. We were constantly falling or tripping on tree stumps hidden under the snow. My mother was nearly at the end of her strength. She was stopping increasingly often, panting for breath and eating snow to cool her parched mouth. Our guide took Mother's rucksack and went on slowly pushing her way through the snow.

The sun rose and climbed slowly higher in the sky. The birds began to twitter. Our guide was by now several dozen paces ahead of us. We could just see her red skirt flickering between the tree trunks. Suddenly she stopped, gazed ahead, then ran back to us.

'The border, the border,' she shouted, almost out of breath. 'The Sestra river is at the bottom of the next slope.'

Instantly our tiredness was forgotten and we, too, pressed forward almost at a run. After about a hundred paces we found ourselves at the top of the high bank of the river. It was still covered with ice, but in places the ice was beginning to crack. Would we fail to cross the river, now that we were so near to our goal? There was no choice. After shaking our guide by the hand we clambered down the bank and set foot on the ice. It gave a crack or two, but it held us. We stumbled headlong across the river and looked back only when we had reached the far side. Our guide was sitting under a tall birch tree on the other bank, waving to us. We waved back to her and set off, leaving the river behind us.

We soon came to a road, where the snow was packed tight from considerable use by traffic; it must have been used to carry timber out of the forest. Concealing ourselves from the road behind some trees, we sat down on tree stumps to rest.

While we were resting, two human figures came into view far down the road. As they came closer to us, we recognized them as soldiers. We exchanged glances and read the same thought in each others' eyes:

'Suppose they are Red Army soldiers?' But there was nowhere to go; they had seen us and were coming towards us. We stood up and walked towards them.

When we were a few paces away from them, they crossed their two rifles to bar our way and said, pointing in the direction of the river: '*Pois*,' which meant 'Go away' in Finnish. We tried to explain by gestures that we had just come from across the river and wanted to come to Finland, but they obstinately repeated: '*Pois, pois.*'

Just then a peasant drove out of the forest on a timber-sledge and came towards us. After exchanging a few words with the soldiers in Finnish, he spoke to us in Russian. 'You must be refugees,' he said. 'But the order was given a few days ago that no more refugees will be allowed into Finland unless they have visas. So many of them have been coming over that we can't feed them all.'

'Oh well, the law is the law,' said my uncle. 'In that case these soldiers might as well shoot us here and now, because if we go back we are certain to be shot. It's not worth trudging ten miles back again just to get a Russian bullet in the back of the neck. A Finnish bullet will be just as good.'

The peasant translated this to the soldiers, who scratched the backs of their necks in perplexity. After talking a bit more with the peasant, who was evidently trying to persuade them to do something, they signed to us to follow them. 'They're going to take you to the officer in charge of their frontier post,' the peasant explained to us. He put our rucksacks on to his pile of timber and invited my mother to sit on them. Uncle and I followed on foot.

After a mile or so, we reached a prosperous-looking peasant's house. Several soldiers were clustered round the front porch, and they stared at us with curiosity. The two soldiers escorting us went inside, and soon a young officer came out; speaking in German, he invited us into the house. We went through a large front room and into a smaller one, which evidently served as the headquarters of this sector of the frontier guard. The officer asked us to sit down, repeating what the peasant had told us. We explained to him that our case was somewhat special: we had already been living in Finland and had gone to Petersburg on a visit that should have lasted only a few weeks, but we had got stuck there when the frontier was closed. At this point we were rendered an invaluable service by the certificate issued by General Mannerheim's headquarters, which had been given to us before we left for Petersburg in the autumn of 1918: it confirmed that everything we had said was the truth. Apart from that, we were able to name as referees a number of leading figures in Vyborg, such as the British Vice-Consul, the pastor of the Lutheran church and several others.

While we were talking, a more senior officer came into the room. Having greeted us, he heard what the junior officer had to say about us and said he would telephone to various authorities who would decide what was to become of us.

A long and agonizing wait began. The senior officer spoke on the telephone in Finnish, often repeating our names. At the end of each conversation he noted something on a piece of paper, then made another call. The nervous strain was such that my mother could only weep silently.

Finally, after yet another telephone call (I lost count of them all) the senior officer turned to us with a beaming smile: 'I congratulate you – you may stay in Finland.' We thanked him profusely and went out into the big front room, where we begged the owner to give us something to eat. His efficient wife quickly laid the table and put out bread, butter, Ukrainian bacon, salami and cottage cheese. A coffee pot was bubbling cheerfully on the stove.

Having eaten our fill and offered coffee to both of the officers – I remember thinking it incredible that they drank only two cups each – we said goodbye to them and to our host and hostess. A sledge was already waiting outside, with two tough little Finnish ponies in harness. We took our places, joined by a soldier who was to escort us to the headquarters in Terioki. Officers and soldiers came out on to the porch to wish us well and wave us goodbye as we set off.

Our escape had succeeded. There now began a new life as émigrés in Finland.

13

A Narrow Escape

PROFESSOR YEKATERINA ALEXANDROVNA VOLKONSKAYA

Yekaterina Alexandrovna Volkonskaya (née Olkhina) was born in 1895 into a wealthy family. Her father was a retired general and held the title of Stallmeister *(equerry); her mother owned an estate in Kherson province, and the family owned another estate near St Petersburg as well as property in the capital itself.*

When the war began I was just out of *gymnazia* [high school] and I was trying to obtain a diploma which was called Certificate of Sister of Mercy in Wartime. I received the diploma and then worked as a nurse. When the Revolution began, I was working as a sister in a Red Cross hospital.

In order to save our house in St Petersburg, we rented it to the American Red Cross. It was fictitious, of course – we never received any money from them; it was only done to save the house. The Americans came and lived in the house for two years until the Soviets evicted them. When they were thrown out, the house was completely looted. It was then that we decided it would not be sensible to stay in St Petersburg, since there wasn't enough food and fuel. We decided to go to the south of Russia. We went to Kherson province, where my mother had her estate, but it was dangerous for women to live there. So then we went to the Crimea, where we rented a country house from Yusupov.

When the Civil War began I started working as a nurse in a Red Cross field hospital for the Whites. We went north with the Army and almost reached Chernigov, but then the great retreat started. As we retreated I fell ill with typhus, but, as you see, I survived. After that I had what you might call several narrow escapes . . .

Once, as we retreated in a freight train, on one of the stations in

Poltava province we were approached by an officer who said that he had several field guns and mortars and three or four soldiers. The guns were unserviceable and he wanted them repaired. Since their locomotive wasn't running, the officer asked if he could attach his railway wagon to our train. The director of our hospital allowed him to do this. Then at the next station our locomotive broke down. As the train stood there and the night began to fall, the Reds occupied a nearby cemetery. As the night fell we saw them making a fire. So then we – the hospital staff – gathered together. There were only six nurses and one surgeon, who said that he had some cyanide and advised us to commit suicide in case we were captured by the Reds. However, the officer who was accompanying us with his defective guns put them all around the train and the Reds, thinking that we would put up a fierce fight, did not attack us during the night. In the morning we were provided with a new locomotive and we continued on our way south.

14

A Sudden Flight

NATALYA LEONIDOVNA DUBASOVA

Natalya Leonidovna Dubasova (née Pushchina) was born in 1909, the great-granddaughter of the Decembrist Ivan Pushchin (1798–1859). Because the Bolsheviks regarded the Decembrists as the first revolution-aries,[1] theirs was one of the few families prominent under the old regime to be looked on favourably by the new. None the less, Natalya's father's position as Gentleman of the Bedchamber to Nicholas II and his right-wing political views put them in danger.

[My father] was a very right-wing member of the *Duma*, and although the *Duma* ceased to function after the February Revolution, he belonged to a group strongly opposed to leaving the war . . . Most of the members of this pro-war group were shot sooner or later. We were able to escape because my father had suspected for some time that this might happen, and he acquired false papers for us, according to which we were the family of a French diplomat or something. This was the only thing that saved us. We had a French governess, and we all spoke fluent French, which enabled us to leave on false French passports.

We – my mother, my brother and my sisters – were in Finland when it all started; Father was in Petrograd. We had property in Finland, but one fine day it was seized and we were thrown out by a party of Red sailors from Helsingfors. [They] told us to take nothing with us but simply to leave the house as it was and get out. There wasn't one grown man with us – all the servants were women – but fortunately no one was touched and we all arrived back in Petrograd, to my father's horror.

We lived at Kirochnaya – I was seventeen at the time – and the house was being watched because they wanted to arrest him, so he couldn't go there. But one of our relatives had already been arrested, and his house had been searched and left empty. So Father took us there, because the house was unlikely to be searched again.

That same evening a meeting was held in that house of some committee organized by the group that was in favour of continuing the war . . . In the middle of the meeting, the janitor came in to say that a crowd of soldiers was coming. They were all terrified, and in five minutes not one member of that committee was left in the house. The only people to remain were we children – who were in bed – and our governess. The soldiers searched the house, found no one but us, and went away again. Father and Mother were outside, walking up and down the streets, not knowing what to do. Finally, at four o'clock in the morning, they came back: 'Quickly, quickly, get up!' They dressed us and we went straight to the Finland Station with our false passports, on which we travelled from Petrograd through Finland and across Sweden to Norway, where we spent a whole month waiting for a ship to take us from Bergen to Scotland.

Natalya Dubasova's family settled in London. Her memoirs of childhood in England appear in Chapter 43 and her sister's in Chapter 44.

15

Exiles in Finland

ANASTASIA VALENTINOVNA BECKER

Mrs Becker (née Countess Anastasia Valentinovna Zubova) was born in St Petersburg in 1908. Her mother, a concert pianist, was of Caucasian origin; her father, of a family distinguished since the eighteenth century, was a professor.

My parents separated when I was two. When I was four or so I went to live with my mother in Berlin . . . But one year later my father decided to steal me and arrived with a governess and lawyer and took me away from Berlin to Petersburg. Then came the war, and my mother became a nurse in the front line, with the French Army. I didn't meet her again until several years after the Revolution.

When we got back to Petersburg, I didn't see many changes because of the war – except that we had no more dancing lessons, because that was thought to be unpatriotic; we had to do gymnastics instead! Then there was the Revolution. We lived on St Isaac's Square, and I remember a good deal of shooting, and being told to keep away from the windows. Since the house in Oranienbaum had been taken as a military hospital we couldn't go there, so we went to Finland – myself, my cousin, our two governesses, my bachelor uncle, my grandmother and the maids. [Eventually my mother joined us.]

My father stayed in Petersburg. During the war he had been put in charge of public monuments there, and felt he had to protect them from the mob, so he didn't come with us. He was a professor of the History of Art, though still quite a young man. On one of the floors of our palace in Petersburg he created an Institute of the History of Art, with a gallery, a library and lecture rooms. When the Revolution started, this Institute became something of a refuge for people from the University. Many were Jewish, like Ephraim Schapiro, and I think it is from that time that several of my father's friendships with Jewish people derived. In any case, he never liked to go along with the majority of his own class – or with any majority. Soon he was arrested and spent several years in prison, first in an ordinary jail in Petersburg, then in the Peter-and-Paul Fortress. He was very badly treated in jail – the population was starving, so you can imagine what it was like for prisoners. He was also infected with lice and bugs. He was sometimes so desperate that he even drank the oil in the lamps. He used to write to us once a year and in the letter he would say that he was sick. This meant that he was in prison, but we didn't understand. He was released eventually and married again, and in 1925 he and his wife were allowed to leave Russia.

Just after the Bolshevik Revolution in October, my Uncle Alexander got a phone call from his brother-in-law, who was also in Finland, saying that his advice was to rush to Petersburg and get all the winter coats for the family and remove the valuable jewellery from the bank. That's what he did. He got the stuff, and no sooner had he got it back than the frontier was closed. It was the last moment he could have got out. The house in which we were living was rented for a certain time; when the lease ran out and we had no more money, we had to go to a small hotel in another town. When we arrived there, the grown-ups were sitting on their suitcases crying because they had found bugs in the beds. We fought those bugs for years.

The town was the scene of the last battle in the Finnish Civil War.[1] Before that, the Reds had come often to search us for jewellery, but it was hidden among my toys. During the last battle and bombardment we were hiding in the cellar. Part of the town was burning, and smoke came in. When the Reds were driven out and we emerged, the streets were full of pieces of shrapnel. We collected them to make toys.

My uncle said to us, 'Children, you'll see that the Finns will all welcome the Whites (and it's very good that the Reds have been defeated), but they were helped by the Germans, by von der Goltz and Wolff, and they are our enemies. You may go to see, but don't welcome them.' So we all stood there with our hands behind our backs. As we watched, one of the German soldiers, tired and very dirty, left the column and came up to my uncle and kissed him – it was his godson! You see my uncle was mad about fire-fighting. He'd made quite a study of it. Several of the fire chiefs in Germany were his friends, and the one in Hanover had made him the godfather of his son.

We lived miserably in this Finnish town for several winters, several summers. I don't remember being hungry, but the food was very bad – more straw than bread. Then one day we had a visit from a certain Mr Bucknall, from London [whom my uncle had met while he was doing the rounds of all the embassies, trying to make acquaintances]. He gave us a present of a huge box of chocolates – a very impressive present at that time; we hadn't seen chocolate for years. And he bought all our jewellery. No one had bought it up till then – who was there in Finland to buy? Nobody there had any money.

We put the money into a bank in London. We were able to pay our debts and move to Stockholm – it was terribly difficult to get visas – and then to Berlin, and finally to Switzerland. That was the time of the great inflation in Germany – people were hungry there too. But what I mainly remember about arriving is that in the West all the women had short dresses and short hair, while our grown-ups arrived in the dresses of 1914, and with corsets too! It was an appalling shock for them!

In London too there was inflation – less than half our money remained; but we had enough to live on, so we moved to Baden-Baden, as that was a town my mother knew from before the war – she used to go there to lose weight. We were still living in hotels – she said there was no point in getting a flat, as we would be going home soon. But she died in Baden-Baden.

I had no difficulty from the other pupils at school through being Russian, but I was one girl among twenty-five boys in my class. It was an ordinary German *Gymnasium* – in Germany, unlike Russia, girls' schools only went up to a certain class. They only expect you to know how to sew, and so on. I was able to go to university because of a teacher who went to visit my grandmother sometimes. He had been in Russia and used to tell her stories of his life there and in the mountains of Siberia. She was interested in him, and he persuaded her to agree to my going to university. At first it had been 'No! Impossible!' – in Russia it had certainly not been the done thing for young ladies.

I got to know far more Germans than Russians, though of course I met a lot of émigrés. For the first few years one used to meet families with teenage children, living on nothing, it seemed . . .

16

Through Latvian Eyes

ARVIDS JUREVICS

Arvids Jurevics was born in Tukums in Latvia in 1907.

In 1905, before my birth, there was a Revolution against the Tsar, and the local people rose against the Barons.[1] My father was involved in the Uprising. The revolutionaries went to the Barons' safes and, because he was a blacksmith, my father opened them. Later on, when the Tsarist authorities hit back against the revolutionaries, he was sent, so he said, to every prison along the Volga. After a few years, my grandfather somehow got him out by paying 100 roubles in gold. Then they moved to a small town of between eight and ten thousand inhabitants and established their smithy. I was born there in 1907. We had a smithy and a house next to it. When I was growing up we were free from the Barons, but later my father's involvement with the revolutionaries came out – during the war of 1914, when our country was often a battlefield and the two armies marched back and forth through Latvia: the Russians and the Germans. He suffered for it later. I remember the First World War and how we left the country.

I was eight. Early one morning my father woke me up. The sun had not yet risen, and I could hear cannon pounding in the distance. He said that we had to leave because the Germans were coming in, and we were going to Petersburg. So we packed everything and went to the railway station. But there we had to wait quite a few days. There was a big area covered with refugees and their belongings, and finally they packed them and their belongings into freight trains and we travelled for a whole week. All the trains were coming down from Petersburg on military business, with cannon and supplies, and we had to wait in sidings until there was room on the tracks. And then we arrived in Petersburg – a big city, having come from a small town. The Neva, all those huge granite embankments and the wide streets . . . We were living on Petrogradskaya Storona, Kamenno-ostrovsky Prospekt . . . across the river, near the cathedral of St Peter and St Paul, where the Tsars' tombs are . . . and the prison. So we were in the middle of events.

I don't know how my father managed to find somewhere so central to live. He spoke Russian pretty well because he had attended Russian schools. We were refugees from the Baltic states, and one of the Tsar's daughters, Tatiana, was in charge of these refugees. I think there was some kind of organization – as a little boy, I didn't understand much about it – but we got an apartment quite quickly. It was in a big house, right on a corner, with a courtyard. I remember very vividly the first days when I came out; there were Russian boys all around me, and they started to talk and joke with me, so that after one month I could speak all the Russian necessary for boys' talk. After a few more months, I had no problems. We went to Latvian refugee schools. Everything was organized. The only subjects taught in Russian were Russian itself and history; these were compulsory.

I remember all those wide streets – the Kamenno-ostrovsky Prospekt with its hexagonal wooden blocks, the very fancy carriages, the officers and nobles riding past. I remember one episode very well. We were walking along the pavement where a very dashing officer was walking with a girl, and one soldier failed to salute. The officer grabbed the soldier, hit him, pushed him into the roadway – hit him a couple of times until the man apologized and saluted, then went back to the girl.

My father found skilled work right away, in a Government car-repair shop. Later he worked in an aeroplane factory. He took me a couple of times to see the enormous steelworks, the Obukhovsky Zavod. When the Revolution started, I remember that big heavy hammer pounding the steel, and the whole earth was shaking.

But everything was nice and quiet for three years. Then things went wrong at the front, the food got scarce. We had big queues at the shops.

One day we were sitting in class having a lesson, and something was going on outside. A window was broken. We looked outside. A crowd had been queuing at a flour store, then the store-owner said he had no more left; the crowd didn't believe him. Several men took a big wooden beam and were banging on the door and the windows of the store. They broke in and found something. Everything was looted. That was the first time I saw it. Then I saw military cars on the streets, and soldiers with rifles. I heard they had deserted from the front – even some officers, too – and they were moving around the city, holding meetings in the squares. When that happened, all the police suddenly disappeared. As soon as they saw people talking in squares, machine guns would start firing from the upper storeys of buildings. First they shot to the side, and if the people didn't disperse, they shot straight and people were killed. Many times the crowds caught policemen and lynched them. I saw on our street a man white as a sheet, being pulled away by the crowd. He wore a *shinel*, the long police greatcoat, and a *papakha*, a grey fur hat. The policemen were dressed a little differently from the soldiers and you couldn't mistake them. He was taken away and was shot just around the corner. He had been shooting at a crowd, and they had caught him.

One day I was going home from school, when all of a sudden there were bullets, and brick chips were coming down from above me and from the wall on the other side. I ran home and told my mother. It began to be unsafe – people getting shot here and there. Cars were dashing about the streets loaded with armed soldiers . . . One day the Troitsky Bridge was raised, where the ships came through. All the bridges in Petrograd were raised, so there were no longer any communications across the Neva. I went down to the Troitsky Bridge, which was within walking distance of our apartment. I watched the crowd, who whenever they saw a nobleman's car would jump on it, push it, and sometimes turned it over. I remember one old lady pushing her shopping bag against a car to stop it. All the young people were having fun with those cars. Here and there something was burning. Everything was in chaos.

One of our relatives came in very pale one day. He had been down on Nevsky Prospekt and there had been shooting. He stumbled into a basement and people fell in over him and got shot; they had probably been having a meeting. He came in half dead – he was so upset and out of breath.

One night, suddenly, we heard big guns booming. Then the next day we heard about the sailors of the cruiser *Aurora* firing at the Winter Palace.[2] When everything was almost over we saw here and there the cadets who were still defending the old regime, and the revolutionaries shooting and destroying the cadet schools. The women's battalion was dispersed. There was shooting the whole night, and the next morning we wanted to know what had been going on.

We heard that the revolutionary regime was in power, and that Lenin had established his headquarters in the Smolny Institute. My father took me around to hear the revolutionary speakers. He said, 'That's Trotsky, with the beard.' He was speaking from a balcony. Many people stood and spoke. And while each person spoke, the crowd agreed with him: '*Pravilno, pravilno*' ['He's right, he's right']. Then someone would put a different viewpoint and they would agree with *him*.

Father was against the Barons, definitely. He was against the Tsar and what was going on in his court with Rasputin. He took me to the place where Rasputin was pushed under the ice after he had been shot, and he showed me the place in a church where one of the Tsars had been blown up.[3]

After the Revolution, when everything was over, we went to Marsovo Polye where the dead are buried, and there was music and flowers. I remember the dead were buried in the revolutionary way, and then after a couple of days they felt that this wasn't right, so they called in a priest to bless them. Before the Revolution, driving in a streetcar, you would pass hundreds of little chapels and everyone would cross themselves. Then they took out the icons and smashed them on the streets. How could they? Probably because the whole thing was some-how connected with the Tsar.

After the Revolution, there was hunger and bread was very scarce. I remember once my father took me forty miles south of Petrograd just to hunt for bread. We went from one hut to another. Usually they had huge brick stoves almost up to the ceilings. We went into one place and there was no one in, just some pigs and chickens. We called out. Then above us we heard a voice – a bearded face looked out from on top of the stove and asked what we wanted. We looked up and saw a row of small faces up there as well. It was nice and warm up there. Finally he gave us a small amount of bread. We went all round the village and saw no gardens in front of the houses, except in one where we saw some flowers. My father suggested we go in and see who was in that house, and who should we find but a Latvian, who had left our country a long time before. He had already almost forgotten Latvian, but could understand us. A Latvian *would* be different from the others.

After the Revolution, in 1918, our family packed its bags and returned to Latvia – we had had enough. The war was over and there was a truce at Brest-Litovsk in March 1918 between the Russians and the Germans. The war was still going on in the West. I remember we went by horse-wagon and crossed the neutral zone. That was what is now the eastern part of Latvia. There was some kind of camp for refugees; the Germans were on the other side and let us in. So we came home in 1918 to our own country. There wasn't peace yet. The Civil War was still raging – White groups fighting Red groups, each under their generals. My father still suffered for his old sins. When the German landowners came back – the old Barons – some of them still remembered and were looking for him. He had to hide. Once he hid in our house. We built a double wall, and he was there for weeks, waiting for another side to take over. Every time this happened, somebody got killed . . .

Jurevics's story is continued in Chapter 47.

17

Escape Through Poland

ALEXANDER VASILIEVICH BAKHRAKH

Alexander Vasilievich Bakhrakh was born in 1902 in Kiev, but his parents moved to St Petersburg soon after his birth.

During the February Revolution the first thing I noticed was when I was walking along the Nevsky Prospekt with some friends, and a cab-driver shouted to us, 'Don't go this way – turn on to the Moika, but avoid the Nevsky whatever you do: a demonstration is coming down here and God knows what may happen.' This occurred on 27 or 28 February, and it was completely unexpected. In the summer of 1917 my mother and I were in the Crimea, and apart from the fact that Russia was no longer a monarchy and there was still a war, everything to my young eyes seemed normal. The thought that we might soon lose *everything* was so remote that it never entered my head . . . When it came to the October Revolution, everybody knew what was happening; the telephones kept working, and I was in constant touch with my friends. We mostly stayed at home because of the disorders and shooting in the streets . . .

Throughout the year I spent in Petrograd – from autumn 1917 to 1918 – living conditions got steadily worse. We were often cold and hungry, but still comparatively well-off compared with the privations that were to come in the next two or three years, which we were lucky to escape. Added to this, my mother was ill for much of 1918, so that by autumn we were convinced we would do better to go south and join my grandfather. Kiev was occupied by the Germans, who kept order. When I left Petersburg, I had no idea that for the next year or so things would be as chaotic and as awful as they actually were in Kiev.

[My grandfather, a prominent bourgeois, escaped to Paris in 1919 and a year later I made up my mind to join him.] My father and his brother had some property in Kiev, and a tenant in one of their apartments was some Polish count, who was escaping from the Bolsheviks. It was virtually impossible to get an exit visa from the Polish authorities, but for the childish reason that I had just quarrelled with my girlfriend, I decided to emigrate, so I went to this Polish count, who was a friend of Rydz-Smygly, the Polish Commandant of the city, and he got me a *laissez-passer* to travel through Poland.[1] This scrap of paper was the only document I had when I reached Warsaw.

I spent two or three weeks in Warsaw, waiting for a French visa – at that time, getting a visa was an extremely complicated business. To make matters worse, the Red Army had invaded Poland and was approaching Warsaw; most people expected the city to fall to the Soviets, so all the foreign consulates, including the French, were evacuated from Warsaw. I had no papers, and I simply didn't know what to do. Then I suddenly noticed the Ukrainian Embassy, which had not been evacuated (it was the embassy of the Petlyura regime),[2] and there I was given some sort of a passport.

The next problem was how to get out of Poland, which was in a state of emergency. All movement was restricted, and I was constantly being stopped and searched by Polish gendarmes on the look-out for deserters. Through an uncle of mine, who was a senior official in a Polish bank, I was told that a friend of his had a spare ticket for Paris on the international wagon-lit coach that was leaving Warsaw. There was such bedlam at the station that I didn't manage to get on to the international coach, but only on to an ordinary Polish coach. Halfway to the German frontier, the international coach was uncoupled, and the Polish coaches went no further. The Polish gendarmes wouldn't allow me to get on to the international coach, but I created a terrible fuss and swore at them in Russian (fortunately most Polish officials then still spoke Russian) until I was escorted by two gendarmes – who carried my two suitcases for me, like porters! – to the wagon-lit coach. There I found my uncle's friend, and although I had never met him before, he turned out to be extremely friendly and helpful. He advised me to get up on to the top bunk and sleep, or pretend to sleep; he would deal with any nosey policemen or frontier guards on my behalf. We were indeed checked by patrols several times in the night, but he successfully kept them at bay by saying that I had the plague or something!

At the frontier station there was a long wait and my travelling-companion vanished into the town. He returned only just before the train was due to leave, and asked me if I would like to take one of his umbrellas through the German customs, as he already had another umbrella and a lot of luggage, all of which was difficult to carry. I had no objection, and when we were inside Germany I asked him why he had wanted me to carry such a trivial thing through the customs. He winked and opened the umbrella: the inside of the fabric was thickly lined with $10 bills and £5 notes! With £5 sterling in Poland at that time you could literally buy a house; this man was a high-class smuggler – which was then the only possible form of trade between Poland and Western Europe . . .

From Poland I first went straight to Paris [but in 1922 I visited Berlin] and it was very much to my liking. I found myself in the midst of the highly stimulating Russian literary world of Berlin, and I stayed there for eighteen months. It was the time of the great inflation, and my father sent me a few dollars a month – $10, or it may have been $20 – and on that I lived like a prince. The only essential point, on which I insisted to my father, was that he should always send me the money in $1 bills, so that I didn't have to change it all at once; if that had happened, my allowance wouldn't have lasted a week . . .

18

Destination America . . .

PYOTR ROBERTOVICH KARPUSHKO

Pyotr Robertovich Karpushko was born in 1900. His family belonged to the Moscow nobility and served in the military. He himself was in the Cadet Academy (Kadetsky Korpus). During the Revolution, most Cadets were systematically shot by the Reds. All the men in Karpushko's family (there were eleven of them) died; he was the only one who survived, and after the Civil War he decided to leave Russia.

My father and I moved to Petrograd in 1922. There I wanted to study at the Polytechnic, but when filling out a questionnaire I had to tell who my parents were, so when the administration of the Polytechnic Institute saw that [they] were of aristocratic origin, I was told that they were (and therefore I as well) 'socially alien elements', and as a result of that I was not allowed to study. I decided to leave, to go anywhere, even to Africa, only not to stay in Russia. At that time my father had a heart-attack and died. So, being completely alone, I decided to make my way to Poland.

I was issued with a special paper by the Polish Embassy in Petrograd. Since my father was called Robert and came originally from Lithuania, the document certified that I was not Russian. That was enough to get me across the border. My final destination, though, was California. My two brothers had fought with Kolchak[1] and had eventually left for America. They managed to get my mother there as well; she was fifty-seven years old then. Since all three of them had settled in San Francisco, I decided to join them.

Travelling through Poland, I had a letter with me, addressed to some Russian sailors at Danzig (Gdansk), who were in the crew of a ship called SS *Estonia*. I had to make my way to this ship in order to go to America. Strictly speaking, I was travelling through Poland illegally. I had no passport. That meant I had to stay awake at all times. I always sat in the corridor of a train so I could see when officials or soldiers checking passengers' papers entered the car. Whenever it happened, I walked to the opposite end of the car, opened the door and sat outside on a step waiting for them to leave. Then, after hearing the door slam behind them, I would return to the car. During the second night of my voyage, as the train was approaching a border town, Tczew [or Dirschau], I spotted a free seat. I felt absolutely exhausted and decided to rest a bit. So I sat down and, of course, fell asleep.

I was woken up by the sound of somebody's voice demanding my papers. As I failed to show any papers, I was ordered off the train and taken to the police station. There I was stripped of all my clothes, and in my tie they found dollars, as well as in my 'long johns'. I had sold all my belongings in Russia and with that money I had bought some dollars from Jewish black-marketeers.

I was taken to prison [in Tczew] and interrogated. Suddenly, an inspector who was questioning me started speaking Russian. I was very surprised and asked how he knew Russian. He replied that he had been a former officer in the cavalry of the Tsarist Army. He seemed to be a nice fellow and I very frankly told him of my plans. I said to him, 'What would I do in Poland? I don't know a soul here. All I need is to get to Danzig where I can board the ship, which will take me to America.'

He said, 'Well, I believe your story. But your dollars . . . They are very pretty, and I collect foreign currency.' What was I to do? His allusion was transparent enough, so I gave him the dollars hidden in my long johns. However, I begged him to let me keep the rest – $100 which I needed to continue my journey and for my first days in America. He let me keep the money [and] suggested that I go back to Warsaw to his uncle and wait for a telegram that he (the inspector) would send. He said his uncle was able to cross the border with Danzig at any time and would smuggle me across. I was to wait for the telegram, which would be a signal that all was ready and I could go.

So I went back to Warsaw, where I found the address of this man's uncle. On the eve of my arrival, however, there had been an explosion, in which seventy people were killed. As I entered the house, the first thing I saw was a coffin. Well, thought I to myself, this is probably not the right moment to pursue the matter. I returned to the railway station, went to the market and bought myself a pair of new shoes, then I took the train back to Tczew. I decided to cross the border under cover of night.

I reached Tczew safely, got off the train and went to a restaurant, where I ordered two portions, thinking who knows when I will have a chance to eat again. After that I took off. I walked straight across the fields. It was a wet October night. My feet were completely soaked, and my new shoes became so tight that it was torture to walk in them. Finally, after having walked half the night, I saw the trains. I thought I must be close to the border; I had been told it was only seven kilometres away, but I had walked almost all night. Approaching the railway line, I saw there was a tiny station. As I stepped on to the platform, I realized that each step echoed – it was very quiet around.

Suddenly I heard a door open and somebody shouted. 'Who's there?'

Poles! I jumped across the tracks and ran. Polish police with dogs ran after me. Of course they caught me, and led me to a border post. As I was escorted there I offered a $5 bribe to one of the policemen if he agreed to help me flee. He refused, afraid of getting himself into trouble.

I was put into a cell, in which there was a small window. A sentry spoke Russian and I explained to him that I had to get to America. It was very cold and he plugged the window with straw. I had only one thing on my mind: how to escape. I pushed that straw out of the window and tried to squeeze myself through it, but no more than my head would go through – in fact, I got stuck in that window. Eventually I managed to extricate myself. Then the sentry came to take me to a town called Novogródok, where there was a real prison . . . It was the first time in my life that I was in prison. At least, though, I could take those shoes off and let my swollen feet rest.

After a month in prison, the date for my trial was set. Until then I was alone in my cell. And it was so damp in there! The small bowl of salt that I was given would fill with water overnight. My eyes were swollen from the damp, water was trickling down the walls; it was truly awful. I asked to be transferred to another cell. My request was granted and I was put into a cell with two other people.

At the trial I was not accused of attempting to cross the border illegally but of trying to bribe a gendarme. I was acquitted, and received all my money back.

After my release I went straight to the address given to me by a smuggler [I had met in jail]. The next day I was given a sack full of geese and this time, escorted by a band of experienced smugglers, I safely crossed the border to Danzig. We reached the city at 9 a.m. It was market day, and the smugglers had brought with them lard, geese and butter to sell. Then with the money received from selling the goods, they would buy tobacco. There was no tobacco monopoly in Danzig, and as a result cigarettes were very cheap. They would take the cigarettes back to Poland, where by selling them they would make a profit of two hundred per cent. They even wanted me to join them!

I thought that now I was in a civilized city, I could put all my money into my wallet. The smugglers all went to sell their goods and told me I had to get to a place called Neufahrwasser, eleven kilometres outside Danzig, where the transatlantic ships docked. I went straight to the booking office and, in what little German I knew, asked for a ticket. I handed the woman at the counter a dollar, but she refused to take it, claiming that it exceeded the price of the ticket. 'Take it all, then,' I suggested, for I had no local currency. She was too honest, however, and did not want to take my money. She said I could change it at a bank. I went in the direction of the main square and, before I reached a bank, I saw a woman selling oranges. I immediately decided to buy some and thus solve my problem. I did that and received the desired change. She did not cheat me on the exchange rate; she very honestly consulted the newspaper. After that I ran back to the booking office for my ticket. As I was about to pay I reached into my pocket for the wallet – oh, horror! It was gone. I had lost it! The ship to America was due to sail at 1 p.m. and it was already 11 a.m. What was I to do?

I went back, retracing my steps and asking everyone if they had seen a wallet. The answer, of course, was no. I had probably dropped it, thinking I was putting it in my pocket. Unfortunately, there had not only been money in the wallet, but my birth certificate and other documents as well. Now it was all gone, just like that, in the last moment before my departure.

I decided to go into the railway station, where I could sit down, calm myself and think about what I could do next. While I sat there a beggar came up and asked me for a light. I started searching my pockets and suddenly discovered that my wallet was still on me – but because I had shoved the oranges into my pockets, I had been unable to reach it. I ran to the ticket counter to buy a train ticket; at the booking office I was informed that the next train to Neufahrwasser did not leave for another hour – and it was already noon! Anyway, when I arrived in

Neufahrwasser, I saw a huge ship and ran towards it. Alas, it was too late. The ship was already ten metres away from the pier. The band was playing, everyone was waving their handkerchieves. Goodbye, America . . .

What was I to do next? I realized I was out of cigarettes, and went to a shop to replenish my supplies. The shop was run by a Jew who, as it turned out, spoke Russian quite well and was glad to have an opportunity to practise it. I explained my situation and he told me that there was a Russian church in town, where a service was held on Saturday night.

When I arrived there I saw many Russian émigrés. I also saw a man who was crying. I approached him, asked him the reason for his grief, and he told me the following story. He was a Russian prisoner-of-war, and completely illiterate. Sent to work for some *Bauer* [peasant farmer] who spoke only German, he finally forgot the Russian language. Now, listening to the service in the church, he could not understand a word and that made him cry.

I was next approached by a man who asked me where I came from. I replied that I was from Petrograd. When asked how long ago I had arrived, I said, 'Just now.' I told him I had been a Cadet of the Third Moscow Cadet Corps. Having learnt that I had no place to stay, he offered me a night's lodging at his place. He also told me that a former Tsarist ambassador, a certain Ostrovsky, was there as well. He explained to me that he and several others were living in a barracks originally built for Russian sailors who got sick during their voyage, and after having been discharged from hospital would wait there for the next ship. In that barracks lived the remaining officers of General Yudenich's White Army.[2]

As soon as I arrived they all started asking me where I was from. When I told them I belonged to the Third Moscow Cadet Corps they started asking me who was the chaplain of our Corps, where were the public baths where we used to go, and so on. They were apparently checking me out. I told them we did not go to the public baths, but went to bathe at the neighbouring Military School. Then they said, 'Well, if you studied at the Polytechnic, then solve a mathematical problem.' And they actually gave me an equation in higher mathematics to solve. I solved it.

In the end I spent a whole year with them. We were not allowed to work and did not have any money. We were only allowed to do whatever the Germans were not doing; for example we made ornamental boxes inlaid with wood. The ladies worked at handicrafts, embroidering, making handkerchieves, and then selling them. We also worked as navvies. Once I got a job at a Polish bakery. I had to operate an ice-cream-making machine and then deliver the ice-cream. One evening I saw the owner putting crumbled pies and cakes into a box, which he was going to throw away. I told him that in my barracks there were seventeen hungry people and I would like him to let me take this box with me. It weighed about 5–6 kilos. After that it became a regular routine. By the time I would return from work, the people in the barracks were already waiting for me with tea. We would put the box on the table and split the contents among all the inmates. That was a big help . . .

Karpushko eventually got to Paris with false papers. His life in exile is described in Chapter 38.

19

In the Crimea

MARC MIKHAILOVICH WOLFF

Marc Wolff was born in 1891 into a Jewish family in St Petersburg, where his father was a lawyer with international connections. Mr Wolff eventually settled in London, where he became a successful lawyer and a very well-known figure in the emigration. He died in 1987.

The Wolff family – Marc, his parents, brother and sister – fled from Petrograd in 1918 along with Marc's fiancée Genia and her parents, the Khoroches. They escaped, with some difficulty, to the Ukraine. In Kiev a family friend, Prince Dolgorukov, offered them the use of a house on his wife's estate, Vasil Sarai near Yalta, and, after a brief stay in Odessa, where Marc Wolff and Genia were married, they arrived in the Crimea.

It was the first time that I had seen the southern shore of the Crimea. It is difficult to describe its beauty and charm. Its wonderful sea, the mountains, the sun, the sweet smell of its flowers and shrubs – everything fascinated us. I am absolutely convinced that only because of our surroundings were we able, with comparatively little wear and tear, to live through the year and a half which we were destined to spend in Yalta.

On the way the boat had a longish stop in Sevastopol, the famous naval base and the scene of the Crimean War of the last century. This was the first time I had seen it and I found the town, the port and the landing-stage very attractive. We arrived at Yalta in the evening [and] were met at the harbour by relations of my mother, who usually lived in Moscow but who had two small houses high over Yalta and who invited my parents, sister and brother to stay with them. For Genia and me a room was reserved in the Hotel Dgalita on the main sea promenade of Yalta; [soon afterwards we were given a room in the house of some friends] . . .

The Crimea was ruled by a Government headed by a certain Sulke-vich, supported by the Germans. But the days of the Germans were numbered; very soon they disappeared as revolutionary events happened in Germany. [In their place] units of the Volunteer Army began to appear. The Volunteer Army was created in the south of Russia to fight the Soviet Government and it consisted of very mixed elements: Cossack units, officers' units, and soldiers drafted into it. The aims of the Army were also mixed. Some asserted that they were fighting for a democratic Russia, some were openly clamouring for a monarchy. At that time [the end of 1918] in the Crimea the units of the Volunteer Army were rather quiet about their political aims because, after the departure of the Germans, the civil power passed to a Crimean Regional Government which was bourgeois but leftish, and consisted of Ministers who were in sympathy with the former Provisional Government deposed by the Soviet Government. The Crimean Government still believed that it would be possible to unite Russia on the political platform of the Constituent Assembly. The Allies supported it, but never gave it sufficient effective help.

At the time of our arrival in Yalta all was quiet, and we were not only able to visit its glorious surroundings and enjoy its beauty . . . but we even had the pleasure of theatrical performances given by actors of the Moscow Arts Theatre. The first few weeks we spent there were real bliss . . .

One of our plans with regard to our stay in the Crimea, however, fell to the ground. When my father had a talk to the Chief Manager of the Dolgorukov estate where we were supposed to live, he explained that the main house, which was in fact a small palace, had been completely looted and that altogether there was no possibility of living there. On the whole estate only three people remained: a Russian gardener, Stepan, and his wife, and a Tartar, Memet, who used to work in the house. In a few days Stepan came to fetch us with a rather primitive vehicle with one horse and we went along a road by the sea towards Gursuf and the famous botanical garden, the Nikitsky Garden, a few miles short of which, on a hill, stood Vasil Sarai. Memet was waiting there for us. During the whole period of our time in Yalta both Stepan and Memet were very good to us, brought us vegetables and wine from the estate, and Stepan never failed to fetch us if we expressed a wish to visit Vasil Sarai; but they hated each other and always poured out their mutual complaints to us. It was quite clear that the antagonism between the Russian and the Tartar sections of the population had sharpened during these troubled times and that it would be most unwise for us to get more closely involved in these quarrels.

While we were basking in the wintry rays of the sun in Yalta the Civil War in other parts of Russia became ominous and fierce, especially in the Ukraine where there were numerous changes of government, with the result that gradually the power of the Soviet Government moved southwards . . . Yalta was full of rumours and the atmosphere, so well known to us, of uncertainty and apprehension . . .

Towards the end of January or the middle of February 1919 the Red Army stood at the boundary of the Crimea, but we were continually assured that the Crimean Peninsula was absolutely impregnable. Soon after we heard that small units of the Allies, particularly the Greeks in their skirts, had disembarked at Sevastopol, and speedily re-embarked again, and that the Crimean Regional Government had also embarked on Allied ships. A big naval evacuation began in which substantial help was given by the Royal Navy. One of the battleships took on board the Dowager Empress Maria, sister of Queen Alexandra, and a number of aristocrats who lived in the Crimea.[1] [A great many] transports were loaded with the rest of the units of the Volunteer Army who were still in the Crimea and with large numbers of civilians. We – the Wolffs, the Khoroches and our Moscow relations – remained in Yalta [but were evacuated to less conspicuous lodgings].

In the first half of March the impregnable Crimea became pregnable and units of the Red Army began to occupy the Peninsula. Their appearance in Yalta was for a matter of days, and the very last units of the Volunteer Army, together with the police, embarked on transports and the port became empty. Everything in the town quietened down – it reminded one of the stillness before a thunderstorm . . .

Some kind of local militia functioned and at night the local workers formed some kind of guard, but not even dogs were to be seen in the streets; all houses were locked and no light showed in the windows. At last a mounted unit with light drays called *tachanki*, on which the infantry was transported under the protection of machine guns, entered the town. This first unit was not a unit of the regular Red Army but belonged to the irregular bands of the so-called 'Father Makhno',[2] who was always on the go in the Ukraine and was one of the most feared and dreaded *ataman*s. For some time he had had some kind of agreement with the Red Army command and that is why – luckily for a fleeting moment – we had the pleasure of seeing a unit of his in Yalta. The appearance of the unit was rather picturesque, because quite a part of it wore ladies' fur coats over which bandoliers of ammunition were worn like decorations. One could not expect anything good from a Makhno unit, but they made a very short halt in Yalta and moved somewhere further on. In their place arrived units of the regular Red Army.

The period of occupation – that is, the first sometimes critical days – passed without undue incident. Several commissariats were opened immediately, amongst them a Commissariat of Justice headed by a Latvian,[3] who had nothing to do with law and jurisprudence but who happened to be a decent man. He was prepared to co-operate with a recently organized professional union of jurists, consisting of all the local Yalta lawyers as well as all the lawyers who were temporarily living in Yalta, including my father and myself. We were quite a formidable number and, thanks to the formation of the union, all negotiations on our behalf were conducted collectively. During this first period practically no one representing the civil power arrived from the centre of Russia and the authorities in Yalta had a kind of amateurish appearance. Even the main town of the Crimea, Simferopol, seemed far away and whatever happened took place on the spot.

Unfortunately, as was usual, the Special Extraordinary Commission against Counter-Revolution also made its entry into Yalta, and at its head was a fierce man in a high Caucasian fur hat who galloped all over Yalta on a wild stallion surrounded by his own retinue. There was also the office of the Commandant, with continually changing Commandants. One of the first was a sailor of the Black Sea Fleet, Novikov, whose fame was based on the fact that if one of his petitioners for some reason unduly annoyed him he, like a boxer, gave him a punch on the jaw and the unfortunate petitioner leapt out of the room, often with the loss of a tooth or even teeth. I was a witness of one such scene. Luckily he was very soon relieved of his post and a complete nonentity called Nosikov took his place. The Commissariat of Justice, by comparison, was a quiet haven.

My father refused to accept a paid job, but agreed to act as consultant to private people who applied to the Commissariat for legal help. As head of this consulting office there appeared a young man from Gomel, who introduced himself to my father as the Commander-in-Chief of Gomel, and his friend, who was with him as the President of the

Revolutionary Tribunal. To the amazement of my father these two young men constantly rushed into his room to ask for his advice in solving all kinds of urgent problems. The views of the President of the Revolutionary Tribunal on law were rather muddled and peculiar. For instance, he agreed that murder was undoubtedly a crime, but was sure that theft belonged to civil action contravening the civil law. Nevertheless, it was not difficult to come to terms with them.

I was first appointed as a People's Notary. All the archives of the three private notaries whose offices were closed, together with the three girl secretaries of the departed notaries, were delivered to me in the office of the Commissariat. [But] I had very little work and therefore I was also made a Registrar of births, marriages, divorces and deaths. This was a much more lively activity. However, as Yalta was not a large centre, I still had a lot of free time. The Commissar therefore decided that I could have one more additional function. Very often people came to the Commissariat to find out why one of their relations had been arrested, where they were detained and whether they could see him or her. If those who had been arrested were held by the militia or the Commandant's office, it was very easy to get information and to give the necessary directions to the people who applied to the Commissariat. But if the arrested person was not discovered either in the militia or the Commandant's office, then the only place he could be was the Special Extraordinary Commission, and it was no good sending the applicant there in person. I was therefore given the task of getting in contact with the Commission personally and doing my best to get information from them and seeing whether something could be done. I must confess that this contact with the Commission was an unpleasant task; but if it resulted in proving to them, by some decree or regulation, that the arrested person came under the jurisdiction of the militia and must be transferred to militia headquarters, then it was well worth it.

As always when new authorities came to power, we were obliged to fill in masses of questionnaires about our professions, special qualifications, political views, etc. My father was a member of the Constitutional Democratic Party,[4] which from the point of view of the Bolsheviks was a reactionary bourgeois party, and filled in his questionnaire accordingly without any harmful consequences; but our friend the former President of the Justices of the Peace got cold feet and limited himself to filling in the paragraph with what he thought was a noncommittal statement that he used to be in sympathy with the Constitutional Democratic Party. He avoided arrest with difficulty . . .

Every morning the Government orders appeared on the walls and the sanctions for their contravention most frequently were 'up to shooting'. If all the contraventions had, in fact, been followed by the declared sanctions, probably half the population of Yalta would have been shot and certainly my family would not have survived. Sometimes in the night we heard rifle shots from the direction of the jetty, which, in all probability, were executions; but in comparison with many other places, the terror in Yalta did not reach a mass character and we could be very grateful that we were spared that.

The clocks were moved three hours forward,[5] which made us get up with the cocks, and as there was a curfew from 8 p.m. and nobody was allowed out without a special pass, and as even gardens and balconies were under curfew, the result was that during the lovely, warm, sunny Crimean spring we were confined to our rooms from 5 p.m. normal time. This was very sad and upsetting.

We were cut off from the entire world, even from the rest of Soviet Russia. News from there was scarce and papers from Moscow and Petrograd practically non-existent. The ordinary post did not function and we lived almost exclusively on rumours. Nevertheless, some pattern of life evolved. We managed to meet our friends, to get not very ample foodstuffs, to find some relaxation and amusements to sweeten the pill of a routine existence which any moment could be shattered by some extraordinary event.

After about six weeks, our flat was invaded by a large Commission for the Requisition of Houses and Flats, which informed us that we must vacate the flat in three days because it was required for some governmental body. We looked round for something suitable, but could not find anything. When one of the members of the Commission reappeared and asked why we were still there and what our intentions were, Mother categorically told him that either the Commission must find us adequate alternative accommodation, or they would have to throw us forcibly out into the street. In a few days the same member of the Commission came again and told us that they had found better premises and our flat was no longer needed . . .

The whole atmosphere in Yalta gradually became more and more unsettled. Rumours were constantly spreading that the wheel of fortune had had another turn and that the Volunteer Army had now begun to push the Red Army back northwards. It was quite clear to us that if this continued the Reds would have to evacuate the Crimea. The sea was not in their hands and they would have to retreat in good time beyond the Crimean Peninsula, otherwise the Crimea might become a mousetrap . . .

[In June or July 1919] there came a night when sleep was out of the question; the whole night through we heard the noise of rolling wheels of drays, carts and other vehicles. In the morning I did not find a single Party member in the Commissariat. Crowds poured into the streets, the head of the Extraordinary Commission galloped on his stallion, surrounded by his minions, out of Yalta in the direction of Simferopol, and once more the town was left to cope through its own resources. A well-known writer, Elpatievsky, assembled a few [prominent] inhabitants to create some kind of local organization to preserve law and order, and again we all waited to see what would come next.

In a few days we saw a small destroyer enter the harbour of Yalta; an officer disembarked and declared that he was occupying Yalta in the name of the Supreme Ruler, Kolchak.[6] Our information about Kolchak was rather nebulous. We knew that his base was in Siberia, that he had at one time had connections with a rump of the Constituent Assembly which met in Samara,[7] and that his Government was supposed to be based on democracy. How far our information was correct can now be checked by studying the history of that time, but, be that as it may, there began once more a new period in our life in Yalta.

The new authorities demanded that all those who were working in the Soviet organizations should come for a check-up. We duly presented ourselves and after a few questions about our functions, when we left Petrograd and more general questions about who we were, we were told that this was all and that we could do whatever we liked. In a day or two I met on the promenade, in the uniform of a colonel, the member of the Soviet Requisition Commission who had come to tell us that we need not move. He now stopped me and told me that he had always been a member of a counter-espionage organization. I thanked him for the information, but did not continue the conversation. In a civil war how is it possible to know where the truth is?

We stayed on in the same flat and Yalta filled up with new arrivals – the sea route from Odessa to Batum through Yalta was functioning again. Gradually elegant staff officers, a general commanding the garrison, a Commandant, all occupied their former premises. Besides this,

British naval units again came into the harbour from time to time. All kinds of money circulated freely – Tsarist notes, which for some unknown reason had a high value; the notes of the Provisional Government called '*Duma* notes'[8] and 'Kerensky notes'; notes of the Volunteer Army, from the Don, called 'the little bells'; all kinds of Ukrainian notes. It was difficult to get change and coupons issued by the local shops instead of change circulated as paper money. Once more Yalta became an isolated point because the fortunes of war were being fought for and decided far away from us. In many respects this was certainly a good thing, but it made the chances of earning one's livelihood and finding work most difficult. The three notarial offices reopened; they took back their lady secretaries and their archives and were most grateful when they found everything in good order. The old Justices of the Peace resumed their work, the banks reopened under their old names, and life once more had a new routine. But I had to find some work urgently because our finances were in a very poor state and quite a lot of our clothes and linen, for which there was great demand, had been taken by my mother to the market for sale.

As I have mentioned, British men-of-war paid frequent visits to Yalta and at their first appearance the Yalta Town Hall even organized a dinner in their honour. As I knew English I was asked to act as interpreter. During this dinner I had an idea which I carried out. I saw the editor of the local paper, the *Voice of Yalta*, and asked him whether he would accept from me material for the paper based on information I would get from English newspapers, because effectively Yalta continued to be isolated. The post functioned extremely badly, news arrived only with the boats and was very unreliable, especially concerning anything that happened abroad. Having got his willing consent, I organized myself so that when a British man-of-war appeared in the Yalta waters I took a boat – or when the smaller ones were at the jetty I just walked – and asked to see the officer on duty. I explained who I was and asked whether they could supply me with a batch of newspapers they no longer required. The officers supplied me with the *Morning Post* or *The Times*, and the sailors brought me without fail the *News of the World*. Many of the officers came to have tea with us and, I hope, enjoyed our hospitality.

For me those papers were the most valuable material I could have hoped for. I read them through with the greatest attention. From the most important political news I concocted telegrams 'from our own

Political Correspondent' which appeared in the *Voice of Yalta*. In this way I informed Yalta about the St Germain Peace Treaty with Austria, about the flight over the Atlantic of Alcock and Brown, and so on. Then I used the same events for articles, often under my own signature. In addition, from the *News of the World* I selected all kinds of sensational love-affairs, scandals, crimes, etc., and altogether sometimes filled quite a substantial part of the paper with my writings, [bringing] in a very desirable and considerable income.

In Yalta at that time it was very difficult to get writing paper and I arranged that the printing offices of the *Voice of Yalta* should supply me with reams of glossy paper, on the reverse side of which were printed the names of various famous Crimean wines from estates which were now more or less derelict and the vineyards in poor shape. These glossy sheets of paper had been prepared long ago and would have been cut up as appellation labels for wine bottles, but for the time being they were useless for this purpose. I remember very vividly that many of my telegrams and articles were written on paper which had on the back, at regular intervals, the name of the wine Malaga . . .

As mentioned previously, the possibilities of earning one's living in Yalta were very limited and my father-in-law decided that the time had come when he and his family must move to some more central spot in the south of Russia. In the autumn [they] embarked for Novorossiysk, from where they had the intention of going on to Rostov-on-Don. However, soon after this the fate of the Volunteer Army took a final turn for the worse and the whole of southern Russia was gradually occupied by the Soviet Government. The Khoroches, with a vast number of others, were evacuated to Constantinople and for a long time we lost all contact with them. Our Moscow relations also went abroad, but we remained in Yalta, hoping that perhaps we might manage to return to Petrograd, although the chances of such a journey at that time were very poor. The whole of Russia was boiling as if it were in a pressure cooker and the Civil War sometimes took quite unexpected twists and flared up sporadically in various places. Nevertheless, towards the end of 1919 it became clear that the final victory of the Soviet Government was near, while we ourselves were isolated in the Crimea.

At about this time a very extraordinary coincidence happened which was of great advantage to my family. One morning I read in one of the official notices pasted on the walls that a new military Commandant of

Yalta had been appointed; his surname was the same as that of an officer of the Guards who, in 1915, went to Krasnoye Selo with me to introduce me to the adjutant of the infantry battalion to which I had been posted. The officer now occupying the post of Commandant was a colonel, but during this period promotions were not subject to normal rules and it was theoretically possible that it was my friend who had come as overlord to Yalta. I decided to go to the quarters of the Commandant to have a look. It was not easy to get admitted to see the Commandant, but I stated firmly that I must see him personally on a very important matter, taking the risk that if he was not my old friend I would have to invent something in connection with my work on the *Voice of Yalta*. I sent in my visiting card and in a minute the Commandant rushed out of his room and greeted me with joy and effusion. The next day he came to see my parents and told us . . . that he intended to retire from the Army and leave for Poland. In his opinion he had fought in the Civil War long enough. At the same time, he told us that he would issue all the members of our family with passports for foreign travel, which at that time were difficult to obtain. Then, if we should see that the journey to Petrograd could not be undertaken, and if life in Yalta became unbearable, we should be able to avail ourselves of a rather problematical chance to go abroad. This was an enormous help and we were most grateful to him.

At this time the authorities had moved into our flat a very nice young lawyer, who was procurator [a prosecutor] and had been evacuated from Gomel; an elderly official from the same town; and an elderly woman who was probably a cook. The winter of 1919–20 was exceptionally cold with masses of snow, which was most unusual for the southern shores of the Crimea . . . During that winter the Volunteer Army headed by General Denikin was evacuated from various southern ports of Russia to foreign lands and only on the Crimean Peninsula was the Civil War not yet over, because it was held by General Wrangel and his Army units. To add to all these tribulations, the south of Russia suffered from an epidemic of spotted typhus and cases of this terrible illness were discovered in Yalta.

One very nasty cold night our procurator asked permission for a friend of his who came from Simferopol to spend the night in the flat. Mother supplied this visitor with a blanket and a cushion, and in the morning the procurator knocked at the door of my parents' room in great excitement to tell my mother that his friend had a high fever and was delirious. We called our doctor, who said at once that our guest had spotted typhus, and gave us the encouraging news that every hospital was full to its maximum capacity and that our guest would have to stay in our flat at least for a few days. As the main carrier of spotted typhus is lice, all the things which the guest was wearing were taken away for disinfection; his bed was placed in the middle of the room and round the bed there was constantly poured out of a kettle a little rivulet of water or oil, because it was alleged that lice could not cross a stream of liquid. This was the only protection we had from infection. My mother and our elderly lodger helped to nurse the unfortunate patient, who was taken to hospital on the sixth day. The elderly lodger in a few days also developed a high fever and was also taken to hospital, from which she returned in a few weeks looking like a corpse. No one else fell ill.

At last the year 1920 was ushered in – a cold, hungry and particularly unpleasant year. The Wrangel regime showed every sign of disintegration. Some generals became ferocious in their endeavours to maintain discipline. They were brutal to the workers. They saw Red danger everywhere. Field courts martial became the order of the day. A young friend of my brother's, a boy of seventeen, was hanged. His surname was Bronstein, which was also the surname of Trotsky, who at that time was the War Commissar of the victorious Red Army. The death of this youth made a deep impression on all those who had not lost the capacity to think independently and for me it was like a Rubicon which made it quite clear that one must quit Wrangel Crimea at the first opportunity.

Should we even succeed in getting through and beginning our trek to Petrograd, life [in the rest of Russia] was also at its lowest ebb as the result of the last two disastrous years. The only solution for us at the time was to embark on one of the very few boats which from time to time came to Yalta, go to Constantinople and from there to Poland by any route, because in Warsaw were our nearest relations on my mother's side who would do everything possible for all of us. Besides, my parents had some property in Warsaw and hoped to realize at least part of it to provide means for some time, which would give us a breathing space before resuming the struggle for existence. However, in order to be able to carry out these plans, apart from the difficulty of finding a boat, there was the enormous obstacle of the fact that we had no money for the journey because by then the few valuables which we had had been sold to enable us to pay for our current living expenses, and my earnings on the *Voice of Yalta* were obviously insufficient to keep six people.

Several times in my life I have had proof that the life of men depends on pure chance, and just such a chance came to our assistance in this crucial moment. In the first days of March 1920 a boat, *Trini*, under a Panama flag, entered the harbour of Yalta and the Captain announced that for £11 sterling he was ready to provide room for a passenger in the ship's holds, that the boat had two holds for three hundred passengers each, and that he would take them to Constantinople. There is a Russian proverb that, in the absence of fish, a crayfish is also a fish; and on this principle we were prepared to climb down into a hold. But where to find £66?

The General Manager of the estates of Princess Dolgorukov and of Count Orlov-Davydov very often visited my father and was well aware of our friendship with the Dolgorukovs, and he and his son-in-law had the following idea. Although the main house in Vasil Sarai had been completely looted, there were in the stables by pure chance several old carriages still standing, and such carriages were much valued by the local Tartars. The Manager's son-in-law suggested that he would try to sell these carriages and that we should use the money to buy the tickets for our journey. Prince Dolgorukov was by that time already abroad, so that there would be no difficulty in paying him the money if we should succeed.

What would happen first – the sale of the carriages or the sailing of *Trini* for Constantinople? All our belongings were packed 'on chance', all our household things were conditionally distributed amongst friends, the precious travelling passports were in our pockets . . . The tension reached its peak when the captain of *Trini* fixed his departure for two days' time. Then, the evening before, the Manager's son-in-law rushed in with a sack containing in various Russian notes the equivalent of £70 . . . Until late into the night friends were coming to see us to wish us happiness in the next chapter of our lives.

In the morning we went with our luggage to the jetty [and] at last we passed safely through the scrutiny of the passport commission . . . The hold was already full of passengers; however, we managed to find space in one of the corners and, as best we could, settled on the floor and on our cases. The centre of the hold presented a most peculiar picture, for installed there was a big double bed with copper balls at the corners on which reclined a young married couple: they obviously thought that it was much more pleasant to use their bed than to sit on the floor. What supplementary price they had had to pay the Captain for this privilege I do not know, but the bed was an unforgettable sight.

The whole day we remained in harbour and the whole day the boat was guarded by the British sailors; and in the evening *Trini* was floodlit by searchlights from a British destroyer. Then, without warning, the boat's screw began to churn the water. Slowly we moved away from the jetty, and the Russian land gradually began to disappear from our sight.

No one who has not left his fatherland in similar conditions can know or fully understand the thoughts and feelings which gripped me, and my wife, my parents, sister and brother standing by me. Would we again, and in what conditions, see Russia? What would happen to each of us in the interval? What would even the next few days bring us?

Another half hour and around us, in utter darkness, there was only a tempestuous Black Sea . . .

Except for hot water for the teapot, we could not get anything on the boat and every family or group of people had their own provisions with them. Next to us on the floor sat a family with small children, and at night when the sea got very rough one of the little girls kept repeating that she would like to move to another flat. In the daytime their nurse incessantly fed the whole family with hot cocoa. We knew very many of the passengers and, when the sea at last showed mercy, impressions and thoughts were exchanged. The sanitary arrangements on board were miserable: there were only two lavatories for six hundred passengers, and long queues were permanently standing by their doors.

It was difficult to concentrate on anything. The unknown future was shrouded in fog and uncertainty. [But eventually, on the fifth morning,] we were moving along the Bosphorus and were enchanted by its shores, palaces and gardens. At last we entered the Golden Horn and an exquisite panorama spread before us. On the left we saw Istanbul, with its unforgettable mosques . . . In front of us was a bridge floating on barges connecting Istanbul with [the port town of] Galata, over the whole width of which stood a line of men in long robes. Through them crowds of people were shoving, dropping small coins into containers held by the men – the toll price for the right to use the bridge. Along the water little steamers, naval launches, sailing and rowing boats, were speeding in all directions; imposing Allied men-of-war stood at anchor. The noise was deafening and after the quiet of Yalta we felt bewildered and even scared.

We were met by friends who had landed in Constantinople some time ago and who, like us, were very short of money. They explained that the prices in the few hotels situated in Pera were exorbitant and that we would have to find accommodation in Galata. It was also explained to us that usually the regular customers of all small hotels in Galata were whores waiting for their clients – the sailors of all nations – but that now many owners of these hotels had thrown out their regular clients to make room for the refugees, who proved to be quieter and more desirable guests. We were directed to one of these small houses round the corner from the main street, bearing the proud name of Hotel Parthenon. With difficulty we got two rooms for the six of us. When my mother looked with horror at the dirty linen which covered the beds, [the servant] tried to reassure her by saying, 'It is clean, really clean, only three slept in these beds before you.' In the rooms some peculiar black spots were continually jumping from the floor, which on observation proved to be fleas . . . At night we sometimes heard frantic knocking at the front doors; these were the clients of the former inhabitants of the Hotel Parthenon who were not yet aware of the transformation of the sailors' brothel into a home for refugees, in their great majority representing the professional intelligentsia of Russia.

It is hardly to be believed, but in a very short time there was even some kind of cosy atmosphere in the Parthenon and during the evening, when it was unsafe to venture into the streets, parties assembled in each others' rooms, sat in groups on beds, discussed various current problems, argued, sometimes hopefully and sometimes in despair. The chief problem was a visa, how to get it and be able to leave Constantinople for Europe; and this was a tough proposition. The then Allied Supreme Command[9] and the diplomatic representatives of the Allies put all kinds of obstacles in our way.

It became clear to us that our stay in Constantinople might be a fairly long one and therefore it became absolutely essential to get some money. The first offer of help came from a young friend of ours, who, with her husband, had come from Yalta much earlier than we and was very well provided with funds. Without being asked she offered to lend us £100 and added that there was no hurry to repay the loan. This first unsolicited offer of assistance raised our spirits. When my father visited the Pera Palace Hotel he found several of his clients there who supplied him with sufficient money for a fairly long stay in Constantinople and for a journey to Warsaw by whatever route we should be able to reach it.

Life became fairly regular . . . Part of the day was spent in long queues with the object of getting a visa to Poland and all kinds of transit visas, and for the remaining part of the day we struggled through the line of men in robes on the bridge between Galata and Istanbul and rested there, for in comparison with Galata and Pera it was an oasis of quiet and dignity. We strolled from one mosque to another, admired their blues, greens and other colours, looked at the ancient tombs, were fascinated by the wonderful proportions of Aia Sophia, and got new strength for our tired nerves from the contemplation of so much beauty. We visited the covered bazaar, caravanserais, and generally steeped ourselves in the previously unknown and peculiar ways of the East . . .

Everything was going on fairly well when suddenly my father developed a very high temperature. We were given the name of a Russian doctor, who came at once to see him and began to calculate whether there was any possibility of his having caught spotted typhus in Yalta from the people who fell ill in our flat there. It seemed that all the incubation periods were over, and what the doctor feared most was that the Turkish authorities would hear about my father's illness, because then they would remove him without further ado to an isolation hospital and there, even if he had not got typhus, he would most certainly get it. We lived through three very anxious days, but then his temperature became normal; the Turkish authorities never heard of the illness and we breathed again.

At last, after a three-week stay in Constantinople and after many hours of standing in various queues for visas, our route was fixed. The easiest way to get to Warsaw was to take a boat of the former Austrian Lloyd line from Constantinople to the Romanian port of Constanta on the Black Sea, to go from there by train via Bucharest to the Polish frontier through Chernovtsy and a Polish frontier post, Śniatyń, and from there through Lvov to Warsaw.

The boat, now under an Italian flag, reflected the disturbed position of the world in 1920. The crew sold their cabins privately to passengers; in these cabins the place of honour on the walls was occupied by photographs of Lenin and Trotsky. Some members of the crew, half in jest, perhaps seriously, told us that it would be much better, instead of sailing to Constanta, to sail straight to Odessa and to hand the boat over to the Bolsheviks. Some of the passengers got into a state of panic on hearing this. In general the mood on the boat was revolutionary, or perhaps just anarchistic. Nevertheless, in the end we arrived in Constanta harbour and bade a final goodbye to the Black Sea.

In Romania we saw everywhere the sad results of the war. Destruction was all round us, the population looked poor and dejected, the stations were packed with people struggling to get into the overcrowded trains. The train carriages were dilapidated and worn, the window panes were broken and often replaced by boards. We made a stop in Bucharest [and] from our [hotel] window we could see the side-entrance to the [Royal] Palace. In front of this entrance stood, sat or lay on the pavement crowds of peasants in country dress and when I asked what they were doing there I was told that they had presented petitions to the King. What the further fate of these petitions was, and what the grievances were against, I could not establish. I retained only three other memories of Bucharest: painted and powdered young officers standing in and strolling along the main street, Calea Victoria, and occupying all the best cafés; cabmen of the Russian Castrates sect with hairless faces, all talking Russian in high-pitched voices; all kinds of small Government employees who expected an appropriate bribe for anything they were supposed to do for us, which included getting a reserved compartment on the train to Chernovtsy, which was full to the very brim.

Chernovtsy, then in Romania, was a Galician Jewish centre, where for the first time I saw Galician Jewish men *en masse*, some of them in almost medieval costumes, spending their time either in synagogues or on various Exchanges where extraordinary transactions took place. In particular, we were several times accosted by individuals who assured us that at the Polish frontier post at Śniatyń all foreign currency would be taken away from us and that we would therefore be well advised to hand over the currency to them, and that their agents would return it to us in Poland with an appropriate discount. They were very disappointed when we declined their kind offers.

The next morning we travelled the short distance to Śniatyń. It was a small frontier station and the train to Poland left half an hour before our train arrived from Romania – a clear indication of the kind of cooperation that existed between neighbours. The passport and customs inspections were short and no one showed any interest in the modest amount of foreign currency we possessed . . .

By the evening we reached Lvov, then a big Polish centre, and got tickets in the sleeping car on the night train to Warsaw. In the corridor of the sleeping car stood a Polish lady who was returning to Poland for the first time since the war and was full of natural enthusiasm that her country was now free and that everything round her was Polish and therefore wonderful. Next morning I came out of my compartment into the corridor. The train was standing at a small station and I saw a disgusting picture – a young Polish soldier was pulling with all his strength the beard of an old Jew, and nobody was taking any notice of it. The Polish lady of last night was also in the corridor and I asked her whether this sight was also wonderful; she was embarrassed by my question, muttered something and retired into her compartment. This picture stuck in my mind and influenced my attitude to Poland and my stay there. Even before reaching Warsaw I was mentally deciding that Genia and I would leave Poland at the first opportunity, though how and to what country I obviously did not even contemplate at that moment.

My aunt and my cousins gave us a most wonderful welcome, which warmed my heart. I shall never forget their love and attention to our needs . . . My mother had many relations in Warsaw [and] to all of them we were welcome guests. During the Second World War those of them who were still alive perished either in the Ghetto or in the gas chambers or in German concentration camps, and the least I can do is to honour their memory and to think of them with gratitude.

During the first weeks of our life in Warsaw we constantly took hot baths, delighted in the comfortable flat and relished the good food provided for us. Then we began to try to find some work or occupation.

So far as I was concerned, I was told that in Warsaw there was an active branch of the enormous American Welfare Organization, the Joint Distribution Committee, which had organized assistance to the impoverished Jewish population. The task of one department was to help poor Polish Jews to find their relations in the USA. I went to see the Manager of the Warsaw JDC and explained to him who I was and that being by profession a lawyer I had a certain amount of experience in interrogating people and in getting from them important facts for compiling the necessary questionnaires, on the basis of which I could prepare English summaries to be sent to the USA. The office of the

JDC was in the Jewish centre of Warsaw . . . which reminded me of Chernovtsy with Jews in traditional dress [and at first] I was slightly apprehensive about how I would succeed in my task, particularly as I could not speak Yiddish and my Polish was very limited. However, my apprehensions were misplaced because my clients, the number of which grew daily, were quite happy to talk to me in Russian, and often confessed that it was more pleasant and easier for them to answer the questions I put to them than to understand and reply to the young Americans who interrogated them in Yiddish, but with the addition of English words in a way and manner which often embarrassed them. My relations with these applicants became excellent, the queues in front of my desk grew longer and the number of questionnaires and summaries I prepared constantly increased.

In about six weeks I was summoned to the Manager of the JDC, who said that he was informed that I conducted my interrogations in Russian, which I confirmed. To my surprise he told me that I must stop this at once, that I must interrogate in Yiddish and, in the last resort, in Polish. I replied that this I could not do, but that as he was so well informed about my activities he probably also knew that I got quick and exact results and that if he was not aware of this he could look through the questionnaires I had filled in and through my summaries. The Manager repeated that no interrogations could be conducted in Russian, whereupon I retorted that I was leaving and did not intend to return. My activity in the JDC came to a sudden end and I once more saw that Poland was not the place for me . . . Even many Poles who had formerly lived in Russia found it difficult to acclimatize themselves to the nationalistic and narrow views predominating in the new Poland . . .

During the summer of 1920 we spent a couple of weeks in the country near Warsaw, but then the Soviet–Polish War took an unfavourable turn for the Poles and anti-Russian tendencies became even sharper. This just coincided with an offer I received from my father's former Yalta clients, who were important timber people and who had a company in London. It was suggested that I should work in their London company to assist as a Russian legal expert. The remuneration which they offered was not sufficient for the living expenses of Genia and myself, but we both decided that this was an opportunity not to be missed and that with luck I should be able to find some further legal work in London. I accepted the offer. The only thing which worried me very much was that if Warsaw should be occupied by the Russians I should be cut off, at least for a time, from my family. However, my parents categorically insisted that I had no right to drop such an opportunity [and so], with the blessings of my family, Genia and I started on our way sometime in August [and, after visits to Berlin and Paris, arrived on 20 October 1920].

England had always attracted me. I considered myself an anglophile, although my knowledge of life there was very limited. I had only been there once, as a tourist for a couple of weeks in 1913. Nevertheless, this was the country to which I had an urge to go and I am glad to say at once that I made no mistake and that I must be very grateful to Fate for my choice of England, where I succeeded in establishing my new home and where I have lived ever since.

20

The War in the Caucasus

COUNTESS OLGA BOBRINSKAYA

Olga Bobrinskaya (née de Bertran) was born in 1899 into a distinguished Franco-Russian family. Her second husband's memories are recounted in Chapters 8 and 11.

I was in Derbent when the Revolution broke out. We went there from the Crimea. My grandmother was a very big landowner in the Caucasus; she had an estate called Gidzhou, a Georgian name, about fifty miles from Derbent, which she sold to Vorontsov-Dashkov.[1] After the Revolution, when Father had no money or anything, he went back to the Caucasus, because that estate had been bought from Vorontsov-Dashkov by another man, I think either Estonian or Lithuanian, [and] this man engaged my father to run it. It was huge: thousands of acres and vineyards. We stayed there until we had to leave. Just after we left, the people of the mountains came and destroyed the estate, burned the house and everything in it, all our books and everything we had. Hordes of Caucasians came to pillage, and took all our lovely horses . . .

My brother at the age of sixteen had fought the Bolsheviks, was captured and sent to prison. He escaped to St Petersburg and was brought back on foot from St Petersburg to Derbent, and the whole town went to plead for him because he was under age. My father went to identify him in prison and passed him by because he was so swollen from hunger and lice and everything. Can you imagine walking from St Petersburg to Derbent on foot, in chains? The peasants used to come and give them food.

[In 1918 I went from Derbent to Baku to visit my uncle, who was part of Denikin's Army,[2] and then went on to Batum with him. Batum, like Baku and the Caucasus, was free at the time.] There were French and English forces of occupation there, who had thrown the Bolsheviks out. The great oil pipeline from Baku finished in Batum, where all kinds of merchant ships and the British and American fleets used to visit. But there was a good deal of fighting between the Caucasian peoples,[3] the Georgians and the Bolsheviks; all the bridges were blown up to stop the advance of the Bolsheviks, and so my return to my parents was cut off. I stayed two years in Batum working for the British [as an interpreter].

My first fiancé was a Russian. During the Civil War, being an officer, he had to hide in a cellar. He was imprisoned and freed when Denikin's Army arrived. To celebrate his release we had a picnic in a big cart full of straw, covered with rugs, a samovar and everything, and we were dancing the *lezghinka*. He had a Georgian friend with us and – you know the Georgians: they are really mad – they started drinking, dancing the *lezghinka* and firing in the air; and Dmitry, my fiancé, took the revolver from his [friend's] hand, started playing with it and put it against his head. Russian roulette. There was one bullet left, and that bullet pierced his head and he fell dead at my feet . . . We went back carrying his body in the cart filled with hay . . . His mother nearly went mad. She thought he'd killed himself because he was jealous of me, but it wasn't true. It was just his foolish Georgian blood. He wasn't drunk or anything . . .

[In Batum] I met and married my first husband, who was a British officer. [He and I, and my uncle, left with the British in 1920 and came to England.] I found it very difficult to adapt to life in England having been used to servants – I even had my own personal maid who came with me to Batum. But I had a wonderful mother-in-law who lived in Langley, in Buckinghamshire. We lived with her for two years, if not more. [She] was a very good woman, very sweet, very religious, but the whole way of life was middle-class, British middle-class. She had a daily help, but I had to help her around the house. And then, the life was rather narrow . . .

21

The Departure of an Empress

COUNTESS YEKATERINA PETROVNA KLEINMICHEL

Countess Yekaterina Petrovna Kleinmichel was a lady-in-waiting to the Dowager Empress Maria Fyodorovna.

In early October 1917 we left our home in the country to go to my estate in the Crimea, near the village of Koreiz. To my great sorrow, I was unable to request an audience of Her Majesty the Dowager Empress, because since 30 August entry into Ai-Todor and Dynlberg was forbidden to everyone except the closest members of the suite.

The Empress had arrived in the Crimea on 25 March 1917 and taken up residence in Ai-Todor, the estate of the Grand Duke Alexander Mikhailovich. From the time of Her Majesty's arrival until 30 August all members of the Imperial Family were free to enter and leave. Their first deprivation of freedom, on 30 August, coincided with Kornilov's campaign.[1] On 27 April a search was made of Ai-Todor and Dynlberg, to which all members of the Imperial Family were obliged to submit, on the orders of the Provisional Government. On 4 May sailors burst into Her Majesty's apartments and in the rudest manner ordered the Dowager Empress to get out of bed; and Her request to be allowed to get up and dress without witnesses was impudently refused. Half-dressed, She sat behind a screen with two sentries standing beside Her, while the remaining sailors opened all the desks, chests of drawers and cupboards, from which they removed everything that seemed to them important and interesting. All the letters from Her Parents and Family, the letters of His Late Majesty Alexander III, Her Majesty's diaries and Her Bible – in a word everything that was dear to Her, and which She had preserved as relics – was thrown indiscriminately into some dirty sacks. (Only a portion of the above-named objects were returned to Her Majesty much later.) Then they summoned a woman whom they had brought with them and ordered her to search the mattresses and pillows for money, jewellery or important documents.

A few days after the search, a car arrived from Sevastopol bringing a commission led by Ketritsa, President of the Sevastopol Naval Court Martial, with the excuse of offering apologies for the search. Instead, however, the visit took the form of an interrogation of all members of the Imperial Family, including Her Majesty. On about 20 October the inhabitants of Ai-Todor and Dynlberg were allowed to go out of doors, and on 26 October members of the Ai-Todor suite were able to take tea with us; but on returning to the Palace they were informed that they had once again been placed under close arrest.

On 26 February the Dowager Empress, together with the Grand Duke Alexander Mikhailovich with all his family and suite were moved to Dynlberg, on the pretext that it would be easier to look after them there; in fact, however, this was to make it easier to guard them (as was the wish of Commissar Zagoratsky, a sailor, who was entrusted with the task of guarding all the palaces and estates in Koreiz).

A car [was sent] for the Dowager Empress and the Grand Duchess Xenia Alexandrovna, which drove them to Dynlberg. The Grand Duke, the children and the suite walked there, escorted by sailors. The owner of Dynlberg gave over the whole upper floor to the Dowager Empress and the other inhabitants of Ai-Todor, herself moving down to the lower floor. Except for Her Majesty, two or three people were accommodated in each room. For exercise, members of the Imperial Family and others were restricted to the lawn in front of the Palace. The Dowager Empress did not once go out of doors.

From February onwards we all lived in constant expectation of being arrested or searched again, since not a day passed without one or another of our neighbours being searched or summoned for interrogation; often they were driven to Yalta in lorries, where the unfortunate creatures were subjected to the ultimate punishment. Thank God, however, no one touched us. The general mood became ever grimmer and more despairing, and although the Tartars continued secretly to bring news of the expected early arrival of an Allied naval squadron, or of the approach of the White Army, the arrests and murders grew more and more frequent and the terror more severe.

In every house, in Yalta and in the surrounding estates, the men took it in turns to stand watch, although they were well aware of the uselessness of such guard duty, given their complete lack of weapons.

One morning in the sixth week of Lent, however, I was told that the Grand Duchess Olga Alexandrovna, with her husband and child, were begging us to give them refuge as they had been obliged to flee from their little house at Kharaks. There, nearby, an attempt had been made to arrest and kill Prince Orlov; since all neighbouring houses were being searched and ransacked, the Grand Duchess and her family had been advised to flee. They had run to us just as they were, hatless and with nothing but the clothes they wore. I was only too glad to accommodate them as best I could, turning our drawing room into a bedroom for them. The Grand Duchess told us that as they had walked past Dynlberg they had seen the Dowager Empress and the Grand Duchess Xenia standing at the window, and that she had so longed at that moment to go in and join them. Her Majesty later told me that on seeing Olga Alexandrovna with her husband and child She had been strangely delighted, thinking that they, too, were being moved to Dynlberg – and how terribly sad She was when She saw them walk past.

Having spent the night with us, next day the Grand Duchess Olga wanted to go back home, but on reflection she realized that the mood was still very unsettled, and she preferred to return and spend the next few days with us. The disorders and disturbances grew steadily worse. Among other events, two commissars were arrested, one of whom was gravely wounded, the other brutally murdered and flung out of a moving car. Every day we expected a nocturnal attack on all bourgeois, even children – a plan that was later discovered in some documents found by the Germans.

Easter was approaching, though there cannot have been many of us who expected to be alive to celebrate it. We began fasting in Holy Week, and then on the Tuesday morning we were told that German troops had reached Yalta together with their supply wagons, and that they would soon be passing along the road past our house. It later transpired that some Tartars had sent word warning the Germans to make haste, as it was planned to kill us all that night. People living near Yalta, along the Simferopol Road, told us that the Germans had been running in order to seize the local Bolshevik Government in time to save the inhabitants of Yalta and the environs. Many of the German soldiers had collapsed from exhaustion and heat. The Bolshevik Soviets had escaped that night on a steamer headed for Novorossiysk, taking with them all the money, gold and even cars that they had stolen. It was terrible to think that we were being saved by our enemies from those very same Bolsheviks that the Germans themselves had created by allowing them into Russia.

For a long time the Dowager Empress and the Grand Dukes refused to be guarded by the Germans and preferred to appoint their own guards, but all these later had to be replaced by German sentries.

At the beginning of the Dowager Empress's sojourn at Ai-Todor, when the squad of sailors guarding them was due to be replaced by some soldiers, one sailor asked permission to see Her Majesty. She called him in; on entering he fell to his knees before Her and asked the Empress's forgiveness for his unintentionally rude behaviour. Her Majesty graciously allowed him to kiss Her hand. He told Her how much he had suffered at seeing Her Majesty and not daring to show Her due respect. The Dowager Empress asked him why he wasn't wearing a Cross around his neck, to which he replied that they had been forbidden to wear Crosses; but he produced his purse and took his Cross out of it. Her Majesty then put it round his neck for him and begged him always to wear it and never to take it off. At his request, She blessed him and he took his farewell of Her in tears.

On Easter Monday, my cousin Goncharova and I had the good fortune to be received by Her Majesty. After all that we had been through, I was profoundly moved as I awaited the happy moment of seeing Her, and I could not restrain my tears on meeting the Royal Martyr. I was surprised and touched to observe the calm and fortitude with which the Dowager Empress described all the tribulations that She had suffered since the fateful day of the Revolution.

In May the Empress moved back to Kharaks, while the Grand Duke Alexander Mikhailovich and his family returned to Ai-Todor. Since then they had all been quite free, but it was an intolerable thought that they had been granted this freedom by the enemy.

The whole of the summer and the autumn passed in relative calm. Her Majesty went for walks and carriage rides in the surrounding countryside, visited Her neighbours, and received calls from Her relatives and others who came to the Crimea for the pleasure of seeing Her. In late autumn, after the German defeat, their troops began to withdraw.[2] Once again came disturbing rumours of Bolshevik movements in the Ukraine and alarm began to be felt among the inhabitants of the Crimea. A guard was formed from ex-officers living in Yalta, the majority of whom were wounded and shell-shocked. At first they were quartered in villas near the palaces; later they were distributed and housed in the palaces – Kharaks, Dynlberg and Ai-Todor. The Malan *dacha*, previously occupied by the Germans, became the headquarters of a unit of the Volunteer Army. The Dowager Empress showed great concern for the officers who were guarding Her at Kharaks. She gave orders that warm sweaters, gloves and socks be bought for each one of them to wear on night duty; in winter She forbade them to patrol the Palace out of doors and instead put Her dining room at the disposal of the officers guarding Her at night, having arranged that they should always be supplied with tea and sandwiches.

When the Germans finally withdrew and a unit of the Allied fleet – awaited for more than a year – arrived in the Black Sea, the Empress was visited several times by British naval officers, who brought Her letters from England. The first letter was from Her sister, Queen Alexandra; this was a great consolation to Her Majesty, having been for so long deprived of direct communication with Her family.

In January talk began to be heard of the threat of danger and, in consequence, of the need for members of the Imperial Family to leave the Crimea and to go abroad. The Empress was indignant at these rumours, saying that in Her opinion to go abroad was unthinkable, and that She could not imagine leaving Russia nor where to go. The Volunteer Army's victory over the Bolsheviks in the Caucasus aroused new hopes and for a time our minds were set at rest – but, unfortunately, not for long. The Bolshevik seizure of Kiev and the Ukraine, and later of Kharkov, once more caused us to be alarmed and after that the fall of Nikolayev and Kherson frightened us even more, especially when we soon learned that the Bolsheviks were approaching the Crimean Peninsula.

One day in early March I arrived at Kharaks at the time appointed by Her Majesty and saw a very dusty car standing in front of the Palace. A Cossack told me that a naval officer from Sevastopol had come to see the Empress, and that I was to wait until he had left before going in to Her Majesty. Prince Dolgoruky came out, looking very worried. When I was finally permitted to see the Empress I found Her in a state of great agitation; She told me indignantly that a British officer had come from the Admiral to warn Her Majesty that the Bolsheviks were approaching the Crimea, that it was useless to count on being able to defend the isthmus of Perekop, and therefore it was time for the Dowager Empress to depart. The Admiral would either come himself or would send a ship to take Her away. The Empress repeated several times, *'Mais je ne puis pas partir, je ne veux pas quitter la Russie'* ['But I cannot go, I do not want to leave Russia']. She was so upset that Her beautiful, expressive eyes several times filled with tears.

As I was leaving Her Majesty, She said to me, *'Je ne bougerai qu'à la dernière extrémité, ou quand on me dira que ma présence gêne les mouvements de notre Armée'* ['I will go only as a last resort, or when they tell me that my presence is hindering the movements of our Army'].

That evening the news was more reassuring; the Bolsheviks had been pushed back, the Allies were fortifying the isthmus and their warships were guarding it. There followed a few days of calm, then on 24 March came alarming news and on the morning of the 25th we learned that a large dreadnought had been sent to take off Her Majesty and the Grand Duke Nikolai Nikolayevich. On 2 April Her Majesty was informed that She must be on board by 5 April. At that grim moment Her Majesty, like a true Mother of Her country, informed the Captain of the warship that She would not leave the Crimea unless all the sick and wounded, the priests and doctors, and any other inhabitants of Yalta and its environs who might be in danger from the Bolsheviks were evacuated with Her. The Captain said that this was impossible at present, since he did not have enough suitable vessels. The Empress repeated that She would stay where She was until the last person of the categories She had named were found a berth on some vessel or another. At that, some British passenger ships and warships, including destroyers, were sent from Sevastopol, and on the next day everyone who wished to leave assembled on the mole at Yalta.

It was a sad sight: all those refugees, most of whom were old and sick, and all of whom were crushed by grief at leaving their homeland, sitting on bundles and rugs (trunks were forbidden) as they waited to be taken aboard the steamers.

At first we were taken to Sevastopol, being told that there we could have the choice of going to the Caucasus or abroad. The Dowager Empress kept Her promise to the end, and only gave Her consent to the departure of HMS *Marlborough* when the last steamer had taken on its cargo of refugees. Instead of the rest of the squadron allowing HMS *Marlborough*, with the Empress on board, to sail first, it was She who, like a Mother, covered the retreat of Her children.

In Sevastopol we were told that it was impossible to go to the Caucasus, so after being transferred to other vessels we were taken to

Constantinople, then to the Princes Islands for three days and back to Constantinople, where we had the consolation of seeing HMS *Marlborough* in the distance and of knowing that our dear Empress was with us! There, right opposite St Sophia, we spent the last two days of Holy Week and . . . on Saturday, almost all of us without exception were granted the great joy of receiving the Holy Sacraments. That Communion was a profoundly moving experience – in very truth were fulfilled the words of our loving Saviour: 'Come unto Me all ye that travail and are heavy laden and I will give you rest'. Little and great, young and old came to Him, all heavy laden with grief and suffering. Truly, peace and light entered into our anguished hearts and we were able to greet Easter Night with a radiant feeling of spiritual joy and hope for the future . . .

The next day we set off for Malta, which we reached after a very stormy, two-day passage. There we were quartered in barracks and huts, two or three people to one room. In Malta we were again fortunate enough to see the Dowager Empress and to express to Her our profound and sincere gratitude for the gracious care that She had taken of us all.

Her Majesty received us in a villa that had been put at Her disposal just outside Valetta. On the eve of Her departure for England the Empress announced Her wish to visit all the barracks and camps in which we were accommodated in the environs of the city. Our happiness at seeing Her was clouded by inexpressible sorrow at parting from Her. The next day, with heavy hearts, we watched as the dreadnought sailed away into the distance, bearing our Mother Empress!

22

An Unexpected Rescue

ESTHER MARKISH

Esther Markish (née Lazebnikovna) was born in 1912 into a Jewish family living in Baku in the Caucasus. In the early years of the century Baku was the centre of Russia's new oil industry and, through their involvement in the oil business, the family prospered. But 1917 saw an end to their way of life, as they became victims of the new wave of anti-Semitism that followed in the wake of the Revolution.

My father, Yefim Lazebnikov, was an oil man [in Baku] and the owner of oil-bearing land. We lived well. My father made huge profits from the oil business. He loved the good life and beautiful things. He had received a technical education in France and had a good grasp of the problems connected with the oil business. It was in France that he had met my mother, where she was studying medicine. The year before she met my father, my mother had gone to the south of France with her family in order to escape from the 1905 pogroms in Russia. My parents were married in 1907, and my mother left with my father for Baku without finishing her studies.

A great many Jews in Baku disapproved of our family's lifestyle: we lived too luxuriously. In 1914, my father was one of the first people in Baku to buy a motor car. A host of neighbours eyed this latest progeny of the technical revolution with envy and soon our vehicle was bespattered with black mud mixed with oil. 'It serves him right for buying that car,' said the Jews of Baku. He was also envied for buying a luxury apartment in the very centre of Baku, for spoiling his wife so much and for indulging all her whims. Her diamonds gave even more glamour to her beauty and she drew admiring looks, not only from the Jews but also from the Christians and Muslims. My mother's beauty was such that whenever my father's name was mentioned, the question that invariably followed was, 'Which Lazebnikov? The one whose wife is so beautiful?'

Unconcerned by criticism, my father continued to live as he pleased. Our house in the Black Town and then our apartment in Birzhevaya Ulitsa [Stock Exchange Street] were always filled with guests and our cook Kondratievna was famous all over Baku.

My parents were not religious, although my father had his place reserved in the local synagogue, which he supported very generously. The only feast day we celebrated solemnly and in accordance with tradition was Passover.

The Russian Revolution put an end to our way of life. My father regarded the Revolution as an inevitable fact to which one must adapt for the sake of the future, but it was difficult to adapt: his oil business was confiscated. My father joked bitterly, 'After all, I was right, and those Jews who criticized me were wrong. The Bolsheviks have taken everything from them – and from me. But at least we were able to live like human beings.'

In 1918, my mother took my brother and me [to Ekaterinoslav, in the Dnieper basin] to see her parents, of whom she had had no news for a long time. My father stayed in Baku. The great events of the year 1917 in Russia – the two Revolutions then the Civil War – were a source of anguish and anxiety for the Jews of Ekaterinoslav. Their long history had shown indisputably that, whatever changes occurred in the surrounding society, they always led to persecution of the Jews, to looting, pogroms and murders. That was why, when gangs, inflamed by vodka, rushed into the streets of Ekaterinoslav, the Jews, fore-warned by the bitter memories of previous generations, began to pre-pare themselves for a pogrom. The first step they took was apparently insignificant: it was to tear down and clear away the wooden fences which separated the houses. This operation was prompted by past experience and had an important practical significance: to enable people to flee as fast as possible from the looting *pogromshchiki* and to escape unhindered by obstacles. To jump over wooden fences with little children is difficult, not to say impossible.

The pogroms were not long in starting, immediately after the rabble-rousing speeches on future freedom and the wonderful equality between men in a new society.

Our family – my mother, my nine-year-old brother and I, the young-est – stayed in the porter's lodge of the house in Shirokaya Street belonging to the banker Kaufmann [for whom my grandfather worked]. This was a street inhabited mostly by Jews, and there was a smell of burning.

Gavrila, the concierge who worked faithfully and conscientiously for my grandfather, showed signs of great nervousness. He listened anxiously to the approaching shouts of a crowd of people who were crying, 'Help!'

'They're really on the rampage today,' Gavrila said at last. 'I'll go and have a look.'

He went out. The cries of 'Help!' grew nearer and nearer, reverberating around the neighbouring houses.

'Gavrila will not give us away,' said my mother. 'But if they manage to get in here . . . ' She was hoping the rioters would pass us by, for they did not attack each house.

Gavrila returned, looking grim. 'Fly,' he said. 'Get away . . . They have already killed the Rabinoviches.'

The Rabinoviches were our neighbours, who lived a few houses away from us. My mother got up, clasped our hands: 'Come, children!'

We went out of the overheated house into the black damp of the night, slithering about in the autumn mud. We fled through the courtyards of houses, pursued by that fearful groaning: 'Help!' One of the houses seemed to have been abandoned by the owners. My mother pushed us through a big open door and hurried into a room.

In a corner of that room, half covered by a torn-down curtain, as if in a shroud, a corpse lay on the ground. A looter was kneeling over the body: he was rifling through the pockets. Turning round as he heard our footsteps, he noticed a jewel glistening in a ring on my mother's finger. He got up, seized my mother's hand, took hold of her finger and tried to snatch the ring.

'Take your hands off!' said my mother calmly. 'I will give it to you myself.'

Then someone called to the looter from another room: 'Hey, Pasha!' Pasha, who was drunk, turned round and ran out.

We jumped out of the window and ran further, searching for a nook or cranny where we could hide at least until morning.

My memories of the Ekaterinoslav pogrom are undoubtedly the first event in my life that I remember fairly precisely. My awareness of time began with that autumn night when the streets were slimy with mud and blood. One's first memory is like the first imprint of an engraving: the clearest, the best defined.

Who was doing the killing? The Whites? The Greens? Makhno's partisans?[1] Petlyura's partisans?[2]

In Ekaterinoslav power changed hands every day. It would happen that one quarter of the town was occupied by the monarchists, the other by the anarchists. It must even seem funny to people today. The anarchists would leave, the Reds would arrive; then the Whites decimated the Reds, after which a band of peasants would approach the town, drawn by the prospect of looting. All these comings and goings took place at night. Two groups of men would clash and fight, one of which would retreat, abandoning their dead and wounded.

Pogroms also took place at night, as did the Jews' silent flight from house to house, over unfenced land. By day, victors and vanquished alike slept off their drunkenness, and we could then sleep too – those Jews who had managed to escape the jubilation of the victors and the fury of the vanquished.

It was on one such day that my father came from Baku to look for us. He had intended to get us out at whatever cost from this town which had gone crazy and to take us back home. However, this was no simple matter. My father spent whole days at a time in town to obtain all the necessary permits and passes for us.

One day, in the midst of negotiations for a pass, [he] was caught by the early autumn nightfall. The night was black as ink. The blank windows gaped – black outlines against a distant background of fire. The clatter of horses' hooves and the shuffling of feet could be heard coming from a nearby street, the boom of gunfire from somewhere else . . . By sticking close to the walls of buildings, my father managed to escape towards the house. He had only about one block to go when the sound of boots echoed behind him and made him flatten himself to the ground. A second later the lash of a *nagaika* [whip] came down on his back and a horse kicked him, almost causing him to roll over. Leaning from his saddle, the rider examined my father's face. His breath smelt of onions and vodka.

'A Yid,' said the rider, as if to confirm his supposition. 'Go on, get a move on, Yid!'

And after tickling my father once more with his *nagaika*, he chased him along in front of him. There was nowhere to flee, it was impossible to escape. Trembling, and slipping on the sticky mud, my father ran in front of the horse. At the end of the road they turned to the left, through a gateway. It led into a courtyard that ended in a cul-de-sac with no way out.

A huge fire was burning in the courtyard. A dozen or so soldiers in bizarre uniforms – baggy red trousers, green and blue tunics, sheepskin jerkins, luxurious ladies' cloaks and astrakhan hats with or without red ribbons – were clustered around the fire. There was also a machine gun mounted on a tripod. A little further on, twenty or so Jews were sitting in a circle on the snow. My father knew several of them: some of the best-known, wealthiest and most respected men in the town. He nodded his head in greeting to a bearded old Jew – the head of the Jewish high school. The second one, the owner of a dye factory, did not answer his greeting: his eyes were closed, his face was nothing but one bruise. Near the prisoners a sentry was pacing up and down smoking a cigarette.

'So, shall we call it a day?' said the horseman who had chased my father. 'It will soon be daylight . . . On your feet!' he yelled to the Jews who were sitting in the mud.

They got up slowly, like a flock of sheep.

'Take off your clothes,' the sentry ordered lazily, without insisting, prodding the nearest prisoners with his bayonet. 'Take off your clothes and get into a line along the wall . . . Hey you, Yid!' he shouted in a terrifying voice to a middle-aged Jew who was being slow to undress.

The trooper who had chased my father, without dismounting from the saddle, snatched off his coat. My father took off his shoes and, squelching up to his ankles in liquid mud mixed with horse piss, approached the wall.

'Why?' said my father, scarcely moving his lips. Then he shouted: 'Why?'

One of the soldiers was already lying down on a mattress spread out behind the machine gun.

Their faces turned against the birchwood wall of the enclosure, some Jews were praying, rocking their bodies. One slipped into the mud, but no one picked him up again.

Suddenly, a man on horseback with long brown hair trotted into the courtyard. From the speed and zeal with which the soldiers turned to him, the new arrival was obviously their commanding officer.

With one bound, my father leapt away from the wall and ran towards the mounted man.

'Sir,' he asked, hanging on to the reins of the horse, 'why do they want to shoot us?'

'Yes, why? Hm'm?' the officer asked the soldiers, imitating my father.

'Well, boss, they're Yids,' explained the one who was lying behind the machine gun. 'We'll make an end of them.'

'Let us live, Sir,' said my father, still holding the reins. 'What are we guilty of? Just of being Jews?'

'We'll let them go, shall we?' said the chief to his men, as if seeking advice. They were silent, not daring to speak up.

'All right, go to the devil, all of you!' said the chief, pulling up his horse. 'Go on, run!'

The Jews fled. Their clothes were heaped up like a black ball in the middle of the courtyard.

My father fled too, finally having let go of the reins. 'Hey, Jew!' shouted the officer in his turn. 'Stop!'

My father stopped, rooted to the spot. What did this mean?

'Put on your galoshes and clothes, Jew, or else you'll catch cold!' And he began to laugh, pleased with himself.

My father ran as far as the gateway and disappeared, hidden by the darkness.

The man who had freed him from death and torture was Makhno himself.

After his fortunate reprieve, Yefim Lazebnikov succeeded in bringing his family back to Baku, but conditions had changed so drastically that they decided to leave Russia.

23

'We'll Be Going Back Soon . . .'

COUNTESS NATALYA SUMAROKOV-ELSTON

When the First World War broke out Natalya Sumarokov-Elston's father, a colonel of cavalry, was posted to the Turkish front and the family lived in the Caucasus from 1914 until after the Revolution.

Her grandfather, also a military man, had spent his entire career in the Caucasus and had been appointed Nachalnik Chechenskovo Naroda *– a sort of district officer or official representative responsible for the welfare of the Chechens. The grateful memories which the local people retained of him and of his wife (a Terek Cossack girl) led them to help his descendants escape as the Red Army advanced.*

[When the Revolution came] it just seemed to me that suddenly one day the soldiers changed, their shirts were hanging out, their belts were round their necks and they were eating sunflower seeds; everything was dirty – all of a sudden, from one day to another.

We owe [the local people, the Chechens] a lot – they must have saved our lives.

We were in Chesvlonaya and someone came out and said, 'I don't know what you're doing here – all the [White] soldiers are gone, there's no one between you and the Bolsheviks; you'd better pack your bags and clear out.' So anything that was handy was thrown into potato sacks. The horses wouldn't co-operate, there was slush everywhere. We arrived at a ford where the Army was crossing. It was dark, it was packed with refugees, horses, carts, people shouting – pandemonium. We were told to wait our turn. No one knew anyone else. Then someone said, 'Here comes the *Chechensky Svyatoi*' – he was a sort of ayatollah, spiritual leader of the Chechens. He'd heard we were trying to cross from the Russian to the Chechen side. He invited us to his village, and guaranteed us protection. He escorted us with his own retinue. We spent quite a few days in that village. Then he reappeared and said he couldn't guarantee our safety any longer. He gave us light carriages and told us to make no noise: 'No cigarettes, no children crying, even if you have to smother them.' He gave us an escort of *abreki* [cut-throats, highwaymen]. At one point we heard a shot and some of our men galloped off to tell another band to keep off. They took us to where the White Army was regrouping . . . It was all great fun for me as a child.

The worst journey by train was from Kislovodsk to Novorossiysk. There were three families in the truck; one of them was Polish – they knew my parents. That was a very risky, dangerous trip. We didn't know how close the Reds were. The train would stop anywhere. A knock on the door – we didn't know if it was the Reds. Usually it was White troops looking for their units or trying to get away.

Novorossiysk was bursting at the seams. We got two rooms. We all slept in one room – there were people there I'd never seen before, I don't know who they were – and in the other was a samovar. Outside they were sleeping on the pavement. There was nothing to eat. Absolute hell. I rather enjoyed it. There was nothing in the market – we would get a little flour and a bit of lard. My nanny would throw this into the samovar and call it soup. People would just come in and have some – anyone from the street. Then the samovar was emptied and refilled and it was called tea. But I never remember being hungry – hot water is very filling!

The wind in Novorossiysk is terrible. This was about January 1920 – we were afraid the Reds were about to arrive. Everyone was asking, 'Where will *you* go?' Nobody knew where. Most went to Prinkipo, but my father wanted to go to Batum so that we stayed in Russia. We got on to a passenger boat with British permission – it was crammed. I had measles; they thought it was typhus and therefore we wouldn't be let into Batum. But when the doctor came on board at Batum my mother gave me crumbs to feed the seagulls to pretend I was all right. Dr Chertkov had been our doctor [when we were previously] in Batum, so she knew him and made conversation: 'What a surprise! How are you?' and so on. Then we were sitting in the snow on the quay – we didn't know where to go. There was no money. Quite by chance my father met someone he'd known in the war. They took us in, although my father told them I had an unknown disease. We stayed with them for weeks until we found somewhere of our own. A few days after we arrived, Dr Chertkov came and examined me and said I only had measles, so that was all right.

Before, we had made money by selling all sorts of things – shoes, for instance. My father sold some of my mother's shoes in the market while we were in the Caucasus. We used to carry all our things round in potato sacks. One time on the road from Chesvlonaya we met another family we knew by the roadside – they had no transport. We threw out some of our sacks to make rooom for them in our cart – and it so happened the ones we had left were full of shoes!

We were in Batum for one year (1920–1), and then got out just before the Bolsheviks arrived. We were able to get out because Shell was going to buy our oil shares (in the Grozny oil-fields) and they gave us a deposit. You see, everyone thought the Bolsheviks wouldn't last. My uncle to the end of his life kept his suitcase under the bed so that he would be able to go back quickly. A friend's mother always refused (in exile) to tidy up her house – 'What's the point? We'll be going back soon!' . . .

Countess Sumarokov-Elston's memories of emigration are recorded in Chapter 36.

PART TWO

Refugees
1922–1945

After the Revolution of 1917 a great wave of Russian émigrés settled in various countries, where they stood out and developed a thriving life all of their own. Those few who had hard currency and friends abroad could still flourish; there were some famous parties; there were still Grand Dukes on the Riviera. But life for most was harsh, as many of the stories that follow will tell.

The strangest of all émigré communities was that of Harbin, a city in Manchuria which had become Russian when the Tsarist Government built the Trans-Siberian railway in the 1890s. It was a Chinese city, but the Russian element became very numerous; with the troubles of China under the War Lords, the Japanese invasion of 1931, the Sino-Japanese War of the 1930s and 1940s, and a new accommodation between China and the Soviet Union, these émigrés' lives became precarious and many of them escaped, first to Shanghai or Hong Kong, and then, after 1945, to California, western Canada or – a great number – Australia.

One striking feature of these stories is the vast difference that there was between the Russia of pre-Revolutionary times and post-war circumstances. Our oldest informants reveal a world that no doubt becomes, in memory, rather more of a magic garden than it really was. On the other hand, the Russia of before 1914 was an exciting place to live. It was booming, quite obviously set on course to becoming what we should now call a super-power. The Government, though still a great nuisance, was improving in its ways. There was still ugly anti-Semitism, as we have seen, but Russian liberalism seemed to be growing in strength, and left-wing parties spoke an internationalist language that had obvious attractions for Jews.

The convulsion of war from 1914 to 1917, the breakdown of order, and the rise of terror and civil war came as a great shock to Russians, who had many grounds, before 1914, for hoping that their country would progress in nineteenth-century style. Some, both inside and outside the Soviet Union, eventually hoped that the Bolsheviks could be 'tamed' by responsibility. There was always something of a movement 'back': the writers Alexey Tolstoy and Andrey Bely, the composer Sergey Prokofiev and (perhaps strangest of all) the one-time Tsarist military attaché in Paris, Count Alexander Ignatieff (who, unlike others who went back, survived in fine style, ending up as Major-General in the Red Army). Even beyond the borders a certain feeling was ineradicable that the Soviet Union was, after all, Russia, and such 'Soviet patriotism' did cause a number of émigrés to return. Most of these suffered very badly in camps as a result, and were not released until after Stalin's death in 1953, or in some cases not until the Khrushchev 'thaw' began in 1956.

In Western countries, the great question which faced the émigrés was whether to support Hitler against Stalin. The émigrés had set up their own military organizations, which had functions of charity and education. Usually they were scrupulous in avoiding involvement with their host countries' politics, and merely kept together in the hope (in the early 1920s, the expectation) of returning to Russia. When the second German war began, the émigrés divided: many of them fought in the Resistance movements, but others offered their services to the Germans (who were neither effective in making use of it, nor very grateful).

During the Second World War, there were volunteer corps in Yugoslavia and some veterans of the Russian Civil War joined up with the anti-Stalin, formerly Soviet, soldiers to establish the Russian Liberation Army, under General Vlasov. Towards the end of the war, Vlasov tried to use his force in a sort of Pan-Slav sense, but this did not save him from recapture by the Soviet machine, along with a great number of his lieutenants and some well-known men of Civil War vintage. The part played by the British Army in returning these thousands of men, as well as their wives and children, and including people with non-Soviet passports who should not have been handed over at all under international law, has attracted some heavily condemnatory literature, of which Nicholas Bethell's *The Last Secret* (1973) was the first. However, it is worth pointing out that other countries also handed over Russian émigrés whose non-Soviet passports ought to have entitled them to protection. In Yugoslavia, for instance, the prominent conservative politician Dmitry Shulgin was arrested, sent to the USSR and imprisoned until 1956 (he continued, nevertheless, to live there after his release). There were similar cases in Romania, Czechoslovakia and Finland.

24

The Russian Church Abroad

METROPOLITAN ANTHONY BLOOM

Anthony Bloom left Russia as a child when his parents decided to emigrate after the Revolution. He grew up in France, taking Holy Orders after the Second World War. In 1949 he came to England as a priest and has remained in London ever since, becoming Metropolitan (equivalent to Archbishop) of the Moscow Patriarchal Orthodox Church in the United Kingdom.

I was born in June 1914 in Lausanne, because my grandfather, who had been in the Diplomatic Corps, had settled in Lausanne after he retired and my father, who was also in the Russian Diplomatic Corps, was on leave at the time, and he and my mother were staying with my grandfather and grandmother in Lausanne. After that – in August, I think – we travelled back to Russia via the south, because of course it was impossible to go via the north, and for a year or two we settled in Moscow, with my maternal grandfather's family. He and my father were both from Moscow.

[My mother was a Skryabin]: I am the nephew of Alexander Nikolayevich [Skryabin, the composer. I am also related to Molotov], but he belongs to a cadet branch of the family.[1] My father's forebears came over to Russia from Scotland at the time of Peter the Great, and when I came to England – in 1949 – a priest from Scotland wrote to me to say that he and I were namesakes and that we were the only people left with the name of Bloom. My grandfather on my father's side still had a second cousin in the northern Highlands; he spelt his name with two 'u's in place of the two 'o's . . . But since the Revolution most of these things have been lost; not only have people died, not only letters but even memories have been lost, because people had no time for such things . . .

I have an endless number of cousins, because my grandfather had six brothers and one sister. The sister never married, but the brothers were all married and each of them had at least five children, so in my generation the family expanded enormously . . . But I am the only one who became a priest and they were all very put out about it. They were all of the officer class, and I remember when I decided to become a priest they all said to me, 'You will be the subordinate of some fool of a bishop!' It was very amusing, because when I became a priest they considered me to be the equivalent of . . . a lieutenant. Then when I became an archimandrite, I turned out to be something like a captain. Then I became a bishop and that was quite different. They considered me to be the same rank as they were. And when I became a metropolitan, they began to stand up when I came in! Because that's already the equivalent of the rank of general, and they were only colonels . . .

We left Russia in 1916 because my father had been posted to Persia [and that's where we were in 1917 when the Revolution began]. It was impossible to return [to Russia], because my father refused to serve the new Bolshevik Government. Until 1920 the embassy [in Persia] remained as it had been before. In 1920 the Soviet authorities began to recall the ambassadors and consuls who had been appointed under the old régime. It was then that my father refused to serve, and of course he had to leave.

We left separately. My grandmother, my mother and I left earlier than my father. I think it was in February 1920. We travelled through northern Persia, through the mountains of Kurdistan, along the Tigris and the Euphrates to Basra, and thence to Bombay. From there we were supposed to travel via Alexandria to Southampton; we never arrived at Southampton, however, because when we boarded the steamship at Alexandria they warned us that it was a very old ship and that if there were a storm it would fall apart. For this reason they allocated each of us to a lifeboat. Of course, having read *Robinson Crusoe* and so on, I dreamt of being shipwrecked and I couldn't understand why my mother was so unromantic. In the end, we weren't shipwrecked, but when the ship stopped at Gibraltar it said, 'I am never going to leave here again.' So we disembarked at Gibraltar and did not reach England. However, some of our luggage nevertheless did arrive in England without us, and we got it back about ten years later with a letter which said, 'Here is your luggage. You owe £1 for transport and storage'!

So, having disembarked, we travelled through Spain to France, where my mother's brother Vladimir was; he had been sent by the Tsar on a mission to the French Government and had been stranded there by the Revolution. From there we travelled to Austria, and from Austria for a short time to the north of Yugoslavia, to Zagreb and Maribor, and then we returned to Vienna – my grandmother had a married sister there and she took us in. I went to school [there] for the first time.

There was hope that my mother might find some kind of work in Vienna, although at that time, in the early 1920s, there was terrible unemployment all over Europe. But that came to nothing, and so my mother left my grandmother and me in Vienna and went to look for work in Paris. And since, besides Russian, she knew French, English and German, she found secretarial work and in 1922 she summoned us to Paris, where we settled until the beginning of 1949.

My father had meanwhile landed in Constantinople, where he had got stranded simply because he had no money to travel further. Then in 1921 he came to Vienna, and from there to France, where he also began to look for work. And so we were reunited [though not under one roof]. We didn't have any money to rent anything. My father worked in one place, my mother worked in another place, and I was a boarder at a French *lycée*.

I began at the Lycée Michelet, which is on the outskirts of Paris, and then after three years I moved to another *lycée* for a while, but basically I would say I was a pupil of the Lycée Condorcet, because when I went there I was already a boy of fifteen or more and I was conscious that it was 'my school'.

I had always been taught French. From my very earliest childhood I used to speak Russian with my father, French with my grandmother and one or the other with my mother. With the local people in Persia I spoke Persian, but my Persian, of course, disappeared very quickly . . . [though] even after I could no longer speak or understand a word of Persian, whenever I used to talk in my sleep at night I would speak in Persian – it remained in my subconscious. And perhaps it's still there somewhere!

I left the *lycée* in 1931, when I was about seventeen, and I entered the Faculty of Science at Paris University. I took a diploma there in physics, chemistry and biology, and then I entered the Faculty of Medicine. [I did not have French citizenship] because I hadn't wanted to become French. I had always dreamt of Russia. All my generation was brought up like that. We lived Russia, dreamed Russia, waking and sleeping. [The world of our parents' memories was] a very accessible world, but I think it was to some extent unreal . . . But it was unreal like a lost paradise. Everything that our parents remembered about Russia was beautiful, great, virtuous, glorious, honourable . . . The dark side, the unattractive, grey things, had somehow vanished from their minds. We, too, were brought up with this dream: we learned the language, the history, the geography, the literature, the culture of Russia and we lived within that culture. I remember, when I was about fifteen years old someone asked me why I didn't want to become a French citizen, and I replied that I wanted to remain Russian and that I would prefer to die in Russia than to live abroad . . .

From the age of ten I was a scout, and then when I was about twelve I joined the Russian Student Christian Movement[2] as a *vityaz* [knight]. And I remained in it, first as a boy, then as a leader, until the period after the war. There were interruptions, of course, particularly for the duration of the war, when times were simply very uncertain. I did go to a young persons' camp in 1939, but then there was an interval until 1943 or 1944, when I visited a camp again, but not to take part in it. I was simply there for three or four days, and I think that was my last camp in France. I didn't take part in political movements. Politics has never interested me. I did have strong monarchist feelings, which have remained to this day. When I went to the Soviet Union for the first time, they invited me to the Committee for Religious Affairs and they asked, 'Have you any political convictions?' 'Yes,' I said, 'I have. I'm a Russian monarchist!' But that's more sentimental than political. I'm not a political animal in that sense. But I used to participate very passionately in everything Russian. I wasn't in the *Mladorossi*. I knew only a few people who belonged to the NTS of the New Generation – what later became the NTS.[3]

[In 1939 when war broke out I was in my last year in the Faculty of Medicine, so I was able to join the French Army as a doctor.] I served for a year, until the moment when France was defeated. I had the rank of Warrant Officer. Then I was in the French Resistance for three years in Paris, [then] after the Liberation of Paris [I rejoined the Army]. I wasn't a hero. I didn't do anything remarkable . . . nobody killed me, nobody took me prisoner, nobody wounded me, so you might say I was wasting my time!

[During the German occupation of France I was not deported to Germany. I was] demobilized in Unoccupied France [and] I went to a young persons' camp [at Pau] because I had to have some address to which to be demobilized. From there I returned to Occupied France, but at the border I had to obtain a pass. I remember I went to the local *maire* and asked him to give me a pass. He said, 'I can't because they will shoot me for it.' I spent a long time trying to persuade him. 'All right,' he said, 'I'm leaving the room. There are the papers. You can steal them and fill them in yourself. If they arrest you, I will say that you stole them.'

And so with these papers I returned to Paris without declaring myself and simply went back and lived in our flat. But since I couldn't live on air, I had to earn my living and so I got work in a hospital as a doctor. I had to leave after a while, because I had been working in the radiological department where the Germans sent people whom they wanted to deport to Germany; we had worked out a whole system whereby we falsified X-ray photographs so that these people would not be able to go. The Germans were terribly afraid of tuberculosis and so we found a way of making symptoms of tuberculosis appear on the X-rays. After a while one had to leave that sort of work, because one never knew when one might be caught. At that point the French Préfecture of Police offered me the job of taking charge of two ambulances and driving to places which had been bombed to bring first aid. This meant that I had a cover, but it wasn't a paid job, so at the same time I taught for a year at the Russian *gymnazia*.

The *gymnazia* was a mixed school, where the basic teaching language was Russian, except, of course, for purely French subjects, and in the senior classes those of us who were more innovative taught in French so that the pupils could sit the Baccalauréat. Before us, all subjects had been taught in Russian, and when the pupils had to produce work in French they lacked the necessary command of the language. I taught there almost up until the Liberation of Paris . . .

But the thing that saved me was the Préfecture giving me those two ambulances. They would warn me that bombs had been seen dropping on such and such a place and I would drive there. If I was lucky I would arrive five minutes after the bombing stopped, and if I wasn't so lucky, five minutes before. Well, I would do my work and drive away. But the job also allowed me, first of all, to drive people who had no means of transport, and secondly, God forgive me, to steal things for the Resistance. [I took medicines and surgical instruments and did not bother about the Communist element in the Resistance]: it wasn't a question then of internal politics, it was a question of fighting the Germans, it was part of the war. We didn't ask 'Who?' I was a doctor at the time and so I tended anyone who was wounded, without asking who he was. For example, during the Liberation of Paris, I tended both German and non-German soldiers. And for that they wanted to shoot me – our people, that is. They said, 'You treat Germans the same, so that means you are a traitor!' But all that passed. It was more amusing than frightening. I had certain convictions. If someone was standing there with a weapon, you shot him. If he wasn't standing there with a weapon, he was a wounded man. I was not interested in who he was by birth or conviction. He was simply a soldier.

I wanted to take Holy Orders, even if only in the long term, from the age of about seventeen, but then I decided to become a doctor so that one day I could go away into the remote provinces and practise as a doctor there, while being a priest at the same time. In that way I would not be a burden to the Orthodox community, and I could found a church at my own expense where the people were too poor or too few in number to support a priest. That, of course, was just a brilliant idea that never came to anything. When the war ended, I didn't even have money for the Métro, let alone to travel anywhere else. I began my medical practice [in Paris] by buying an instrument for measuring blood pressure, a syringe and one needle, because I hadn't enough money for a second, then going to the butcher, the baker and the milkman and saying, 'I'm a doctor. If you have any patients, send them to me.'

But all the time I was dreaming, somehow, somewhere, of becoming a priest. And later I did become a priest, when I was thirty-five. I tried for three months to be a priest and a doctor at the same time, but that turned out to be out of the question, because with a large practice it is impossible to be something else as well; I was either in the church when there were patients waiting for me, or I was with my patients when they were waiting for me in the church. And then I had a stroke of luck. I was invited to come here [to England].

I never went to theological school. I had read a lot, and at one time I had worked with young people, and so I had given talks and had tried to teach other people what I didn't really know myself, but they decided that I knew enough to become a priest. [I was ordained by Metropolitan

Serafim in] a tiny church in the Latin Quarter called Mother of God of All Sorrows and Joys at Ste-Geneviève. It was in a house that you were simply scared to go near, because all around there were tumble-down houses, rubbish dumps, cat fights . . . [Our church there was about two-thirds the size of an average room.] I became a deacon there. But I was ordained priest in a French parish church on the Boulevard Auguste Blanqui – also by Metropolitan Serafim.

I preferred to join the Moscow Patriarchal Church.[4] When the separation happened in 1931, I chose the Patriarchal Church because I was convinced that so long as the Church in Russia preaches Orthodoxy, there is no reason to leave her. And if she is imprisoned under Soviet rule, then it is our business to remain free. We are abroad, no one can force us to do anything whatsoever. If any of us gives in to bribery, or fear, or does something out of stupidity, one must not blame the Russian Church, but the person who does it. I remember one of our bishops expressed it, not very elegantly but very clearly, when he said, 'If my mother became a prostitute, I wouldn't disown her!'

In those days there were very few of us – not more than fifty in Paris. There was tremendous poverty among the priests. But there was simply a great spiritual fervour. It was remarkable. [The other branch was richer and] more numerous. And unfortunately between us and them there was a great deal of tension and unfriendliness, which need not have been so. When I think now, at more than seventy years of age, of what I was like then, and what my contemporaries and elders were like, I am simply sorry. We Russians have a great gift for splitting into factions, and for dividing not only ideologically but immediately transferring our differences to the personal level. 'If you don't agree with me, you're probably not a good person' – that is a prevalent attitude. And, unfortunately, it was very strong in these early 1930s and up to and including the war. It's a pity, because now I think we could all have stayed together, despite our different points of view, and not have split up.

The first split was in 1925, when a group of bishops in exile addressed a request to the League of Nations for military intervention in Russia. At the time most Russian émigrés disassociated themselves from this group, but the group did continue to exist, in Yugoslavia, for example, and in Bulgaria. Then in 1931 the second schism, or division, happened in Paris. And it's all a great pity. When I read the documents now I think of that Russian proverb: 'The bear was wrong to eat the cow, but the cow was wrong to go into the wood.' We were wrong and they were wrong. We ought to have held out and said 'No! We need to be united.' But then we didn't see that, we didn't understand, we had . . . very strong feelings, very strong, unhealthy feelings.

There are churches [of the Constantinople branch in Paris today], but it is growing smaller and dying away all the time. There are various reasons. The first is that, with one exception, not a single parish was prepared to use the French language; sixty-five years after the Revolution, that means that you are going to lose all the young people. Here in London, for example, if we didn't do anything in English we would have no young people. That's one thing. And the second is that, after the war, and after the change of attitudes which took place then, there is no ideological reason not to be Patriarchal . . .

Thirty-five years ago, statistically, the Patriarchal Church represented one-third of the Russian Orthodox population, but we grew for several reasons. First of all, because we devoted all our energies to caring for individual parishioners, the old, the sick and so on. And we did this more and better than the other church because the priests of the other parish were much older than I was. They didn't do it because they couldn't, but the result was that we gained in numbers. The second reason was that we never attacked them, while the priest of the other church, who was here [in London] when I had just arrived, said such things about us that even his supporters felt he went too far. I remember I once asked him personally, 'What do you think of me?' He replied, 'Since you're an honest man, I'll give you a straight answer. If I wanted to be polite, I would say, "You are not a priest." But I will give you a straight answer: "If you are under Moscow, you are a priest of Satan!"' And of course that did us more good than it did him, because very few people judge so radically and severely. Then people who came into contact with us saw that I didn't have horns, that when I preached or lectured I said nothing which was contrary to Christian belief, and so on.

The third thing was that straight away, even before I could speak English, I began to take services in English for a group of young people who no longer understood Russian. And as I began to learn more and more English, I began to give talks and to work with children. I founded a Sunday School where I taught in English – a small school, of course, but it attracted a whole generation which would otherwise have fallen away. When I arrived, there were grandmothers and grandchildren –

and they were small grandchildren, because as soon as they grew up, they left. But then that gap began to fill up.

Now [in London] we have about 350 people of Russian extraction: that is, people who were either born in Russia or who belong to the 'forgotten generation'. Then, secondly, we have four generations of mixed marriages. One can't call these people 'Russians'; they are British. The first generation may say 'My parents were Russian', but the second generation will not even say that. They will say, rather, 'I have a Russian ancestry'. And besides these, quite a number of English people have converted to the Orthodox faith. So that whereas in 1949 we had about three hundred people in the parish, we now have about a thousand. That is in Greater London, of course, not London in the narrow sense. And as a result of this, priests have begun to emerge from our young people, so that now we have eleven parishes in England, whereas before there was only London. And of the priests in those parishes, Father Mikhail, Father Sergey [in Brighton] and Father Nikolay [in Bristol] are the only Russians. All the others are English, apart from two Americans, but at any rate they are all foreigners. And all our provincial parishes hold their services in English. In Bristol it's half and half . . .

All that was simply the result of our pastoral work and the fact that we didn't attack anyone. Once one of our lady parishioners spoke to me about the priest of the other parish as 'That scoundrel!' I said to her, 'Wait a moment, I'm going to ring him.' And I said to him on the phone, 'I have a parishioner here who has called you a scoundrel. When can she come and apologize to you?' And after that no one did that again . . . We simply went on with our life and said nothing. We have our own task: our faith, prayer and the teaching of our community, young and old. And that is enough. The rest is not our affair. If they criticize, we must listen, because often there is a lot of truth in criticism. Listen. If it's not true, well so much the better. And if it is true, take heed.

I resigned [as Exarch[5]] when I became sixty, because being Exarch meant travelling approximately eight months of the year, to eleven different countries, and, to be honest, without achieving very much. You arrive for two or three days in one place. People bring you all their problems. You take time and trouble with them. You sort a few things out, and you know that as soon as you go away they will begin again, because in three days you wouldn't heal a sick person either, and it's the same situation. So when I became sixty I asked to be allowed to retire, and I concentrated on my work here. There is enough of it to keep me busy without anything else.

[I came to London in 1949 to] an organization called the Fellowship of St Alban and St Sergius. When I was in Paris I was asked to prepare a group of young people to go to a conference organized by the Fellowship in England, because in those days the Fellowship was rich, since the French franc was very low and the pound was very high. So I worked with them for a year and at my last talk the secretary of the Fellowship arrived and asked me, 'Why aren't you coming?' I said that I didn't speak English and she said, 'You can speak French.' And so I came and met them and they invited me to come here as a priest to be chaplain to the Fellowship, on the condition that I somehow support myself. Well, I applied to the French hospital here and said, 'I'm a doctor, young, it's true – thirty-five years old – but with some experience already – five years in the war and five years in practice after that.' They answered, 'By all means come. We'll pay you £5 per month travelling expenses, but we can't pay you a salary.' Well, that was the end of that, as you can understand: £5 a month for me, my mother and grandmother! The next year I came over and they proposed that I come for two years, because someone had given the fellowship £800 and so they could pay me £400 a year for two years. So then I gave up medicine, and brought my grandmother and my mother [to London] and we settled in a small flat, for which we then paid £70 a year. And so for a year and a half I was chaplain to the Fellowship. Then my time came to an end and I presumed that I would return to France and take up medicine again . . . But just then, Father Vladimir Theokritov, who was then priest of this parish, died, and since there was nobody else, they appointed me. You know the saying, 'When there are no fish, a crab is a fish'. . . . And so from that time, since 1950, I have been the priest of this parish.

They demolished [our church in Buckingham Palace Road] and we were lucky that they did, because it was in terrible condition. We didn't have the money to repair it, and I was always expecting the moment when we would be evicted in disgrace. But the Church of England decided to demolish it, asked us to leave and even apologized! They offered us another church in the City, but I turned it down, because it was a small Wren church, which we would have had to maintain just as it was. You can imagine what it means to maintain a Wren church in perfect condition! Besides that, no one would have been able to travel to the City on Sunday. And so in the end we got this church [in Ennismore Gardens] and made of it what we could – a very beautiful, fine place, I think.

[The BBC gives us facilities to broadcast to the Soviet Union] at Easter and at Christmas, and the service is broadcast live, not from a recording which can be edited after it is made, but simply live, direct from the church. Afterwards they broadcast parts of the programme in the course of the next few days, but in shortened form, and only selected extracts. Besides that, I do regular broadcasts to Russia through the BBC. I have now recorded fifteen programmes on 'How to be an Orthodox Christian when you have no church' – about how to live, pray and so on without a church, which is of course a very vital topic for Russia.

I can't travel [to the Soviet Union] freely, of course, but periodically they used to invite me to come. While I was Exarch, they used to invite me every year. After that there was a period of eight years when they didn't invite me and when I wrote to say that I would like to come, they replied, 'No!' Then they invited me twice, and now they have said, 'We can't invite you at the moment.' You see, when I travel to Russia, I have an official programme, according to which I have to travel here and there, but the trouble about it is that I am given such a heavy timetable. For example, I lecture at the theological college in Zagorsk. Usually they arrange for me to give one or two lectures, but they allocate one hour for the lecture and two hours for the questions, so that it ends up being not just a lecture, but a three-hour session, and the last time they gave me in addition three hours for questions from the other teachers, so that made six hours. On top of that I take services almost every day, and I preach every day. That's the official part. The unofficial part involves meeting people, groups of people or individuals, and the last two times there have been unpleasant incidents. My meetings were reported to the authorities and when I went to meet a large group of people in someone's flat there were two police cars there and the police made a note of everyone who came. After that they asked me to be careful and not to arrange meetings. Besides that, a great many people used to come to my hotel. This last time there were not so many, but on one of my trips people kept coming for three whole days, from seven in the morning to three in the morning, so that I never left my room. I drank water from the tap and ate bread which people brought me. All the rest of the time people kept coming, including amongst others Nadezhda Mandelstam[6] . . . I didn't mind that of course!

The last time a Russian delegation came to Britain from the Soviet Union I said some things which were also reported to the authorities, after which relations deteriorated very badly. That was in the early 1980s. Representatives from various churches in the Soviet Union were invited by the British Council of Churches. At first it was decided that the theme would be the life of the Church in England and the Soviet Union. But then they changed it to disarmament. The British Council of Churches presented a report on support for unilateral disarmament, the Russian delegation presented a paper on the same subject. I sat and sat there until finally I exploded and said, 'I'm sorry, but the British Council of Churches is deceiving you. They are telling you that the British people support unilateral disarmament. That is not true. In the first place, the Church represents one-tenth of the population. In the second place, out of that tenth, the majority is against unilateral disarmament. That's one thing. The second thing is that you keep talking about the sanctity of life. Neither England nor the Soviet Union has had the right to talk about the sanctity of life since they legalized abortion, which is the murder of the defenceless. You cannot condone that and still say you are afraid of murdering the guilty in war. Thirdly, you ask us to trust the Soviet Union. We have no reason to do that. The Soviet Union undermines all governments, either by underhand means or by force. We will begin to trust you when you can explain to us in some comprehensible way your bloody repression of the uprising in Germany, and the uprising in Hungary, why you are ready to pounce on Poland, why you occupied Czechoslovakia, why you occupied Afghanistan. When you have explained that, perhaps we may believe you, but at the moment we do not believe you.' And of course, that was reported back to Russia to the necessary people, and when I went to Russia, the first thing they asked, on the very first evening, was: 'What did you say?' Well, I told them what I had said, because I had spoken out of conviction, not because I had had too much to drink! And then there were difficulties, and since that they haven't invited me. Sooner or later they will invite me, or if they don't – well, then they don't.

I think that lectures, sermons, meetings with people [when I visit the Soviet Union] are of some use. If you consider how many people I encounter every day for fourteen days . . . I see, first of all, people in church. When I was preaching in the cathedral in Leningrad, there were twelve hundred people. In London, I'll never find twelve hundred people. So some people hear something. Then there are the students – as I said, I'm not a theologian, but I talk about things from a point of view which they do not have. For example, I gave a lecture on the priesthood in a different way from the way they are taught because I see it from a completely different point of view, in completely different circumstances. And various other subjects . . . Besides this there are the broadcasts . . . and the fact that our existence gives a reason for the Russian Church to send its representatives abroad, to visit their own people [means that we are helping in some way].

There was a time when it would have been impossible for me to have gone to Russia. Then my parishioners themselves said, 'Why not go?' So I go. They trust me not to betray them politically, not to give in if they should somehow try to persuade me to do anything, and so there is no objection [from my parish] to my going.

There are fewer and fewer émigrés nowadays. There was a time when there were eighty thousand of us in Paris. Now there are eight thousand [there] at most, and they are half-Russian, half-French [and Jews] and so on, but even in the sense simply of ethnic Russians, there are very few left. The Church used to be the place where we all gathered, which gave us unity. That is undoubtedly true, because the political parties only divided us. But on the other hand nowadays . . . well, there is no emigration. Bishop Constantine [of the Constantinople branch] used to say to me, 'You realize, of course, that if it weren't for you, they would all come to me!' I would say, 'No, because there is no one to go to either of us.' Nowadays you will not get all our old people together. Perhaps you may for a bazaar or a Christmas party, but they are no longer an ideologically militant emigration. They are a dying emigration. The role of the Church is to look after these people, but to think of making them into a coherent, militant body is useless. Perhaps it might be possible in America, where more of the new emigration have settled, but I would say that the new emigration is far more indifferent to the Church. It is a political emigration, or to some extent – without wanting to offend – it is a selfish emigration, in the sense that they are people who no longer want to live in Soviet conditions. But one way or another it is not an ideological or a religious emigration and it is becoming less and less so all the time. People become dissatisfied and so they leave. They go to Israel, America, wherever you like, not in order to fight Soviet reality but in order to escape from it.

I think that Bishop Constantine still retains the remnants of the old ideology, still believes that we can gather together the emigration, that it represents the 'light of Russia' and so on. I think that he is mistaken and that [in the Constantinople branch] they are making the Orthodox Church very narrow. They now consider that they are the last remaining Orthodox Church which has not defiled itself. They have anathematized those who joined the World Council of Churches and everyone who is from Moscow is also 'untouchable'. And who is there left? It's very sad, because they have such a wealth of piety, of love for the Church, of love for Russia and yet it is so narrow that only a certain type of person can appreciate it. They say that besides themselves, their own people, there are no Christians! For example, if a Roman Catholic or an Anglican or a Protestant wants to join them, they will baptize him, as if he had never been baptized before. I think they are mistaken to do this.

But I think that the main point where they are mistaken is that the emigration of which they think no longer exists. I am sorry that it is so. I myself am an émigré of those years and I remember them as if they were a time of festivity. It was a remarkable time, when there were Russian organizations, young people, ideology, love of Russia, an ardent, passionate Church life . . . But it does not exist any more. And it cannot be created artificially.

25

From the New World

OLEG OLEGOVICH PANTYUKHOV

Oleg Olegovich Pantyukhov (alias John Bates) was born in St Petersburg in 1910. In 1917 the family fled to Yalta, from where they went on to Constantinople. His parents opened a small craft business there and, from the modest living they made, managed to save enough for the passage to America. They sailed in 1922.

There were several times when we thought the ship would overturn. There were other times when we thought we'd die of hunger because the food was absolutely terrible. But we made it, and in New York we were met by a man named Boaz, who gave up a day from his business to meet us. He was a nephew of [an American lady we had known] in Constantinople and he had with him the manager of the Slavonic Home in New York, who put us up. [The Slavonic Home] is no longer in existence. It was a dormitory-type hostel for immigrants, on West 23rd Street. When we were there, we were the only residents. It consisted of several large and some small rooms, immaculately clean. We stayed possibly two or three weeks, then got an apartment . . . That was found for us by a Russian refugee committee in New York – that's about the only thing they did for us. I don't know where the rent came from, unless it all came from the funds from Constantinople . . .

However, very shortly after that, Father went to an address to present a letter from a Miss Mitchell. We knew nothing about her social status or her financial status, but she was a very nice spinster lady from Constantinople helping refugees. The letter was addressed to her nephew and the address was 900 Park Avenue. Father had no idea where it was or how it looked, but when he arrived [he discovered that] it was a Norman-type stone mansion on the corner of Park and 79th. He rang the bell and the footman, who looked like a minister, Father said, took the letter and said, 'Just wait.' And this was the palatial home of Mr and Mrs Sherman Huth, nephew of the Miss Mitchell. They were tremendously nice to Father. Mother went there too, and they showed them the little things they had made in Constantinople. I'm afraid the Huths couldn't do much for Father, and really never did, except that they introduced him to someone else – and that someone else introduced Father to a certain Doctor Somebody. And Father went with an address again to a house on Madison Avenue and 73rd Street, and only on reaching there did he realize that he was not an MD but a minister of the Madison Avenue Presbyterian Church. He turned out to be all outgoing and most helpful . . . After making just one or two phone calls he sent Father to Henry Sloane Coffin on the corner of 5th Avenue and 38th Street. It turned out to be a most palatial furniture store, lamps and accessories, only as fancy and as expensive as things were in those days. Nothing in New York now compares to the store of Sloane's – W. J. Sloane – at that time. He met Mr Coffin, who turned out to be manager and part-owner, who said, 'Yes, I've heard about you – you're an artist. Well, we can use an artist.' And he put Father to work painting very fine decorations on furniture. We don't have furniture like that these days – it was like Italian paintings of rosebuds, for example, on bedsteads. And Father said, 'Yes, I think I could do that, particularly if you would employ my wife as well', because my mother painted much better, and together they made out very well for a number of years at W. J. Sloane's. Amazingly, only three or four years ago some friends told us that Mrs Coffin still lived in Newhaven, so we called on her. It was a very nice meeting, and she produced a coffee table that had been made by my mother in a raised lacquer Japanese style. It's somewhat battered by now, of course, but it was still there . . .

When we got to New York [my brother and I] were very fortunate – again through some kind friends – to be enrolled in a most amazing small private school. I don't think that there were more than forty students, whose families were – I wouldn't say the most wealthy New Yorkers, but possibly the second tier. The school was 17 East 60th Street, which is now a garage across from the Copacabana. We had access to Central Park for our athletics and in the school the classes were minute with the very best teachers. We were there for two or three years, and then I went to Clarke School in New Hampshire, which was the Dartmouth prep. It was known as such but they also took in freshmen from Dartmouth who were a little delinquent in maths.

I graduated from there in 1929, at which point I worked as a sailor on a Belgian ship called the *Caucasien*. [I spent some time travelling around Europe, then, when I returned to America,] I went to night classes at Columbia, while I worked [part time] in New York as an apprentice in the printing business. By 1935 I had a reserve commission in the Army, and I applied for active duty with the Civilian Conservation Corps. [We had been American citizens since 1929.]

In 1939 I was assigned to an anti-aircraft regiment on Long Island, the 62nd Regiment at Fort Cotton. I was there during Pearl Harbor. [Then, after training, I was sent to Tehran as an interpreter] because of my Russian language, which I always kept up. It was the most fascinating assignment anyone could have . . . The Commanding General of the United States troops in the Persian Gulf Command was Major General Connolly. He commanded thirty thousand troops. Our mission was to unload ships in the Persian Gulf and send on the cargo to Stalingrad overland by rail and truck. In doing so we had daily contact with Soviet officers, who were most amiable, wonderful people, because they had instructions to be so. After all, we gave them several billion dollars of stuff. They wanted to thank the General for all that and asked him to come up to Moscow, ostensibly to inspect what was happening to the Lend–Lease supplies, and he took me and several other officers with him. We went to Moscow, where we met Mr Mikoyan, Minister of Foreign Trade, whose guests we were. He gave us a banquet [and asked the General what else we would like to see]. We'd seen enough of ballet and opera by that time, and some dusty factories in Moscow, which we said could not produce a truck, so the General instructed me [to say] that he wanted to see only one other thing: a little bit of the front line, because that was where we were sending the stuff. But I had been born in what was now Leningrad and I wanted to see a bit of that too, so I said, 'You know, General, Leningrad is still under siege. If they would let us in . . . and furthermore, they haven't had any foreigners in Leningrad since the siege, and they have the most extensive anti-aircraft defence . . . ' So when we saw Mikoyan, the General asked for those two things . . . and that's the only time I lied in my many years as an interpreter. Well . . . I didn't lie, but I added another word. Instead of just saying, 'We want to see an active front', I said 'We want to see the Kiev front', because my father was born in Kiev and I had never seen it. Actually the Kiev front was the most active, but if we hadn't specified it they would have sent us somewhere where there was no action.

[We went first to Leningrad, and in fact if we hadn't gone right away we] would not have seen it under siege, because within two weeks after we left the siege was broken, and we didn't see the horror that we sensed. [We were there at the end of December and in the first days of January.] They had broken through one line near Lake Ladoga by that time. It was not a complete siege, but they were still being shelled by artillery.

We were guests of the mayor. We were put up in the Hotel Astoria – it dates back to Tsarist times – and we were feasted. It was very embarrassing. We were feasted during our entire trip [despite starvation all round]. You'd see the Soviet officials and Soviet generals who had been invited to join us – they hadn't had a square meal in a long time.

[I had some memories of] Leningrad, because I was born there and I collected maps of [the city]; I knew where things were. On one occasion when the Soviet guide from Moscow asked what we wanted to see, I said the General wanted to see the house of Peter the Great on the River Neva, and the Soviet officer had no idea where it was. I said, 'I'll tell you where it is – it's just a little way up here on this side.' He looked at me and in his mind he knew that I was a trained spy, which was not too far off the truth . . .

When eventually General Connolly's mission in Tehran ended he took me with him back to Washington because he thought that the War Department would take into consideration his knowledge of Russians and Russian contacts for a period of two or three years and that they would send him to Poland. He would have taken me with him, but on arrival in Washington he was told that he was going to be Commissioner of Surplus Trade [so] eventually he released me to his friend General Clay,[1] who was . . . going to Europe. We weren't quite sure for what, but it turned out that General Clay was to be the Military Governor of Germany, with General Eisenhower as his chief. I got to Berlin on the first occasion that Eisenhower flew in. I was at the first meeting, and at every meeting except one between Zhukov and Eisenhower . . .

26

A Refuge in Manchuria

MARGARITA IVANOVNA FREEMAN

Of all centres of Russian emigration, the town of Harbin was undoubt-edly the most peculiar. It was a Chinese town in Manchuria, on the Rivers Mondiago and Sungari, and was taken over by the Russians when the Trans-Siberian railway was built: it had Russian jurisdiction and schools, although theoretically still part of China. A Russian 'New Town' and a Chinese old town ('The Wharf') co-existed, the Chinese town being plagued by cholera. The Russian town had a factory or two, including Siemens-Schuckert, the German electrical firm; there was a cathedral, two private schools and some public schools. Russians were there in not inconsiderable numbers in connection with the railway, but they tended to speak only shopping-Chinese at best; the buffets were run by Georgi-ans; the railway did not really have timetables. The local hero was one O. P. Pankratov, who went round the world by bicycle in two years.

In November 1917, largely through soldiers, the town acquired a Bolshevized Soviet, but it was taken over shortly afterwards by Whites. The Bolsheviks renounced sovereignty of any kind in Harbin, which then acquired a large refugee colony.

Margarita Ivanovna Freeman (née Zarudnaya) found refuge in Harbin as a child. Her mother was a Socialist Revolutionary who had devoted herself to the education of the working classes; her father was employed in a factory in Magnitogorsk. In 1918, when she was ten, her parents were imprisoned in the town of Ufa, while the children remained at home.

[My parents] were eventually released, but they were forbidden to return to us, so we went to Ufa. With us went my old nanny, my mother's maid and some others. While we were in Ufa, the town was occupied by the Czech Legion (who were fighting on the White side) and my father was offered a post on the governing body of a group of factories in the Urals. We therefore moved to Shubalashovsk. When the Reds arrived there, we went to Chelyabinsk, but when they started to retreat it was back to Shubalashovsk. Again the Bolsheviks drew near, so we moved eastwards to Omsk. There my father met his former classmate from the Naval Academy, Admiral Kolchak,[1] who was now the White Commander-in-Chief in Siberia.

It soon became clear that the Bolsheviks were about to capture Omsk too, and that there would be a massive exodus. At the same time my parents were faced with problems: my mother now had six children, of whom the youngest was only a few months old. To travel in those crowded freight cars, not knowing whether we might come out alive, was clearly impossible. At the same time, it was too dangerous for my father to stay, so he left. For two years after that we had no idea where he was or whether he was alive or dead, as we remained in Omsk while the Bolsheviks occupied it.

To support us, my mother became a teacher; she had a higher education and was able to teach history in classes that lasted all day and all evening. In 1922 she was arrested on suspicion of being one of the organizers of an SR plot to stage an uprising. After three years in prison, she was shot by the Bolsheviks.

We six children were therefore left in the care of my mother's old nanny and of the maid, Manya, a peasant girl of twenty-five who had been a pupil in my mother's school. It was Manya who took our mother's place in most respects. She spent all her money on us. In Omsk we had practically nothing . . . Manya used to grow vegetables: from the cabbages she made sauerkraut for the winter; we gathered mushrooms which she dried; she grew potatoes and carrots and stored them in the cellar – but food was still very short. We kept our own cow, and Manya knew how to milk. We had no meat and very little bread. Once my father sent us a supply of buckwheat, so we ate *kasha* all winter long. My youngest sister had rickets, and there was only enough bread for one person. We had absolutely no heating; in the Siberian winters, when the temperature was permanently at −40°C, we lived in a log cabin that was very poorly caulked up: the wallpaper would flap in the wind. As well as rickets, my youngest sister had lung trouble and we all caught measles and mumps. Manya was wonderful: she did everything for us children – and in a sense she still does. She is alive and well, and lives in Providence, Rhode Island. She has been mother and grandmother to us. She had only a minimal education, but she read a lot. It was she who kept us all together. At one point she wanted to send us to various relatives in Petersburg, but just then we learned that my father was alive and living in Japan.

At that time General Horvath was in Peking; he was married to a Benois, daughter of the famous artist, who was somehow related to us. A very attractive and interesting woman, she got to know the American Ambassador in Peking, a Mr Crane, who had at one time represented the Crane Company, a manufacturer of plumbing equipment. He was a millionaire, a patron of the arts, and was fascinated by Russia – he had been to Russia twenty-six times before the Revolution. He was recalled to America when Woodrow Wilson's administration took over, but had decided to return to Russia via the Pacific to China and thence by rail; this was in 1922. Madame Horvath-Benois had discovered that we were in Omsk and telegraphed my father in Japan. Father hastened to Peking, begged Mr Crane to find us (writing letters to Soviet Siberia was hopeless) and gave him a package of food and clothes for us, which Mr Crane promised to deliver. After an adventurous journey he reached Omsk and found us. We spoke no English, but we both had a little French and managed to converse while Manya found someone who could speak English. Mr Crane handed over our package, took some photographs of us and left; later, on reaching Europe, he sent my father a letter and the photographs.

Father then had to devise a way of getting us out. At that time, émigrés were allowed to bring their families out of Russia to join them. Eventually he found a man who was prepared to escort us, but it took ages and he couldn't decide where to send us. At one time he decided on Latvia, which was now independent, on the strength of having once worked in Libau [Liepāja], but he himself had no right of residence in Latvia. In the end he decided to send us to Harbin. He had just lost his job in Japan, so he went to Harbin and found an engineering job on the Chinese Eastern Railway. Finally he managed to get permission for us to leave. The journey from Omsk to Harbin, normally a matter of a few days, took us three weeks.

Nanny and Manya also joined us in Harbin. We continued our education in Russian schools there; Father wanted us to remain 'Russian' and, like most other émigrés at the time, he thought we would all be going back to Russia before long. Harbin was an extremely interesting centre of Russian emigration; we spent nine years there. There was a railway school called the *Kommercheskoe uchilishche*; also a boys' and a girls' *gymnazia*, each with a superb syllabus and organized entirely on pre-Revolutionary Russian lines [and maintaining pre-Revolutionary standards]; there was even a school chapel with priests who taught us scripture and the catechism. In other words, it was a typical Russian *gymnazia*, where we still had to curtsey to the headmistress. There was also a *real'noe uchilishche*, where modern languages were taught instead of the classics, although in the *gymnazia* we also learned English, French and German.

The city of Harbin was built by the Russian Government to house the technical workshops and the administration of the Chinese Eastern Railway. The railway looped around the Amur river to Vladivostok. It would have been shorter and easier to send the track in a straight line to Vladivostok, but the route was chosen for purely strategic reasons: Harbin was the central point, or pivot, from which a southern branch was built to Port Arthur, the port that Russia had fortified at the turn of the century for fear of an attack by the Japanese.

Manchuria was almost depopulated then, because the Manchu dynasty prohibited the Chinese from settling in Manchuria, while all Manchurians of military age were conscripted into the Army because they were loyal to the dynasty, and their families usually went with them.

When the Chinese Eastern Railway was built, Russia acquired a ninety-nine-year lease on the territory of the railway. This was merely a strip of land along both sides of the track, with larger areas around Harbin and at the various stations and depots; this extra-territorial strip ran all the way across Manchuria to Port Arthur. After the Russo-Japanese War, when Port Arthur was ceded to Japan, half of the railway line, from Port Arthur to Changchung, also went to Japan. A fairly short southward stretch from Harbin remained in Russian hands. Harbin was therefore a city suspended in a kind of territorial vacuum, with a Chinese town alongside it to house the unskilled workforce, small traders, and so on. Everything in Harbin itself – the houses, the cathedral, the city offices, the railway workshops, the railway headquarters – was built by the Russians. The main street intersected with all the others at right angles and ended at the station. As an inducement to work there, the railway employees were given all sorts of privileges: free housing; free education for their children at excellent schools; a railwaymen's club that contained a theatre, a cinema, an opera house and a concert hall. There was a superb Polytechnic to train engineers for the railway. In other words, it was what you would call a 'company town' – and what a town! I loved the place.

When the 1917 Revolution occurred, and before the Chinese Government recognized the Soviet Union, they closed the frontier, but they left the Russian population to its own devices and allowed the Russians to operate the railway as before, since by this time the railway had begun to take on a commercial importance. [This was because] after the Revolution of 1912, which overthrew the Manchu dynasty, the Chinese began to settle along the railway – in fact, the greater part of the population of Manchuria gravitated to the areas around the railway. They began to grow soya beans as a cash crop, which became a major source of income for the province. What had been a purely strategic railway soon became entirely commercial and a valuable element in the economy.

There was a Russian garrison which at one time had defended the whole length of the railway. The commander of this garrison – and head of the railway until 1917 – was the same General Horvath who was then sent to Peking (the one who was married to my father's Benois cousin). After 1917, the soldiers formed an unofficial defence force, because there were many bandits in the surrounding hills. The Russians in Harbin continued to live in the same houses, maintained the railway and kept it going but with a partly Chinese workforce. It was used to export food and other products to China proper, to Korea and Japan – in fact, all over the world.

A few trains were given special permission to go through the closed [Soviet–Manchurian] frontier. That is how we got there, and large numbers of Russians emigrated by that route. Harbin became a large and important *Russian* city; the population grew very quickly and many new buildings were built. A lot of businessmen settled there, and opened up trade links with China and Japan. There were several banks and many rich people. It was more like an old colonial settlement that stayed on after the Empire had fallen. Chinese came and worked on the railway, too, but they had to learn Russian. There was a special two-year course for the Chinese to learn Russian, where they also learned other subjects that would enable them to enter the Polytechnic. The Polytechnic, in fact, had only two faculties: Electro-Mechanical and Railway Construction. One course that was obligatory for all students was to be trained for a licence to drive steam locomotives, for which you had to log a certain amount of mileage, starting as a stoker and working your way up to driver.

Although the town was very closely connected with the railway, it became increasingly important as a general commercial centre. It was also a considerable centre of Russian culture: there was a very good symphony orchestra, an excellent opera, three Russian daily papers, several magazines and a constant succession of visiting lecturers, performers, soloists and so on. It was so active largely because it was totally isolated and cut off from Russia; there was only China to the south and Japan to the east. It made you realize how very *European* Russian culture was; Harbin seemed like an island of civilization.

My father never wanted us to lead a ghetto existence. If ever we went to live abroad, then we should become French, German, American or whatever; we ought never to let ourselves become 'eternal Russian émigrés' in some other country.

[I lived in Harbin until I was a student in my early twenties, when the same Mr Crane who had helped us get out of Russia paid for my brother and me to go to America to finish our education. Our father died in Russia while we were there. When we had got our degrees and found jobs we became sponsors for our sisters and brought them to America too.] They all got scholarships and went to university; they all married Americans, and their children speak only English, so with the second generation our family had become completely assimilated. Such was my father's intention, and we carried it out for him.

27

The Town on the Sungari

VIKTOR PETROV

Viktor Petrov's book on Harbin, The Town on the Sungari, *was published by the Russo-American Historical Society (Washington, DC, 1984).*

Throughout 1918 and 1919, as the Civil War spread across Siberia and the Far East, Harbin, free from Soviet power, became host to troops and refugees of all nations.

Who did Harbiners not see in those days? . . . There were the endless trains of the Japanese, the colourful Americans, with their 'boy-scout' hats. Then came the British and the Italians; the celebrated French Foreign Legion passed through, and even the Chinese. Somehow or other, on their way westwards, the recently formed Polish Legion arrived, the soldiers wearing their distinctive four-cornered *konfederatki*, and always the endless waves of Czechs poured in, first to the west, and then back to the east.

At the end of 1919 came the collapse of the White movement in Siberia. As a result of the catastrophe in Siberia the demoralized remains of the White Army and thousands of foreign refugees flooded into Manchuria. Harbin was bursting at the seams. The refugees could find no help anywhere. The local Soviet appealed to the old inhabitants, to the better part of the population, for help, requesting the allocation of one room in each house for the newcomers.

It should be said that at first this influx of refugees was difficult to deal with, but somehow or other everything was gradually resolved and everyone found accommodation. It is a paradox that the terrible catastrophe in Siberia and the ejection of tens of thousands of refugees to the east was of great benefit to Harbin. The town suddenly came to life and grew; its Russian population increased by two hundred thousand. This new population, in the majority of cases drawn from the Government and intelligentsia, raised the cultural level of this Russian town on Chinese soil to an unusual height.

Professors of large Russian universities, important lawyers, journalists and students refused readmission to their faculties were rescued from Red territory and poured into Harbin . . . Merchants, small traders and artisans, they all swelled the ranks of the town's Russian contingent and gradually transformed its peaceful provincial atmosphere. Many religious figures also arrived, including several members of the higher clergy.

The town came to life at once. Little by little the new immigrants began to settle down. They spread outside the town proper and busied themselves constructing new *dacha*-like houses – what were called 'brick and lining' dwellings. The bricks were made from clay-like, partly fired material, and the lining – insulation – was sawdust poured between two walls of thin boards hurriedly knocked together. Such houses could be built quickly and cheaply, but they were terribly cold in the winter.

In houses like these the refugee mass spread out, mostly around the town. Soon these suburban dwellers surrounded Harbin on all sides. Former Harbiners, now scattered all over the world, will remember their names: Modiago, Gondatev'ka, the Brick District, Chinkhe, the Hospital District, Block District – and even the Cheeky Woman. They used to chuckle over the 'Cheeky Woman' – quietly and in a good-natured way: 'There's nothing here at all, no running water, no bridges, no pavements . . .'

This unique Russian refugee town grew to an extraordinary extent, and in a very short space of time. Simultaneously, the administration of the region passed into the hands of the Chinese. The chief disadvantage as far as the Russians were concerned was the loss of extra-territorial rights: Russians were now directly under the Chinese administration and subject to Chinese law.

The Chinese, suddenly inheriting the administration of the Russian 'foreign zone', did not make a very confident display of their powers. At first they limited themselves to changing the traffic regulations; all vehicles now had to drive on the left instead of the right. To enforce this new regulation they placed signs in ungrammatical Russian on each street corner: 'Everything is to be going by the left-hand side'.

In essence, there were no really fundamental changes. Even the names of the streets stayed the same, written in Russian. All the big changes came later on, by degrees. In the course of time the Russian city Soviet withered away and the town administration became Chinese. The Chinese also took control of the telegraph and assumed responsibility for the Chinese and Far Eastern Railway Company's shipping interests.

What was particularly striking was the way the town's cultural life changed. With uncharacteristic energy the Russian expatriates set about opening new schools to meet the needs of the newly arrived population. They began, as an act of benevolence, to build places of worship for the new immigrants. But the main reason for this flowering of cultural activity was the sense of sudden and complete liberation, the complete absence of Red terror.

Harbin became, to all intents and purposes, a really free Russian town; a place where life continued as previously, in the old Russian way, a place of calm and contentment. As in old Russia, the deep solemn tones of the cathedral bell called the congregation to early morning service, and in the evening people crossed themselves as once more its measured tolling summoned them to Mass. And Easter, when the cathedral bells rang out disordered peals all day, was a time of legitimate delight for the boys – the one day in the year when they could climb into the bell-tower and ring the bells to their hearts' delight.

Russian émigrés in the West had nothing similar. There the Russians were, by nature of their emigrant status, also foreigners. They had bigger communities, organizations and churches than the Harbiners, but nevertheless they remained an alien element.

The Russians were masters of Manchuria before the Revolution and thus they remained dominant after the Revolution – no longer by virtue of force, but because of their dominant economic position. The real political masters of Harbin – the Chinese – were in a minority. There were very few in the town. They were, for the most part, small traders, shopkeepers, artisans and, of course, administrators. As a rule the great mass of Chinese lived huddled together in hovels – *fanzas*, or peasant huts – in the Chinese suburb called Fundziadian.

The entire decade of the 1920s was a period of extraordinary cultural blossoming in Harbin. New journals and newspapers were founded in the town. Some of them, it is true, turned out to be ephemeral and quickly disappeared; others continued right up to the very end of the sojourn of the Russian colony in the city. Before the Revolution there were two newspapers: the *Harbin Herald*, edited by P. Tishenko, taken by the chief inhabitants of the town, and *News of Life*, edited by Cherniavsky. The first was the mouthpiece of official Harbin; Cherniavsky's paper was somewhat liberal in tone and reflected the views of the commercial world in particular.

After the collapse of the White movement in Siberia and with the subsequent influx of refugees, many important journalists arrived in the town. They began to publish new journals and newspapers. First of all the old *Harbin Herald* passed into new hands, took on a new slant, and was renamed the *Manchurian Herald*. *News of Life* continued to be published for many years. At that time many completely new papers, run on commercial principles, made their appearance, and thus carved out a popular readership for themselves.

Dawn, owned by Lembich, a city journalist from St Petersburg, became the most successful of the popular newspapers. Lembich began to broaden his publishing activities: by the end of the 1920s he had already founded a new paper, *Our Dawn*, in the town of Tien'tsin, and he quickly established yet another of his publications, *Shanghai Dawn*, in Shanghai. In the fullness of time, when waves of Russians flooded into Shanghai from Harbin, the *Shanghai Dawn* assumed the role of the most important Russian newspaper in the Far East.

Another very popular newspaper in Harbin was *Mouthpiece*, whose publisher and editor was one Kaufman, a journalist from the Amur region. And last of all there was the cheap newssheet, *Penny Paper*, published and edited by another former St Petersburg journalist, Chilikin, a man who strove for cheap effects and loud sensationalism. Several other newspapers were founded, flourished for a short while, and then closed down. The journals found themselves in the same position. Of the several journals founded in the first years of the emigration only one lasted: *The Border*, owned by Kaufman.

In those first years, Harbin experienced an exceptional blossoming in the world of theatre. This was because a considerable part of the artistic talent of Russia came to the region. Dramatic theatre made its appearance, along with opera and musical comedy. Because there was no proper theatre in the town arrangements were made for performances to be staged, first on the fine stage in the Railway Assembly Rooms in New Town and later in the Commercial Building in The Wharf. Operatic performances were staged regularly throughout the winter season. The most memorable were those given by artists famous all over Russia, Mozzhukhin and Lipovsky. Their appearances, of course, were quite rare, for they soon left Harbin. Sometime later on devotees of opera were delighted by the arrival of a new talent, Lemshev. The opera season usually opened with a performance of *Aida*. After that came other, no less popular operas: *Tosca*, *Madame Butterfly* ('Cho-Cho-San') and of course *Carmen*. Of the Russian operas, I recall that they regularly staged *Eugene Onegin* and *The Queen of Spades*. Rarely – not every season – they put on *Prince Igor* and *Sadko*. This list, of course, is far from complete.

Harbin's musical comedies always resulted in a full house. Devotees were entertained by performances of the unfailingly popular *Bayaderki*, amongst others. On the streets the boys whistled or hummed arias from *Sylvia* in harmony. Concerts given by the symphony orchestra in the Railway Assembly Rooms were also highly popular.

All this undoubtedly refined the musical sensibilities of Harbin's population, and so a demand arose for the instruction of those youngsters hoping for a career in music. This in turn led to the foundation of Harbin's first Higher Musical School – the founders of the school were chary of naming a school on someone else's territory a 'conservatory', and so decided on the more modest appellation 'Higher Musical School'. If my memory is correct, this school trained the young Yul Brynner, subsequently the famous Hollywood film star.

The most illustrious names in Harbin's musical world were the pianists O. A. Kolchina and Aptekareva. Later on Kolchina moved to Shanghai, where she took a part in directing Shanghai's musical comedies. Before the Second World War, along with her husband I. A. Kolchin, she moved to San Francisco.

It would be wrong to omit mention of one highly popular entertainment in Harbin – Iazko's circus. It had a permanent home, not a tarpaulin tent. The circus was open to the public every evening. There were the usual circus attractions – performers with 'world-famous' names. There were horse riders, clowns, ballerinas, athletes, acrobats, trapeze artists . . . During the finale, wrestlers with names like 'Black Mask', 'Red Mask', and so on, paraded round the ring . . . loud voices could be heard shouting 'Parade!' And after that, of course, the unforgettable circus smell of sawdust, horse hair and stables, and the cages of the wild animals.

With the influx of a cultured population Harbin became a university town. Professors arrived, refugees from Russia, and this made it possible to found institutes of higher education. Because Russia was now under the domination of the Bolsheviks, all contact was broken and all communications severed, so Harbin's youngsters had nowhere to go to complete their education after finishing high school, unless they went abroad. But many were unable to go; the average Harbin family did not have the necessary funds. Wages were not very generous, and those who were able to go probably lived very moderately; in all events, few went abroad. These few students, drawn from wealthy families of the commercial world or from the families of the most important employees of the railway, left for a prolonged education in the higher institutions of Czechoslovakia, Belgium or France. In 1921-2 several groups went to the USA from Harbin, but this did not last long, as the Americans passed laws restricting immigration.

It was entirely natural, therefore, to open an institute of higher education in Harbin. There was no shortage of staff, and within a few years it bloomed like the desert after a shower. First of all a Medical School was founded, then a technical institute, which soon grew into a fully fledged Polytechnic. Next came an Institute of Oriental and Commercial Studies, also with a separate Legal Faculty – in essence a fully functioning university. In the Institute of Oriental and Commercial Studies there were two departments: oriental and commercial. The Legal Faculty [usually known as 'Legfac'] had subsections for jurisprudence, business law and Eastern law. Thus two higher educational institutes were opened at once. The Institute was headed by the senior lecturer, Marakulin. Professor Golovochev, a well-known lawyer, gave courses on the general theory of law, state law and jurisprudence. The famous Sinologist Shkmurkin also gave lectures. The Legfac gradually became the largest of all the higher educational institutes and had a whole series of famous and distinguished professors. The director was Professor Riazanovsky. Professors Ustrialov, Gins, Tal'berg, Nikiforov and Chepurkovsky, amongst others, gave courses.

The Medical School closed down within a year or so of its foundation, it seems, and on reflection it could not really be otherwise. It could scarcely survive in a condition of emigration: passing doctors with only theoretical knowledge was a waste of talent, and the school could do little else, having no possibility of securing the necessary medical equipment and thus no way of giving the doctors practical experience and practical training.

Like Legfac and the Institute of Oriental and Commercial Studies, the Polytechnic flourished. Of all these institutes only the Polytechnic had its own buildings; it was situated in what was formerly the Russian Consulate General. In Legfac lectures were read in the evening in the buildings of the Commercial School. The Institute of Oriental and Commercial Studies gave classes initially in the buildings of Oksakovsky's Academy, and later in another place.

Despite many difficulties – not least inappropriate accommodation and lack of equipment – all three schools gave their students a fine higher education. Graduates of the Polytechnic – mechanical and civil engineers – were recognized as competently trained and obtained responsible positions when they left for other centres of the Russian diaspora. And the same is true of the other two institutes. Later on some of them gained higher qualifications abroad and became professors in the faculties of foreign universities.

Harbin's young students set the tone of the town's life with their youthful exuberance, enthusiasm, sincere good humour and corporate spirit. They attended lectures, studied assiduously, gave seminars and took their yearly examinations, but on the other hand they never forgot the demands of youth. Student pranks, parties and escapades livened up the life of the town. The traditional Thief's Day of 12/25 January – once the holiday of Moscow University and of all Russian students in general – became an annual occurence in Harbin. Students enjoyed ceremonies, attended sparkling student balls, and celebrated the first fall of the winter snows by walking the town's streets . . . and throwing parties. They celebrated all night, and the whole town celebrated with them. From every part of Harbin one could hear the strains of the unforgettable student anthem, 'Gaudeamus Igitur'.

The influx of immigrants resulted in the opening of additional schools, mainly of the secondary type. The previously existing Commercial Institute – the General Horvath High School – and the various private academies for boys and girls, proved to be insufficient. New ones were therefore founded, at first non-classical secondary schools, then other high schools, including the Ukrainian High School. Rofast's private academy became known as Drizul's Academy.

The religious life of Harbin flourished. The town's pre-Revolutionary contingent of clergy was headed by the Manchurian rural dean and cathedral superior, Archpriest Leonty Pekrasky. Officiating with him in the St Nikolayev Cathedral were the priests Konstantin Tsivilev and Mikhail Tregubov, along with the deacon, Porfiry Petrov. Down in The

Wharf, at the Iversky Church, the priest Braduchan and deacon Surmeli officiated, and the priest Chistiakov could be found in the Church of St Sofia. The beautiful cathedral in the centre of New Town, constructed in the old Volga style, developed out of St Sofia's. St Sofia's was in the town's commercial sector, and the Iversky Church had once been the barracks for the border guards. There was still another church in old Harbin, this one run by a priest named Savateyev.

The ranks of Harbin's established clergy were reinforced by a massive influx of new clergy and associated officials, many of whom had previously received theological training. In former days Harbin did not have its own higher clergy, but was subsumed in the see of the Archbishop of Primorsk and Kamchatka, Eusebius. Now it was the residence of three hierarchs of the Church, headed by Archbishop Methodius, formerly the Archbishop of Orenburg and Turgay. Apart from Methodius, Archbishop Melety and the Suffragan Bishop of Kamchatka, Nestor, came to the town. The young Bishop Nestor quickly became known for his energy and philanthropic endeavours; he founded a House of Mercy in Harbin for orphans.

Because of the presence of so many church dignitaries, the émigré synod of the Orthodox Church permitted the formation of a separate metropolitanate in Manchuria headed by Archbishop Methodius, who became Metropolitan of Harbin and Manchuria. At the same time the highest Church authorities elevated the status of the Russian Spiritual Mission to Peking by promoting its head, Innocent, from Archbishop to Metropolitan of Peking and China.

Many brilliant theologians resided in Harbin during these years. Amongst those to be remembered are the energetic Archpriest Rozhdestvensky, superior of the church in Modiago, and, of course, Archpriest Pekrasky, since 1906 Superior of the St Nikolayev Cathedral. A popular missionary, the silver-tongued Archpriest Demidov, soon to depart for America, was very well known. His post of diocesan missionary passed to a cathedral official, Archpriest Ponomarev, who, incidentally, was a graduate of the Legal Faculty in Harbin. The current head of the Orthodox Church Synod in Emigration, Metropolitan Filaret, also received a higher education in Harbin; he is a graduate of the Polytechnic. Another Harbiner, a classmate of the present writer in secondary school, Vasia L'vov, is now Bishop Nathaniel in Western Europe. There were also other famous clergymen – Storozhev, Viktorov, and a whole host of others.

Many new churches were built in the suburbs, including one on the far shore of the River Sungari, in Zaton. A monastery was also established in New Modiago.

Besides the Orthodox churches, there was also a large Catholic church in the High Street. There was a Lutheran chapel a little further on, and a synagogue in The Wharf. The Old Believers also had their own church, and in addition there was a whole series of prayer houses belonging to various sects: Methodists, Baptists, Molokans and others.

The enterprising Russian immigrants not only managed to open a mass of small concerns in Harbin – snack bars, confectionary shops, cafés, restaurants, pawn shops and various others – but also large industrial undertakings. Dairies and tobacco factories opened up first. I recollect the largest of them: Borodin's Creamery, Gerasim's Vodka Factory, the rolling mill belonging to Buzanov, Lopato's tobacco factory and a whole series of others. According to foreign observers, the first flour mill in China was built by Russians from Manchuria. Much later on, profiting from the Russians' experience, the Chinese began to construct similar plants and factories in other districts of China. That miracle of Russian engineering – the delicate, lattice-work railway bridge spanning the River Sungari at Harbin – attracted the attention of the Italian civil engineers in the south of China: [they] came to Harbin to learn the art of bridge-building from Russian engineers.

As one would expect, Harbin's return to normality made it possible for people to take up all kinds of sports. Track events and horse races in the Modiago Hippodrome were very popular. Many successful merchants kept their own stables. Sometimes they took part in the so-called 'gentleman's race', when the owners themselves competed against one another in sulkies.

There was a stadium in The Wharf where it was possible to hold the entire range of athletic events. Bicycle races were especially popular. In Washington today there lives a G. Titov, in former times one of the Harbin 'stars' of cycle sport.

It is impossible, of course, to neglect a mention of the water sports held along the banks of the yellow-watered River Sungari. Members of the Harbin Yacht Club took part in various competitions – swimming, sailing and rowing races. In summer the river simply swarmed with rowing boats. Youngsters out to earn extra money, especially students on vacation, ferried the public across the river, mostly to Solnechny

Island – a popular destination for a Sunday outing. The cost of the ferry was insignificant – 5 kopecks per person – but it was no easy matter to row across the fast-flowing river. In winter people indulged in tumbling and tobogganing from the banks of the high shores down to the frozen river below. And there, in the Sungari, on the holiday of Epiphany – the time of baptism – several bold spirits plunged through holes cut through the ice into the frozen waters below, ignoring the biting frost.

There was an abundance of restaurants, cafés and simple snack bars in the town, especially in The Wharf. Rogozinsky's wine cellars – in both New Town and The Wharf – were popular with the young students. The wine was produced locally, a red Manchurian made from local wild vines which grew prolifically in the taiga and on the slopes of the volcanoes of eastern Manchuria. 'Filipov' pies, made in the café in The Wharf by a family famous throughout all Russia for their pies, were renowned in Harbin; they were sold everywhere.

The travelling public, especially foreigners, stayed in first-class hotels: the Moderne in The Wharf, the Orient on New Trade Street, or the Grand Hotel by the station.

Literary activity in the town was focused on circles of poets and writers, on Harbin's 'Churaevka'. Members of these groups were young writers just starting out on their careers, especially poets. For many years the well-known writer N. A. Baikov lived in Harbin. The literary world was powerfully strengthened by the arrival of Gusev-Orenburgsky and Petrov-Skitalets from the Far Eastern Republic in 1921. Neither writer, however, stayed for long in Harbin. Gusev-Orenburgsky soon found it possible to leave for Japan, and from there he went to New York. Petrov-Skitalets threw his weight around for a time in Harbin, and then began to be oppressed by 'the call of the Motherland'; unbeknown to anyone, saying not one word he left for the Soviet Union in 1934. The most famous of the Harbin poets were Arseny Nesmelov and Aleksey Achair. Their lines were regularly published in national newspapers and journals. The young learned from them. I will always keep in my memory Achair's heartfelt words:

> Because our Motherland drove us away,
> We carry her light within us . . .

It is impossible to write everything about the blessed, serene and peaceful life of the Harbiners in one brief account. One could go on to describe how, just as in former times in Russia, but in fact many years after the disappearance of normal life in the Motherland, a Harbin girl, 'a high-school girl in white aprons' with a bouquet of blue violets or soft white lilies, would meet some slim, well-proportioned schoolboy by Churin's store in New Town, or on the Chinese Street in The Wharf, and walk for hours with him, perhaps hand in hand for the first time, shyly . . . And how, somewhere or other in the suburbs, perhaps in Modiago, in the evening, when we were made drowsy by the heavy aroma of flowers, we might hear the enchanting sound of a piano drifting from the open window of a modest 'clapboard' house.

And it is just as impossible to forget the journey along the line to one of the small railway stations to the west, perhaps the fabulous spa of Chzhalantun', the place about which they sometimes sang softly: 'O Chzhalantun', such wonderful views, O Chzhalantun', such beauty!' Or a visit to hilly Barim, with its ice-cold, crystal-clear streams, its abundant trout, and then – the unforgettable vista of hills and spurs, and of the gigantic, majestic Great Khingan.

In the twinkling of an eye I can find myself carried along the eastern line of the railway, with its tiny stations, clean and tidy: Ertsendiandzy, Siaolin, Maoershan', the tracks winding through the districts full of summerhouses, where Chinese children came running towards each approaching train to sell scarlet wild raspberries, ripe and overflowing in green wicker baskets. In my mind's eye I can walk along neverending meadows, full of orange-coloured wild lilies – *saranok* – into low, cool places leading into a field of fairytale blue irises. For all this, and about much more besides in Manchuria, it would be necessary to write a whole book. And it is the same for the region's unique wildlife – its gigantic wild boars, handsome wild goats and regal tigers. And the Manchurian hunt, summer and winter, and, of course, the spring and autumn migrations of ducks and geese, and the exhilarating autumn hunting of the multi-hued pheasant.

Until now I have said almost nothing about the chief source of income for the Russians in Manchuria – the Chinese and Far Eastern Railway, or KVZhD. Strange as it may seem, the cardinal change in the history of the line, the introduction of dual administration, dual ownership of the line by the Chinese and Soviet Governments in 1924, had very little effect on the lives of the Russian community in general, or on the émigrés in particular. The émigrés found work with private firms, or even opened their own personal trading concerns or small workshops. A vast number of shops, tailors, restaurants – or rather, moderately priced dining rooms – started up. The young began work as taxi-drivers or bus-drivers. None of these people, of course, worked directly for the railway, but they did depend on it indirectly; they were dependent on the privileged position of those who managed the line, those employees who received a good salary.

But nevertheless a fundamental change in the fortunes of the railway did come about in the autumn of 1924. The Soviet Government signed an agreement with the Chinese administration of the region – modelled on the previous Tsarist treaty – concerning the transfer of the line's management into the hands of both States on, at first, a basis of parity. As a result the executive (the former controlling organ of the railway) and the management (the technical administration) were subject to orders from the personnel of both Governments. The chairman of the executive remained Chinese, but his assistant was a Soviet citizen. Similarly the director of the technical administration was Soviet, and his assistant Chinese.

The problem of parity amongst all the other employees proved to be a more difficult matter. All Russian employees were invited to take Soviet citizenship, or to lose their jobs. There was no great wish to change, but many did keep their places by accepting Soviet citizenship. The numbers leaving the railway, however, turned out to be small: the Chinese did not have a sufficiently large contingent of experienced railway employees, and so those Russians who did not wish to take a Soviet passport and were thus liable to dismissal, proffered letters of recommendation to the authorities asking for Chinese citizenship. And once having received Chinese citizenship, they remained where they were as Chinese employees.

The upshot of all this was that the workforce was virtually unchanged, aside from the fact that half the employees worked for the Soviet part of the railway, the other half for the Chinese. Nor was there any change in the way in which they related to one another. The contacts between employees remained correct and formal.

This is an appropriate point to note that the first director of the railway, General Horvath, resigned from his post in 1920. At the insistence of the trade union for technical control, Engineer Ostroumov was appointed in his place, a man who at once set about establishing discipline and order on the line. The trains began to run properly and according to the timetable. If they were even a little late he flew into a rage with the workers, stationmasters and controllers! Ostroumov introduced a new 'American' style of work to the line. He administered his fief not in the free and easy way of General Horvath, but with severity and an iron fist. Every employee was made to answer for every little mistake, and not infrequently sacked.

Ostroumov found his way into all corners of the railway's administration, poked his nose into everything, searched out and criticized inefficiency – a whirlwind flying along the track in his own special carriage, almost always concentrating on the goods trains . . . He bawled out the stationmasters, the station staff and the signalmen, he ran round the employees' backyards and sheds, and made a fuss if they were like pigsties. Immediately and everywhere along the line everything became cleaner. Not only were the station platforms sprinkled with fine sand, but the employees' houses were also brought up to the mark. Ostroumov was a terror . . . he fired people without batting an eyelid, but the trains began to run properly and to time – and not only the passenger trains, but the freight trains as well.

On all the stations the platforms were beautified with flowerbeds, and in front of the Harbin station, where previously there was merely a huge, ugly square paved with cobblestones, he ordered the construction of a small public garden with flowerbeds. The station improved at once.

Ostroumov did not remain at his post for long. He was removed as a result of the Sino-Soviet agreement of 1924 and replaced by a Soviet director. The newly arrived Soviet administrators tried to introduce their own Soviet ways of doing things on the line, but, for the most part, and due to the opposition of the Chinese, things did not work out their way. Many former Harbiners will well remember a characteristic occasion which provoked conflict on the line. The Soviets decided to remove the highly revered icon of St Nicholas the Thaumaturge from the hall, where it stood in a corner in a beautiful icon-case. The Chinese protested. They declared that St Nicholas was their 'grand old man', and insisted that the icon should remain in the station. And so it came to pass that the icon remained in the waiting room until the very end of the Russian émigré presence in Harbin. One could see people coming to touch the icon, old Chinese peasants who came into the station, purchased candles and lit them before the icon of the 'grand old man'.

*

The Russians, of course, did not live just in Harbin, but also around the stations along the line and in settlements in the foreign zone . . . many were thriving, not only employees of the railway but also those with their own businesses. Large entrepreneurs could be found down the line. To the east were the large and well-known Mulinsk coal mines. Also in the east was the big forestry concession of the famous lumber company of Skindel' and Koval'. Closer to Harbin, in the little village of Ashikh, there was a large sugar factory, and at the Shitokufetsy station vast plantations, famous for their strawberries.

To the west the very largest enterprises were at the Manchuria and Khailar stations. Here the famous names Ganin, Sapelkin, and many others could be found. In these boundless steppes they skinned animals for their meat and furs, and not far from the Manchuria station, on the large Lake of Dalai-Nor, were a whole series of Russian fisheries. Looking at a map of Lake Dalai-Nor in those days, you would see a vast number of Russian-named settlements, especially on the western shores – settlements with names like Kataev, Zlobin, Sapelkin, Borisov, Tamashin, Gorbunov and Gantimurov. On the eastern shore and along the River Arshun-gol, one would discover settlements given over to fishing and preserving fish: Borisov, Shil'nikov, Mikheev.

One should not, of course, forget to note the existence of an entire district of Cossacks from the Lake Baikal region who fled to Manchuria from the Bolsheviks. They settled on a large plain, not far from the Russian border, and established farmsteads and settlements similar in style to the Cossack villages – *stanitsy* – of the Baikal region. This district, far from the railway line, was called Trekhrech'. It was possible to reach Trekhrech' from Khailar along rural byways, but only with difficulty. The Trekhrech' folk quickly built big settlements . . . constructed churches, schools . . . They lived by the old Russian traditions. Their old rural ways flourished in the forest steppe, in low-lying places, in the basins of the Rivers Gan, Derbul and Khaul, where the soil is of a very rich black-earth type. The names of their villages were for the most part Russian: Dragotsenka, Pokrovka, Odinoky, Chernous, St Kliuch, Shuch'e, Ust'-Kuli and so on.

For a further eight years, following the changes in 1924, Harbin continued to live a free-and-easy life. At first, there was no open hostility between the two camps, White and Red. The shops traded, people enjoyed themselves, celebrated their name-days, went to their *dachas* in summer – one could say they simply continued to live a normal, pleasant Russian life. They celebrated the traditional church festivals in the old way. Inexperienced youngsters, after indispensable and innumerable preparatory visits, got blind drunk in the bars and woke up with an aching head the following day.

A radical change in Harbin's life occurred in 1932 – that is, in the thirty-fifth year of the town's existence. Japanese troops occupied northern Manchuria, and, under various pretexts and guises – chiefly the excuse that the soldiers were guaranteeing the independent state of Manchukuo – the region fell under the sway of Japanese militarists. Domination by the Japanese lasted for the next thirteen years. Life became intolerable. The Russians began to desert this familiar haunt in droves, leaving for the south, mainly for Shanghai, under the protection of the foreign concessions.

When Harbin's rights to the railway were sold in 1935, the town was abandoned by a second wave of Russians. This was the mass evacuation of the line's Soviet employees 'to the Motherland', a place which many of them, born in Harbin, had never seen in their lives. Some former Soviet officials, discovering that their passports had expired, formally renounced their Soviet nationality and took on the status of emigrants.

Harbin lost the greater part of its Russian population in these two exoduses. But there remained in the town a third group of people – people who had no wish to go to Russia and decided not to leave for Shanghai. For various reasons they decided to stay on in Harbin, firm in the optimistic belief that, as always, everything would go back to normal and nothing untoward would affect them. These people went through the entire period of the terrible Japanese occupation, and in 1945 suffered a still more dreadful fate. In August 1945 the 'liberating' Soviet troops forced their way into Manchuria. In numberless streams, in endless trains, the Russian population of Harbin was evacuated to Soviet labour camps. All the adult male population was taken . . . Just as the terrible destroying hordes of Genghis Khan and Tamurlane had swept across this border, so the villagers living all along the line, including the folk from Trekhrech', disappeared into Russia.

Nevertheless there were still three thousand – chiefly women and children – untouched by the hand of Soviet Nemesis, who continued to live on somehow. The young studied and even received a higher education from the Polytechnic, which was still functioning. But gradually the remaining youngsters grew up, matured, and yearned to leave for some other place. Few wished to go to the Soviet Union. They wanted to go abroad, especially to Australia. Russian Harbin had come to an end.

With the exodus of Russians to Shanghai (the numbers there increased to forty thousand), cultural activity in Harbin ceased. Shanghai – 'the Yellow Babylon' – became, just like Harbin previously, and thanks to the many thousands of new immigrants, the Russian cultural centre in the Far East.

Of Russian Harbin virtually nothing now remains. Of the previous population of two hundred thousand there were no more than forty people [by 1982]. Harbiners, and Far Easterners in general, are now scattered across the whole world, with sad and nostalgic memories of their life in Harbin and the days of their youth.

28

Disaster in Harbin

IVAN ALEXANDROVICH YUKHOTSKY

Yukhotsky's memoirs of arrest and imprisonment in Tsarist Russia appear in Chapter 9. In 1921–2 he was living in Blagoveshchensk and teaching sciences at the Polytechnic there; but conditions were harsh.

From spring of 1922 they began giving out passports quite freely to go abroad to China. If you brought 3 roubles 50 kopecks to the Ispolkom [Executive Committee] (the large roubles made of silver[1]) you received a passport three days later. The Government took the attitude: 'If you want to live with the bourgeois, off with you and good riddance!' This went on till the autumn of 1922. The song was going round at the time: 'Oh, little apple where are you rolling to? You will end up in Harbin, never to return!'

Misha and Valya [my son and daughter] and Olga Alexandrovna Serebryanikova [my sister] took advantage of the opportunity to get a passport to China and left in March 1922. [My wife and I] decided to wait and see if they got settled, and then join them in Harbin. Life in Blagoveshchensk was getting worse and worse all the time, but rumours about Harbin were not too good: to settle there and get yourself a job on the Chinese Eastern Railway was difficult – you had to pay 200,000 roubles. Harbin was overflowing with refugees and there were more than six hundred people out of work, or so the rumours went.

But life in Blagoveshchensk was not wonderful. We had sold everything of even the slightest value. My wife, Elizaveta Moiseyevna, took care of this side of things. I used to carry a small light table I had knocked together for her out into the bazaar; she would spread out her 'wares' on it and wait for a customer, usually a peasant from the Zazeisk villages. In the end everything was sold off, and only the clothes on our backs were left. Then Elizaveta Moiseyevna, who had a pass to

Sakhalin, began getting cotton thread from there and she made ladies'
knitted jackets on her machine. This business went very well . . . Each
jacket was sold for 5 roubles in gold and 4 roubles were pure profit,
When I was there this was only beginning, but Elizaveta Moiseyevna
really got down to it after I left for Harbin.

Somehow Misha got himself fixed up very quickly in Harbin. He
went to the *Harbin News* as a proofreader and earned 100 roubles a
month. In Blagoveshchensk he had been both secretary and proofreader
[on a newspaper], so he already knew the job and loved it. Olga
Alexandrovna soon got a job and Valya was their housekeeper and
cook. So now I could travel to Harbin; we decided, however, that my
wife and [younger daughter] Nadya should stay in Blagoveshchensk for
the time being.

At the end of June I got my passport without any fuss and a few
days later left for Harbin. When the steamer sailed along the river past
Blagoveshchensk I remembered Lermontov's poem:

> Farewell unwashed Russia
> Land of slaves, land of lords
> and you, in your blue uniformed coats
> and you who humble yourselves to them.
> Perhaps beyond the Caucasus wall,
> I shall escape from your leaders,
> From their all-seeing eye
> and all-hearing ears.

So I left Russia, with such a feeling of sadness . . . and calm . . .

[There was nothing very remarkable about the journey down the Amur
to the Sungari. After eight or nine days we reached Harbin.]

The flat where our family was living was [in a creek on the left bank
of the Sungari. It was] very small – just one room and a kitchen. When
I arrived there Olga Alexandrovna was working in the laboratory of
the Railway Traction Department Workshops; she was the main breadwinner, earning 200,000 roubles [a year]. Misha continued his work at
the newspaper [while Valya looked after them] . . . We had Sunday
off and friends used to come round and see us at the *dacha* (the creek
was a place where people had *dacha*s); they bathed in the muddy water
of the Sungari and enjoyed themselves. Around September we moved
into the town [and were joined by] Elizaveta Moiseyevna and Nadya.

After our move into town I began looking for employment. I did not dare to count on work with the Chinese Eastern Railway. I was even scared to go into the Head Office, as all over the place were hanging notices saying 'No Vacancies'. I discovered from someone that there was a commission for the development of a water-system project for Harbin on the railway; this happened to be my kind of work. They pointed out the engineer whose job it was to set up the project and I went to see him at the Head Office. He showed me his project and I did not like it; it was obvious that some person had cobbled it together, having no interest at all in this type of work. [Through a friend, I managed to obtain an interview with the chief engineer of the railway, who had great influence with Ostroumov, the head of the railway,[2]] and told him that I had been awarded first prize in the Petersburg Technological Society for my plan for water systems for Stavropol province; he was particularly impressed by this. Then we started talking about the plan for Harbin's water supplies and I gave my opinion about it. He expressed his regret that I had not come to Harbin earlier. All the same he wanted to talk to Ostroumov and see if he could find any way of giving me another project, as an alternative to the project of the Water Systems Commission – and there our talks ended . . .

Someone advised me to go and see the Director of the Polytechnic, A. A. Shchelkov. He received me politely (there were people who slammed the door quite categorically in your face when they discovered you were looking for work) and started asking me where I had graduated from. I told him and he said, 'I know that school – I was Head there after 1905.' He knew my surname from copies of drawings which were hanging on the school walls and as an instigator of revolutionary propaganda in the school. 'I will give you a job in the Polytechnic but just watch that you don't spread any Bolshevik propaganda,' he said. A few days afterwards he fixed me up on a low wage (75 roubles a month) in the workshops of the Institute. Not long after I was transferred into the workshop offices and then suddenly A. A. [as Shchelkov was known] called me into the office and said, 'There is no more work in the workshops, but I am going to appoint you as a lecturer in water supplies with a salary of about 125 to 150 roubles for four hours a week.' I was very pleased . . .

My 'lectureship' lasted all of a month. The students did not like being taught by a non-graduate and registered a protest. The Teachers' Council also protested (in truth there was scarcely one real teacher there; they were all engineers with diplomas) and A. A., somewhat embarrassed and severe [told me that I would have to leave.]

Olga Alexandrovna advised me to apply to Ostroumov's private secretary, Obolsky, saying that he was an accessible and attentive person. I went off to see him, intending to ask for a job on the railway, but there was such a long queue in the waiting room that I had to wait until two o'clock and so had plenty of time for reflection. All around there hung notices saying 'No Vacancies'. When it was my turn, Obolsky wrung his hands and said, 'I still haven't had a bite to eat today. Come back tomorrow.' I sighed with relief. I now realized that the job application I had prepared was hopeless and I had thought of another way out. I would ask Ostroumov to allow me to familiarize myself with the water-supply project, saying that I was the specialist who won first prize in the Petersburg Technological Society for my work on the water systems in Stavropol province; it was quite possible that having acquainted myself with the plan, I would be able to suggest something better. The next day I went up to Obolsky with this proposal. He read through the paper and said, 'Very good, I will pass it on to Ostroumov.' [Ostroumov agreed and I was taken on by the railway as Inspector of Water Supplies.]

In 1929 the Russo-Chinese 'incident' took place, as that war was called between the three eastern provinces of China and Soviet Russia. This war flared up because the Chinese wanted once and for all to take the Chinese Eastern Railway away from the Russians and introduce White emigrant organization, as it used to be before the arrival of the Bolsheviks; the Whites would be the heirs of the Russian pre-Revolutionary regime. There was an inconsistency on the part of the Chinese, for once China recognized the Bolshevik Government as the legal Government of Russia, they then had to recognize too Russia's rights on the Chinese Eastern Railway. It actually did recognize them from October of 1924 to July of 1929; but in 1929 on one night the whole USSR administration was arrested and part of it (chiefly the most senior administration) was put into railway carriages and transported to Russia; some were confined to house arrest and the small fry were shut up in a concentration camp in Sumbei (not far from Harbin). The USSR could not let such a situation continue and tried to smooth over the affair peacefully, but this was not successful. For at least four or five months, however, there was no military action. The Chinese kept up the rumours that Japan would not allow the Soviets to resolve the question by force, but the Japanese ambiguously kept silent. Dzhan-Su-E-Lyan, the son of the ruler of Manchuria who had been murdered by the Japanese, was not very inclined to follow the dictates of the Japanese. In the end the USSR invaded and routed the Chinese within a few days at the western and eastern ends of the railway; Khailar in the west and Mulin in the east were taken by Soviet forces and the Chinese were forced to beg for peace. The conditions imposed by the USSR were extremely lenient – to restore the status quo that existed before the 'conflict'. The conditions were accepted by the Chinese . . . The new (Soviet) regime came into force from 1 January 1930.

On 12 August 1932 the water in the River Sungari rose to a record height of 134.31 metres above sea-level, higher than the average summer level of 130–1 metres, flooding the whole of the lower part of Harbin . . . The Wharf started to flood in the afternoon; there was no loss of life there, but the flood reached Fundziadian [the Chinese town next to The Wharf] at night, tearing down the surrounding flood barriers. It flooded in very quickly and there were hundreds, if not thousands, of deaths there. The flooding lasted a very long time, as the Sungari fell very slowly and water stayed in the streets of the town for about three months. When it left the streets, it remained for a long time in all the cellars, so that the inhabitants had to live not only in damp houses, but in wet ones too. In total about a hundred thousand people were affected: they sheltered in the streets, squares and parks of the New Town, in barracks built by the railway specially for the inhabitants of Fundziadian (about eleven thousand people), in the upper floors of houses whose lower floors had been flooded, on The Wharf and in attics and the roofs of houses . . .

This was not the only unexpected disaster to befall Harbin. As the streets first of all were flooded with sewage water, which poured across, filling up the wells and the water system, so the sanitary situation of the town worsened rapidly. Although the water on the streets was plentiful, it was not suitable for drinking. Water was brought in on boats from the New Town and sold, but not everybody had access to it, so that willy-nilly they also drank the water from the streets, whose purity was very dubious . . .

Apart from the flooding, yet another disaster afflicted the town at the beginning of 1932: the Japanese occupied Harbin by force. The battle took place in Old Harbin, between the main part of the town and Chenkhe. Stray bullets were flying around into the centre of the town – shrapnel fell in the room where the railway employees were sitting, for example. The Japanese poked their noses into everything, even into the affairs of the railway . . . However, their hold on the surroundings of Harbin was not secure and the same went for the railway line. For the whole time that I was working on the railway (I left on 1 February 1934), the Japanese held only the large stations; there they were fully armed and even the trains were armoured, but the line was in the hands of the partisans, who derailed the trains, killed the guards and often the employees, blew up engines and so on. The result was that travelling outwards on the trains became quite dangerous and the old outgoing crews, who hoped to receive a guarantee from the railway, started to leave the service. I tried as far as possible not to travel down the line, [and] as I was the only person working on the water systems, I was successful in this: the management considered that I should not travel out on the line at all. I used to try to travel during the day and, if possible, only short distances. The eastern line was the most dangerous. Here the partisans were right on the border with the USSR and could get arms and explosives to damage the railway; their path up to the border led through dense taiga, where they were on home ground, and the Japanese did not dare to follow them with infantry or aeroplanes.

Before the Japanese occupation there was no kidnapping [in Harbin], but after their arrival this flourished. A gang of 'patriots' was formed, which abducted people, shut them up in a cellar, or simply in a pit in the forest, and then the blackmail began. Usually they abducted those who were quite wealthy. Relatives would receive a letter from the person who had been kidnapped, saying that if by such and such a date there was no ransom (usually in Chinese dollars), then they would cut off an ear or nose from the victim. The relative bargained, because the ransom figure did not correspond to their financial situation, but they gave in and the affair usually ended peacefully, [though] with some mutilation to the victim and real nervous and physical exhaustion.

However, things did not always turn out so well. I remember one rich man who disappeared without any news. At first there were letters about a ransom, but these soon stopped. He was ill and no longer a young man; obviously he could not withstand the regime of the kidnappers, and he died. Tarasenko, the owner of a shop on China Street, was abducted and kept for about a week and a half. He was a fit chap of about thirty-five, but he returned having aged ten years.

The most outrageous incident was the kidnapping of the son of one of Harbin's wealthiest merchants, Kaspe. One night, returning home with a young lady friend, he was dragged into a car and abducted. Kaspe was faced with a demand for several hundred thousand roubles. Outraged, he thought he could come to some agreement to pay less, but the robbers would not reduce it very much. Kaspe was a French subject; the consular authorities stepped in and detectives were hired, but in the end his son was murdered in the taiga, several dozen versts from Harbin. They found his mutilated body. The robbers had scattered, but several people were arrested and gave the ringleaders away. It transpired that the head of the gang was in the police – although the police were Chinese, they were heavily influenced by the Japanese. At first they wanted to hush up the whole affair, but when a loud outcry against kidnapping began, especially in the foreign press, echoes reached the Japanese and a trial was held, resulting in the court sentencing several men to death. The kidnappers announced loudly that the court had acted under the influence of Jews and Communists, and said that the murders had been carried out for patriotic reasons, in order to get money for the struggle against Communism; they could not believe that the puppet Emperor of Manchukuo, would not repeal the sentence. It was indeed repealed, and the kidnappers were released. This was the 'new order' of public safety.

As far as hygiene was concerned, the Japanese beat the record in Harbin. During the winter [of 1933–4] they took it upon themselves to clean up the streets of the town and also the courtyards. So on the square near the Catholic church there towered a mountain some two storeys high of manure, snow, stuff from the rubbish pits and so on. The inhabitants were surprised . . . they said that they were going to take this mountain out on to the ice on the Sungari and, when the river melted, the stuff would be carried off downstream. The ice began cracking at the end of March, but April and half of May passed and the mountain remained at two-thirds of its height. All this time streams of stinking liquid trickled from underneath, running down the streets into the square; they never thought of clearing the pile away . . .

*

Under the old regime, ice-breaking on the Sungari was not taxed. In 1934 the Harbiners began taking off the ice in February [as usual]. One day when this was going on, several Japanese appeared [at the place] where they were bringing the carts up on to the bank. They began stopping them, counting the carts and collecting taxes; I do not remember how much – about 1½ dayans a cart. The citizens were furious and rushed off to the Town Hall to straighten things out. It turned out that the Town Hall had not levied any tax; it was all done by people who were lining their own pockets by frightening the inhabitants. After the visit to the Town Hall, they disappeared.

Life [under the Japanese] was alarming. You went out not knowing if you would return, or in what state. At the end of 1933 I was so exhausted that I asked for two months' leave. I was entitled to this, as during ten years' service I had had none; but I was refused. Then I began asking for sick leave and was told I had to have a medical examination. [The doctor who examined me gave me a choice of sick leave or termination of employment: I chose the latter and so retired from the railway.]

After his retirement, Yukhotsky left Harbin for Tsindao in China, where his son Misha was by that time working as an engineer. In 1937 the family emigrated to Australia, where Yukhotsky died in 1947.

29

Turning-Points

IRINA ILOVAISKAYA-ALBERTI

Irina Ilovaiskaya-Alberti is editor-in-chief of Russkaya Mysl', *the weekly Russian newspaper published in Paris.*

[My parents] lived part of their lives as émigrés – my mother the greater part of her life, and my father a lesser part. He was much older than my mother. He was from a Don Cossack family – landowners who preferred to live in towns rather than on their own land, as was often the case. My father lived practically the whole of his life in Moscow, although he was from a family who had a big estate and coal mines in the Don region. He was a barrister . . . and he was, as far as I know, the only man in the family who did not go into the Army.

He emigrated in 1920 or 1921 from Sevastopol to Constantinople . . . and in Constantinople he met my mother, who had also emigrated. I think they left [Constantinople] fairly quickly, because I was born in 1924 in Belgrade. My father had friends in Yugoslavia, who officially invited him there . . .

My parents divorced when I was still quite young. I saw quite a lot of my father when I was a child and teenager, but I never really questioned him about his life, because at that time I was still uninterested in it all. My interest in Russia came to me later. All I remember is that he very often talked to me about the Russian judicial system and law courts of that period – let's say from 1905 to the Revolution – and he often praised them.[1] I can remember that very distinctly, because it was repeated to me like a lesson, that Russian law was at a height which had not yet been achieved in Europe and that, in his opinion, the courts were unusually just, unusually humane and objective, and I remember that he was devoted to this idea with all his heart. When he emigrated he suffered most of all because he could no longer practise his profession. He didn't suffer at all from the loss of money – he was a fairly rich man – it was all the same to him, he was able to bear émigré poverty very easily, but he suffered from the fact that his work was really over and he was unable to work as a barrister in Yugoslavia. He did work as a legal consultant, but for the Russian colony.

In about 1938 or 1939 he left [Yugoslavia for Belgium, where his eldest son was living] and he died in Belgium very soon after the end of the Second World War.

Mother was born near Petersburg – in a town called Luga, quite a small town – because her father was stationed there. Then they moved to Kiev, [where] they lived through the arrival of the Bolsheviks – I remember my mother talking about how, after Kiev fell into the hands of the Bolsheviks, she found work in some sort of Soviet-organized institution and there she worked because they had no other means of living. But it seems to me that their standard of living [before 1914] had been remarkably good. These were moderately off people whose only income was what my grandfather earned at the Academy. Nevertheless, they had a cook, maid and governess for the children; a huge flat; they travelled abroad every year, to France and Germany – travel was a normal part of their lives – yet it was only an average family.

They emigrated to Constantinople and there my grandfather found himself a job as a cashier in a Russian restaurant – thanks to the fact that he was a Professor of Mathematics. My mother had to forget university and start to earn some money. [When they got to Belgrade] her knowledge of languages helped her; she had an excellent knowledge of French, English and German so she quickly found a job because there was great demand for such people in Yugoslavia. It was a country which had only just started to establish links with the outside world, and there was a crying need for people who could read, write and speak Western languages. There simply weren't any Serbs with such qualifications. She learnt [Serbo-Croat] when she got there, very quickly too, because she was very young when they arrived – twenty-one or twenty-two. She wrote Serbo-Croat and worked in this language without any difficulty – it's not difficult for a Russian, although I must add that my grandfather and grandmother never learnt it, all their lives. They talked in some strange mixture of Russian and Serbo-Croat. It was impossible for them to learn because they were too elderly.

Mother worked all day and I never saw her. [After my parents] divorced my grandparents brought me up. We all lived together in the old Russian way. I don't think it occurred to anybody that it would be possible to live separately. The flat was fine . . . Mother soon started to earn good money. She belonged to that section of Russian émigrés who were very successful [and who] didn't live badly, in the material sense, in Belgrade. There was a part of the colony which was poor and needed help – Mother was very active in this sphere. She was a very socially active person and always took part in organizations which supported old, ill and poor Russians. I remember that a great solidarity existed. I observe with great bitterness the lack of charity and social cohesion among today's émigrés. If someone is badly off nowadays, there is no one to help him, but it wasn't like that at all in Yugoslavia at that time. People were quick to help and everything was extremely well organized.

The Church was very active. It was an Orthodox country. The Serbian Orthodox Church supported the Russian Church; although they were both independent, they existed in complete friendship and complete agreement – there was always full support.

[In 1930 or 1931 my grandparents managed to sell a house they still owned in Lithuania and with the proceeds built a house in Dubrovnik on the Dalmatian coast. I lived with them there, on the sea, until my mother decided it was time for me to go to the Russian *gymnazia* in Belgrade.]

My mother had remarried. My stepfather was also Russian . . . the son of a merchant family which at some point had changed from being traders to being factory owners; they had owned a big cloth factory near Tambov. [My stepfather was also in the cloth business.] He sold materials sent to him by English firms . . . and he was a very good businessman. Not only did he survive the war and the German Occupation – because the value of those materials increased enormously and so he was able to live on that – but he even saved my mother's life [when she] was arrested by the Germans, accused of hiding Jewish property.

She really did hide Jewish property. People knew that she was very friendly with the Jewish family that owned the factory where she worked as head of the Export Department. The Germans confiscated Jewish-owned factories, but nevertheless she carried on working there. They didn't touch her because she was too valuable to them, not only because she knew languages but also because she knew the business and was able to run the place. But someone informed on her and she was arrested, and we really thought that we would never see her again. However, my stepfather negotiated with the Gestapo officer who had arrested her and gave him all the remnants of the English materials that we had, which were very valuable at that time, and for these my mother was released.

[I went to the *gymnazia* in Belgrade and finished my education there in 1942, during the Nazi Occupation. The school remained Russian, but] there were many changes . . . many [teachers] left and many stopped teaching. Others, whom the Germans considered 'reliable', took their places . . . [they were still all Russians but] those whom the Germans considered apolitical, I suppose, so that they wouldn't cause a disturbance. I managed to take my school-leaving exams – what they call the *matura* – [then] a few months after I left the Germans closed the *gymnazia* down.

We stayed until 1944 when Tito's troops were already almost on the outskirts of Belgrade. Then we decided to get away. I remember that very well, because I was then twenty years old and I clearly understood the situation. I remember it was very much discussed by the family and we had big arguments about whether to go or not. Her many Serbian friends kept telling my mother not to go: they would testify to the fact that she'd never been on the Germans' side, and that she had no links with the Germans, etc., etc. My mother said that she didn't believe their testimony would carry any weight with the Communists and that she had already run away from Communist rule once and why now, after twenty years, should she fall under it again? And so she decided to leave. My grandfather had died during the war and my mother had managed to get my grandmother out of Dalmatia to rejoin us. So there was my mother, stepfather, grandmother, my stepfather's widowed mother and myself. We escaped in the only direction possible – to Austria.

It was winter . . . We left Belgrade by train which took us almost to the frontier. I remember how the train stood for a long time across the river from Belgrade, and my mother and I looked at Belgrade from the train window, and I said to my mother that we wouldn't go back there again. She said, 'Why do you say that and think such things?' I said that I didn't know why but it just seemed to me that we would never return there. That turned out to be the truth, because we never did go back. And then, I remember, we went on foot, along long, narrow roads, having put the two grandmothers on some sort of horse-drawn carriages, while we just went on foot. Sometimes we got a lift on a lorry, but generally it was a rather chaotic journey.

Our aim was, in fact, to go to Italy, because I had met my future husband while I was in Yugoslavia – he was at the Italian Embassy in Belgrade during the war. He left Belgrade when there was upheaval in Italy – when they threw out Mussolini.[2] My future husband was under strong suspicion as someone who had helped Serbian people against the Germans. That was true: he really did help many people, using his official position . . . [The Germans] couldn't touch him while [the Italians were allies and] he was a member of the Italian Embassy, but it was known that they would seize him as soon as the possibility arose . . . He got away a few days after they started arresting all the Italians in Yugoslavia.

So we tried to get to Italy, but were unsuccessful, because when we got as far as the Italian–Austrian frontier the war ended and we stopped there . . . in a small Austrian mountain village called Igls, in the mountains above Innsbruck. Before that, my only memory is of stopping in another mountain village in Austria – I've forgotten the name of it – where we listened to Hitler's last speech, which he gave before the Soviet Army took Berlin and he committed suicide. This speech was transmitted by loudspeaker and the whole population of the little town came out on to the street to listen to it. He spoke in his crazy voice – it was more like a wail than a speech, about how 'We will take back Berlin, no we will not hand over Berlin. We will take back Vienna.' Vienna was already occupied then and yet he ranted on about how 'We will take everything back and we will be victorious.' What I remember most vividly, and which completely paralysed me – because it was clear to us that the war was over: not only lost, but over – was that the Austrian people around us listened to this mad speech and embraced each other, cried and sobbed – they really believed him.

Anyway – we didn't manage to get to Italy. When the war ended it became more difficult than before to cross borders. We didn't want to disobey the occupying powers because we considered them our allies and so if we were going to do something we wanted to do it by legal means. In any case, we no longer had a reason to escape, because we were running away from Soviet troops and by then it was clear that Soviet troops wouldn't get that far. Some kind of 'democratic' line between what was Soviet and what was not had become recognizable.

We were already on the Western side, so the fear of being caught by the Soviet authorities no longer worried us. First of all it was occupied by the Americans and then the French arrived – at which point a lot of Russians left immediately, because they didn't trust the French at all. The general feeling was such that the French might send us back and the Americans would not, therefore it was felt essential to be in the American zone.

My family was afraid of [being sent back to Russia]. I remember my mother saying that if we were repatriated, then we would all be repatriated to different parts of the world. I would be repatriated to Yugoslavia, as I was born there; they would be repatriated to Russia, and then everyone was born in different parts of Russia . . . In fact, it was totally unclear what would happen: [all that was clear was] that it was awful under Soviet rule and Communism – my family never had any doubt about that. When we ran away from Yugoslavia [it was a very different matter from my family's first emigration from Russia]. They had lived [in Yugoslavia] for twenty-five years and had made a life for themselves there; they were no longer unhappy, helpless refugees and my mother was aware of the harsh realities of escaping and emigrating for the second time. But she was prepared to do it because she was sure that nothing good could come out of the Soviet social system.

So we left for Salzburg, because Salzburg was under American occupation, and I myself spent a year there, until 1946 when I managed to obtain my official *laissez-passer*, with which I could go to Italy. Meanwhile, I looked for my future husband – I looked for him because he didn't know where to look for me . . . I sent him a letter through the Italian military government, which had assumed power – it was impossible to send a letter by post. He sent me a reply and I joined him in Italy in 1946, where we were married.

The rest of my family stayed in Austria . . . In 1948 when the Berlin Airlift crisis began, they were very frightened because they were living in Salzburg and the Soviet Army was in Linz.[3] They then decided that they wouldn't stay in Europe any more – they emigrated to South America, to Paraguay [where] they had some old Russian friends. My mother died in Paraguay in 1966, my grandmother just before that – she lived to the age of ninety-five or ninety-six. Just imagine – she was born in the Caucasus and died in Paraguay . . .

*

After the end of the war, after all that we had lived through, I turned away very sharply from everything Russian. I had a sad conviction that Russia no longer existed. I mistakenly believed that Russia had turned into the Soviet Union, that the population of Russia had completely absorbed the Communist ideology and outlook and that the Russia which I had once loved, which I believed in, and which had formed my character, remained only in the past. It existed in Russian literature, in Russian philosophy and Russian cultural traditions, but it no longer existed in the present. Therefore there was no point in taking an interest in Russia; it was, so to speak, Utopia. I lived many years of my life, a married adult, a product of Russian society who no longer had anything in common with it. Nothing, that is, apart from my family . . . This conviction of mine was so strong that I made no effort for my children to know Russian – the person in our family who insisted that they learn it was my husband, who didn't have a drop of Russian blood in him. He always told them that they were half Russian and that they must hold on to that tradition and guard it . . .

In 1964 or 1965, when people started leaving Russia for the West, when *samizdat* began and then Solzhenitsyn's works appeared – that was really the turning-point in my life: Solzhenitsyn. I suddenly understood, with dismay and very deep emotion, that I had made a mistake, that in the Soviet Union there is of course the Soviet system, and there are people who have completely adapted to it, but there is something else too – something living, free – a free soul, a vitality in a kind of Russian tradition, something spiritual and cultural . . . That explains my quick decision when Solzhenitsyn suggested that I work with him.

His wife's mother came to Italy and I met her. At that time I was very active in all things Russian in Italy – I wrote a lot of things in the Italian press; I often did translations, mainly from Russian into Italian when something important or serious came up, and besides that, I worked a lot with émigrés and helped them. Many people emigrated from the USSR at that time, and all those who didn't go to Israel ended up in Rome. I worked with a group who helped these people in all sorts of ways – financially, morally, by explaining to them about the world in which they had arrived, and by being there and giving them the feeling of human solidarity and closeness. Therefore lots of the new émigrés knew me, and when Natasha Solzhenitsyn's mother came to Italy we were introduced through mutual friends. That was my first contact with their family. I became very friendly with her – she is a remarkable person. She was an electronic engineer, specializing in aircraft design. She had worked in the Soviet Union for the whole of her life. Then she was sacked because her daughter dared to be associated with Solzhenitsyn. She emigrated – that is, she was made to leave because of her family . . .

When my husband died [in 1976, the Solzhenitsyns had] decided to go to America. They had the idea that I would perhaps be interested in working for them. When Solzhenitsyn asked, I didn't have any doubts – of course I wanted to.[4] I went to stay with them in Switzerland [where they lived], to meet them and discuss things with them. Then they emigrated on their own and I left from Italy a month or two afterwards.

My role was that of a bridge between them and the outside world. It was at a time when everything was very difficult for them. For all people who arrive in the West not knowing the West, it's incredibly difficult and complicated at first. And it was made even more difficult for them, because it was like being under siege – on the one side the press, on the other side people who were just curious, people who admired him a lot and aspired to be like him. All that greatly complicated their situation. They needed somebody who could take this part of the burden from them – 'public relations' in a sense. I was also his secretary. I did a lot of translating as well. No one ever laid down my hours of work. There wasn't anyone else, just the family and me, so everyone shared everything – I did everything that they did.

[Solzhenitsyn is not the kind of person who does the cooking]: if he *had* to cook he would do so very, very simply – really frugal food; he considered his time too valuable to waste on such stupid things.

His wife basically edits his works. They have their own typesetting machine [which she has] learnt to work like a professional linotype operator and typesetter, and on it she transcribes and edits all his works. That's her main job and she does it really well. She's learnt English pretty well by now.

I came to them in autumn 1976, and Alexander Ginzburg was arrested in February 1977. Ginzburg was the representative of the Solzhenitsyn Fund in Russia,[5] and so when he was arrested a very big campaign was organized in his defence and I worked a lot for that because [of my languages]. Natasha [Solzhenitsyn] herself led the campaign. It was a serious business, organizing a campaign of such a size, as it was largely aimed at America and people in America are somewhat remote from these problems. Now they understand them better and

With the Russian Corps

VLADIMIR ALEXEYEVICH GRIGORIEV

Vladimir Alexeyevich Grigoriev emigrated to the United States in 1958 and works for the Tolstoy Foundation, the organization which provides help for Russian immigrants in America.

His father was an engineering student in Kharkov at the time of the Revolution, but in 1918 joined the White movement and fought in the Drozdovsky Regiment[1] with the Volunteer Army. He left Russia for Constantinople after the evacuation of the Crimea, and eventually moved with his regiment to Bulgaria. Vladimir was born in Sofia in 1923.

There was a large Russian colony in Bulgaria, most of its members being employed in manual labour. Grigoriev's father, however, managed to complete his studies and found work as an engineer, earning a reasonably good salary. Grigoriev attended a Russian school and had begun studying at Sofia University when Bulgaria entered the Second World War.

In 1942 I joined the Russian Corps [*Russky Korpus*].[2] The formation of the Corps began in September 1941 [in Yugoslavia] but in March 1942 recruitment to it was extended to Bulgaria. When representatives of the Corps came to Sofia from Belgrade, there was a mass influx of Russian émigrés to its ranks. Fortunately for those who later wanted to emigrate to America, the Russian Corps was not listed by the Allies as a 'criminal organization', as were, for instance, the SS and the Croation *Ustaša*.[3] The Corps was already in being before the USA entered the war.

I came to Yugoslavia with the first group to be recruited from Russians in Bulgaria. Our initial training took place in Belgrade; it was hastily organized and pretty superficial. We were then sent to a camp in the south of Serbia, where we were given a fuller course of training.

[Many of the officers were Whites.] Those who had come from Bulgaria, however, were greatly disappointed. There was a tendency not to promote former Russian officers to ranks higher than those they had formerly held in the White Army. In Yugoslavia there were a lot of émigrés who had originated in Tsarist times from the Baltic provinces – Baltic Germans, that is – and they seemed to be the ones who were initially appointed officers. Later, though, the younger Bulgarian-based émigrés, my generation, were promoted and given commissions, but our fathers, so to speak, were not. This was resented by many of those who had come from Bulgaria, and after a while they left and went back. When this unwelcome news got around, many people refrained from joining. I stayed, because that problem didn't bother me. For me the important thing was the fight against Communism. I took the view that if I was competent I would be promoted, and if not – then I wouldn't, and my duty was to soldier on in the ranks.

I reached the rank of *podporuchik* – second lieutenant. In fact, I wasn't given command of a platoon until later, when I was transferred to a unit of Vlasov's Army – the ROA, *Russkaya Osvoboditel'naya Armiya* [Russian Liberation Army].[4] For some time I ran a school for radio operators, which trained men recruited into the ROA. Because I spoke German, I was employed in retraining Russians in the use of German equipment – tank radios, aircraft radios and so on.

In the end I found myself with 260 men under me – no longer radio operators but just ordinary infantrymen, and we were posted to defensive and guard duties about sixty kilometres behind the front line. By then the Soviet Armies had penetrated quite far into Germany, and we were retreating. I ended up with only twelve men. Everything at that time was very fluid, the situation was changing all the time; the usual chain of command – division, regiment, battalion and so on – often broke down, and you couldn't even rely on having the normal thirty-six men in a platoon.

From the very first there was great disappointment among the Russian Corps, because its first commander, General Skorodumov, in his introductory speech, assumed that he would have the right to co-ordinate the actions of the Corps with the Germans in a fairly active role – that is, to fight on the main front against the Red Army. But it was soon obvious that there was a big discrepancy between his ambitious plans and what was realistically possible, and he was dismissed from command of the Corps. As a result it was explained to us that we were to support the German rear services and guard the lines of communication – a vital task in the unpredictable conditions of guerrilla warfare in Yugoslavia, where the German depots, stores and supply convoys were the favourite targets of Tito's partisans. We were not, in any case, trained or equipped to stand and face the Red Army. It was twenty years since most of our officers and many of our rankers had been in battle; our weapons were not of the best; we were full of idealism, but our training was inadequate. So the job of guard and convoy troops in the fight against the Communist partisans in Yugoslavia was one of the fronts in the struggle against Bolshevism – at least, that is what we told ourselves, and it helped to keep up our morale.

When Vlasov began to form his units of the ROA, that was a different matter. Many Germans were greatly in favour of it – I know that from a number of personal contacts (although they were invariably in the Wehrmacht and not in the Nazi Party; the Party was always extremely lukewarm and ambiguous about the Vlasov Army). To some people in the Russian Corps, joining a Vlasov unit seemed a much better way of getting to grips with the Reds. At the same time, the Germans did not want the Corps simply to melt away, as would have happened if all its best men had transferred to Vlasov. In particular, the German general commanding the south-eastern front, to whom the Russian Corps was subordinate, was very keen not to lose the Corps or have it disintegrate: we were doing valuable work by releasing thousands of his men – a complete division in fact – for front-line fighting against the Red Army.

On the other hand, no one could stop people like myself getting an official German Army travel warrant, taking a train and going to some place for entirely legitimate reasons – and that was how I and others made contacts with the Vlasovites. Then in 1943 I was in charge of the radio communications of the Russian Corps at its headquarters in Belgrade when a party of Vlasov's officers arrived in order to draw up lists of the people they needed to train the cadres of Vlasov's Army.

[I was put in charge of] a school to retrain Soviet soldiers who had been radio operators before being taken prisoner by the Germans and who had then enlisted under Vlasov. We trained them in the use of German equipment and in German radio procedure, such as the German encoding system, which had to be adapted to the Cyrillic alphabet. Of course, messages were only encoded from battalion level upwards; from battalion HQ down to companies, transmissions were *en clair*.

[I fought] against both Tito's partisans and the Red Army. We were, for instance, involved in some very heavy fighting in August 1943 on the River Drina, the boundary along which the Russian Corps was deployed to prevent the Communist partisans from penetrating into Serbia. The Četniks under Draža Mihailović were also operating in that area,[5] but because they were aware of the ideological position of the Corps they left us alone. In fact, when the British withdrew their support from Mihailović *we* supported him; we kept him supplied with food, we brought him ammunition, and so on. I had personal experience of this: I would be put in command of a convoy of trucks loaded with ammunition; we would drive to a certain spot and leave the trucks for an hour or so, and then when we went back to them the ammunition was gone – collected by the Četniks. At other times we co-operated with them even more closely. When Mihailović fell out of favour with the Allies because he regarded the Communists as his main enemy, he linked up with us for support and supplies – not with the Germans but with the Russian Corps.

[There were links between the Russian Corps and Croatian forces] only in late 1944, when Soviet troops began advancing towards Croatia. I can't tell you anything about that from personal experience, because by October 1944 I had moved to Germany, but *before* that our relations with the Croats were not at all friendly. First, the Croats laid great stress on the religious aspect of their differences with the Serbs; they were, you might say, aggressively Catholic, while both we and the Serbs were Orthodox. Apart from that, however, we Russians always seem to have had a kind of inborn affinity with the Serbs, which affected our attitude to them in a positive sense, and it was largely reciprocated by the Serbian population. For instance, when units of the Russian Corps were stationed on the border between Serbia and Croatia, and the Croats burned Serbian villages on the Croatian side of the border simply because they were Orthodox, our Russian units crossed the border to defend the Serbs and to help in evacuating them to Serbia.

It is interesting to note that the German liaison officers attached to our regiments wholly sympathized with our action. The German liaison officer at our battalion HQ, for example, was married to a Russian woman. I know for a fact, too, that one of them was in the group of German officers who attempted to assassinate Hitler in July 1944. The whole of von Stauffenberg's[6] staff and the officers assigned to liaison with Vlasov, acting as the 'eyes' of the German Command at Vlasov's headquarters, were sympathetic to the aims of the ROA. They all spoke excellent Russian, which greatly assisted mutual understanding. They helped Vlasov without the knowledge of the Nazi Party or of the Supreme Command. It was all done at the level of the various front commanders, and not at the level of the OKW [*Oberkommando der Wehrmacht*].

I went to Vienna; our Corps had a small staff stationed there. It was merely a reporting-point for our people who went there after being discharged from one or another of the military hospitals in Austria, and for those being sent on official journeys; there they were given the necessary travel documents. This was in early October 1944. From Vienna I was sent to Chemnitz . . . In Chemnitz I was arrested by the Gestapo, who put me in a prison camp and interrogated me. They questioned me about my origins – my place of birth, who and what were my parents, and had I ever been a member of the Communist Party, at which I laughed. My interrogator said he was simply asking me because he had to fill in all the blanks in a printed questionnaire! [My] uniform had various badges and insignia indicating that I didn't belong to a normal, hundred-per-cent German unit. By then I was wearing Vlasov's ROA shoulder-patches with Russian-type officers' epaulettes, and we didn't wear the German eagle above our right-hand breast pocket, as did all branches of the German armed forces.

Anyway, they released me. I reported to the Wehrmacht HQ in Chemnitz, and from there they sent me to Breslau, where I organized our unit, which consisted of myself, the other radio instructor, a quartermaster, a cook and a driver. We were given a large truck, full of radio equipment and converted into a training classroom.

My radio school existed until January 1945, when the Red Army broke through at Kielce and the general retreat began. Scratch units were formed, made up of individual units of the ROA in company or even platoon strength, and we found ourselves exchanging fire with our fellow Russians on the enemy side. Often when our men were badly wounded in these clashes, they would beg to be finished off with a *coup de grâce* from a pistol rather than fall into the hands of Soviet troops. In the town of Oppeln, for instance, in January 1945, we held the bridge over the River Oder for a long time, until all our units had safely crossed to the west bank. The bridge was mined with explosives, as we knew, but about thirty of us held it on the east bank. We were on the far side when the bridge was blown up, and on 30 January – my birthday, by the way! – we had to swim back across the freezing Oder, each man with two empty jerricans tied to his belt as lifebelts to keep afloat, wearing thick greatcoats that weighed us down as soon as they became soaked with water. We reached the west bank looking like drowned rats, but with the loss of only one man out of thirty.

When we finally reached Breslau, I submitted an application to be returned to the Russian Corps [which was] still in Yugoslavia. This was at the end of March 1945. I was given permission to go, and travelled by train from Breslau to Munich, under strafing or bombing attacks for a lot of the way. Everything in Munich was in such chaos that I was held up in a transit camp there for nearly three weeks before I was able to move on to Salzburg on 28 April.

[In Salzburg I found an ROA unit and managed to obtain the necessary papers to enable me to travel to Yugoslavia to rejoin the Russian Corps at Ljubljana.] I met an officer whom I knew, and he informed me that there was, as it happened, another White Russian unit in that area, the so-called Varangian Regiment. This and a Cossack regiment were just about to withdraw, and the Russian Corps units planned to join up with them and pull out.

The intention was to move up into the mountains, where we would sit it out for a while and wait and see what was happening. It was my job to set up a radio network between all three elements in order to keep in touch and co-ordinate the move. The Germans were pulling out too (by now it was 3 or 4 May), so I had no difficulty in getting from them two medium-power transmitters. One battalion of the Varangians arrived, with a lot of wounded and some female auxiliary personnel. This battalion linked up with some Russian Corps units, and we were joined a day later by the other two battalions of the Varangian Regiment and the Cossacks. At the same time we acquired some Germans – stray companies from various units, an anti-aircraft battery, and so on. We decided to move north into Austria and surrender to the British, having heard from local Slovenes that Carinthia, the adjacent Austrian province, was in British hands.

The German headquarters and staff officers had already left, using whatever means they could. They had abandoned their hospitals along with all the patients, so we loaded all the wounded – Germans, Croats, Slovenes, Russians – into railway wagons and slowly this huge trainload made its way northward towards the frontier. We were supposed to meet up with several Russian Corps units at a station called Ratmannsdorf [the Slovene name of the town is Radovljica]. By the time we reached that station the war had officially ended, but the Yugoslav partisans and a unit of their regular Army started firing on our patrol, which we had sent out on reconnaissance to find out whether Ratmannsdorf was safe for our link-up with the Russian Corps units. Our train had halted short of the station, under the reverse slope of a hill; after the hill came a slight downward gradient and then there was the station. As soon as our patrol approached the station, they came under fire. We realized that the Corps obviously hadn't yet reached Ratmannsdorf, because they should have been waiting for us at the station, but the Yugoslavs were also in for a surprise, because they hadn't counted on our group being in such strength. We were determined to get through at all costs; the very last thing we wanted to do was to surrender to the Yugoslavs, because we knew exactly what would happen to us if we did. Two companies of the Varangians deployed, stormed the station, and took it.

The Yugoslavs were driven out and, most importantly, our men captured a Yugoslav colonel, who was, as it happened, a former officer of the Royal Yugoslav Army. We escorted him to the senior officer of our group, Colonel Semyonov, who commanded the Varangian Regiment. (Semyonov, by the way, used to look rather like a pirate chief, with at least half a box of ammunition draped around his torso in bandoliers. He was a holder of the Finnish Order of the White Eagle for having distinguished himself against the Red Army in the Russo-Finnish War of 1939–40, as well as seven other decorations.) I was present at this encounter and heard everything that went on. Semyonov said to the Yugoslav colonel: 'You will remain with us as a hostage. You will also telephone from this station to your headquarters and give orders that no one is to fire on our train. We are carrying a large number of wounded – and in any case, hostilities have ceased. You will be answerable with your life if our train is attacked before it enters the tunnel through which we have to pass to reach the British-held zone of Austria.'

So we set off again for the frontier station, Jesenice. The distance is only about thirty kilometres, but it took us a day and a half because the track was damaged. We repaired it; and on the way, as a safety precaution, we also hitched on an armoured train that had been abandoned by the Germans. When we reached Jesenice, we found that the station housed a big headquarters of Tito's Army and the whole place was heavily occupied by Yugoslav troops.

We held lengthy negotiations with the Yugoslavs, in which we offered to hand over our weapons in exchange for being allowed to proceed, together with our wounded, through the tunnel and into Austria. We reminded the Yugoslav commander that our train included sixteen German 88mm anti-aircraft guns mounted on flat cars; this was possibly the best and most versatile gun to have been developed by any country in the Second World War, and if the barrel were depressed to fire in a horizontal trajectory it was very accurate and absolutely devastating. We also had a troop of field artillery. We assured them that, if forced to, we would not only fight to the last man but we would also destroy the modern steel mills that the Germans had built in Jesenice and which had so far survived undamaged because until recently they had been out of range of Allied bombers. Semyonov was patient and reasonable, arguing that not only was the war now over but that Yugoslavia needed to protect and restore its industrial plant; it was therefore pointless for the Yugoslavs to risk an armed confrontation in Jesenice that could be both physically and politically extremely damaging.

At first the Yugoslavs said they couldn't let us proceed because the railway track through the tunnel was mined. One of the younger Russian officers, who had been a sapper in the Red Army, thereupon offered personally to check the track for mines and, if necessary, to remove and defuse them. I gave him a portable radio set and kept in touch with him all the way as he and three of his sappers walked the entire length of the tunnel (a distance of five or six kilometres), probing for mines, until he reached the far side and reported by radio that the track was completely 'clean'.

We therefore reached an agreement with the Yugoslav commander: we gave up the armoured train, the AA guns and the field artillery, and in return we were allowed to walk over the mountains into Austria, carrying light arms – rifles, revolvers, sub-machine guns. As a form of guarantee, the Yugoslavs sent with us a detachment of fifty partisans; theoretically they were to escort us, but in fact, since we were still armed, they were also our hostages – of which both sides were tacitly aware. As I spoke German, English and Serbo-Croat, I acted as interpreter for the Yugoslav captain in command of our escort, and we went on ahead of the column in a captured German staff car until we reached Austrian territory, where I explained the situation to the local British commander.

When our column arrived on foot, the British had already called up a fleet of trucks to take us to Villach. There the Russians, Germans and Yugoslavs were separated out; after a delay of a day or so we, the Russians, were loaded into another convoy of trucks and packed off to Italy. On the way, at Udine, we were again separated out, and those who could prove Yugoslavian citizenship were sent there;[7] to the rest of us, our escort commander gave us his word of honour as a British officer that we would not be handed over to the Soviets . . . We were put on a train and continued our journey in a pretty cheerful mood – helped by the fact that Colonel Semyonov had somehow managed to acquire a huge drum of British army-issue rum!

We travelled slowly for several days until we reached a town where a unit of General Anders' Polish Corps was stationed.[8] Some of us got out of the train to buy food and drink on the platform, and while we were doing so we met a group of Polish officers, who said, 'If you value your lives, get off that train and come and join us, because they are taking you to the Soviets; you will be handed over to them and you know what *that* means. Don't believe what the British tell you; they are under orders to lie to you about your real destination.'

Several of our Russians were persuaded; they slipped away with the Poles and were quietly absorbed into Polish units. The rest of us continued on our journey, which ended at Taranto, the port in the 'heel' of Italy. We arrived there in the middle of the night, and as we tumbled out of the train half asleep we were faced by a row of truck headlamps and searchlights directed straight at us. In this somewhat dazed and disorientated state we were immediately handed over to the Soviet 'Repatriation Commission'. So much for the 'word of honour' of a British officer . . .

Officers and lower ranks were ordered by megaphone to divide into separate parties, although we were so dazzled that we could hardly see what we were doing. When we were lined up in ranks, a very spruce and good-looking Red Army captain came up to us and started by apologizing: 'I'm sorry, gentlemen . . . your arrival was so unexpected that we haven't prepared anything for you, but I hope you won't be too uncomfortable. To make things easier for yourselves as well as for us, I would therefore be grateful if you would kindly hand over any weapons you may be carrying.' I think we were all so amazed by his

unexpected politeness that, although many of us had concealed weapons, we all handed them over like good little boys; I had two hand-
grenades and a revolver. We were not searched, but were taken to
some wooden huts. Once inside, we looked out of the windows and
saw that the huts were surrounded by Soviet troops pointing sub-
machine guns at us.

Later I learned from the other officers, most of whom were from the
Varangian Regiment, that all the lower ranks – privates and NCOs –
were shot out of hand by the Soviets as deserters from the Red Army,
although these wretched men had only been ordinary prisoners-of-war.

We immediately began to prepare ourselves for interrogation,
rehearsing to each other the detailed facts about our respective origins:
I produced documents showing that I was a Bulgarian citizen by birth,
I recalled the street in Sofia where I had been born, listed the schools
I had attended, and so on. Next morning we were told to parade outside
the hut, where the same polite Soviet captain announced that we would
now be addressed by the Mission's *politruk* [political commissar] and
then we would have to wait and see what our subsequent fate was to
be.

The *politruk*, a short, fat man with the rank of major, approached
and said, 'Step forward anyone who was formerly an officer in the Red
Army. There is no point in anyone concealing that fact, because we
know all about you from the lists we have received.' One unfortunate
officer stepped forward; he was immediately placed under arrest, marched off and never seen again.

A little while after that episode one of the younger officers in our
party said, 'May I ask a question, Major? We were all born outside
Russia. None of us has ever been in the Soviet Union, but we are
curious about it: most of our parents are Russian, and it would be most
interesting to be able to go there and see what it's like in reality. What
is the reality of the USSR? Our parents tell us one thing, you tell us
another.' That young man was playing the fool a bit. The major looked
at him and said, 'First, Lieutenant, although you and I are enemies,
we are both officers and belong to the same caste. When you are
speaking to a senior officer, kindly stand to attention.' The young man
apologized and stood to attention. 'Second, we are *not* representatives
of Intourist. The Captain here will give you any further information
you may need. But I warn you – if any of you conceals or falsifies his

place of origin, we will find him out, even if we have to dig him out of the grave. That is all.' And he drove away in his jeep.

The captain took over: 'Stand at ease, gentlemen. I must now inform you of the following. The Major was quite right in saying that we do not fulfil the functions of Intourist. There are, however, Intourist offices in Rome and in Munich, and if any of you really does want to go to the Soviet Union, you can always write to them. For the time being, though, I advise you not to try – it could lead to a misunderstanding on both sides, with consequences that you might come to regret. Stay where you are for a while and *then* decide what you want to do.'

With that he dismissed us; we went back to our huts to collect our few belongings and were transferred to the British internment camp. There we felt perpetually under the threat of being called back to the Soviet Mission; every so often we would be summoned and interrogated, but by British officers and within the British camp.

We stayed in Taranto for about eight months, after which we were transferred to Rimini and thence to Bavaria, where the Americans assumed responsibility for us. There, after two weeks, they started to release all those who had a profession that could be usefully integrated into the German economy. I and a Russian friend from Bulgaria had a bit of luck one day when we met in the American-run DP Employment Office and saw an advertisement calling for men to work as market gardeners. Bulgaria being regarded as 'the kitchen garden of Eastern Europe', we were readily taken on. We were picked up by an American military escort and taken to our place of work, bringing with us our unsigned discharge papers. If at the end of six months our employer found us to be satisfactory workers, our discharge papers would be signed and we would be formally released as free men. As neither of us, however, knew the first thing about gardening, we were terribly worried that the whole business would end in fiasco and we would find ourselves back in the internment camp.

Since our status was that of stateless internees, we had the right to be maintained and fed on the same standard as American troops. We were issued with a certain amount of 'dollar scrip' – the paper currency used by the American occupation forces, which enabled us to buy whatever we liked in the PX. We mostly bought cigarettes, the only real currency for Germans in those days – they could buy you anything. Anyway, we arrived at the station with our escort, a black American corporal, whom I always purposely addressed as 'Sergeant'. I went and bought a bottle of schnapps with my cigarettes, sat the corporal down under a tree with the bottle and persuaded him to part with the folder that contained our papers. We had decided that our future did not lie in horticulture; instead, we took the train to Munich, after I had offered up a prayer asking God not to be too hard on the corporal when he returned to his unit without us and without our papers.

In Munich there was an organization that helped people who had escaped from or been released from concentration camps, which was under the aegis of the IRO [International Refugee Agency]. Thanks to my knowledge of languages, I quite easily got a job in the administrative offices of this organization. When I eventually wanted to come to America, the fact of having been an IRO employee weighed considerably in my favour; it seemed to 'cancel out', so to speak, the fact that I had spent most of the Second World War as a volunteer fighting on the German side.

31

'Your Motherland Awaits You'

BORIS GEORGIEVICH MILLER

Boris Georgievich Miller's parents met on board an evacuation ship during the exodus from the Crimea in 1920. They emigrated to Yugoslavia, where Boris was born in 1929. He studied at the military school at Belaya Tserkov, on the Romanian border, until 1944 when the Soviet Army was drawing close. An attempt was made to evacuate the entire school to Germany. They travelled in goods wagons through Hungary to Austria, where they were left in a young persons' camp for the remaining months of the war.

At the end of the war I ran away from the Germans and looked for my mother, who I knew was in the town of Villach in Carinthia, near the Yugoslav border – a very beautiful place. I managed to find her and we were evacuated in April, virtually on the last train. We made our way from Villach towards Salzburg because we had heard that there was a concentration of Russians there. General Turkul was there, in command of one of Vlasov's detachments[1] which was in Austrian territory. Despite the fact that there had recently been very heavy bombing of Germany, you had to give the Germans their due: they are certainly punctual. The trains left exactly on time and arrived precisely on time if bombing did not prevent it. Of course, if the line was completely destroyed we had to go on foot, or in carts – we covered large parts of the way in this manner – and people were abandoning their belongings on the road . . .

On the way, there is a long tunnel between Spittal and Bad Gastein, about nine kilometres, and it ran under the British zone. We managed to cross over – our train stopped at Bad Gastein and that was our last stop. We lived a few days at the station. This is one of the smartest resorts in Austria, but at that time we weren't very interested in that.

There were huge crowds living in tents there. Then the Americans arrived and we were given a school temporarily, three kilometres from Bad Gastein, right by the tunnel itself. After a few weeks there, we were given the opportunity to go to Salzburg. When we got there, we settled in a camp called Paz. Everything was organized there very quickly; we had a Russian church straight away, our own hospital, a football field, a sports team, a primary school, a secondary school and workshops.

It was very interesting: when we arrived, the place seemed absolutely dead – there was no life in it at all; but as soon as we Russians settled down in our camp, the Austrians started coming to have their radios repaired in our workshops. We didn't have any resistance wire or any valves, but the Russian technicians somehow managed to improvise without having any replacements for damaged parts. In spite of this the workshops flourished, thanks to the ingenuity of these Russian people.

Soon Soviet repatriation missions started to appear, and we often saw a large red bus arriving which had painted on it in Russian in golden letters:

'YOUR MOTHERLAND AWAITS YOU'

And then the interrogations began, and all those who had lived on Soviet territory had to return, according to the agreement between the Soviet Union and the Western Allies at Yalta. There was a commission and we had to appear before it with our documents. There were American, British, French and Soviet officers. Every man was interrogated. And the most important occupation of every man who lived in our camp was to get himself forged documents to prove that he had been born in Yugoslavia, Poland – anywhere but the Soviet Union. These documents were beautifully made and people learned very quickly to say a few words in the relevant languages.

There were sometimes tragi-comic episodes: for example, a man came, showed all his documents and was even able to say a few words in the language of the country where he claimed to have been born and bred; he had already been told that he could go, but on his way out the Soviet officer called out to him, 'Just a minute – when did you say you were captured?' And the man answered: '1942' or '1943' – in Russian. He had dropped his guard. When the Soviet commissioner then said, 'Did you complete your schooling?' it became clear that his documents were false.

In our camp, however, the only ones who were extradited were those against whom the Soviets could prove that they had collaborated with the Germans, or had been in the German Army, and then they had always been warned what would happen if they ran away . . .

32

Masaryk's Guests

GEORGY MIKHAILOVICH KATKOV

Georgy Mikhailovich Katkov was born in 1903. His family emigrated to Prague, where he studied and became a research student. In the late 1930s he left Czechoslovakia for England, living there until his death in 1985. A Fellow of St Antony's College, Oxford, he was the author of several books, including February 1917, *which describes the early stages of the Revolution.*

We left illegally, to Poland, across the border. We were arrested there and sent to a place called Uniec, and from there to Warsaw. The Poles said we could stay there a little while, but my father had acquired a Yugoslav visa, because our surname, Katkov, had a special meaning for the Serbs – it was that of some famous Serbian freedom-fighter and we could have made use of this, but we didn't. We passed through Prague, and there were many Russians there who had been invited by the Czech Government. They asked us to stay, so we did. My parents thought that we could obtain a better education in Prague, and in effect I went to a German university – the Deutsche Universität in Prague.[1]

I studied with Krauss and Ehrenfels;[2] they both knew Masaryk[3] as a philosopher and they introduced me to him. He took an interest in me for a long time, and gave them money for teaching me. It was his own money – or rather, the Czech Government gave it to him to use in whatever way he chose. He didn't take anything for himself; he was a very modest man. The only thing he spent money on was horses. He liked to ride . . . He cut a very elegant figure – majestic, even.

He disliked Russians. [He helped] simply because the Russians had helped Czech refugees. Whether he liked them or not didn't enter into the question. They were deserving people, so he helped them, that's all.

[The Czech Government] thought that the Bolsheviks wouldn't hold their ground. Four months, six months, maybe a year, but they couldn't possibly hold out any longer than that. Who were these Bolsheviks? Nobodies. Trotsky? Lenin? Why, Russia is a great country, a brilliant country . . . You've got professors who are émigrés . . . While back there you had just an insignificant gang of thieves and robbers . . . They reckoned that within a year, or two at the most, the old regime would be reinstated, all these old émigrés would become bigwigs in Moscow and would show extreme gratitude. Because the Czechs were always afraid of the Germans. That's the only reason they helped us. Ironically, the results – in 1948 and again in 1968 – were not exactly what they had hoped for . . .

[The Czechs also felt a need to fill the ranks of the intelligentsia with brother Slavs, to replace the Germans now that Czechoslovakia had freed itself from the Austrian Empire.] But their reasoning was unsound. Educated Czechs see themselves as Europeans. But Russians feel they are different from them. They see the Czechs as a nation of petty bourgeois – 'How dare they call themselves professors? We are a great nation, we have brilliance.' And so no good could come of this . . .

33

A Lonely Exile

VERA FYODOROVNA KALINOVSKA

Vera Fyodorovna Kalinovska's parents left Russia in 1920 and settled in Prague, where Vera was born in 1924.

My father was a Cossack officer. When he left Russia at the age of thirty-two he was still a junior officer, with the Cossack rank of *podyesaul* [lieutenant]. I'm of Cossack descent on both sides of my family: the Ryabovs and Uryadnikovs came from the same *stanitsa* [settlement] on the Don. I still have an eighty-three-year-old aunt in the Soviet Union and I correspond with her fairly regularly . . . she writes nice long letters, five or six pages, and they're very interesting . . .

It's been difficult for me to live here in Czechoslovakia. I've been alone for fourteen years and my life is rather tough. I get a good pension, but the loneliness is killing me.

[When he came to Czechoslovakia, my father worked] as a librarian, helping build up the very big and important Russian section of the Clementinum, the library of the Charles University here in Prague. So with his Civil Service pay he was able to send me to the Russian school in Moravski Čebel. In the early years of the emigration, in the 1920s and early 1930s, there were many children at the school, but inevitably the numbers dwindled until there were so few that they couldn't afford the upkeep of Moravski Čebel and had to close it down. Living in exile and feeling uncertain about the future, the first generation of Russian émigrés (my parents' generation) did not have many children [I have no brothers or sisters] – partly because they were often very poor, partly because many were too old; also because many of those who were young enough to have children were convinced that they would go back to Russia and wanted their children to be born in Russia . . .

Émigré life is never exactly easy. But I survived and got an education. Because of my father's position, my parents were better off than many of their fellow Russians. There were émigrés who had to work as drivers or porters, and there were members of the intelligentsia who could find work only as unskilled labourers on building sites, for instance.

During the Second World War I first did clerical and business training, then I worked in technology. When they closed the school, all the men born in 1920 had to go to work in Germany, and the women born in 1924 who had no children also had to go to Germany. So the day before my birthday, 25 March 1943, they took me off to Germany. They stamped my identity card so that I couldn't remain in Czechoslovakia, then they transported me to Germany. On this paper are the signatures of witnesses testifying that I was a Czech citizen by marriage, so that I could return after the war.

I lived with my mother in Berlin, right to the end of the war. When the Russians came, I worked for them as a translator and interpreter. I stayed on for another three months, then I came home.

[Berlin during the war was terrible.] If I wrote a novel about it now, people would be horrified. But if anything it was even worse after the Russians arrived. It was a nightmare . . . it was nothing but murder, looting and rape. I had to cut off my hair, wear men's clothes and pretend I was a teenage boy. There wasn't a single woman – German or any other – who wasn't raped or killed, often both. Even Soviet officers [for whom I worked] warned me that if I didn't dress as a man I would be harmed. In the block where I lived was a Soviet military headquarters, and this is what saved me.

There were some Frenchmen there, too, whom I saved from being shot by the Russians as collaborators. I still keep in contact with my friends who were there – they write to me from Paris . . .

When I returned from Germany I had typhus, because often there was no water, so we couldn't wash and got lice. I caught typhus from the lice. Once I had to cut meat off a horse barely dead. It was so awful, it's difficult to describe.

I didn't return under the official repatriation scheme. I avoided going through official channels because I might have been arrested at any point. The Soviets were stopping all the trains and rounding up every Russian, Soviet citizens and émigrés alike, even if like me they had been born outside Russia. I had no proper Czech passport. We Russians had only a German identity document [with] no photo on it. If I had been heard speaking Russian while travelling, the Soviet military police might simply have shipped me off to the Soviet Union and I would have perished in a labour camp. When I worked at the Soviet military headquarters in Berlin, there were Russians there who were sympathetic and told me frankly *not* to go to the Czech repatriation mission because if the mission officials discovered I was of Russian descent on both sides of my family, they were under orders to hand any Russian over to the Soviet authorities. The officers who were friendly to me said, 'Take your Czech husband, find a horse and make your own way home.'

At that time you could pick up a horse anywhere – [they] were wandering around loose. Both the German and Soviet Armies used a lot of horses, and we found one with no trouble. We also found a small abandoned cart – the sort that butchers used to use, a small two-wheeler with two seats. [We rode all the way back to Czechoslovakia in that cart.] Four of our horses died on the journey and four times we found another one . . . My husband was Czech, and Czechs are cowards, but I have Cossack blood in my veins. It was I who found the horses. Perhaps it's because I'd already suffered so much that I'm still alive to tell you about it. Another person who experienced what I did might not have survived . . .

Of course, very many Russian émigrés in Czechoslovakia did *not* survive the arrival of Soviet troops in 1945 and the Communist takeover in 1948. The luckier ones were women who, like myself, had married Czechs and so acquired Czech names and nationality. The Soviet repatriation teams were very active then – and 'repatriation' usually meant a one-way ticket to Siberia in a cattle truck. So there are very few of us Russians left here now, from what was, at one time, one of the biggest and – all things considered – one of the happiest Russian émigré communities in Europe, chiefly thanks to President Masaryk and his wish to help us. The really fortunate ones were those who managed to re-emigrate between 1945 and 1948 and who found another home in America, France, Switzerland . . .

I always wanted to leave, too, but I stayed here because of my parents – they only had me. My father died in 1967, my mother in 1975 and my daughter has emigrated to England. Since then I've been alone and it's terribly difficult . . . I could go and live with Milena in England, but then I would lose my Czech pension and become a burden to her.

Also, I have a daughter-in-law and three grandchildren here. It's really because of these children that I don't want to emigrate . . .

My father loved Russia very much. Having been forced to leave his homeland when he was still quite young, he always longed to see it again, if only once. He did, in fact, go back, having acquired a Czech passport. He went for the first time when they allowed Russian émigrés to visit their relatives. He visited his sister in Moscow, then went to the Don and the Volga country, to Volgograd to see his other sister – the one I still correspond with. When he returned he made me give my word of honour that I would never go to Russia. I would have liked to have gone, you know; my aunts kept urging me to go: 'Vera, come and see us.' But I am the sort of person who, if I've given my word, I keep it.

Czechs are very unlike us, you know. They have a different attitude to life. Although I was born here, to the Czechs I have always been an émigré, although I speak Czech fluently and, apart from my relatives, hardly anyone knows I'm Russian. But it's written in my papers, and the authorities never forget it.

Both my mother and my father went back to Russia several times. They were drawn to something that had never existed. Their ideal never existed – or, if it did, it had perished. Although my father wanted so much to see his homeland, he nevertheless wanted to die in Czechoslovakia. Everyone loves Prague, it's so beautiful, so full of history; people who come here, even on a visit, always return again.

But I'll tell you one thing: if I had the opportunity, I wouldn't stay here. Here your hands are tied – tongue, hands, everything is tied. And Czechs are two-faced: they talk to you as a friend, and then as soon as they leave you they say something bad or unkind about you. That's why I lead a solitary life. It's hard to find real friends, and the friends I had have all left. There are so very few of us Russians left. I have two Russian friends – women – but if you saw them! They're my age, but they're really *old*, they're dirty, and they've let themselves go. I understand them, but you should live by the standards to which you were brought up . . .

34

A Russian Life Abroad

MICHEL GORDEY

*Michel Gordey was born Mikhail Samoilovich Rappoport in St Peters-
burg in 1913. His parents disapproved of the Bolshevik Revolution and,
as life became more dangerous for bourgeois and Jews, the family fled
to Latvia, then on to Germany and France. Like many émigrés, the life
they led in their new homes continued to be almost exclusively Russian.*

As a child [in Petrograd] I remember trucks going by the house carrying
soldiers with raised rifles with bayonets and red flags and singing. On
the ceilings we had gold plasterwork – one could see it from the street;
but during the evening we never put the light on because once, when
we had it on, they started shooting.

The food became strange. My mother managed to feed me. My
father and she probably didn't eat as well as I did, but she managed to
do different things for me. There was very little meat. I remember that
we took in a tenant because otherwise some space would have been
requisitioned. He was a real tenant. He was probably a Bolshevik, or
at any rate on good terms with the authorities, because he had food,
and I was once scolded terribly by my mother because she found out
that this man was giving me the crusts of his cheese . . . She didn't like
that at all, both from the point of view of humiliation and that it could
be unhealthy. But this man had sausages, and cheese, and so on, which
we didn't have. And then a peasant woman would come in and ring at
the door, and my mother would give away some of her clothing – cheap
jewels, things like that – in exchange for food, butter, eggs, milk, but
in very small quantities.

Somehow we could heat at least a small part of our apartment. We
had an enormous Dutch stove in the corridor behind the main rooms,
so we slept mostly there, next to the stove. We had heat in the kitchen

too. Maybe we were getting some fuel from my father's job. We also had clothing – there was no problem with that. Probably the nights were not very agreeable. As far as I remember there were no visits of any kind – those nightly visits by the Cheka that I later read about. But there must have been a reason that we slept in this corridor, rather than in my parents' room – [it was partly for warmth] but there was some kind of security in it too . . .

There were [safety] measures decreed in the city. One had to sit in front of the building and guard it – I don't know whether it was against robbery. All the tenants in the building had to take turns. I remember that my mother used to sit on her *tumba*[1] in front of the building and I would sit with her for two or three hours. What we were watching for, I still don't remember . . .

We had no political protection or anything like that, so I think that my parents got more and more scared. My father was warned at his place of work that there would be a check on people of bourgeois origin and Jews, that he would be in trouble, and he got hints that he had better get out. He took the hints. My mother had been born in Riga, and Latvia at that time had become an independent state. It was arranged between the Soviet Government and the Latvian Government that people who had been born in Latvia could be repatriated there as if they were citizens of the newly constituted country. My mother applied, and for my father as being the husband of such a person; they probably had to bribe someone. Anyhow, we left legally, unlike many others who had to flee, in a very long train of box cars – and we travelled a very long time in the winter, in December 1920. I think it took ten or twelve days to go from Petrograd to the border, because the train [moved for only one or two hours a day and] stopped all the time and was put in sidings. We had taken food with us and all our belongings. I remember the men getting out very early, probably to pee, but they were also bringing back snow from the plains around the train, and it was heated so that we would have water. We had an iron stove in the middle of the box car.

But personally I remember liking it a lot on that train. I was very close to my mother and father all the time. They kept me between them. We were lying on *nary*, which were big planks – there were two levels in the car and we had a place on the higher. There were no disputes in the car – people were all very nice.

[In Riga we had] quite a lot of family. One of [my mother's uncles] lived there, so we found him. He was not a wealthy man but he was a man of means and still engaged in the timber business, and our financial problems were solved by the fact that my mother managed to get her jewels out. They were hidden away and were sold one after the other, and probably provided enough for us to live on and for some business enterprises for four or five years.

I remember some of the towers and some of the architecture of the Hanseatic city [Riga], churches, the beaches (which were very nice) where we spent the summer . . .

Almost exactly a year after we had arrived, there were discussions. If we had stayed we would have had to become Latvian citizens. Neither my mother nor my father wanted that, so they moved on to Germany. Both spoke German absolutely flawlessly. They went to Berlin and joined what was at that time a very big Russian émigré colony; I don't know about numbers: the Paris colony was already probably more numerous. But in the Berlin crowd there were some political–intellectual groups – perhaps even more than in Paris – and many of them moved to Paris.

We stayed [in Berlin] for almost five years, until June 1926. We had a good life so far as material things go. We had a very nice apartment in Schoeneberg near the Stadtpark. It was very luxurious. My father and mother were rather elegant people. When I think back, I don't think that they were very sensible with their money . . . However, in the last year we had to leave that apartment because I think it was too expensive. They moved to a much smaller apartment, also in Schoeneberg but much less luxurious.

They had many Russian émigré friends – many of them were Russian Jews, but there were also non-Jews. They didn't mix with the Germans much. [They lived a Russian life.] I don't know if it was so much Russian food, or Russian music or Russian theatre, though there was a lot of that. But their friends were all Russian. The language spoken at home was always Russian. And sometimes they would bring people back from some trip – even then these would be Dutch or Danes, but not Germans.

For me it was different, because I was in a German school, so I had some German friends, but in my school there were also quite a few Russian Jewish children like myself, including two of my cousins. I played more with these. I don't remember having German pals. I would go home with one or two of them, but in general I didn't bring them home or go to their homes.

I was a very good student. After one or two years, I was *primus* – first in the class. At that time anti-Semitism started in Germany and in that school there were a few future Nazis, among the pupils and the teachers, as I found out later. I never personally felt anything, because since I was such a good student some of the dumb boys would copy from me or get help from me, so I had a sort of bodyguard all the time. In the courtyard during breaktime there was some jeering at Jews, but I remember this bodyguard saying, 'This is our Jew. Leave him alone.' So I didn't feel threatened. The teachers didn't attack the Jews in class, but one of them was definitely a Nazi [even] then.

As far as German culture was concerned, I saw all the Schiller plays in the Berlin theatres – I knew them quite well. I would also read Dietrich, Heine and other authors, not only in school but at home. I was also taking in Russian as well – I think my favourite reading was still in Russian. My father would buy me books from Russian book-shops. Russian publishers were established there. Even in my parents' library they had lots of books in Russian that were published in Berlin. My parents brought a lot of books on that train from Petrograd.

I think [things] changed later on in Germany. I think that in the 1950s they were more curious about foreigners – they were going out to meet them. In the period that I'm talking about, I remember that the German Jews were rather proud of German citizenship, that they rather despised the *Auslandsjuden* or *Ostjuden*, though if you take the milieu of my parents and my uncle they were as well, if not better, educated than the Germans were. But there was still a sort of despising attitude to the East European Jews, which had always been the case with the German non-Jews but was also true of the German Jews. What they meant by *Ostjuden* were the poorer, so-called '*Bauchladenjuden*' [street-trading Jews]. These were the Polish Jews with their outlandish garb, black hats and locks, but they were all mixed in it, Russian Jews as well.

My father started several businesses [in Berlin, still using money from my mother's jewellery]. At first he went into film production – silent movies – with a partner and lost all his money. And then, I think, the last attempt also failed. He bought two taxis which were driven by White Army officers with whom he had a very friendly relationship. I think they cheated him terribly . . . It lasted one year, and then the taxis were gone and the officers were gone, and my father I think still didn't realize that they had cheated him. He was at that time a bad businessman. Later on, in France, he became a good businessman, but it took many, many years before he learnt. Anyhow, by that time we had lost all our money . . .

In Berlin we had lots of relatives. My father's sister, who had gone with her husband and children through Constantinople and Yugoslavia to Paris, had moved to Berlin from Paris. My uncle, Herr Doktor Rossen-Bernstein, [was] a lawyer and a businessman [and also] a very famous chess-player. [In 1926 he] was again in big business in Paris and finally called my father there and said, 'I have a job for you.' My father didn't have anything left in Berlin and my mother wanted to go to Paris anyway – she liked Paris and wanted to bring me up in France. So they moved there.

I think at the end of their stay in Germany, my parents, at least my father, had completely given up any idea of returning to Russia. He never believed – as at that time I know that many Russian refugees believed – that they would return and that Bolshevik rule would collapse. He had gone from Russia to Riga, from Riga to Germany, from Germany to France; these were all major changes in his life.

My father, when they came to Paris, spoke very little French. He did speak some, but with great difficulty and with an accent and it took him several years to speak it better. My mother, on the other hand, spoke French very well, and she had no difficulties, but my father had to fight for a living and he didn't think about the future very much. He had to think about the present and next week, and next month and how to pay the rent and how to keep his family. I don't think that he suffered very much from the exile. He was an exile – that was his condition. He didn't think that he would ever leave that condition. He was rather glad later on when he became a French citizen by naturalization [in 1937], though that was not because he had integrated into French life but because from the administrative and legal point of view this citizenship made life normal and easy for him. Before, he had difficulties – for work, for business, for the French had all sorts of restrictive laws for foreigners.

Not that my parents had integrated well, but there was just no other place to go. At that time nobody thought of going to America, which I did later on under other circumstances. They thought that they would stay in France, which they hadn't thought in Germany; from the beginning they had had the feeling that that was a temporary stay, that they hadn't completely settled down . . .

When we got here to Paris, I [was thirteen and] had only a few months to get ready for the French school. I was given some tutoring by two French women teachers, mother and daughter, who taught me several subjects, and by some linguistic magic, because I didn't speak French (I had learned French in school at Germany but very little), in a few months I was ready to enter that French school. Though I had some difficulty in the first six or seven months, pretty soon I was a very good student, especially in French.

In the mid-1920s in Paris there were two or three main centres of Russian emigration. There were people who lived in the 16th *arrondissement*, which is Les Beaux Quartiers – that's Auteuil and Passy. The poorer people were living in the 15th *arrondissement*, which was much cheaper – the rents were cheaper and the standard of living was lower there; that was more a working section. Some people lived in Boulogne, near Paris. We lived at the Porte de St-Cloud, which was on the city limits of Paris – Auteuil. [Our house] was in a complex of houses – a whole group of buildings belonging to the city of Paris. There were probably a thousand people living in this group of houses, more than half of whom were Russians. There were doctors, painters, all kinds of professions . . . And they stuck together. There was not one but four Russian food shops in the neighbourhood. There were Russian restaurants.

Again, what happened was that my parents had very few French friends. They went on living among their Russian friends. They had *some* French friends – more than they had German friends when they were in Germany – but very few and not really good personal friends. Some Russian friends from Berlin had followed them there. And there was our family which had moved on from Berlin . . . My father and mother read the Russian paper every day – *Posledniye Novosti*. They took part in the Russian cultural life, I think – there was the Russian theatre, they went to concerts and in general read Russian books, though also French books.

[Once again], it was completely different for me because I had my school friends, though my very best friend in Paris was a Russian Jewish boy who was killed at Dunkirk in the French Army. I was in a group of Russian Jewish boys. We played chess a lot [and] went together to different things. We even had a Russian informal gathering – a *kruzhok* – of boys and girls who were all Russian or Russian Jewish and spoke Russian and recited poetry and sang and there was Russian music, though we were all going to French schools. Some became lawyers, some doctors; some went back to Russia and had very tragic fates.

In 1935–6 there was a movement among the young Russians – those who were then twenty or twenty-one: a strange nostalgia for Russia developed and the Soviets did take them back. One girl went back and six months later was arrested and spent seventeen years in a concentration camp in the Gulag (where she met Solzhenitsyn, by the way). She also met in the different Gulags two of the former members of this *kruzhok*. Both of them died. They had gone back because they felt Russian. I never even thought of doing this. It bewilders me even now, how these people went back . . .

35

Gaiety . . . and Despair

COUNTESS EKATERINA NIEROTH

Countess Ekaterina Nieroth (née Kleinmichel) was born into the Russian aristocracy in St Petersburg in 1902. Her father was killed fighting the Bolsheviks during the Civil War. The rest of the family went to Finland in 1917, then to the Ukraine. From there they journeyed to Yalta to join Countess Nieroth's grandmother, Yekaterina Petrovna Kleinmichel, whose memories of the evacuation of the Crimea, and the departure of the Dowager Empress Maria Fyodorovna from Yalta, are recounted in Chapter 21.

After leaving the Crimea, the family was taken to Malta and from there went on to Berlin, where they had relatives.

In Germany I married my husband, Count Nieroth. When the great inflation came, and life in Germany became impossible, we went to his relations in Paris, and then to the Côte d'Azur . . . I worked in a *maison de mode*; my sister had a *maison de lingerie*. In the 1920s, it wasn't difficult to get a *permis de travail*, or a visa. You had only to ask for them – and pay, of course. My husband got a job with the Garanty Trust Bank. First he was a cashier, then a sorter. After that, he was with the Listerine Company. To get into these firms, you had to know someone already there. We were very poor: my husband was earning 600 francs a month – much less than our friends driving taxis were getting. He would work from 6 p.m. to midnight because it paid better. When he bought his first pair of shoes in France – that was years after we arrived there – we looked at them for weeks before he put them on. In those firms, if you made a mistake you were fined, and if you made three mistakes you were kicked out. For the Russians in France, life was easier under Léon Blum – I have to say that, though I don't like his politics. He was much more lenient. It was easier to get papers, identity cards and so on, which you needed if you were to work and find lodgings.

For us young Russians in France, life was gay. We remembered Russia only vaguely. We were poor, but we were all in the same boat. We went out in the evenings to parties, to Russian restaurants – where the waiter might be your best friend. Among the older generation, though, there was much despair when little by little their hopes that the Bolsheviks would disappear and they would go back were disappointed . . .

36

The Russian Dustmen of Cannes

COUNTESS NATALYA SUMAROKOV-ELSTON

Countess Sumarokov-Elston's earlier recollections appear in Chapter 23. After leaving Russia in 1921 the family sailed to Constantinople, then travelled on to Venice and finally settled in the south of France.

The Russian dustmen of Cannes were famous: they were very elegant and glamorous in their military tunics! Everyone loved them. I knew an English woman who lived below a Russian colonel who was working as a dustman, and he used to give her copies of the *Tatler* every week. She asked him why on earth he got the *Tatler* – 'Oh, to keep track of my friends.'

Some of the French whom Russians had known before the war were very kind. My husband went instinctively to the Hôtel Meurice when he arrived. After three days he realized they were charging him the same price they had in 1914, despite the fact that in the meantime inflation had made that sum almost ridiculous. He couldn't pay the real price, so he left. Another friend went to Dusé to get some new shirts and he told them he owed them money from before the war. They told him they'd torn up all those bills. Nor did they want him to pay for the new shirts – he'd been a good customer in the past.

Russians adapted very quickly, but very few made fortunes. They're very bad at money. But they soon found jobs: couture for the women; nursing; embroidery. The men started driving taxis, acting as guides for American tourists – anything. In Constantinople, when we were there, there was already a Russian restaurant – the Doré – with *baryshni* [well-brought-up girls] acting as waitresses. So there was no sitting around. But the Russian restaurants I knew in France mostly went bankrupt. People would be eating in front, while at the back there would be a room where old Russian generals would sit drinking vodka and eating the restaurant's food, talking politics and fighting battles: 'Now if I'd put my cavalry *there* and my guns *there* . . . ' – it was a stock joke.

The women mostly started work first; the men had been through the war, then the Civil War – they were still dazed. But there was no loss of self-respect in taking any job that was going: 'Man must have bread!'

Mother and Father bought a farm and Father teamed up with a childhood friend he met. It was an absolute disaster. They knew nothing about farming. He'd been a soldier all his life. He did know something about horses, but not about cows. Then he trained dogs for a while. After that he collected bills for the Gas and Electricity Company. His friend Baron Prittwitz[1] read the meters. They'd meet on the street: 'How are you, my dear fellow?' 'I live like a moth, you know – first I eat my trousers, then the jacket!' There was no gloom and no suicides. Russians become gloomy only when they have nothing to be gloomy about and have time to sit around and think.

For two years my cousin and I had private lessons. Then, aged fifteen, we were put into school with the *Sœurs Laïques*. That was very difficult. In maths and so on I had of course to translate from the Russian terms, despite the fact that my French was good. They were very strict and hypercritical, didn't even want you to laugh. And then they taught such rubbish about Russia – that Russian women were veiled, that they had to go round in closed carriages. How could we believe them about anything else when they taught things like that? One trouble was that people in the West tended to say to the Russian émigrés, 'Well, you got your just deserts,' because we had supposedly oppressed the people so terribly.

After that I went to the École des Arts Décoratifs, and then became a mannequin. For a while I worked as an extra for Rex Ingram's films[2] – the whole of Russian Nice was working as extras. When he was making a film of *The White Devil* my father had a glorious two weeks. They made a village in the mountains above Cannes into a complete *aul* [Caucasian village] for the time of the making of the film, and he had the illusion that he was home again.

Around Cannes there were many Cossacks who kept chicken farms. They never learnt French – there was one famous mistranslation from Russian in an advertisement: '*Cosaque d'Amour Divorce les Poules*'.[3] My nanny never learnt either French or English, although she died only twelve years ago – yet she always understood what was going on and somehow people understood her; and she always knew all the gossip. There were many like that.

Countess Sumarokov-Elston moved to England in 1937 with her husband, a professional tennis player (and cousin of Prince Yusupov, involved in the murder of Rasputin in 1917) who came to help found the Russian Sports Club in Chiswick in London.

37

A Second Flight

IONA SOLOMONOVICH HALPERIN

The memoirs of Iona Halperin's mother are recorded in Chapter 7. When the family left Russia, they went first to Constantinople, then on to Marseilles, Lausanne and Montreux; from there they moved to Berlin, then to Wiesbaden, eventually settling in Paris in 1924/5.

I was three years old when the family moved to Paris, so you could say that I am French: I consider myself a Frenchman, but not quite – although I have a French passport. I follow French politics very closely and vote with care when there are elections; I consider myself a citizen of France with full rights. However, my Jewish origins and Russian upbringing cannot be denied. I remember when I was a child in Paris, taking notes in a history lesson. The teacher was speaking of the French Revolution and all the time referring to 'us', 'we' – and somehow, as I scribbled down my notes, it was difficult to consider myself a true French boy!

[I went to] a French State grammar school: Lycée Sainte-Cécile, in Paris in the 16th *arrondissement*. And (to illustrate my parents' approach to such things) once a week a private tutor would come to our home to give us lessons in Russian. Evgenia Mikhailovna – I forget her surname – read Russian literature with us and taught us the language. She was an émigrée herself.

Some time later, the Russian émigré community organized a kind of Sunday School for the children, with lessons in Russian literature, under the leadership of General Golovin – Nikolay Nikolayevich.[1] In my room I have the complete works of Pushkin, beautifully illustrated, which I received for outstanding marks in my Russian lessons. It was obvious that our teacher was a former general. As it was a voluntary organization, I don't know what his status would have been in the

French school system, but he had his own class and would teach about twenty hours of Russian literature every week. He was an incredible character. Although a born soldier, he behaved as a true aristocrat of the intellect – a member of the Tsarist intelligentsia. He was a tall, well-built man. I remember that he wore a French Order, awarded to him in the First World War. He was a very precise man and carried out his duties in the classroom with much devotion – which cannot have been easy as we were all children of about fifteen or sixteen. But you could feel that he was happy to pass on his love for Russian history and literature to these young foreigners – and there were also others like me, second-generation Russian émigrés. Those classes were no ordinary, formal lectures either! He was an unconventional character. He would come into the room and start talking. We would take notes, but at the end, they would generally read back as – nonsense! He died during the Second World War.

Mother was also friends, through her parents, with the famous General Miller,[2] who was kidnapped by the Soviets. The Soviets were very worried about the international situation at that time, when they kidnapped Miller.

When we arrived in Paris my father was forty-five years of age and a professional man. I think he very much hoped to find a responsible job, but it didn't happen that way. He occupied himself with some business affairs, but without much enthusiasm and somewhat irregularly. He relied heavily on his parents for everything – his parents moved to Paris at the same time as we did, and they lived in a two-floored flat in the same block. So he gave all his time to his parents and his children. He was always at home and was very involved in our upbringing. He never gave us any lessons, but he kept us in order. Although my parents never complained in front of us, I think that he suffered from the fact that the Revolution had deprived him of his professional career.

I was eighteen or nineteen when the war started in 1939. I was not called up for the French Army. My elder brother took French citizenship before us, and did his military service in the Army at Le Havre, 129th Battalion, in 1938–9. As for myself and my twin [brother], we completed a study course at the Military Academy from 1939 to 1940, to prepare ourselves for Army service. Our year should have been called up just at that time, when the war started, so we escaped conscription involuntarily.

I became a French citizen only after the war. My parents also did not wish to cut the crucial tie to their Russian identity; it wouldn't even have entered into their heads to ask for a French passport. People are amused at this stubborn Russian patriotism – especially since we are not even Russian, but Jews. But you must remember that during the war, in spite of Stalin, Communism, and so on, my father regarded himself first and foremost as Russian. In the Great Patriotic War, we were *all* Russian patriots.

We left Paris around June 1940, on practically the last normal train, and travelled to Vichy. We knew that we would get a car there, and planned on using this to travel to the centre of France. We lived there, in Vichy, through June, July, August and September. Then in autumn, my parents moved to Orange. They more or less set themselves up there, but my brother and I stayed on in Lyons [to complete our university degrees].

There were troubles [with Vichy legislation].³ They came to look for us once or twice to make us fulfil our quota of compulsory labour. But our people would say that we were not at home, or sometimes we sought the help of the Resistance. On 22 June 1941, when the Russo-German War began, the French arrested both of us, because we were considered half Russian. It was the same for my parents in Orange; they also were put in prison. This did not continue for long because we were able to explain that we were refugees from Soviet Russia. But on principle, at that time they arrested all of us: Russians, half Russians. If you had any trace of Russian blood, you were regarded as a possible enemy.

Towards the end of 1942, one of my mother's sisters was married in Basel. We were then still in contact by phone and letter and, being in France, we told her how much of a threat there was to her if she tried to join us. It was clear to us that the best thing to do was to stay put – we weren't even too keen on going to Paris, because it still seemed unsafe to expose yourself by travelling.

Then my mother's sister began to insist doggedly that we should get out fast, otherwise it could only end badly for us all. They were starting to round up the Jews, to arrest them. So, on her own initiative, she somehow obtained visas and travel passes to Switzerland for us. Towards the end of 1942, she persuaded us to leave France for Switzerland illegally – and how we did this is a story in itself.

I had to make contact and come to an agreement with a secret organization – French, not Jewish, a branch of the Resistance. They got hold of an ambulance for us as a car, for our father was already sixty-two years old and was suffering from a weak heart. Maybe sixty-two seems young, but he had already undergone much hardship. It seemed that everything was in order, and we decided that it would be best to travel across part of France not by train, nor by car, but by ambulance. So [in December] Father, Mother, my twin brother and I (my elder brother remained in France) set off. We were not driven right up to the border, of course, but somewhere about fifty kilometres from Geneva. It was night. There was a full moon. The '*passeur*' was waiting for us there as agreed. When we all climbed out of the ambulance, our guide took us by the hand and led us along byways that were so familiar to him. It was still a terrifying risk, for we were totally in the hands of this *contrabandiste* – he could have taken us anywhere. These *contrabandistes* always assumed that people who were fleeing from France must have gold, jewels and valuables, but we had only fake stones, cut-glass and trinkets. We knew that it was necessary to give him some contraband; a little suitcase full of trinkets, perhaps, and that would be all.

They led us for several hours through the forest, until we came to a small, fast-running stream. Then they took us on a little further and said, 'You're on your own now – get moving! The border is over there. Be careful because the Germans are there, with dogs . . . ' But we were very lucky. We set off across country and suddenly saw some soldiers in uniform. We were convinced that they were Germans, but they turned out to be Swiss. [We were] not far from Geneva.

We told them that we were escaping from France but our visas were at Berne. They then telephoned the authorities and took us by lorry to a camp at Geneva – Camp Chernis. We stayed there for less than an hour, for as soon as they had confirmed that we did indeed have visas we were allowed to leave. It was lucky that the visas were there, because otherwise they could have sent us back – to certain death.

Halperin stayed in Switzerland after the war, taking his doctorate at Zurich University and becoming a teacher of Economic and Social History at the University. He also worked as an interpreter for the United Nations and in 1966/7 became Head of the Languages Division. He retired in 1981.

38

Surviving

PYOTR ROBERTOVICH KARPUSHKO

The story of Karpushko's escape from Russia is told in Chapter 18. His attempts to emigrate to the United States to join his mother and brothers having failed, he made his way instead to France, where he built up a new life.

Eventually my cousin, who was in Paris in the Foreign Legion, helped me. He provided me with false documents and arranged a job for me [as an electrician] at a chocolate factory in Paris. That is how I came to Paris. There was no more chance to get to the United States. My brothers and my mother sent me money from America and that helped me to survive. [Later] I worked for Citroën.[1] He was a Russian Jew – Tsitron – and helped Russian refugees a great deal. I found working at his factory very unpleasant, though, because I was suffocating from the smell of burning machine oil. After that I left to work for other private businesses on a contract basis. That lasted eleven years, until Gorgulov assassinated the French President,[2] when I became jobless again.

By that time I was already married and had a child. My wife was a teacher, who taught the children of a very rich publisher, and he found out that I was unemployed. This publishing house was very big – it employed eighteen hundred people – and the head of the firm took me on. I worked at the [company's] power station. I had to deal with the station, generators, motors and all the electric equipment.

[The firm] was called 'Éditions Monsouris'. The head of the firm – Monsieur de Cognières – was very nice to me and my wife. He helped us a lot. I was told at the personnel office that they could not keep foreigners, and that we had to get naturalized as soon as possible. We started the procedure, went to the doctors and so on, but we still got no reply to our application. One day I was telling this to the head of one of the departments of the firm; he told me that his brother worked at the Ministry of Foreign Affairs and asked me to write down my name. The next day he brought the decree of our naturalization.

We lived near the Place d'Italie [in Paris]. It was a great time! We almost never had a chance to speak French. At work it was only 'Hello' and 'Goodbye'. Everything else was Russian. Russian schools, Russian churches, Russian conferences, Russian balls. Later, in order to help the Russian unemployed in Paris, I lectured at the so-called Russian People's University. It was organized by a certain Dmitriev, a Russian architect. I taught electrical theory and installation techniques: I had to work during weekends. I was very proud of it. My students obtained jobs at the Métro as electricians.

[In the 1930s] I belonged to the Russian Peasant Movement [*Russkoye Krestyanskoye Dvizheniye*]. I was a youth leader there. And since I loved the sea we had a sailboat, which we sailed along the Mediterranean coast during the school holidays. We would stop at all the Russian youth summer camps on the coast. We would play volleyball and afterwards have tea. Then we were invited for supper; we would take part in another volleyball match and have more tea, and so it went on for days on end. Thus we cruised along the Côte d'Azur and spoke only Russian day after day. Until Léon Blum introduced *vacances payées* in 1937 there were no Frenchmen, just Russian émigrés.[3] If somebody were to speak French on the beach, he would be gawped at in surprise. The Russians, though, would arrive at the Côte d'Azur in trains not only full of children, but of grandparents as well. [They were] just simple people, who from the bottom of their hearts wanted their parents and grandparents to have a bit of sun. In such a way people put together trainloads of Russians. Of course, after you arrived you had to put up a tent, stuff a mattress with straw and sew it up – in other words, conditions there were very primitive. But none the less, everybody was content. In the evening we would have a fire, gather round it and sing songs, drink tea and eat watermelons or grapes. All this still exists . . .

I was affiliated with the Russian Student Christian Movement, because they believed that the Soviets could not be destroyed by machine guns but by ideas. You cannot kill ideas. Our church did not recognize the Patriarch of Moscow, since there was not any freedom. The then Patriarch Tikhon collected money for the restoration of churches and people gave their last pennies, but instead of this they would use the money to build a Komsomol club. It was robbery!

During the Second World War we hid Soviet soldiers who escaped from the construction sites of the so-called Atlantic Wall – the fortifications [which the Germans were building] on the Atlantic coast. Some of them we visited in hospital. They had tuberculosis. We would bring them a tie and say, 'Look here, Seryozha, what a beautiful tie! When you get well, you will wear it.' But, of course, in a month the fellow would die. There were also Georgians among them. Around Christmas time one of them, called Misha, told me that he was going to go to a French peasant who had helped him immediately after his escape from the Germans. He hoped to get some produce from the peasant, a hare or maybe some eggs. He asked me to give him a suitcase for that purpose. My wife gave him one that belonged to my younger son, Vanya. The suitcase had all Vanya's particulars written on it: name, address, etc. Then Misha disappeared. In fact a Czech *homme de liaison* took him to see a peasant, where they had a good time and then returned to Paris. This Czech worked as a gas-fitter in Paris and he had secretly put gas-pipes into his flat for heating purposes. So the two men had a little celebration for Christmas; they drank, fell asleep and never woke up. During the night the gas was temporarily cut off, which apparently was the cause of the incident. In the morning a neighbour came knocking on the door, surprised that they were still asleep. She had been asked to cook lunch for them. Then she smelled the gas and called for the concierge. She opened the door and they all saw that the two men were already blue in the face. When the police arrived, they naturally found my son's suitcase in the room. The police immediately became suspicious, since the dead men were foreigners. They thought they might have been connected with the Resistance movement. Imagine what would have happened if the police had found my address on the ill-fated suitcase . . . But luckily my wife had had the sense to rip that piece of paper with the address on it off the suitcase, so I did not have to worry about being hanged.

[In the war] a lot of Russians were put behind bars – professors, clergymen, etc. Mother Maria, a Russian nun, was put in jail by the Germans because she signed certificates of baptism for Jews. And Father Dmitry Klepinin, a friend of ours, also signed certificates of baptism for Jews in order to save them. They were sent to concentration camps. Mother Maria died there. A young Jewish woman was very afraid of death and was weeping and crying, so Mother Maria offered to exchange passports and went to die instead of her.

[I served in the French Army until] after the treaty signed by Marshal Pétain on the border.[4] He issued a statement to the effect that the French Army and Air Force were destroyed and therefore there was no sense in continuing the massacre. At that moment we started to retreat. I was retreating with my wife and my little son, who was only eight months old. During this march we were bombed six times by the Germans. When this happened we would head for cover, which we found in the ditch by the roadside, and pull a thick blanket over our bodies to shelter ourselves from bomb splinters. Once I was shot at from a German plane while I was rolling myself a cigarette, but I managed to escape unscathed.

At first we moved in the direction of Spain. Then we thought we could get away to the French colonies, such as Algiers. We reached the border region near Pau, in the Pyrenees. There we found ourselves in an abandoned car park. I found an empty Rolls-Royce and we slept in it for two days. Then we went looking for wood to make a fire. My little son was crawling on the ground where lots of snakes were creeping as well, but they did not touch him.

Then came the Armistice. Demobilization. I received some money for that. I needed a seat on the train to return to Paris. By chance I met a friend of mine, Anthony Bloom; he was the son of the former Russian Ambassador to Persia.[5] When I asked him what was he doing there, he explained to me that he was escorting the staff of a hospital, which used to be in the central part of France. Anthony was a doctor there. All the other doctors had fled from the Germans and he was the only one to have stayed behind, so he had evacuated all the staff to the south of France and now he was returning. I told him I had been stung by a bee and he, having said it was very dangerous, extracted the sting. Then he gave me all his money so that I could return to Paris . . . When he was young, he was very much loved by children and even more by young women. He was very handsome when he was young. I asked him once why didn't he pay attention to any of the women and he said that he did not want to offend any of them. So thus he remained a monk. He is a very remarkable person.

In Paris I returned to the same publishing house where I had worked before the war [and] I continued to work there for another twenty-seven years. In recent years I have been chiefly engaged in fundraising for our local Russian Society . . . for funerals, flowers, wreaths, for help for the needy. We have a small committee, of which [my wife] Nadezhda Antonovna is the secretary. I also conduct cultural and educational work. We get together about three times a year, for Christmas, Easter and Mardi Gras [*maslennitsa*]. We put together plays, organize conferences, balls, dances, dinners – everything Russian still lives on here. On an average evening about ten people will turn up. But many people send in their donations for charity. It's a wonderful manifestation of solidarity. We have learned this from the Jews. They have a very well-developed sense of solidarity. The Russians often distinguish people by their political or other beliefs, but I think all that is irrelevant; the most important thing is that we are all first and foremost human beings.

In our family there have been many tragedies. [I am the only survivor.]

My uncle was in the Army during the First World War. He was wounded and captured by the Germans. When he returned after the war to Russia, the Soviet authorities, who were already in power, told him that he ought to join the Red Army at once. He pleaded with them, begging to be allowed to return to his family for a while, since he had not seen them for a long time. He wanted to see his mother, wife and children. He tried to explain that he had spent three and a half years as a prisoner-of-war and it was only natural that he should want to see his family. But the Soviets called it sabotage and put him in jail. There he lost his sanity. When he went mad, he was let free. He returned to our family home, and we found him one winter morning – dead, on a nearby bench. He still had a piece of bread in his pocket, so he had died not from hunger but from exposure.

My sister Katya was engaged during the First World War. I remember her fiancé was very cheerful, young and handsome. Two months after the war had begun he returned home to Moscow, but in what a state! His arms and legs had been amputated, because they had been frostbitten. Katya visited him every Sunday at the military hospital. On one of her visits he asked her if she was still willing to be his wife, and she replied that as long as she lived she would not change her mind. A week later she stopped coming to the hospital. Two weeks passed and she still did not appear, so her fiancé sent his batman to find out why she was not coming and was told that Katya had shot herself two weeks ago – immediately after that conversation about her keeping her promise to marry him. When the man found this out, this is what he did. His room in the hospital was on the sixth floor; he sent his batman to get him some cigarettes, but first he asked him to bring him closer to the window. As the batman reached street-level he heard a big thump and something fell down right next to him. It was my sister's fiancé, who had rolled over the window-sill to his death.

I had another sister – Natasha. She married a certain Markov in Odessa. The Markov family had been famous since the time of Peter the Great: they were very rich merchants – real millionaires. Natasha had to give birth to a baby in Odessa. It was in winter; outside it was −17°C and at the same time the city was being bombed. All the windows in their house were shattered from the bombing and she had to deliver in the cold. She caught peritonitis and died. The new-born baby died as well and her husband was shot by the Reds as a saboteur.

My brother Vanya, who lived in the United States, had a very beautiful daughter, Xenia, who was so pretty that she even entered a beauty contest. On the way to the contest she had an accident, fractured her spine and died. My brother could not reconcile himself to the death of his beloved daughter, so he killed himself. My other brother, Pavel, a former officer, came to Paris to visit us for the Easter holidays. The weather was superb and I suggested that we go to the Côte d'Azur and take a cruise aboard a ship, but he refused and preferred to stay in Paris. As we were saying our goodbyes, he embraced and kissed me in a very strange way, and I did not like the way he looked at me. When we returned from our trip we could not open the door to the flat, since it was kept shut from inside with what we thought was a chair. My wife and I went to the neighbours; they came with us and we managed to open the door. As we entered the flat we saw my brother lying on the kitchen floor – dead. He had shot himself. He had cancer of the stomach; he left behind a note explaining everything.

So I am the only survivor; [I have already survived a great deal] and I think that if God gives me the chance to continue living, I should go on.

39

'Ces Sales Russes'

TATYANA IVANOVNA GABARD

Tatyana Ivanovna Gabard's father was a lecturer in the St Petersburg Naval Academy and the family was living in Kronstadt[1] when the Revolution began in 1917. As conditions in the capital worsened, they moved south, eventually settling in Sevastopol, where a new Naval Academy was planned. After only a year there, they were forced to flee again as the Red Army closed in on the Crimea. With hundreds of others, they sailed for Constantinople, thence to Tunisia, where the family was accommodated in the refugee camp at Bizerta.

Bizerta was surrounded by forts. Those who arrived with the Naval Academy were placed in Kibir-Kibir, while all the families were placed in a camp at Svayak. There were several cadet divisions, two *garde-marine* [naval warrant officers] who lived in the old barracks. They even had their own church there. They had their instructors and their teachers; for example, there were very good professors of physics, history, natural sciences, astronomy, two excellent mathematicians . . . In this way the young men and boys received a very good education up to the level of the top class in a *gymnazia*. Parallel with the general education they studied navigation and other maritime subjects. The only thing they could not do was go to sea. They had their own rifles, and they practised marching. They also had uniforms made out of material sent to us by the Americans. Many women in our camp, including my mother, sewed trousers, shirts and caps for them. In fact, the American Red Cross sent not only materials but ready-made clothes, since we had practically nothing. They also helped during the holidays and I remember that, for example, Christmas could be celebrated with a Christmas tree and various good things, thanks to American gifts. We even had a dance on Christmas Day.

I had a good time there, but it was not the same for the adults. They were the ones who had to bear the burden of everyday life in a refugee camp. We did not have separate quarters. Our family was separated from the neighbours only by a blanket, and it was much more difficult for adults to live in those conditions. And even then we still did not think we could stay away for ever, we still thought we would go back, we dreamed that we would return . . .

We left Bizerta in 1924 and the others stayed there for another two years. As the boys graduated from the Academy they left. Many went to Paris, where numerous charity organizations existed which provided help and scholarships. Many of those young men went to study further at Nancy, Strasbourg and other places. Some went to the United States. The camp was closed in 1925–6. Admiral Dmitriev, who was Russian naval attaché in Paris under the Tsar, remained in Paris after the Revolution and he in particular helped the families of naval officers, using the funds left over from the old regime.

When we left Bizerta we went to France. France was experiencing a labour shortage, and many people were in fact invited to go and work there on a contract basis, among them my father. He got a job at the Delage automobile factory. He learnt to operate a certain machine, but he worked there only a short period. A year after he started work, he was going home one evening by tram and a lorry collided with the tram just at the point where my father was standing. As a result, his right arm was crushed and had to be amputated immediately, and for the rest of his life he was an invalid. This, of course, affected his employment. At first he found a job at the same factory, doing something very simple: operating a lift. But then the times changed, the economic situation grew worse – it was the time of the economic crisis – and it became harder for him to find employment. Nevertheless, Father learnt to write with his left hand very well indeed, and for some time he worked for the father of one of my schoolmates, who had a construction firm. My father kept the books for him. He did all this work in French. [He did not know it well] but he worked at it very hard and managed to learn it well enough. He spoke very good English, since his dream had always been to settle in England . . . but of course we couldn't go to England, because we had no relatives there and England was not accepting anybody.

When we came to Paris I was fourteen. I was placed in a *lycée* with the help of Admiral Dmitriev. Anna Pavlova, the famous ballerina, opened a small *pension* for girls in the suburbs of Paris, in a place called St-Cloud. It provided for only fifteen girls, but even that was a great help. I was one of the fifteen and I was fully provided for; everything was paid for by Anna Pavlova, and that meant that my parents did not have to worry about finding the means to support me. I went to the Lycée de St-Cloud; other girls went to a real Russian school, which existed in Paris for a long time. It had been steadily declining until Countess Donskaya – Lady Olga Deterding[2] – donated a large sum of money, which revived it.

We were not received very well in France. We were invited into the country, that is true, but only because we were needed. The attitude of the common people was awful. Whenever we had to get papers at the Préfecture it was a real drama. We were treated like dogs. There were many uneducated Russians – soldiers, for example – who did not speak French, so they were bounced from one counter to another, yelled at, treated in the worst possible manner. Their papers were thrown at them if something was missing or seemed unsatisfactory to the French bureaucrats. And as for the people in the street, they were not too keen on us either. First of all, they bore a grudge against us for their lost money. Tsarist Russia received a big loan from France, and of course after the Revolution it was never repaid. So all those Frenchmen who had bought Russian bonds lost their money, and I don't think they ever forgave us for this loss.

Once, I remember, I visited an American doctor in Paris, who wanted me to give him French lessons. I was barely seventeen then. His housekeeper, an ordinary Frenchwoman, but quite nice, once gave me a piece of her mind. I noticed her treating me in a rather peculiar way, as if she were angry with me. When I asked her what was the matter, she screamed, 'You Russians, you came here! But it is because of you that we lost all our savings!' So I tried to explain to her that we, too, lost all our savings, and that I had nothing to do with it anyway. But it was in vain. Others used to say, 'Go away, get lost,' and one could hear the words '*Ces sales russes*' at every turn.

It got worse when the economic situation worsened. You can read many such stories in the books by Teffi[3] and other Russian émigré writers. As the economic situation got worse, the Russians were the first to lose their jobs, as there were plenty of unemployed Frenchmen. Then the authorities said they would issue a work permit if you could bring a note from a prospective employer stating that he was willing to employ you. But when people applied for one of these notes, employers said they couldn't engage anyone without a work permit. So it was a vicious circle. Some Russians were so desperate, they didn't know what to do, and there were cases of suicide. Don't forget that at that time – 1929–30 – there was no social security, no supplementary benefits. Only later, in 1936, were some rudimentary welfare benefits introduced. I, for example, could not work in France simply because I didn't have a work permit. Finally, it was an American firm that employed me without asking who I was and where I was from.

[When war broke out the French] conscripted those same Russians to whom they had denied a work permit. And we greatly resented that . . .

40

Exiles in America

DMITRY VLADIMIROVICH LEKHOVICH

Dmitry Vladimirovich Lekhovich was born in 1901. His father was an officer of the Guards Artillery. In 1918 Dmitry joined the Volunteer Army, but his service was brought to an abrupt end when he caught typhus. Although still ill, he managed to join his parents as they were evacuated from Novorossiysk in March 1920 and went with them to Yugoslavia. Once he had recovered his health he returned to Russia to fight with Wrangel's Army in the Crimea. When the Civil War ended he was evacuated from Sevastopol to Gallipoli, where he spent eight months until his father obtained a Yugoslav visa for him.

When I reached Yugoslavia, I was offered a post – it was very touching, the Serbs in those days were extremely pro-White Russian – in the *Granichna Trupa*: the Yugoslav Frontier Guard; the post was on the Albanian frontier. I'm afraid I wasn't very attracted to it, but at the same time I was offered the job of messenger in the *Serbska Zadruzhna Banka*. I took it, and from messenger I was promoted to bookkeeper; there I stayed until late 1923. After that I spent ten months in England, and from there I went to the USA.

My stay [in England] was due to visa problems. The American immigration laws were changed – the Russian quota was reduced from twenty-six thousand to two thousand and it was very quickly filled. I had to wait until there was a place for me. But because the White Star Line had already undertaken to transport us to America, we lived at the company's expense at Atlantic Park in Eastleigh, near Southampton, until our visas came through. It was nothing but an enormous hangar which had been used to house blimps during the First World War. We slept on long rows of bunks – for ten months.

I had a very good time. I hired a bicycle and explored a large part of Hampshire and southern England. Most of [the others] were Jews who had come from various parts of Eastern Europe. Some were from Russia, but most from Poland – and in particular from the former Russian Poland. I spoke Russian with them – indeed, most of them didn't even speak Polish.

I was invited [to America. My 'sponsor' was] a relative who had already emigrated. I arrived in New York [in September 1925] and, apart from the years of the Second World War when I was in Washington, I have lived in New York ever since . . .

Soon after my arrival, I enrolled at Columbia University and in due course graduated. From there I went into banking, where I stayed until retirement, having reached the position of a Vice-President of the Manufacturers' Hanover Trust Bank.

I didn't renounce my past. One's past is too closely bound up with one's whole life. I did, however, renounce any involvement in Russian émigré politics. Among the émigrés there were, of course, people of all political persuasions, but I would have nothing to do with their politics, while maintaining excellent personal relations with many of them, of all political colours. I was, for instance, on very friendly terms with Nabokov,[1] and through him I got to know Kerensky.

One day before the war Nabokov invited me to his home, he was a lecturer in those days and not too well off – he had a room in his sister-in-law's apartment, a walk-up on 60th Street on the fourth floor, near Madison Avenue. We were sitting around – it was quite late; I arrived only after most of the other guests had already left – when suddenly the doorbell rang. Heavy footsteps on the stairs. Nabokov said, 'That must be Alexander Fyodorovich.' The door opened and Kerensky said, as he looked around the room, 'Ah, I see that whenever I arrive somewhere all "decent" people leave!' It was said in such an amusing, self-deprecating way that I decided to stay and see what Kerensky was like at close quarters. Nabokov wanted to draw me into the conversation, and mentioned to Kerensky that I had been at the Lycée.[2] 'Ah,' said Kerensky, 'did you leave Russia right after the February Revolution?' (I suppose he thought I was a confirmed monarchist.) I replied, 'No, I stayed until 1920 and lived right through the mess you created!' I immediately felt very ashamed of myself for this remark; he was, after all, a man considerably older than me, and I was a guest in someone else's house. When we were leaving, Kerensky offered me a lift home – at that time he was living in the house of a very rich

American woman [and he] very kindly took me home in the chauffeur-driven car that his hostess had put at his disposal.

I met him later, too, here in America. I remember an occasion in 1927, when a book that he had written was translated into English and published. It was in the Century Theater, where Kerensky was to make a speech to an audience of Russian émigrés. The theatre was full, and I could only get a seat at the very back, but I saw Kerensky come on stage, to be greeted by a mixture of applause and a sort of hostile buzz. Then some woman came up on stage with a huge bouquet of red flowers. Kerensky accepted the bouquet with great pleasure, at which moment the woman gave him the most resounding box on the ears. The place immediately broke into an uproar; the police had to take action and they arrested the woman. It later transpired that her brother had been killed at the very beginning of the Revolution; he was a naval officer, who was killed by revolutionary sailors in Kronstadt[3] . . .

I knew Nabokov well, but it was hard for anyone to say that they had a *close* friendship with Nabokov . . . Although he could often be a very amusing companion, a large part of his nature was made up of what one might call profound self-love, although in those days, before the publication of *Lolita*, it was unjustified in other people's eyes. Still, as far as I'm concerned, I was always on very good terms with him . . .

At one time I was very friendly with another émigré writer and critic, Georgy Dmitrievich Adamovich;[4] he had been my tutor in Russia. He settled in France, and the only time, unfortunately, that he came to America was in 1971. He spent an evening here with us, and then a few weeks later he died. I'm afraid Nabokov couldn't stand Adamovich, and Georgy Dmitrievich greatly disliked Nabokov too . . .

On his retirement in 1966 Dr Lekhovich devoted his time to writing his History of the Volunteer Army *(published in 1973). His interest in the White movement stemmed originally from his own participation in its collapse; in addition, in America he got to know Denikin during the final years of his life. When the former general died, his widow granted Dr Lekhovich complete access to his archive – a source of priceless material on the Civil War.*

41

'Here Is Imperial Russia . . . '

PYOTR PETROVICH SHILOVSKY

Pyotr Petrovich Shilovsky's account of the Russian Revolution is given in Chapter 5. He and his wife arrived in England in 1922. After about eighteen months his engineering projects began to be well received and in time the couple settled into the close-knit Russian community in London. The recollections of Shilovsky's daughter are recorded in Chapter 42.

For a long time we held aloof from the Russian colony in London. Those who have not lived under the Soviet regime must find it hard to imagine the psychology of persons who left that paradise during the first decade of the new order. I don't know how it may be today but, at that time, nobody who had previously belonged to the old Russia could be sure of his life and well-being, right down to the last minute of his existence. A careless word spoken in the street might give rise to a denunciation, arrest and imprisonment. A sharp knock at the door meant a visit by the Cheka, and caused those within to tremble. A carelessly written letter, if it fell into the hands of the censor, would lead to the arrest of both writer and addressee.

Even when we had spent some time in London, under the protection of English laws, in complete confidence that we were beyond the reach of the Soviet system, we could not shake off our instinctive reactions of fear. We trembled at a knock on the door, and spoke in whispers when we wanted to say something that was contrary to Soviet orthodoxy. Before I left Russia not only I but also two professors who were colleagues of mine had signed assurances that we would maintain a 'correct attitude' towards the Soviet regime when abroad. And two of my brothers were still on Soviet territory . . .

[After I had been in England for eighteen months, I stopped my regular visits to the Soviet Embassy to get my passport endorsed for a further period. This evoked no reaction from the Soviet authorities.] Thank God, they had simply forgotten me. After a while, the absence of those Soviet endorsements came to the attention of the Home Office, and when I explained that it was difficult for me to approach the Soviet authorities, I was told that, in these circumstances, I should apply for a League of Nations passport. Such a passport was granted to me, and thereby I became a member of the Russian emigration.

For two years, however, we had kept away from the Russian émigré colony – and the members of it had looked at us with a certain perplexity. My wife's brother, Alexander Nikolayevich Bryanchaninov, happened to be in London and reproached me for not having called on the head of the colony, E. V. Sablin, former Counsellor of the Imperial Russian Embassy. Next day I went along to a big house in Cromwell Road and asked to be announced. Some embarrassment was shown, and then I was told that Sablin was busy and could not receive me. I frowned at the servant or messenger who conveyed that decision to me, but when I was in the street again I understood and approved: undoubtedly I should have informed Sablin [who is now a friend] of my intention to call on him, and obtained his consent.

This affair showed, though, that my reserved attitude towards the Russian colony was justified. At this point I must give an instance of that reserve, the memory of which still to this day brings me bitterness and sometimes self-reproach . . .

[When we lived in Russia we appreciated] the kind and gracious attitude of the Empress Maria Fyodorovna to my wife, and also, to some extent, to me. During the second year of our residence in London the Empress was also there for a time. On Sundays we used to go to the Orthodox church in Buckingham Palace Road, a Protestant church that had been transformed into an Orthodox one during the war, before the fall of the Tsar, and was adorned with an iconostasis and holy pictures. At the entrance to the church we were struck by the sight of a tall, handsome Cossack in uniform – a spectacle we had not beheld since the Revolution. The Empress was in the church. With her was her lady-in-waiting, Countess Mengden, who knew my wife. In normal times we would have had to remain at a distance and wait for the Empress to give a sign that she wished to speak to us.

My wife was intending to approach the Empress. But through my mind flashed the words: 'I guarantee that P. P. Shilovsky will behave correctly in relation to the Soviet Government while abroad . . . ' Did my 'conciliatory' (even though only in a technical sense) attitude to the Soviet regime give me the right to approach the Empress as naturally and easily as she was being approached by other members of the colony – people who had not known Bolshevism or had escaped from it?

That there were Soviet agents in the church on this occasion, watching everyone present, was beyond doubt.

I made a sign to my wife that we ought not to approach the Empress . . .

Some time later my wife received a letter from her friend, sent from France, saying that our failure to greet the Empress had been noticed and had caused surprise . . . It is very painful to recall all that. Painful even now, when many years have passed and we have become recognized as long-established members of the Russian colony in London. To this day I don't know whether I could have put my brothers and my guarantors at risk.

The Russian colony in London was an interesting place, both historically and, so to speak, sociologically.

We had all lost our country. We were 'stateless persons', as they now call the millions of citizens of various countries, both civilized and uncivilized, whose governments have found it necessary to create within those countries conditions such that certain groups of their population are no longer allowed to run off in a carefree way wherever they choose. Fortunately, 'stateless persons' have found countries where they are tolerated, even if without any great enthusiasm. When he is in one of these philanthropic countries a refugee who in his homeland possessed some property and social privileges finds himself on an equal footing as regards rights and living conditions with a refugee of no particular distinction. The refugee's passport reduces everyone to the same level. And the population of a country that gives shelter to these refugees usually looks upon them, not without some grounds, with condescending contempt. The organs of democracy make sure that these refugees do not become too numerous and do not compete with the native working class. All that is perfectly understandable.

But, despite the indisputable logic of all the above, the Russian colony in London strove to maintain, in their new and alien conditions, the structure of the old, pre-Revolutionary Russia, complete and in every detail.

All of the old Russia was to be found in this London microcosm, beginning with the Court. The sister of the late Tsar, Grand Duchess Xenia Alexandrovna lived in a small villa. Modest, with sad, pensive eyes, and surrounded by her sons and grandsons, she would sometimes appear at church services. If what had happened in our country had happened in England, England's representatives would have met with generous hospitality in our palaces. Young émigrés would have been accepted, at State expense, into privileged educational institutions and our most brilliant regiments. Undoubtedly, King George would have liked to help his cousin the Grand Duchess, but in this matter it was necessary to reckon with Parliament, the democratic parties, parliamentary questions . . . Thanks be to God, the Grand Duchess did not have to suffer: her children, such as Prince Nikita Alexandrovich, did not disdain to take jobs in British firms and thereby contributed to the household expenses.

Under English law the Grand Duchess was accorded no privileges that were not possessed by an ordinary Russian refugee. Yet, when we saw her, none of us, whoever he might be, dared to speak of her as the 'former' Grand Duchess. She remained for us – and also, to their honour be it said, to the English – a Grand Duchess. She did not go out much, but kept within a small circle of friends. To be invited to her house was considered a great honour.

The London colony also had its Faubourg St-Germain, in the form of a few bearers of the greatest Russian names: Golitsyns, Meshcherskys, Byeloselskys, Trubetskoys, Volkovs, Kutaissovs, Shipovs, and so on.

There was, too, a professorial, cultured set, always cool and restrained, even when engaged in altercations with Soviet opponents: Baron A. F. Meyendorff, Deputy Speaker of the last State *Duma*; Professor Korenchevsky, a member of the Lister Institute; Professor Struve. These were all outstanding men of the old Russia. But what of that brilliant representative of the Cadet Party, A. V. Tyrkova, who had now, of course, corrected her views? And the former liberal Mayor Braikevich? And the publisher of an interesting little patriotic newspaper in London, A. V. Baikalov, once an active member of the Socialist Revolutionary Party? It was not only 'die-hards' who had fled to London from the Soviet paradise. These were all representatives of 'progressive' Russia. And there was also T. Byelaev, Professor of Metallurgy.

From the ranks of former high officials there were the former Minister of Finance, P. L. Bark,[1] and his deputy, S. A. Shatalin; from the armed forces there were General Prince Byeloselsky, General Galfter and Admiral Smirnov.

Finally, from the world of *haut commerce*, Valnov and Ampenov. These were respectable, cultured men who had directed large enterprises in Russia.

The material situation of the colony was, of course, considerably better than that of Russians in Paris or, say, the Belgrade Russian colony. On the one hand, the British Government did not grant 'extensions' to residence permits as easily as other governments did; but, on the other hand, nowhere else, apparently, were Russian émigrés so free to take up occupation and engage in businesses, or to reside wherever they liked, as was the case in Britain. Here there was nothing comparable to the tedious restrictions on employment that prevailed in France, and we ought, of course, to have valued that circumstance very highly. Nor was there any obligation to go to the police station or to pay dues. That also counted for something.

In Britain before the Second World War there were two million unemployed, and that fact naturally affected the chances of Russian émigrés finding work. All other things being equal, preference would, of course, be given to a British citizen. None of the Russians made a grand, successful career in Britain. Still, P. L. Bark had a well-paid appointment in a bank, and some of the Russian Jews who had moved to Britain before the Revolution became prosperous. Professor Korenchevsky, honoured in scientific circles, commanded a big salary. Braikevich ran a building firm. All the rest made their living through various small-scale crafts and trade – millinery, underclothes and toilet articles. No work was below the dignity of an émigré: Admiral Smirnov, who had been Kolchak's Chief of Staff, lived by making ladies' hats; the Volkovs kept a restaurant;[2] and the Golitsyns went into the antiques business.

Many of the Russians had British friends. Once or twice these would give practical help, but after that the Russians looked after themselves. Our youngsters, or the more talented of them, succeeded in getting, free of charge or on favourable conditions, into good schools, and then, through scholarships, into universities. Soon a number of young Russians, both men and women, were working in cultural occupations. All of them, as a general rule, had to become British subjects. Many of the older generation did the same. Curiously enough, this did not mean severing their links with the nucleus of the Russian colony. They still attended the Orthodox Church, came to our meetings and took part in the work of charitable institutions. For us they were still Russians. More than a dozen of our young men gave their lives, as British subjects, on the field of battle.

Besides the above-mentioned persons, who were at one time the more privileged group among the London émigrés, there was a wide circle of Russians centred on what was called the Northern Society. When the British occupation forces left Archangel, a substantial number of members of the middle classes went with them, headed by local businessmen and timber merchants who would have been in danger when the Soviet troops appeared. Many of these arrived in Britain with certain resources, and some carried on small businesses in London.

What deserves special mention is the effort made by the Northern Society to keep the younger generation of the émigrés, so far as possible, within the orbit of Russian interests and love for Russian culture. Theatrical performance, dance parties in a fine building, literary gatherings, a Russian school, all played an important role in fulfilling this task.

I am describing things as they were before the war. The war put an end, or at least suspended, all this activity, as it also suspended the existence of the well-run, progressive, but definitely anti-Soviet Russian newspaper published in London by Baikalov.

For the young people there was the 'Young Russia' club led by I. I. Bilibin, which could be described as a Russian nationalist circle. However, it must be admitted that a rather marked degree of de-nationalization took place in our second and third generation. Also to be mentioned is the fact that if a young member of the colony managed, for example, through a brilliant marriage, to escape into a way of life very different from the straitened circumstances he had endured until then, he became irrecoverably de-nationalized. But marriages with educated middle-class British girls occurred quite often, and these were mostly successful. To the honour of the British be it said that they showed respect for the Orthodox Church and usually made no objection to the children being brought up in it.

I think it may be of some interest to the reader to learn the names of members of the colony who worked hard to preserve for the Russian émigrés the distinctive atmosphere of the old Russia and, also, as far as possible, to help those who fell on hard times.

This two-sided activity was centred on the Church and the Red Cross Society. The London colony did not escape a split in its congregation between the more conservative Karlovtsy section of our church and the more moderate Paris section led by Metropolitan Eulogius. However, to the great credit of both sections, the dissension, which was historically inevitable, remained free, or almost free, from any sharply expressed mutual unpleasantness of a personal character. The great church building was common to both sections, as was also the principal financial resource for its upkeep, the big concert held every year. And, unless I am mistaken, the choir, too, was common to both.

Attending more or less regularly either one or both of the services of these factions was a sign that one belonged to the colony. Non-attendance at the Orthodox Church meant either that one was inclined towards the Soviet orientation or that one had become de-nationalized and was no longer concerned with the interests and honour of the Russian emigration.

I stress the word 'honour'. To by no means all of us was it clear that to be a refugee, in the given historical situation, was a matter of honour and pride: that we were, in spite of everything, representatives of that epoch of Russia's history which had given the world some great geniuses of science, philosophy, literature and art. There is in Britain a limited circle of persons who know and have studied Russian culture and esteem it highly: but the conception of the old Russia held by the mass of the population, the intelligentsia included, is depressing . . .

I remember how amazed I was when we attended the charity concert in support of the church, in a spacious and elegant room in the Park Lane Hotel in Knightsbridge by S. L. Bark, wife of our last Minister of Finance, whom I have already mentioned. These concerts were a major event in the life of the emigration. All our society ladies, forgetting for a few hours their poverty, worries and in some cases hard work, appeared at the concert as they had been ten years earlier, in elegant *toilettes*. Jewellery, alas, was not much in evidence, but its place was taken by those features of refined education and manners characteristic of the old Russia, the social value of which is probably greater than the outstandingly fashionable dresses and unconstrainedly free behaviour we observed among the ladies of the well-to-do class in Britain. As a rule, one of the older members of the Royal Family came to these concerts. P. L. Bark wore his ribbon and star. General Kholodovsky, elderly and rather comical, would be there with his full array of Russian stars and crosses. Some British military men would come, in uniform. In short, for a few hours there was brought back to life something that had seemed dead – a colourful assembly of the refined society of the old Russia. Mrs Bark, herself a good musician, ensured that the programme of the concerts was always artistic. The collection met the expenses of the church.

No less successful were the bazaars of the Red Cross. Here I must mention Princess Ekaterina Georgievna Golitsyna. Granddaughter of Grand Duchess Ekaterina Mikhailovna and daughter of the Duke of Mecklenburg-Strelitz, she lost everything after the Revolution, but managed, along with her husband, to set up a successful small antiques business in London [as I have mentioned]. Her commercial activity did not prevent her from maintaining excellent relations with the British Court and high society; but her spiritual concerns, her disinterested desire to be useful, were focused on the needs of the Russian colony. A typical great lady of Petersburg society, educated, musical, upright, somewhat ardent in her opinions and her way of expressing them, she enjoyed respect in British circles no less than in Russian. It was in response to her invitation that some of the most distinguished Englishmen came to our gatherings.

Colonel D. A. Zinoviev[3] looked after the business and accounts side of the Red Cross. The bazaars were opened, elegantly and ceremonially, either by Grand Duchess Xenia Alexandrovna or by Princess Palovskaya, the wife of Prince Vsevolod Ioannovich (grandson of Grand Duke Konstantin Konstantinovich). At these gatherings, too, one was aware of the distinctive atmosphere in old Russia. British people who were friends of that old Russia unfailingly attended and supported these bazaars, and a member of the Red Cross, Mrs Carrington-Wild, sometimes made a friendly speech appropriate to the occasion.

Worthy of no less notice were the well-attended meetings of the Northern Society. This, too, was Russia, the Russia of the past, and at these meetings one met quite a few British friends. But the atmosphere at them was free and easy, simple and cordial. Amateur dramatics, dances, a Russian buffet with *pirozhki*, and vodka, for which British people who had lived in Russia also had a certain weakness: all this recalled to us our own dear provinces – Archangel, Morshansk or Kirsanov. At these meetings you could enter the room smoking a cigarette, and it was all right to wear your everyday clothes. A hearty welcome awaited everyone.

Earlier, there was an academic group in London, whose members gave interesting lectures. Alas, this broke up.

Among the persons who devoted much love and care to charitable work and the education of the young I must mention V. N. Volkova, the wife of the naval attaché at the Imperial Embassy; Princess Meshcherskaya, author of tales about the early period of the Revolution; and E. A. Korenchevskaya. Many of our young people owe something to them.

It will be seen from what I have written that the colony was extremely varied, both socially and intellectually. The position of its President was therefore very difficult and complicated. I remember that when I first made the acquaintance of the colony, its upper strata were against Sablin. That opposition somehow faded away. How this happened, to what it could be attributed, is hard to say. I think the chief role was played by E. V. Sablin's diplomatic tact and the generous, kindly hospitality of Nadezhda Ivanovna, his wife.

Possessing a delightful house, private means and possibly a small subsidy from previous Imperial resources, the Sablins made their home the centre of the Russian émigrés' business, cultural and social life. In no other European capital was there such a centre, on entering which both Russians and foreigners found that the Russia of the past was not so insignificant, and – who knows – that it might have, deep within itself, the possibility of coming back one happy day.

Enormous portraits of our Emperors, covering a whole wall, gazed majestically down on the visitor, and Empresses greeted them with kindly smiles. Prints showing regimental uniforms, buildings in Petersburg and Moscow, and old maps were hung on the walls. On the table old Court silverware was to be seen . . .

'Here is Imperial Russia, here we breathe its air.'

42

Getting By in England

OLGA PETROVNA LAWRENCE

*When Pyotr Petrovich Shilovsky (whose memoirs appear in Chapters 5
and 41) and his wife were given permission to leave the Soviet Union
for England in 1922, the authorities insisted that their three children
remain behind to ensure their parents' return. Once in London, their
mother exerted all her energies to get a visa for them and, as Russia had
been struck by famine and the children – all girls – were regarded as
three superfluous mouths to feed, in 1923 she finally succeeded. Olga,
who was born in 1914, has lived in England ever since.*

[When at last Mother got a visa for us, our governess brought us out
through Stettin, where Mother met us.] She kissed us and gave us
chocolate, which we ate and suffered for it. We didn't know what
chocolate was. It hadn't existed. We were all sick. It was not what you
might call a successful reunion for my poor mother. We looked so
awful and she had had time to forget how Russian children had suffered
in their rags.

Well, almost in rags. One didn't wear clothes that fitted, but whatever
there was or would keep one warm. I had a pair of boots which had
been my cousin's, who was aged seven; she had a kind of woman's hat
which was too small but which served its purpose. It was November
and we had to wear what there was. My mother wasn't used to this
because she had been living in England where the children, even of
the poor or those of modest means, had been dressed in children's
clothes . . . We were all lousy . . . And so for our poor mother seeing
her children again was a mixed pleasure, although, of course, a pleasure
it was.

In London we rented a modest house in Upper Norwood. My
mother's friend helped us a lot; Mother had met [her] in Dresden in a

finishing school, an Englishwoman who was from a quite comfortably off family, although not so well off as Mother when she was eighteen. Now, of course, the position was reversed and this lady said she would help until my father got on his feet again. We were luckier than many other émigrés. Many came with nothing.

[Father] was offered a job with Vickers-Armstrong after eighteen months or two years.[1] I have a vague memory of him coming home very happy, saying he had a contract as a consulting engineer. However, the contract proved very unsatisfactory because he never gave any consultations. It was simply to prevent him taking a job with another firm and so that they could gain access to his gyroscopic research. Of course, if we had known more of what we know now he would have inveigled his way into the firm. He could have gone to the right places, invited people for 'drinks in the pub' and done the right things because he could have helped them. For them, however, he was just another Russian with no great command of the English language and who had invented something. It was all very interesting but what the English call 'peripheral'. Of course, my father, like the captain of an ocean-going ship who is used to the open sea, simply couldn't or didn't know how to circumnavigate these obstacles and, what's more, he wasn't temperamentally suited. He did what he wanted to do and that's how he continued. [He didn't] want any talk or 'arrangements' or any of this 'Invite that chap you work with to my place. We'll have something nice to eat. We'll relax and there'll be interesting conversation. It could be a great help to you.' He couldn't grasp how much is done and arranged and, what's more, done well, without any suggestion of brib- ery, 'over a glass of beer'.

Mother and Father felt that from what they had seen of the Revolution there would be no changes permitting a return. Many émigrés, it's true, believed that their children and grandchildren would return, perhaps even in their (the parents') lifetime, but my parents never thought so. They had mentally put a full stop at the end of their existence in Russia and had decided to settle in England. Not to become English, though – neither of my parents took British nationality, although they could have done; nor did anyone put any pressure on them to do so.

The question did arise, however, when I was eighteen or nineteen. I wanted to go to university and there was no money for the fees, but one could get scholarships and there were private charities that helped able but needy children. I won an Exhibition to Oxford, so I was eligible for other forms of financial aid. I was given a list of various charitable societies to which I wrote, telling them that I needed a maintenance grant of £50 per term to live in college at Lady Margaret Hall. I was awarded a grant of £50 per year, so I somehow had to get another £100. I remember with gratitude the very kind Mrs Stobart who had money and helped refugees; she gave me £50, leaving me to find another £50. There was one society that offered £500, which was a significant amount in those days, but on one condition: the recipient had to be British. I was still a minor, so could not be naturalized; the minimum age was twenty-one. 'No matter,' they said. 'You can have the grant now if you promise to become a British subject when you reach your majority.' I went home and explained this, and my father said straight away, 'Your life is going to be in England and not in Russia. Personally, I don't intend to take British nationality, neither for you nor for anyone else. But since they have given you a promise, then agree.' For him the sacrifices didn't count; the most important thing was that I should go to university, which he thought completely right and proper. Unlike many Russians of his generation, he had absolutely no prejudices against higher education for women. So I received my British passport when I was twenty-one.

Now there are Russian Orthodox churches in Ennismore Gardens and Emperor's Gate, the latter being the Orthodox Church-in-Exile, whose members don't acknowledge the Patriarch of Moscow. The church in Ennismore Gardens is under Metropolitan Anthony Bloom and is in communion with Moscow.[2] I remember the terrible arguments that went on, even in England, between the two branches of the Church. They were even worse in Paris; in England, thank goodness, it was much calmer. We belonged to the Church-in-Exile, together with the Pushchins, the Golitsyns and others. Later Bishop Bloom appeared and did a lot to unite the two sides . . . but malicious people said that Bloom and his clergy were simply commissars in cassocks, because they recognized the Moscow Patriarch, who was completely under the thumb of the Soviet Government.

Our religious instruction in Russian Orthodoxy was rather haphazard and inadequate. My mother had been properly taught by the chaplain at the Smolny Institute [in St Petersburg], and she simply didn't understand that we had no one to learn from. She seemed to think that knowledge would somehow fall on us from Heaven – like snow or something! We went to church, knelt down, crossed ourselves and knew some of the prayers, but that was about all. We didn't go to church every Sunday because it was rather far away and difficult, though we went often enough to know the services. It may surprise you when I say that I knew the Catholic Mass better than the Orthodox liturgy, because I went to a convent as a boarder and there we went to church twice a day, so I got to know the services as well as any priest. The differences between Catholicism and Orthodoxy mattered little to us in the end: prayers are all much the same.

[Mother] had never [coped with a household] in her life before, but she managed very well. During our time in Russia after the Revolution she had decided to learn how to cook, having never previously done so much as boil an egg. Then in England she went to a domestic science college in Buckingham Palace Road. It wasn't very convenient, but she nevertheless learned the basic essentials of cookery; the college was very well run and the teaching was absolutely professional. As well as cooking, she learned how to run a household. She was a naturally good organizer and realized that she had to make do with a fixed and limited amount of money.

Things soon improved when Vickers started paying [Father] for his invention, and before that we were helped by another Russian woman, a friend of my mother's. She had brought out some jewellery and, although she didn't sell it all, she would sell some of her valuables and make us a loan whenever we were faced with a bill for gas or electricity or unexpected personal expenses. But we lived very modestly. I don't remember there being a time when there wasn't *any* money – as often happened with other émigrés, like some friends of ours who rented a large house and let out rooms, and when their lodgers didn't pay the rent, there would be no money to buy food for dinner. If two or three failed to pay, there would be a terrible to-do. There was no such thing as social security in those days, but in an emergency friends would rally round and help.

43

A Woman of Resource

NATALYA LEONIDOVNA DUBASOVA

Natalya Leonidovna Dubasova's account of her family's flight from Petrograd appears in Chapter 14. Her younger sister's recollections of their English childhood are given in Chapter 44.

[My mother, Alexandra Fyodorovna Pushchina,] was unique – quite unique. There she was in England with a husband and five children on her hands. When we first arrived we managed quite well, because there was still enough money. We thought we would just stay here for about six months and then go back to Russia, so at first we lived very comfortably in a splendid hotel; then gradually we started to go downhill, and after six months our resources had dwindled to the point where we had nowhere to live.

In those days there was still a Russian Consul, Mr Onul, a remarkable man. Of course, he was no longer officially Consul, but he apparently still had some funds and he looked after the Russian refugees. The British Government allowed him to continue functioning *as if* he still had consular status, and he did a very great deal to help the many Russians stranded in England. My mother went to him and said, 'What am I to do?'

My father was much older than she. He had never done a day's real work in his life and didn't even know how to set about finding work – he simply didn't belong in the twentieth century. He was a wonderfully talented artist, but he had only ever drawn and painted as a hobby. He painted the most beautiful miniatures, but he was quite incapable of doing anything in England. The war was still on, the only work available was war-work – and all he could do was paint miniatures.

So my mother said to Onul, 'What am I to do?' He said, 'The first thing you must do is to learn English. While you're doing that, all I can offer you is a job as one of my secretaries.' Mother started this work at once.

Father simply sat at home and did nothing. It was awful for him to see his wife going out to work and supporting the entire family while he could only twiddle his thumbs. Then a friend of his called Lodizhensky arrived from America and convinced him that in America the streets were paved with gold and he could easily find work there. So Father went to America. When he got there, it was worse than in England; he found nothing. He kept alive by staying with rich people and painting miniatures of the whole family one after another – but he didn't understand that he then had to present them with his bill. If someone happened to pay him without being asked or prompted, he accepted it, but if they didn't pay him he would simply depart – he just *could not* ask for money, so as a rule he was never paid.

There were masses of Russian refugees going to America then. One was a general who was lucky to get a job as doorman at the Sherry-Netherlands Hotel; another was an admiral who swept the floors at the Diamond Match Factory. Their lives began only when they came home and could behave as if they were still in Russia, with all their ranks and titles. But for Father the worst thing was that he couldn't help *us*. We had stayed in England.

But my mother taught herself English – by reading Dickens – and became a superb secretary. She already knew French and German. She could do shorthand and typing equally well in four languages and could even translate from the shorthand of one language directly into another language, and she eventually got an excellent job. She was quite amazing. But in those days secretaries were paid terribly little; a secretary was a mere nobody. Fortunately, we children somehow all went to very good schools – boarding schools. It was simply amazing how we of the 'first emigration' were helped. My brother went to Sherborne. So Mother had to keep us only during school holidays [because] the schools took us completely free – free tuition, free boarding. All the schools arranged for us to be awarded scholarships. Masha [my younger sister] and my elder sister were at school in Wantage. It was a convent. My other sister, Varvara, and I went to St Hilda's at Whitby in Yorkshire.

In order to do the utmost for us children, during the school terms my mother would move into some tiny little room, where she lived in real poverty, saving every penny, so that when we, all five of us, were due to come home for the holidays she could find and rent a flat. We would come together three times a year, and each time we never knew where we would be going to live. One of our flats was over a garage; we had great fun peering through the cracks in the wooden floor and watching the mechanics repairing cars. When Mother went off in the morning to work, my brother would look after us and take us out, perhaps to the circus, perhaps for walks in Richmond Park – we were always together. We would wait impatiently for Mother to come home. She would at once cook supper for us; there was usually a geyser to heat the water and always one or two little gas-rings. Mother was a hopeless cook. She simply threw whatever there was into one huge saucepan and we ate the result. But it must have been a perfectly healthy diet and we accepted all this as absolutely normal. Before we came to England, Mother had never so much as set foot in a kitchen in her life, so she had never learned to cook, and she never could cook properly to her dying day.

It was amazing that it never occurred to any of us to question this style of living – it just seemed natural that, because we were in another country, everything was different. And our flat was always bursting with people – there were masses of our Russian friends, all living in equally difficult circumstances, so we just assumed that everyone lived like that.

44

Pride Among the Packing Cases

LADY MASHA WILLIAMS

*Lady Williams (née Masha Leonidovna Pushchina) was born in 1914
in St Petersburg. She is author of* White Among the Reds.
Her elder sister's memoirs appear in Chapters 14 and 43.

We left in 1917. [My father] was outlawed right at the beginning of the
Revolution. The mob seized a lot of officers, and they marched them
to the *Duma* and nobody was there. My father happened to be the
most senior man present, so he went out and met the mob and said,
'Justice will be done. Hand them over to us.' So they handed the
officers over, and he opened the doors at the other end and let them
go. And he had to run too. So he was outlawed. This would have been
February or March 1917. A great friend, who was in the Ministry of
Foreign Affairs, said he would get him a false passport.

In what seemed to me the middle of the night, my godfather came
in and put the light on and picked me up. Of course I began to cry,
and my mother came in and asked what he was doing. He said that he
was saying goodbye and put a chain with a gold cross round my neck,
and that was my only memory. It was the last time I saw him. Next
day, he had the passports ready. I think we came out as the French
Ambassador and family. We had a French governess and all spoke
French. Once out of St Petersburg we were all right.

We came to England via Finland and Norway. We were going to
Paris, because my father knew French, but he was on the Committee
to continue war against Germany, so he was persuaded by the British
Government to stay on here. He had brought out a bit of money, and
thought it would be a question of three or four months and so he spent,
of course, and helped those that arrived. And then the crash came and
there was no money.

My father disapproved of the Provisional Government in Russia. He later met Kerensky in London, and put his hand behind his back as he would not shake hands with him. He remained a monarchist to the end of his life . . . I think like many men he couldn't take it – they felt that what had happened was dishonourable. He felt guilty that they had let the Emperor down, and couldn't take the fact that the Emperor was murdered at all.[1] He simply couldn't accept the fact that my mother had to work, and that his daughters would have to work. I think it literally killed him – he just couldn't take life. Whereas my mother just got on with it: the children had to be fed. I don't think women are troubled quite so much with honour; they are more practical.

She had a terrible time. She went first as a charwoman, although she didn't know the work, to give herself a chance to learn the language. Then [when the former] Russian Consul found out she was there, he asked her to go and help him with his work. So she worked in the consulate, and at night she studied English, typing and shorthand and looked after five children. Then she got a job as a foreign correspondent [i.e. writing in and translating from foreign languages] in Throgmorton Street in the City, where she spent the rest of her life.

[In the lives of the Russian émigrés] the main thing was the Church. I think to survive you have got to have a pride in yourself, to be somebody in a community. In the British community, we were nothing; we had no money, no position, no friends. So if we were mixed with the British we were the lowest of the low. But if we mixed with Russians, we still had our titles (those of us that had had them) and our old positions and so on. I think that's why the community has to hold together. It gives you a position in life.

The whole of life centred around the Church and, of course, it was the only pleasure that we had, really, because we had no books, no toys, no possessions. Nobody had anything. We dressed in other people's cast-offs and that was it. Whereas the Church was beautiful, the music was lovely, the candles, the icons, the priests' garments, the wonderful atmosphere. And for the children, that was our greatest pleasure and was what we looked forward to. And of course on Sunday we all met there. They kept up the old traditions; at Easter we all had white silk dresses whatever the weather. If it snowed or not, we had white silk dresses, with no coat on top because that would spoil the effect. We four girls would stand there, with my brother in a white sailor suit, because that was traditional, and so did all the other children. So really we lived for the Church. That's where we met, and after church we'd all go to someone's house and have tea there, or bread and butter or whatever they had.

We all spoke Russian at home, because our parents did not speak anything else. Although my mother's English was very good, and she spoke English all the time at work, she spoke with an accent and not as easily as she spoke Russian. You have to be proud of something, and there was nothing to be proud of here as nobody had achieved anything here. So they all lived in the past.

I think we were all brought up to think it was our duty to bring back the monarchy and to cause the downfall of the Soviet State. On the day of the assassination of the Emperor, we always held a service which we all attended. Even when I was abroad, I was expected to attend the services there – in Switzerland and so on. That was a duty that was understood.

I had an uncle in Prague [who belonged to an organization which] trained young people to go and commit acts of sabotage in the Soviet Union. He tried to enrol us; I was then in Switzerland with my aunt. We were sixteen or seventeen, and somehow we couldn't go in for that violence; we were brought up differently. None of us, not even my boy cousins, could bear the thought.

Katya Golitsyn[2] was the centre of the Russian colony. The Sablins were a bit to one side. Sablin was the official representative of the Russians to the British Government.[3] He owed his position to the fact that he had been a diplomat. But socially, it was the Golitsyns who were the centre of it all. She was a very remarkable woman, very interesting and clever, and was a relation to the Royal Family here, so she had a position here at Court. She was a very humanitarian woman. She had three very wild sons, Emanuel, George and Nicholas. Emanuel and George live here in London. The parents are both dead now. We whirled round them, and we obeyed them. For instance, I was unemployed, and I was offered a job to go as governess to a little boy, the son of an Indian rajah, to teach him English. I thought it would be very exciting. And Katya Golitsyn said, 'You do not go as a governess anywhere. Once you go as a governess, you *are* a governess and the British in India will not accept you.' And we obeyed. She ruled the roost to that extent, trying to do her best for everybody. She felt responsible for the Russian colony.

We were very snobby, there was no doubt about that. There was a man here, a ship's captain [who] had continued working for the Soviets because he felt that Russia was Russia, whatever; he wasn't concerned in politics. In the end, he left and came to London, and nobody would know him because he had worked with the Soviets. He worked in the City as a porter or something and my mother met him secretly and had lunch with him in the City. She didn't dare admit to her friends that she was associating with him, but she was terribly sorry for him, because here was a Russian alone, whom nobody wanted to know, as much in distress as any one of us. All right, he had made a mistake . . . To that extent, it was very strict.

[The hierarchy of titles] was kept up. Like Katya Golitsyn – her husband called her Katya, but I called her Princess Golitsyn. [We observed all these niceties, even though we were hard up and hungry.] I remember even when I went up to Oxford and a young man invited me to dinner and to the theatre in London, and his parents came to the theatre and dinner afterwards, I said to my mother that I really should ask them back. So she said that by all means I should invite them for coffee another time, which I did – without thinking, because we Russians are totally impractical. So we came, all in evening dress – I had an evening dress which somebody must have given to me – and they had lovely furs on. So we sailed into our room, and I suddenly realized that all our furniture was packing cases. And there were all these people pouring in in evening dress. There was my mother sitting there in an ancient garment, probably her dressing gown. The table was a packing case. The chairs were packing cases, our beds were up against the walls. Well, I was never asked again, either to the theatre or anywhere else. But that was how we lived. It never occurred to me, and I didn't even realize what I was doing, until they walked in and I saw their faces.

It was a very nice clergyman, Fynes-Clinton, who arranged for [Anglican] convents to take two of us, and another convent took the other two and we were educated there free. Fynes-Clinton was a clergyman in the East End of London. Why he was interested in Russian émigrés I don't know, but he made enquiries about who had children, and who needed help, and someone, maybe Katya Golitsyn, told him about us. He had an icon in his church with candles in front of it; Russian sailors used to go there, as it was near the docks.

I think I got Responsions on my School Certificate and then I sat for the Oxford exam and I got an Exhibition. We were still foreigners [and] there weren't any scholarships for foreigners. In Lady Margaret Hall, where Olga [Shilovskaya – see Chapter 42] went, you had to be Church of England to get a scholarship, and in fact it was very difficult to get in but they took us. The Exhibition covered only part of the money; personally I had nothing else, but I was determined to get in. I applied literally everywhere and I got £10 here, £5 there and £20 there . . . In the end somebody told me about a man in Oxford called Spalding who knew about all these things. [I wrote] and said to him that I needed so much money to get into Oxford, and asked if he could advise me where I might apply to get it. He wrote back and said that he didn't know of any other organization, but his wife and he would be delighted to help me in this way. They had never met me or heard of me in any way before . . .

When I was in Oxford, I had my first meeting with the Soviets. There was an agricultural conference and they asked me to interpret at it. I didn't want to because I had been brought up to have nothing to do with the Soviets [but] I couldn't refuse because the University authorities had been very kind, making excuses when I couldn't pay, and it was the least I could do. So these Soviet professors arrived, old men with long beards, which at that time nobody had, and there was also a Russian professor, an émigré, from Paris, because this was an international conference. These Soviet professors wanted to get together with this émigré professor, because they had been at university together and were old friends, and asked me to organize it so that nobody knew about it. So I organized it, and set my friends to watch the corridors because there was a young man who was obviously watching them, and they helped to keep him occupied so he wouldn't find out. They got in wine and so on, and then I brought this Russian from France there and there was this terrific reunion. Then they started arguing in a friendly way. The Paris professor was saying, 'How can you stay in the Soviet Union? You've got no freedom, you can't think for yourselves, you can't go where you want to.' The Soviets were saying, 'And where has your freedom got you? You have no equipment, nowhere to work, the French don't recognize your work. *We* know more about what you have achieved than the French. You've got no opportunities . . . ' Afterwards, I realized they did not bring up the fact that they had good food, clothing or material things – the conversation was exclusively about work, who could produce the best job.

You know British people suffer terribly from loneliness. Well, no

Russian does, because there's so much affection from the parents and the children and the relations and the families clinging together. I think this helped the Jews under Hitler. It saved some of them from going mad. I think it's what saved the Russians here. Nobody was lonely in spite of difficult times. We didn't notice it because we were all happy together – we were very happy as children. Outsiders, foreigners, I think notice this particularly. I think it's true today amongst Russians in the Soviet Union – the peculiar, unusual warmth of personal relations, and how Russians mercifully lack all these extraordinary inhibiting factors which the English display over personal relations from the most superficial to the most profound. They are perfectly willing to articulate their feelings about people and to be frank about their feelings.

I think as an emigration, we all looked down on the British. It helps keep up morale to feel superior to the British around you, who may have money and everything. It took years to get over that and to realize that the British were worth associating with! When we were naturalized, it was a terrible tragedy. My mother naturalized in order that I should stay up at Oxford, otherwise I couldn't as a foreigner. We felt that we were betraying Russia, and the monarchy. In fact, we concealed it from the other Russians.

Of course, I'm considered a bit of a Bolshie among my Russian colleagues because I was one of the first to go back to the Soviet Union to visit. We were all brought up on this hatred and, frankly, hatred is destructive. I felt it was wrong; enough is enough and we have to look to the future. It's no good thinking about monarchies and so on. There is the Soviet Union; one has to accept it, make the best of it and use what little influence one has in one's own way.

45

Living With the English

PROFESSOR ALEXANDER KENNAWAY

Alexander Kennaway was born in 1923 in Vienna of Russian parents, who emigrated to England. He was educated at St Paul's School, London, and Cambridge University. During the Second World War he was commissioned in the Royal Navy, and has since made a distinguished career as a Professor of Mechanical Engineering at Imperial College of Science, Technology and Medicine, London.

I changed my name in about 1952 from my Russian given name of Kalmanovsky. My father was Jewish; his first cousin is Edward Kalmanovsky, the composer of pop songs in the Soviet Union. I was born in Vienna [in 1923], on the way out of Russia. My parents were, of course, Russian. My mother was a nurse at the front during the First World War and was engaged to my father, who was an Army officer. He found himself on the White side of the lines, did not wish to fight a civil war, demobilized himself and managed to escape through Poland to Vienna. My mother decided to join him, and she got out in the usual circumstances – in a cattle truck with only the clothes she stood up in – and they both arrived penniless in Vienna. They married, I was born there, and then they brought me here.

My mother was ethnic Russian, from Mogilyov, but lived in Moscow and went to university in Moscow. In Russia it was normal for the middle classes and the upper-middle classes to receive an education, including the women, but what was not normal was to find them any useful work. For the men, by that generation, it wasn't too difficult. From the 1860s to the 1890s it was very difficult. For the women it remained difficult, although, as far as my aunts who remained in the Soviet Union all their lives were concerned, Aunt Marya, who graduated from Lausanne University, in fact became Professor of German and Spanish at the Military Academy in Moscow. Aunt Slava worked with Ivy Litvinova (wife of the later Foreign Minister, Maxim Litvinov[1]) in the cosmetics industry. She went to study with Helena Rubinstein, of all people, in Paris in the early 1930s to bring cosmetics to Russian factory girls. Stalin suddenly decided that factory girls should have lipstick, that the Hitler *Mädchen in Uniform* thing didn't work, and Aunt Slava was the lady chosen to go and do it . . .

I was brought up on four languages because we lived in England and in France. My mother and father spoke Russian to each other and to me, and when I was born my mother took a Viennese girl to look after me; they spoke German to her. So I heard German around me, French all the time, the common language at home was always Russian and of course I went to school in England and so consequently my language of education was English.

I never grew up thinking that I was Jewish. I always felt that I was Russian because it was the cultural dimension that mattered to me – the language, the literature and, in fact, I was always drawn much more to Russian Orthodoxy than to the Church of England. Judaism never occurred to me.

My mother was Orthodox – not desperately religious, but religious in that superstitious way that Russians have. For example, when she yawned, she would make the sign of the Cross over her mouth in order not to let the Devil in. But my mother, who was a tremendous anglophile, put me into an English prep. school as a boarder for my own good, and insisted that I went to Church of England services. But they frightened me, because to go into the English upper-middle-class social and educational system in the 1920s and the 1930s was a very curious experience; they were still suffering from the hellfire and damnation of the Victorians in many ways, and I found that English church services frightened me and made me miserable and I always wanted to cry. I'm afraid this antipathy has lasted the whole of my life. Then again there is the liturgy – it's not a liturgical religion, and Orthodoxy is. I always liked the Russian form of the Byzantine chant; I've retained this all my life . . .

When my parents came here, my father never really settled down as an engineer. He had rather bitty jobs – first as a draughtsman, then as an engineer – and he never really made a success of his life in emigration. I got the impression from my mother that she thought he had been the spoilt darling of a very wealthy Russian family and, like so many people, he hankered back to it and never really lived in reality. Although he wasn't living in a world of illusion, he did rather hanker after the past. But my mother did settle down . . .

My mother and father divorced when I was about six, and she remarried – a Ukrainian Jewish left-wing economist called Noah Baruch, who in fact was one of the co-founders of the World Jewish Congress. He was an interesting man because he was one of the only non-Communists in the first Congress of the Soviets, as a representative of *Poale Zion*, the Zionist Jewish workers' movement.[2] He was an economist and he got his PhD from the LSE, after which he became manager of the Moscow Narodny Bank in London. My mother learned to type and do shorthand, and she typed all his books and articles. He had a tremendous influence on me – a thoroughly unreligious man . . . [but] he thought that Jews needed somewhere. He was all practicality. It was his idea to get reparations for Jews from the Germans after the Second World War and he negotiated it all with Adenauer. He had to make hundreds and hundreds of journeys, because he had to convince both the Jewish fanatics (who said it was blood money) and the Germans that they were doing the right thing, to build up the State of Israel with the money, which is what was achieved . . .

I came here as a baby and went to an English prep. school – Downton in Leatherhead – and from there to St Paul's. I wasn't particularly happy at either school. At St Paul's, I was a boarder for the first year and a day-boy for the rest. The English upper-middle class at the time assumed that everyone else was very much a second-class human being and they made you try to feel that you should despise yourself. It was very difficult as an émigré child, because you didn't know who you were. They were very insensitive people, very insular, very smug; everything British was best when it manifestly wasn't – they really had a very curious view of the rest of the world. It's owing to that experience that if you look up my entry in *Who's Who*, it says under leisure pursuits 'Enlarging the bounds of an insular and specialist education.' In other words, getting rid of the lies I was told in things like *Our Island Story*. As a Russian, of course, I was going to reject all this instinctively, but it hurt.

My mother admired [English education] from the sort of standpoint of an Edwardian Russian lady. In a sense I don't think she saw the snags, but in a sense I think she did but reckoned it would be good for me. I had a scholarship to St Paul's, and also to Cambridge, but it was a quite definite decision on my parents' part that I was to stay there, regardless of the fact that I said I was thoroughly miserable . . .

I don't think I really enjoyed the English until I went up to Cambridge in 1940. Cambridge was the first time I really met civilized, cosmopolitan, cultured Englishmen. At an ordinary prep. school and at St Paul's at the time, one wasn't meeting those people. One was meeting people who were going to have an education simply as a prelude to a vocation, a profession. They despised foreigners of course, and were saying things and thinking things and talking about the world and politics and Europe in a manner that one knew was untrue and would lead to disaster, and of course it did lead to disaster. But Cambridge was an eye-opener to me. It was lovely – the first time I ever really felt at home in England.

As holders of Nansen passports, we were under the protection of the Spanish crown; later we had a Romanian protective passport, and I had a Romanian passport until I naturalized at the age of sixteen. That caused some problems, because when Romania came into the war on the German side, in spite of the fact that I was by then a naval officer, I was listed as an enemy alien! The Home Office was so inefficient that they hadn't listed my naturalization. The English were terribly funny about it all. I remember when war broke out I thought I would do something, so I offered my services filling sandbags at the local fire station, and I was told that I couldn't do that because I was only a *naturalized* British subject! Then, when I went down from Cambridge, and was commissioned into the Royal Navy, I had the greatest of pleasure in returning to the Town Clerk at Hampstead Town Hall, from Malta, a letter which said that unless I reported for fire-watching duties I would be prosecuted. I simply said that I had a prior engagement with His Majesty's Fleet.

I chose the Navy because I had always had a tremendous admiration for it, was interested in it and I was interested in things maritime. I was right, because the Navy was and still is a society which is accustomed to taking in people of all kinds and nationalities. After all, it tolerated Mountbatten and Prince Philip. Tolerance is the wrong word – it implies contempt; this was an automatic acceptance of you as you were, and it didn't matter what your background was. Provided you were socially acceptable, did your duty and became a member of the team, it didn't matter if you came from Timbuctoo. This immediate camaraderie and acceptance, and the professionalism, suited me. Of course I was in the

Fleet as an RN officer, not as an RNVR officer, and therefore I was with professionals, and I liked it.

I was commissioned in 1942. The questions at my commission interview were terribly funny. They didn't ask me about my degree, because they saw I had it, and they asked me one technical question about marine engineering to which I said I didn't know the answer. Then they asked if I was very keen on the Navy, and I said that I was. One of the admirals said, 'I see you've got a half-blue for fencing,' so I said that I had, and he said, 'Well, I don't think there are any more questions. Cut along and see the doctor, my dear chap.' Of course, the other interesting thing – looking back on the time and remembering who were the dons when I was an undergraduate (it was the days of the Apostles, the English Communist treason) – was that I was accepted into security duties, as far as I can see without question. I was required to pass the Foreign Service language examination in Russian, which was rather funny. I was sat down at the Admiralty, with a four-stripe captain invigilating at the other end of the room. I looked at these exam papers and I took them to him and said, 'Sir, I honestly don't think I can sit these papers.' He said, 'Why not?' and I said, 'Well, I proofread them.' This was because Professor Boyanus (a sweet man and a friend of my mother's) was Professor of Russian at Dartmouth. He set these papers, and one day at a weekend he handed them to me and said, 'Sasha, would you mind proofreading this lot for me?' But I was required to do the exam.

I had a very interesting experience [connected with Boyanus] years later. I was on an exchange from Roehampton, where I was working, to the Prosthetics Research Institute in Leningrad. I was on the team developing rather advanced artificial limbs for amputees. I'd come out of the operating theatre and went into the director's room; there were a lot of people, and there was a sort of translation going on into Italian and I was sitting next to a small, frail, elderly gentleman on the sofa, who whispered to me, 'That's not the right Italian word for "muscle" – what is it?' So I told him, and he whispered to me several times. In the end, he took to me, and we walked out up the road together, and he said, 'You speak Russian in a very familiar way. Where have you come from?' So I said innocently, 'Moscow.' It turned out that he was Professor of Philology at Leningrad University. He'd just come out of eighteen years in a concentration camp because his special interest was Spanish and Portuguese religious documents of the sixteenth century and Stalin had him jailed because he had had correspondence with Jesuits. I said, 'Well, in that case, you can probably hear overtones of the man who preceded you in your post – Boyanus.' He said, 'Yes. I recognize some of his speech patterns.' So I'd obviously unconsciously been listening. Boyanus was a marvellous man. I remember one day when I had been complaining about the English prostituting their language, he said to me, 'You will realize one day that anything an Englishman says will sooner or later become correct.' All prostitutions of language become accepted in time. A tragic remark, but true.

I stayed on the active list until 1947 and then went on the reserve with duties connected with Russian. I stayed on the reserve for quite a long time, and then resigned from it at the minimum age because my name appeared in the Navy List in a fashion that made it dangerous for me to go to the Soviet Union. Dagger: advanced engineering course; two stars: first-class Russian interpreter . . . reserve duty . . . But I wanted to go to Russia very much. I wanted to see my family, whom I had never seen, so I took every possible opportunity to go – scientific exchange, official delegations, with a private visa with a right to stay with my family, and I stayed privately as a Soviet citizen and that's not so easy . . .

I went to work in the research department of ICI, then I got interested in orthopaedics, became a consultant at Roehampton and worked on artificial limbs. I was materials adviser to the Medical Research Council on implantation.

I went to the Soviet Union twice during the war and since then I must have been about a dozen times. A lot of my relatives are still there.

My mother's brother, who is now retired, of course, [is in the USSR]. He had a very unpleasant history. He was jailed under Stalin twice, became a colonel in the Red Army with two Orders of Lenin, wrote the standard Red Army handbook on supply of an army in the field, retired after the war and became deputy to Mikoyan as Internal Trade Minister. That didn't save him from going to jail again under Stalin. Then, having been the director of some enormous organization, he ran a bread shop in Moscow. And because he had all these connections, he had the best bread shop in Moscow. I said to him, 'How did you manage with the drop in salary?' and he replied that he made it up in bonuses. After he retired, he ran the four foreign-currency food shops.

It was very funny: my cousin, who's a psychiatrist and an Olympic oarsman, happened to be doing his MD thesis when I was in Moscow. He got his MD, which was on schizophrenia, and you can imagine the party. My uncle said to me, 'Sasha, you will go to the foreign-currency food shops and you will buy the following things: forty-eight bottles of vodka, six hams, twelve tongues . . . ' The party went on for forty-eight hours, and can you imagine the mixture of the psychiatric establishment of Moscow and all the oarsmen – the hearties! It was unbelievable . . .

I was told an incredible story by my cousin Lyosha's boss, who was at [the sinister Dr] Lunts's Central Psychiatric Hospital in Moscow.[3] He said that a female colleague of his had a patient who was deemed to be well enough to go to a psychiatric outworker, and the patient used to go up to her flat in the lift once a week and talk to this woman. And one day he pressed the bell, went into the kitchen, took a knife, cut off her head and put it on the kitchen table. He then went round the block, made a matrix of four heads and then called the police and said, 'Come and see what I've done!' The police were apparently quite annoyed because one of the heads belonged to the superintendent of the area police. So they prosecuted the psychiatrist for dereliction of duty. Of course, the Moscow medical establishment, just like the London one, ganged together and got him off. I said to him, 'What happened to this lunatic?' 'Oh, they shot him.' I said, 'Forgive me, but am I not right in thinking that there is no capital punishment for murder in the Soviet Union?' 'Yes,' he said, 'but this was such a bad case that they made an exception for him.' So I said, 'Do you realize what you're saying? You're a senior member of this establishment, a professional man, and you're saying that the State is above its own law?' He said, 'Yes, I realize what I'm saying.'

What is marvellous about having an intelligent, responsible, involved family in Russia is that you have these incredible conversations with their relations and friends with whom they've been at school or university or they've worked for, and you're totally vouched for. It's uninhibited on both sides, because they can't shop you, and they know you won't shop them.

I'm slightly *persona non grata* in the Soviet Union at the moment because of provocative broadcasts here. I've always known the BBC people – I grew up with them, old émigrés . . . But my programme started when my wife and I were on holiday in Paris about three or four years ago, and I bought a copy of *Russkaya Mysl'* and there was a letter in it, smuggled out of the Soviet Union: 'Please, Voice of America and BBC, give us broadcasts about the life of disabled people in your country.'[4] So when I got back to London, I rang up and talked to Diran Magreblyan [of the BBC] and he said that they would broadcast such a programme, provided I did it. I said, 'Don't be silly, I'm just an engineer.' He replied that of course I could do it; I had been talking fluent Russian to him for the last half-hour. So I did three programmes. I started off my first one by saying: 'The English are a fairly sentimental lot. Thirty years ago, they left all their money to cats' homes and didn't worry about disabled people very much. That's all changed. Not because the State in its munificence has seen the light on the road to Damascus, but because of the pressure from the voluntary societies, and the free press putting pressure on the State . . . ' I finished up my broadcast saying: 'Now, dear listeners, you realize that all this has gone a long way, but here in Derbyshire we have some people whom we interviewed who said to the local authorities: "To hell with your social workers – they don't know how to cope with paraplegics like us. We know it better than you do. Give us the money you spend on them and we'll run our own affairs." And the county authority agreed. And they're now running their own housing, their own caring arrangements, their own work, their own schooling, without the help of the professionals. Now you see, dear listeners, this is the second stage of the Revolution. All power to the people against the bureaucracy!'

After that, I'm afraid that my mail to my cousins got held up. They connected – I didn't think the KGB was clever enough – Professor Kennaway at London University with Sasha writing to Alyosha . . .

The British should stop worrying about Communism; it's bureaucracy that's the real enemy. It's the proximate enemy.

The English are proud of not having an intelligentsia, though they are sometimes clever in little boxes. They don't like to cross boundaries. In my job as a director of a national public authority, I have suffered from under-secretaries and permanent secretaries who say, 'Of course, I'm thoroughly unpractical. I couldn't even change a fuse!' And they're proud of it. This sort of contempt for technology is disastrous. This is why we fall behind other countries. I'd like very much to try to create an intelligentsia – not an English word; in fact, it's held in contempt. I was asked to talk to the boys at Eton about this at a careers meeting and said, 'You know you actually ought to think about technology and engineering as a study and a profession, because it is the best liberal arts education for the modern world.' And that, when you add to culture and breeding, ought to be right for an Etonian. Because we suffer from technologists in blinkers, without culture, without religion and without humanity. After all, why did the Germans build concentration camps? People who have no heart and no soul we don't need in this world, and technologists without it are a menace. As a professor in a university, I believe in helping people to extend their bounds. The English like to typecast you, like the Americans – you're a plastics engineer, or you're a surgeon of the left gut halfway up on the right-hand side. You're never a medical man or a human being. It seems to me that the English have to learn to unify the intellectual establishment.

Although it took me a long time to enjoy being with the English, the one thing I've always insisted upon is that I never will let the English submerge me. I'm still a Russian. I insist on retaining my Russianness in every way – in literature, religion, music, culture, conversation, in everything that matters in the way I feel about myself. The Russian word *dusha* [soul] comes to me and there's no English equivalent. The word 'spiritual' is wrong – it doesn't mean the same thing at all. The important thing is you've got to know who you are. If somebody says to me, 'What are you?' I would say that I'm Russian. I've got a British passport, but it would be foolish to say that I'm English because I'm not. If the answer is 'You're British', what exactly does it mean? You can't be, because the Britons are up in North Wales, having been pushed out by the Angles. I think that, like a lot of Russians, England represents to me a country in which it is nowadays easy to live because the English leave you alone to be yourself – they don't force you to be someone else any more [like] they did when I was a child . . .

PART THREE

The Soviet Experience and Beyond
1946–1986

It is only now, with the extraordinary changes that have occurred in the Soviet Union since 1986, that we can make a proper start on documenting a large part of the Soviet experience under the Stalinist tyranny; even now, more is promised than has as yet been performed. For generations even the most basic facts, known in outline in the West, were not revealed to the Soviet public.

The second wave of emigration came to the West as a result of the Soviet–German war, when German armies reached far into the country, to the Caucasus, the lower Volga, and the outskirts of Moscow and Leningrad. The Ukraine in particular was under German occupation for over two years; the Soviet Army lost six million men as prisoners in the first disastrous year of the war. A great many people were dragged off to forced labour in Germany and, in the wake of the German defeat, a great many others went to Central Europe of their own volition.

In the early 1920s many well-meaning commentators and hard-headed businessmen (including the young Armand Hammer) supposed that the Communist State would settle down. However, after Lenin's death in 1924 there was much dissension among the Communists: some supported Trotsky in advocating revolutionary crusades abroad and at home; others supported Nikolay Bukharin, who wanted what we might now call 'market socialism' or 'socialism with a human face'. The victor in these disputes was Joseph Stalin, who presided over the Party's administration and who allowed the secret police to flourish. After 1926 he was easily the dominant figure in the Party, expelling Trotsky from it and eventually also from the country. (Trotsky was exiled, in the end, in Mexico, where Stalin's assassin killed him.) Dissent was no longer tolerated even in the Communist Party leadership and, with ruthless use of the means of power of the twentieth century, Stalin acquired autocratic dominion over this vast country. In it, one-sixth of the world's land surface, one-sixth of the population was directly employed by the NKVD (literally, 'People's Commissariat of the Interior') – millions and millions of them in camps, working to death as slave labour.

The 'justification' for this was that the Soviet Union had to be 'modernized'. Commentators exaggerated the extent of old Russia's backwardness – in 1914 she had after all been overtaking France to become the world's fourth economic power – and the real argument for 'modernization' was that Communism could not thrive except by control of any elements likely to be difficult – the peasantry above all. In the later 1920s, difficulties between Government and peasants grew and grew. Harsh taxation, excessive petty controls, price-stops led to food shortages in the cities, and Stalin responded in effect by requisitioning the peasants' land and using them as forced labour on the new collective farms. These were set up virtually as plantations, and the process, in circumstances which have never adequately been explained, led to a great famine in 1933. Grain output did not return to the levels of 1914 until 1951, and in many ways agriculture seems never to have recovered at all. Shortages of basic goods and long queues at shops marked the Stalinist era (and much of the time beyond).

However, collectivization did have one great advantage for the Soviet Union, in that it forced in the end some forty million peasants to leave their land. This supplied an enormous force of unskilled labour, which allowed for a programme of building and canal digging which in turn gave the infrastructure for large factories. This process, now also known to have been heavily expensive in human life and living conditions, is normally referred to as The Plan. It achieved prodigies of military output; but it was driven along by a strong element of idealism, with an effort to show that 'the Workers' State' could catch up with the capitalists and the Fascists. Many of the people who rose through the Party at this time – they include some of our informants – had cause to bless the 1930s; recognition of the truth came only later.

These enormous social convulsions could be controlled only through a State and Party machine of great power – the NKVD, which is ancestor, at least in its secret-police functions, of the KGB ('Committee of State Security'). In the later 1930s, this machine rolled over the Soviet population with crushing force: these were the years of the Great

Purge, and of the famous trials of 1937–9 at which prominent old Bolsheviks, Stalin's possible rivals for power, confessed to impossible crimes. For ordinary people, there was an atmosphere of constant denunciation; virtually no family failed to have its experience of the vast imprisonments on piddling or trumped-up charges which enabled the Terror to go on.

Accordingly, when Hitler invaded the Soviet Union in June 1941, there were a great many demoralized and hostile people who might have collaborated, in order to get rid of Stalin. This may account for the collapse of the Red Army in the first months of the war: certainly its defeat was not caused by lack of military hardware, in which it enjoyed a very comfortable superiority. However, German rule was also harsh; Russian patriotism came to the fore and Stalin was able to rely on wide support, on national, patriotic grounds, for a prodigious war-effort. People hoped, in 1945, that this new atmosphere might allow the Terror to be lessened; but by 1947 the brief moment of hope was ended, and Stalin's last years were marked by the constant fear that a new great purge would be under way.

Stalin died on 6 March 1953, and gradually the atmosphere improved. In 1956 Nikita Khrushchev denounced Stalin before the Party Congress in a speech which was at once leaked to the West, and a 'thaw' in foreign affairs set in. Writers were encouraged to publish; millions of people were released from the prison camps; and the standard of living rose beyond the dismal levels of Stalinist times. There were setbacks of a mysterious kind, one of them being the rise in anti-Semitism. Our informants of the third wave of emigration – which is still going on – were mainly people of Jewish origin, some in Israel, some in the United States. We have not used the memories of all of them, because very often they have exactly the same dreadful story: an institute; some mysterious denunciation; some stupid people being rude in a corridor; the KGB harassing them, opening their post, listening to their telephone calls, making things difficult if they want to learn Hebrew. Brave souls apply for emigration, face enormous waits at various bureaucratic hurdles, and eventually, often after pressure from sympathetic people in the West, manage to take the plane to Vienna. The less fortunate – Anatoly Shcharansky – face years and years of imprisonment. Their resilience is remarkable.

The 1960s and 1970s saw the end to Khrushchev's fond hope that the Soviet Union would 'overtake' the West economically, and life, though better than in Stalin's time, continued to be a grey, grim round for most people. On the other hand, the strength of the country's intellectual tradition is very great – perhaps simply because other distractions are so much less tempting. The result was a combination of stagnation and powerful literature denouncing it. In 1985, with a new leader in Mikhail Gorbachev, the strongest note of reform and criticism in Soviet history was sounded. The promise now is that Soviet Communism will follow the better sides of the West; already Soviet television has been filming the lives of emigrants, and some of them have made successful returns to their home country.

46

The Peasant's Tale

VASSILY ARKHIPOVICH SOKOLOV

Vassily Arkhipovich Sokolov was born in 1921, the son of a Cossack farmer in the Kuban.

My father, Arkhip Sokolov, was a private in the Imperial Army, and came home to the Kuban when that Army was disbanded. When the Communists came to our area and started their propaganda, at first many people believed them; but after three to four months they saw through them and started to fight against them. My father fought with the other Kuban Cossacks in the White Army for several years. When the Whites finally left, he was sick and could not accompany them. He stayed at home, and then after a year or so he organized some of the ex-soldiers of the White Army and others into a large group to revolt against the Communists. They fought for a while and then he led them over the Caucasus mountains into Georgia, which was then an independent republic. That was early in 1921, about two months before I was born. From Georgia they went to Turkey and from there to France, leaving my mother behind.

In the 1920s my father used to write to my mother and she to reply, which in the Communists' eyes made her in principle a spy. He could write fairly freely, but each time they arrested her for one or two days, demanding to know what he had written and what she had replied. This would happen three or four times a year. So after 1927 she wrote no more. But I knew he was there in France and wanted to join him, which I did after 1945.

My mother took over the farm and when I was old enough I helped her. Since the age of six I've always worked. When she was under arrest I had to look after everything. In summer I helped bring in the harvest and in winter I tended the animals after I came home from school. I had time to go to school only in winter and not very often. After collectivization started it was almost impossible; I had no clothes and we had to spend our whole time looking for food.[1]

At school, of course, there was a lot of propaganda. Despite everything, some of it had an effect on me for a while – then suddenly I saw through it. No one I knew at school became a Communist through conviction. The members of the Young Communist League used to spy on the others, wanted to know what books you were reading and so on.

All through the 1920s – the period of NEP [New Economic Policy] – the Party was working gradually to bring the people completely under their control. They feared the workers and they gave them privileges, but the peasants they always intended to destroy. There was a Cossack village – a *stanitsa* – in the Kuban, which I was told had 2800 people before the Revolution. By the end of the Civil War it had only 921. Then all through the 1920s, gradually more and more people were taken away. Each year after the Revolution a few more disappeared: first all the artisans, then all the traders, all the shopkeepers, until by the time of collectivization all the shops were kept closed by order. All the old schoolteachers went; in their place came ordinary workers from the towns, who knew nothing.

There were perhaps 1.8 million people in the whole Kuban area in 1929 when collectivization started, and when it finished there were only about 390,000 left. The rest were sent to Siberia or died of starvation. For years children had been taught and organized by their teachers to go round their families agitating for collectivization. They also tried to organize the poor peasants to carry it out. In other areas this succeeded, and detachments of the landless peasants played a big part, but in the Kuban not a single person wanted collectivization. There it was NKVD troops and groups of workers – many were from Baku – who were responsible, led by commissars who were almost all Jewish. As far as I know, the Army itself wasn't used. A few villages took up arms against collectivization, and were destroyed. I know of three big *stanitsa*s in our area – Urubskaya, Poltavskaya and Novonikolayevskaya – which fought back. In the night troops surrounded them, and two days later they had been completely destroyed – every single person was rounded up.

Sometimes we ate, sometimes we didn't eat for weeks on end in these years. In 1931–2, when the population was starving, there were big heaps of maize under guard in the middle of the village squares, waiting to be taken away. No one ever collected it, and when winter came it rotted where it was. Then they'd clear it away and collect more. Women went and stole the maize – and that meant risking being shot – and hid it in their skirts and petticoats. My mother could not do that because she was known to the Communists as a spy and the wife of a White Guard. So I used to go and run after the women and pick up any of the maize they dropped from their skirts, and eat it as it was. My mother's legs swelled up because of hunger until she could hardly walk, but we used to follow carts for miles, and search along the roads, hoping to find potatoes, which sometimes used to fall out. In winter these would be frozen, but we ate them as they were.

I was never arrested; I saw what had happened to other people, so I kept my head down and worked. On the *kolkhoz*es one would work a year for one month's wages in food – one month's supply was all the *kolkhoz* managers had to give after the rest had been collected and taken away. These managers usually came from outside, though some were from nearby towns. They called themselves 'specialists', but anyone with a good grounding in Communism was thought to be qualified to run an agricultural enterprise, and they thought so themselves. They made incredible mistakes and ruined a lot of equipment.

I tried after that to go to an aeronautics institute, but they wouldn't let me in because of my father. So I went to the towns, where I became a worker, and did a correspondence course. And in those years, if they needed a technician, they just declared you to be one! I lived in Armavir, then in Rostov-on-Don, and worked and tried to study at the same time. There was more to eat there than in the villages, so the peasants tried to come into the towns. They were forbidden to do so, and were issued with internal passports that had to be stamped by the police before they could go to a town, but they came all the same. You'd see them bringing in a kilo of potatoes or a few eggs and trying to exchange them for bread, because there was no bread in the countryside. The towns were packed and the villages empty. All the young men who had finished their service in the Army used to stay in the towns and find work, and did not go home to their villages.

There was no general revolt for several reasons: first, all the peasants clever enough to have thought things out had been sent to Siberia – the equivalent of the whole population of France! Second, there were informers everywhere. A man couldn't talk to his wife. If he trusted his wife, he was afraid of his children. I had a friend who was a Party member and he told me himself he was spying on me. I knew lots of Communists, but very few who were Communists by conviction. After all, they even mobilized *me* for propaganda work! During the war I met only one man who was a convinced Communist. He was a teacher in a village in the Ukraine, where we spent some time, and we had long arguments. I met far more men who said, 'We're Communists, so we'll do what we like, and there's —— all you can do about it.' They had no ideology; their only idea was '*Nous sommes de la force . . .*' Generally they came from the big cities, from the slums.

In 1939 I got into a technical college in Rostov. I was there for two years, and then when the war started I was conscripted into a labour army as a technician. We were in the eastern Ukraine when the Germans overran the area. We didn't retreat with the Soviet Army but we didn't want to be made prisoners by the Germans either, so the sergeant in our 'brigade' organized us into a private group to build bath-houses in the villages. Most of them had been destroyed during collectivization. The villagers needed new ones and the German Army needed them as well. So we travelled around, a small group of us, from one village to another in the Ukraine. They paid us with food.

The peasants thought that when the Germans arrived the Soviet Government would fall, the *kolkhoz*es would be dissolved and they would go back to farming in the way they had done before. But I saw the Germans arrive in the Ukraine. They saw that the *kolkhoz*es were a good system for them. They sent their man along with a stick and he said: 'Work!'

Several old Communist officials stayed on under the Germans as *kolkhoz* chiefs – they knew their job. All produce was requisitioned. Under the Soviets the peasants were allowed a patch of land beside their house where they could keep ten or twenty chickens, a goat or even a cow. Often the Germans took even these; they *made* people into partisans. In the German POW camps you were starved; either you fought or worked for them and received rations, or you escaped and became a partisan, or you starved where you were. I came into contact with the partisans a lot as we travelled around. They were of three sorts: the pro-Soviet ones, sometimes actually under regular military command; the Ukrainian nationalists, who sometimes collaborated with the Germans and sometimes fought them; and the ones who wanted nothing to do with either side and fought for themselves. Many of these were either deserters from the Red Army or escaped prisoners – criminals as well as POWs. As time went on, the Soviets gained more and more influence and control over this sort. How much harm any of these various types of partisans did to the Germans I'm not sure, but every now and then the Germans would descend on a village and shoot one man out of every five or ten, saying that partisans had been hiding there.

I had a Cossack friend who was the leader of a group of partisans. He had been a captain in the Red Army, in command of a cavalry squadron, and when the Germans attacked he had taken his whole squadron over to them – arms, horses and all. The Germans wanted these men on their side, so they let them go home on leave to the Ukraine, still with their rifles, sabres and horses. But when this man reached their home village, he held a meeting of the peasants and told them they must get arms from the Germans in order to use them eventually against both the Germans and the Soviets. When we were in that area I got to know this man quite well, and I was talking to him in the village where he was based when the Germans came and rounded up him and his band. I was arrested too, and spent three weeks with him before he was shot. They let me go – I don't know why. We used to talk about what was to be done – how to fight both the Germans and the Soviets. Personally, I could see no future in an independent 'Cossackdom': Cossacks are Russians in the final analysis.

My friend's family, too, had come to a tragic end, which explains why he went over to the Germans in the first place. They had been well-off farmers, and during collectivization the entire family was shot, down to his ten-year-old brother. Being only a small child then, he had escaped by hiding in a hayloft. He had then survived by sneaking into a Red Army camp and living off the food brought to him by soldiers who took pity on him. He pretended he didn't know who his parents were – there were many orphaned or destitute children [*besprizorniki*] like him wandering around at that time – and eventually the Army adopted him and sent him to school. He did well there, joined the Army and in time was promoted to captain. All that time he had been waiting for his moment to strike back. There were probably many like him who hid their *kulak* origins and waited for their revenge – one could hardly find a single peasant family in which someone hadn't been arrested; this was even true of Communist Party members. Most of the people I met were anti-Soviet – not especially anti-Stalin, but anti-

Government in general. I did meet a few who were pro-Soviet, like the teacher I mentioned, but not many.

The ordinary soldiers of the German Wehrmacht were not particularly cruel, but they were all fighting in the front line. Behind the real soldiers came the SS and a horde of civilian officials; they were much worse. They organized forced labour, transported people off to work in Germany, and massacred the Jews. I only once saw Jews actually being killed, and I left in a hurry. Like the Soviet Army, the German Army had special commissars [*Sonderführer*] attached to most military units, and they forced officers and men to do things they wouldn't otherwise have done.

When the German troops started retreating, the group that I was with (still building bath-houses) moved westwards with them. I was still hoping to join my father in France. We made our way through Poland, with considerable difficulty; the roads west were choked with millions of people, not to mention their horses, carts and herds of cattle. Because our presence there was illegal – we had no transit papers – we could get neither work nor food. We had to live on what we had brought with us from the Ukraine. I remember that the Poles we met were then very pro-Communist and they wouldn't listen when I told them what things were really like in the Soviet Union. For a while we had very little to eat. Occasionally, as in one Czech village we passed through, I remember, the German Army quartermasters would give out soup to the refugees.

Behind all retreating armies there is always a rabble of lost troops and stragglers looking for their units, usually mixed with would-be deserters. Sometimes the German military police would set up a checkpoint and take soldiers out of the column at random and check their papers. We were stopped several times and always claimed to be Cossacks in German service searching for our corps. When we reached Prague, we made contact with Russian émigrés of the 'first wave' of emigration, and they found us food and work for a while. Then we went on. At the Austrian frontier we were stopped and asked: 'Who are you?' 'Cossacks,' we replied. 'All Cossacks are to proceed to Italy.' So they set us on the road to Italy, but we skirted round the checkpoint and headed for Germany instead, where we made our way to Berlin. By then – spring 1945 – everything was falling to pieces and no one tried to stop us. Another long trek westwards brought us to a Displaced

47

The Lesser of Two Evils

ARVIDS JUREVICS

Arvids Jurevics's childhood memories of life as a Latvian refugee in Petrograd appear in Chapter 16.

[Our family had lived in independent Latvia since the Revolution, but in 1940 the Soviets returned as occupiers.] They said: 'We are not feeling safe and we need your harbours.' They took Riga and two more, Ventspils and Liepāja (Libau). When they took them, all our banned Communist organizations came out into the open; they saw that the Latvian Government was tottering. Then our military started to disappear. Then freight trains started to stop at our railway stations and undesirable elements suddenly disappeared during the night. Armed Russian and some local soldiers with rifles came in: 'You have to come with us,' and they were taken out in the night with very little preparation and stuffed into a freight train.

One day the whole thing took off; there were all kinds of heartbreaking stories. A husband went away on some kind of business, came home and found nobody there . . . That created very bitter feelings. Some of the men grabbed rifles and disappeared into the woods. When your wife and children are taken away you know what feelings you have. Some men joined the partisans, and they started to shoot at the Russian troops. After a year, they seized a whole company of the Red Army.

Our President Ulmanis was taken away and disappeared in Siberia. We heard many stories of what happened to him . . . Many other members of the Government were taken away. Nobody knows what happened to them: they may have been eliminated, or died of hunger in labour camps. The same thing happened to all the bourgeois element – farmers, and never mind who you were: if you owned something,

Persons camp in one of the Allied Zones in West Germany. After spending a year dodging the attentions of the Soviet Repatriation Commission, I eventually joined my father in France.

you were anti-Communist and without any reason you were taken away.

In the 1930s I had become a history teacher. Latvia was then an independent country, and so my feeling was that history was something objective, a science. Then when first the Germans and then the Russians occupied our country, I saw how history is made and it isn't objective at all.

[In 1941] we were friendly neither with the Russians nor with the Germans, but all of a sudden the Germans came in, and we were free of all those Soviet trains shipping people off to Siberia, all those deportations and prisons. We felt that although the Germans were bad, they were the lesser of two evils; some of our people even joined the German Army, not for any highly idealistic reasons but simply to get our own back on the Russians, because even before the Germans came in we already saw the Red Army retreating. Our partisans were shooting at them from the rooftops along the main roads to Russia. So when the Germans came, many people saw them as liberators and they joined them. The Germans looked to us very friendly people . . . I wouldn't say there was a Nazi movement as such, but a revenge movement against the Russians. Maybe there were some individual elements who behaved like Nazis, but they were exceptional. The majority didn't join any German organization, though some of our young people, such as Army officers who had hidden from the Russians, even joined the SS troops just to fight the Russians. Their brothers, their fathers, their children, their wives had been deported . . .

[Then] the German Army started to retreat, and day and night we heard rumbling along the main roads leading from Leningrad down to Danzig, and onward to Germany – tanks and everything. I was living in Tukums, that's about sixty miles west of Riga, and while that was going on, suddenly on a Sunday morning we heard some rumours that the Russians were coming from the south, from Yaltava. Everything was quiet for a while, but then a couple of times planes came and bombed us. I remember we were digging trenches to hide in, but we didn't even get a chance to get to the trenches – the bombs were falling everywhere. When you are a family man with a wife and children this is especially awful, so we just sat and prayed. Then everything quietened down again.

We had some friends who lived a little bit out of the town in the woods. We lived right on the top of a hill not far from the railroad station and the main road from Yaltava [and] we thought it wasn't safe there right beneath their noses, so we moved to our friends. They had a big basement, a big cellar and several families went there to hide, at least until it was over.

That Sunday morning everything was quiet; I had forgotten something in our house, so I jumped on my bicycle, went home to get those things and started to ride back. I was maybe halfway there [when] all of a sudden I heard noise: Russian tanks were coming along that road, about thirty tanks, shooting at whatever they could, making a surprise attack. And all of a sudden, coming towards me [along the railway track beside the road] was a train. I stopped the bicycle and waved; they saw me and started to put on the brakes. I remember the train going forwards and then trying to go backwards and it was slipping, slipping . . . But I think the Russian tanks saw it. It was quite a distance, but the tank commander saw it and started to shoot. I remember he missed the train, but there was a level-crossing with a man, and the bell was ringing: the crossing-keeper's booth just went to pieces. I jumped on my bicycle and was pedalling like mad towards the woods when the train started going backwards. They got away; they were lucky. I came home.

The Russians advanced and cut the German Army right in half, so the whole retreat was stopped. We were right in the middle now, between the Baltic Sea and a Russian Army in the south moving towards Berlin; we were cut off, like sitting ducks. After a couple of weeks German ships started to bombard from the sea and the Russians withdrew, but after a little while they returned and cut us off again. It was getting worse and worse, we were surrounded, and by now the sea was cleared of Germans and the Russians were coming in from there. We thought, 'Now it's coming – the same thing, the same trains, the same deportations.' I thought I'd be the first candidate for the next train, so we had to get away.

The question was: where to? The only way out was to Germany. So we packed one day, and had to go by horse and carriage, so many trains had been destroyed. Finally we got to Liepāja, one of the ports that was still working. They said we had a chance to get on one of the German Army hospital ships. So there we were, right in the harbour, sitting waiting one day – another day – a third day. I could speak German [so] I could at least make myself understood. I went on board a ship and started to talk to the captain. 'Can you help our family and

two children?' 'Yes, come right away.' We picked up our belongings –
we did not have much – and up we went on board. The German soldiers
were kind; they were wounded men being evacuated from the front,
Wehrmacht, not SS, just ordinary soldiers, and they were so friendly
with the children – they hadn't seen their own children for so many
years.

We were bound, I think, for Danzig. We had alarms several times
during the night because of Russian submarines, but suddenly we got
there. We were taken, like citizens of a friendly country, to the German
authorities; we were promised they would give us jobs in Germany,
because the Germans were very short of factory workers. We were
taken to Merseburg, where I got a job as a bookkeeper in an aeroplane
factory [at Halle-an-der-Saale.]

I was in an office working alongside Czechs, Slovaks and Poles who
had simply been grabbed off the streets – just young people deported
as labour to Germany for having been unfriendly towards the Germans.
With us it was much better. They gave us quarters in a farmhouse in
a small village – just a small room. In that village we watched the
bombing of Merseburg every night. It was like a spectacle: first those
searchlight-beams going up and then the German flak.

A rumour was going around that there was a college in Halle-an-
der-Saale where there was an American professor, which was supposed
to be the reason why the Americans wouldn't bomb the town. [But
then] one day, I remember, I came from the village to the town, for
something I had to do at the town council offices. And all of a sudden
there was an air-raid warning. We'd had our alarms before, many times,
and nothing had happened. But you had to go into the cellar, and in
that establishment there wasn't much of a cellar – just the windows
covered with sandbags. And oh it was a big raid – it was 'carpet
bombing' [a saturation raid]. I was so lucky – the place to which I was
going was situated about a hundred yards from where the 'carpet'
stopped. When I came into the cellar all the Germans were on the
ground, praying; maybe because I'm not a religious man, I just stood
and stared about me. I was the only person standing up. I looked
around, shaking, and I thought maybe my ears were going to burst.
The earth was trembling. All of a sudden it was quiet. I came out. I
didn't believe it. There was no town any more. On both sides the
buildings were just heaps of bricks on the street. Both sides of the
street were burning; you could hardly pass through by climbing over

the bricks. The people getting up from the ground, just to open their eyes, were all covered with earth. You could only see their eyes, looking like zombies. I went past the cemetery, all ruined, where you could see the coffins and some corpses and dead horses. Somehow I scrambled through and got home . . .

Then one day I was coming home from work and all of a sudden a whole squadron – I don't know how many – maybe hundreds, maybe thousands, flew over me, and not too high: the earth was trembling from those aeroplanes. I thought this is it, but they weren't interested in me. I was so impressed that I just lay down on my back in that field and looked up. A couple of times the flak fired and I saw shells bursting in the sky, but even more planes came, and then I heard later that Dresden was bombed. And I saw the whole bunch going over me, and my God, when all those planes had done their bombing there was nothing left of Dresden.

One night some of the younger Czechs [at my place of work] disappeared. They just took off. They knew the Americans were coming. The older men thought they wouldn't risk it; they knew too much, and thought they would wait and see what was going to happen.

Then one day when I was in my little village, all of a sudden from all sides jeeps came pouring in, full of American soldiers. When they came into the village they called out all the German farmers: 'You have to bring out all your shotguns or rifles.' I remember a huge coloured fellow: he took every shotgun and broke it across his knee. The Germans just stood and watched. There wasn't any fighting – the Americans just took over. We were moved right away to Displaced Persons camps.

All of a sudden we heard rumours that, according to the agreement between Stalin and Roosevelt at Yalta, the Americans were going to give away everything to the Russians, all of this territory. The American Army had come that far already – that is, beyond the Elbe; why should they give it up? But it had been laid down in the agreement and we started to fear again.

Our representatives started to go to the US Army generals, to persuade them that we should be moved out, somewhere to the west, to the American zone, or where the zone was going to be. To our surprise, some of the generals were a little bit too – I wouldn't say Red, but very sympathetic to the Russians, and it took quite some time to convince them that we had to go otherwise we were going to be killed or deported. Finally, somehow, they worked things out, and one day we were loaded into US Army trucks, and taken west, far away to Mannheim. We were put in camps there. It took us five years to get to America, to get a sponsor. Others were distributed to all kind of countries – to Australia, to any country that would have them.

I was a teacher in the Displaced Persons camp. There were Jewish children there from those horror camps. I talked to them. I was interested to know their views. They had all lost their religion. Nobody believed in God any more. One boy was sitting in the window one morning, almost naked despite the cold. I said, 'You're going to catch cold.' He said, 'Catch cold? What? Here? If I am still alive, this is nothing.'

One thing in those camps I never can forget. It was an Armenian group. According to those agreements with the Russians, the Armenians were listed as Soviet citizens. They were not like us; we were Latvian but they were from the Soviet Union. And in the agreement they had to be sent back there. My God, I saw a group of Armenian men who had stabbed each other to death with knives, the women in the centre with the children, the American soldiers having received the order to load them into the trucks and take them away to the railroad station or whatever. It was a tragic scene. Finally the leader of the American soldiers couldn't stand the sight and they all slunk away. And the next day again there was some other group; again the trucks would come in and the people would start to jump from high buildings, committing suicide by jumping out of the windows. We tried to hide them in the non-Armenian camps – under the beds, everywhere. Some tried to escape, but I don't know how long they managed to hide or how long they could get away; there were so many . . . In those times we were very angry at those agreements. How could American presidents and other politicians be so stupid?

Jurevics was eventually sponsored by a Latvian woman who had also been a teacher in a Displaced Persons camp. In 1950 he arrived in the United States.

48

Following Alien Paths

GERSHON SOLOMONOVICH SHAPIRO

*Gershon Solomonovich Shapiro was born in 1899 in Rovno, near Zhito-
mir, the son of a self-employed chalk-miner.*

I belong to the generation of Russian-born Jews who are as old as this
century, and who joined Marxist movements under the influence of
certain illusions about socialism.

Born into a poor Jewish family in 1899, I grew up in the days of the
Beylis case.[1] I also witnessed the First World War; living as I did in an
area immediately behind the front line, I saw the tragic slaughter of
the combatants and the almost equally tragic plight of the Jewish population as they were forcibly evacuated from the front-line areas. It was
natural and understandable that socialist ideas should have impressed
me.

In 1915–16 I belonged to a revolutionary socialist group. In 1917,
after the February Revolution, when the discriminatory anti-Jewish
laws and the Pale of Settlement[2] were abolished, I moved to Kiev.
There I frequented the clubs of the Jewish socialist parties – the *Bund*,
Poale Zion,[3] and the Unionists (the joint organization of the Zionist
socialists and the Jewish socialists). In 1918 I joined the left wing of
Poale Zion, then I enrolled in the *Poale Zion* detachment of the Red
Guard and took part in the rout of the 'Green' movement, when the
Red Guard stormed Pushcha-Voditsa near Kiev. In April 1919 the Kiev
branch of *Poale Zion* transferred me to the Red Army, where I fought
against Denikin's White Army; against Petlyura, the Ukrainian
nationalist leader;[4] and against the Poles in the Polish–Soviet War of
1919–20. I was demobilized at the end of 1926.

In October 1920 I joined the All-Russian Communist Party (Bolsheviks). During the purge of August 1921 I was expelled from the Party

for failing to renounce the Zionist ideology of *Poale Zion*. In March 1922 I was readmitted as a probationary member. During a Party comb-out in 1932 I was again expelled, on the same grounds as before, but was soon reinstated. Then, during Stalin's 'Purge' trials of 1936 I was expelled for the third time. On that occasion I did not apply for reinstatement, although ideologically I had not broken with the Party; my rejection of Marxism and Communism did not occur until the 1960s.

During the later 1920s and 1930s I was active in collectivization, and also served as Director of the House of Jewish Culture in Odessa. I then worked as a specialist in livestock-breeding until the Germans invaded the Soviet Union in June 1941 [when] I rejoined the Red Army. [After the war] I returned to Odessa, where I worked in the agricultural-livestock division of the Regional Planning Commission until I retired on pension in July 1959.

My eighty-odd years have been filled with fateful and dramatic events. My journey through life can be divided into two unequal parts: the first, lasting fifty years, along an alien path in which I served alien gods; the second, lasting twenty years, in which I have followed the true path of my people.

The process of turning aside from an alien path on to my own, Jewish, path was difficult and prolonged, lasting at least a decade. From the 1920s onward I was fed on an exclusive diet of biased, dogmatic Marxist literature that was completely out of touch with the currents of social and political thinking in the rest of the world.

Secondly, I lived through the period of the so-called flourishing of Jewish culture in the USSR and the social restructuring of the Jewish population of the Soviet Union: the mass exodus of the Jewish population from the poverty-stricken rural *shtetl*s and ghettos of the Pale of Settlement into the industrial cities and universities of Russia, and into new, voluntarily organized Jewish townships and settlements, where former shopkeepers, small craftsmen and young Jews, whose lives had previously been narrow and devoid of prospects, were metamorphosed into trained professionals with a higher education or became energetic, efficient farmers, successfully cultivating large tracts of land allotted to them by the State. All these former *Luftmenschen* acquired a stable base of relative material security. This inevitably induced many Jews to become convinced supporters of the Soviet regime, of which they, perhaps more than any other ethnic component of the multi-national Soviet State, were the beneficiaries.

Thirdly, we were horrified witnesses to the pre-war and wartime catastrophe, in which Hitler attempted (with, alas, considerable success) to destroy the entire Jewish population of Europe. During those years, my fellow Jews and I tended to divide the world into Fascist and anti-Fascist, regarding those countries with a socialist political structure as anti-Fascist, and all the rest as Fascist.

In fact, it took me years to abandon this false, simplistic picture and to discern the threat to the Jews that was much nearer home: the assimilationist nature of Soviet Jewish culture and the basically predatory, exploitative intention behind the social restructuring of Russian Jewry, which was carried out with the active help of the *Yevsektsiya* (the now abolished 'Jewish Section' of the Soviet Communist Party); to appreciate the regressive character of a socialist as opposed to a capitalist economy; the inhumanity of the Soviet State's *raison d'état*; the expansionist, indeed imperialist behaviour of the Soviet Union in the world arena; and the ingrained anti-Semitism of the Soviet State apparatus. In the end, I could not accept the explanation of what happened as being simply due to Stalin's arbitrary despotism. Nor could I, in view of the harsh, cruel facts of Soviet reality, reject Communism without seeking an answer to what had turned it so sour for me. I had to make a total reappraisal of those ideological values that had formed the very core of my being, my 'ego'; to do this took me the entire decade of the 1950s.

The scarcity and inadequacy of goods and services leads to their inequitable distribution; to a massive degree of bureaucratic abuse of office, embezzlement and plain theft; to endemic popular discontent that is then suppressed by force or the threat of force; to the inevitable strengthening of the apparatus of repression, so creating a self-perpetuating caste whose principal function is coercion and all its accompanying evils: arbitrary power, corruption, the suppression of protest and, worst of all, the profaning of these very ideals in whose name the ruling oligarchy originally took power. Talk of 'socialism with a human face', with which some people hope to find a way out of this situation, is useless. The very foundations, economic and political, of Soviet-type socialism are rotten and must inevitably lead to the lamentable consequences that are to be seen in the USSR and those unfortunate countries under its hegemony.

The problem of ethnic minorities, in particular the Jewish problem, is one of the many challenges that Soviet socialism finds insoluble.

Finally, therefore, I came to the conclusion that in conditions of dispersal the Jewish people would not find the solution to those problems – legal, cultural, even economic – that militate against its ethnic and national integrity. Even when Jews participate freely in the economic, cultural and political life of other nation-states, this does not guarantee their continued existence either as a people or as scattered, assimilated individuals – as the Holocaust of the Hitler era proved.

Therefore, every Jew, wherever he or she may be, should direct every effort towards the security, consolidation and development of the Jewish State on the territory that it possesses.

I finally reached this viewpoint in the 1950s, and since then I have directed my activities towards its realization, within the bounds of my limited strength and abilities.

At my relatively advanced age, I devoted the last years of my time in the USSR to spreading Zionism among Soviet Jews. My wife and I created a centre of 'Jewish *samizdat*'. I translated several dozen books and brochures from Yiddish into Russian – books on Jewish history, books on Jewish life in other countries, on the creation and development of the State of Israel – and my wife typed them all. At the same time I collected material about Jewish participation in the war against Hitler's Germany – in the Allied armies, in the partisan movement, in the Warsaw Ghetto, and on many other fields of battle. The most abundant material was that concerning those Jews who had been decorated with the Soviet Union's highest award – Hero of the Soviet Union; by 1973 we had compiled three volumes, comprising 107 biographies. We brought one typescript copy with us to Israel, and here, at last, it has been published in Russian; the irony of it is that this book, which records some of the most glorious, the most moving and the most self-sacrificial deeds in the whole of Russian military history, is strictly banned in the Soviet Union.

49

Polish Affairs

YAKOV SAMOILOVICH KALETSKY

During the Second World War the Soviet Government summoned a congress of Polish patriots who were then on Soviet soil. For Russia and Europe, it was one of the most significant events of the century.

It is my opinion that, while the war was still in progress, Stalin had already begun to think out, and to put into effect, a long-term political strategy. He began, that is, to develop a plan of how he might, after a successful outcome to the war, in effect annex the countries that had been liberated, and do so in such a way that the Allies would somehow be able to swallow without making too much fuss.

As is well known, Stalin [had] dissolved the Polish Communist Party on the grounds that it was a hotbed of Trotskyism. God help any Polish refugee who fled across the 'green frontier' to the USSR (which was open in 1939 and early 1940) to escape from Hitler, from the Ghetto, from extermination in the pogroms, if he then declared to the Soviet authorities that he had been a member of the PCP or had fought for the Communist cause. He would be mercilessly beaten up, exiled to some distant region at the back of beyond – or very often he would be shot. It was, in fact, the ultimate fate of most Communists who ever escaped to the USSR from Hitler's Germany or from Poland.

[In 1943, however], with the help of the well-known Polish writer Wanda Wasilewska,[1] the Soviet Government decided to create the so-called 'Union of Polish Patriots'. It was supposed to be a spontaneously formed organization, but in fact the delegates were all Soviet nominees from among the Polish refugees in the USSR, many of whom were actually in prison camps. The NKVD issued them with special permits to travel to Moscow, because in 1943 all travel was strictly controlled. They all assembled in a large transit hotel, the Central House of the

Red Army in Moscow. There they lived and did their work. Their first meeting as a formal body took place in April 1943 in the presence of Molotov and other members of the Soviet Government. Chopin's 'Revolutionary Étude' was played, there were speeches, Wanda Wasilewska appeared and it was resolved that this would be the future Provisional Government of Poland. In some unexplained way, the Union was declared to represent and embody the will of the Polish people, suffering under Nazi oppression, [and] the Union of Polish Patriots became the 'Polish Committee for National Liberation'.

Polish affairs have a habit of becoming an international issue. The Poles themselves bear some of the responsibility for this: they have tended to see Poland as the Christ of the nations, to believe that the whole world would be saved by the example of Polish sacrifice and moral grandeur. And so the Poles in the Soviet Union believed that the Polish question was very closely bound up with this traditional mission. They were, of course, deluded, because in reality they were being used as pawns on the European chessboard by that ruthless Grand Master of the game, Stalin.

[Sikorski was already dead and] the Government-in-Exile lost its influence.[2] A new Polish term made its appearance in Russia: 'POP' – standing for the Polish words which mean 'Poles who are fulfilling their obligations'. These were old Poles of the fifth or sixth generation whose forefathers had been exiled to Siberia by the Imperial Russian Government, mostly for political reasons. They had become completely russified, just like the many Germans who settled in Russia in the eighteenth and nineteenth centuries. The Soviet authorities dug out large numbers of POPs and sent them to Poland.

The Committee for National Liberation was installed in Lublin, the temporary capital of liberated Poland, but later moved to Warsaw and, despite the fact that Warsaw had been virtually razed to the ground, the decision was taken to re-establish it as the capital. That is how post-war, contemporary Poland arose and became (although often extremely recalcitrant) a Soviet satellite.

But how is this related to our topic – emigration from Russia? It is because, I believe, one of the most important, fundamental turning-points in the history of Russia is the fact that during and immediately after the Second World War emigration and repatriation from the Soviet Union was permitted – admittedly for reasons of Soviet national interest. What did that repatriation mean? It affected not only those

Poles who had found themselves in the Soviet Union as a result of the events of 1939, who had refused to accept Soviet passports and who had been forcibly settled in Siberia – they had all been released from internal exile after Sikorski flew to Moscow as early as 1942. Having lived under appalling climatic conditions until then, most of them moved to warmer places, such as the Caucasus or Central Asia. Then it was announced, under pressure of the military situation and at the urgent insistence of the London-based Government-in-Exile, that General Anders' Polish Army Corps was to be formed.[3] It was then that the Soviet authorities announced something that was completely unprecedented in Soviet conditions: that Poles would be allowed to return to Poland. This referred, in fact, only to soldiers who agreed to join Soviet-sponsored military units, but gradually, after the founding of the Polish Committee for National Liberation, the concept was broadened, and rumours soon began to circulate about 'repatriation' on a larger scale. By the end of 1944, local Soviet police officials and local NKVD offices were being instructed to take the first steps towards registering former Polish citizens. All those who wanted to be registered, that is; it wasn't compulsory – there were Poles who had made a satisfactory career in Russia, or who had arrived in the USSR as orphaned children and didn't really look upon Poland as their homeland.

So arrangements for repatriation began in 1945. Why? Because Stalin wanted to shape the future of Poland in accordance with the long-term interests of the USSR. He calculated that if these people, who had become at least partially 'sovietized' during their time as refugees, were now allowed to return to Poland, and if to these were added the POPs and the Committee for National Liberation, plus the permanent presence of the Soviet Army, they would form the essential skeleton of the future Poland and that Poland would be Soviet. And – with certain exceptions, such as the persistent strength of the Catholic Church in Poland – he was not mistaken in his calculations.

There is an interesting story, which circulated during the period of Polish repatriation, although I cannot vouch for its truth. There was corrupt administration in some of the parts of the Soviet Union where there were numbers of Polish refugees or those of Polish origin – regions such as the Union Republic of Georgia, where corruption was (and still is) endemic. There, Polish candidates for repatriation didn't wait for formal permission but corruptly acquired locomotives and railway waggons and steamed across Russia to Polish territory. The war was still going on, and there was as yet no proper frontier, while the main bulk of the Soviet Army had already advanced as far as western Poland.

Whatever the truth of that probably apocryphal story, the official repatriation of Poles in 1945, and later, was an event of great importance because for the first time the Soviet authorities allowed people, many of them Soviet citizens, to go abroad and to take with them a knowledge of many discreditable facts about life in the Soviet Union: the low standard of living, the corruption and inefficiency, the cruelty and arbitrary injustice. It must be said, though, that this plan was understood and fully worked out only at the highest level – in the Politburo and the Central Committee, perhaps at the top echelons of certain ministries. But when the orders to implement it filtered down to the lower levels of officialdom, they couldn't understand what was happening. Had the authorities taken leave of their senses? How could they allow it? Why were *Poles* being allowed to go home, when other nationalities who had been suspected of less than hundred per cent loyalty to the Soviet Union were being irrevocably deported from their ancestral homelands and exiled, as a punishment, to the most barren and inhospitable regions of Siberia – the Volga Germans, the Kalmyks, the Chechens, the Crimean Tartars, the Karelian Finns? So wherever they could, Soviet officials at grassroots level did all they could to obstruct the repatriation, as a result of which it was stopped in 1947. Hundreds of thousands of Poles or those of Polish descent remained stuck in the USSR, their applications having been turned down.

Then in 1956 came the outburst of unrest in Poland, at a time when Khrushchev had only recently managed to gain supremacy in the Soviet leadership and had sent shock-waves throughout Soviet-controlled Eastern Europe by the revelations of his 'de-Stalinization' speech at the Twentieth Party Congress of the CPSU. The Polish newspapers were saying openly: 'We don't want any more Moscow appointees ruling the Polish people.' Khrushchev realized that he was facing a national uprising and that this time the USA might be provoked into action by the powerful Polish–American lobby. [As part of his bargaining with the Polish First Secretary, Gomulka,] repatriation to Poland began again that year. It was a further blow at one of the central myths that underlie the Stalinist conception of the State – namely that since Soviet socialism is the closest thing to perfection that mankind has ever known, no one who has tasted the delights of living under that system will ever need, still less want to leave it. Because once they had let the Poles go, the Armenians, the Volga Germans and the Jews – all of whom have national territories or large ethnic communities abroad – began to agitate, gradually but ultimately successfully, for the right to emigrate. It also tended to aggravate feelings of separatist resentment among the Balts and the Ukrainians.

The only essential condition [for repatriation] was to prove that you really had come from Poland, that you had once been a Polish citizen. No one could say for sure that they did or didn't have relatives there, because in the first place the country had suffered under Hitler's terrible policy of genocide, and, secondly, a person obliged to live in the Soviet Union was deprived of the normal means of communication. He knows that his letters are censored and very often never reach their destination, so that virtually no one was in a position to know whether they had any surviving relatives.

There was a secret clause in the agreement on repatriation: the Polish State would guarantee that the 'repatriatees' would not be allowed, for a long time, to emigrate any further. The Soviets were afraid that Poland might become a mere transit-station to other parts of the world. Above all they were aware that among those repatriated there was a significant number of Jews, and they wanted to prevent them from going to Israel and fighting the Arabs as members of the Israeli armed forces. Secondly, they wanted to prevent ethnic Poles from joining up with former members of General Anders' disbanded army in Britain and elsewhere, and from nurturing any dreams in inciting Poland to throw off Soviet domination.

I remember a Polish joke about this. They made exceptions to the 'no further emigration' rule only in the case of old people, so the following story went round Warsaw. A very old man who has been repatriated goes to the passport section of the Ministry of Foreign Affairs and says, 'Please give me a passport. I want to go abroad. None of my relatives are left alive in Poland; I can't even find their gravestones in the cemetery. So let me emigrate – I can't do any useful work and I will only be a burden on the State by drawing my pension.' The official replies, 'By all means. Only young people of working age are not allowed to leave; we don't prevent old people from going. Tell us where you want to go, and we'll give you a passport right away.' The old man says, 'But I don't know where to go. Perhaps you have a globe?' 'Certainly!' They bring him a globe. He examines the globe, then pulls a wry face: 'You know, I still don't know where to go. Perhaps you have another globe?'

[I was repatriated in 1956.] I went to Warsaw, but I wasn't born in Warsaw, although I went to school and university there. I was born in a town that was then part of Russia, but now belongs to Poland – Avgustov, near Grodno. One's place of birth didn't matter. What counted was being able to prove that at one time you had been a Polish citizen. This wasn't always easy. The former *Rzeczpospolita Polska* ceased to exist on 17 September 1939, at the fall of Warsaw; the Government had fled, the Army was captured or disbanded, local government and the civil service no longer existed, civil registration archives were largely destroyed. Yet the Soviet authorities, in 1956, demanded that I produce a valid certificate to show that I had been a Polish citizen on 17 September 1939. 'How can I give you a certificate when at that date Poland was in ruins and most of the population was fleeing in one direction or another?' 'Then give us a certificate from the Soviet authorities to show that you entered western Byelorussia and where you came from . . . '

[The territory in which I was born became Polish in 1918, when I was nine or ten years old, so as a child I was a subject of the Tsar.] When I was eight years old we were living in Bialystok, and I heard Trotsky speak. That must have been in late 1917 or early 1918. I remember what he looked like, and I remember something else: he was a remarkable orator. I am a musician, after all; even as a child I had a good ear and the sound of his voice made a great impression on me. It was in the market square; there was a crowd of thousands, a wooden platform – and on to the platform climbed a handsome man of striking, even pleasant appearance, not very tall, with a little pointed beard, and he began to speak, in a ringing, high-pitched voice, speaking the most beautiful Russian. That was Trotsky. Three weeks later the Cossacks of the White Army were in that market square. Then the Whites fled, the Reds returned and were later expelled when the Polish Army came. With them was de Gaulle, who was then a captain; the French were supporting the Poles in the Polish–Soviet War. De Gaulle was attached to the military mission of General Weygand.

I speak perfect Polish, but Russian is my mother tongue. Even if one is bilingual, one language will always have a slight advantage, however tiny. For me, Russian has that slight advantage over Polish. [My parents spoke Russian.] Later they began to speak Polish, too, but their instinctive language of choice was Russian. They were wholly russified. After all, Poland hadn't existed since the partition of 1772. I wouldn't say they were revolutionaries or militant atheists of any sort. They were just ordinary, reasonably well-educated, non-religious people.

[I was educated in Warsaw and then in 1939] I suddenly found myself in Russia. I escaped to the Soviet Union when Warsaw fell. It had been under siege since 9 September 1939; I had already been smuggling contraband through the German lines. We received the order from the Polish High Command that everyone capable of bearing arms was to go east and there we would be given weapons. So we took to the road. At that time the whole population was on the road, thousands of people – babies, children, women, old men. Everyone who could was fleeing, in one direction: eastwards. There were constant air attacks. Normal values were turned upside down: people were giving away motor cars in exchange for a bicycle. A bicycle was what everyone dreamed of. There was no petrol; the roads were littered with cars. If someone could get hold of a bicycle, he felt as if he had won the lottery, because it meant he could travel farther and faster. We were supposed to be going to get weapons but there were no weapons anywhere; the Army Command had vanished.

So we kept moving eastwards until 17 September, or thereabouts, when it was announced on the radio that Soviet troops were about to occupy Polish territory as far as the River Bug. We were already on the right bank of the Bug by then.

I made my way on to Grodno and Bialystok, because that was my home country. Later I found a Polish officer who had thrown away his uniform; he was making trips to Warsaw on some kind of 'business' and used to bring back Poles who had got stranded in the German-occupied part of Poland. The border wasn't guarded – or rather, for the first few months the Soviet frontier guards turned a blind eye. There was a no man's land in between. When refugees came to no man's land, they would walk forward singing the 'Internationale' and the Soviet guards would let them through. I gave the Polish officer a thousand zlotys (or a thousand roubles, I forget which) and he brought my mother safely from Warsaw. He only did it for payment, of course; it was a sort of industry. The local peasants used to do it, too. Refugees would come as far as a frontier village, where they would find a peasant guide. The peasant would take their suitcases and would lead a party across the frontier by night. Just before the Soviet border, he would start to shout: 'Look out! Nazis! Nazis!' – and run off with the suitcases!

I was in Bialystok [in June 1941 when the Germans invaded the USSR]. I had to flee again and lost everything I had. But what I minded most was the ruin of my intended career as a barrister. I had already finished my period of probationary training [in Warsaw, and] was to have sat my final examinations in September 1939, just when the war began. Of course, if I had wanted it badly enough I could have become a barrister in the Soviet Union, but I decided to avoid the Soviet legal system. I saw that it was deeply flawed. The courts had the reputation of being mere tools of the Party, which were used, above all, as convenient instruments of Stalin's political purges. At that time everyone vividly remembered 1937, the climactic year of terror, the rigged tribunals, and the show trials dominated by that monster Vyshinsky, the Procurator-General. It was all so abhorrent that I didn't want to have anything to do with it . . . Instead, I studied music and later took a literature course. [I became a professional pianist and translator, then later worked for the Moscow branch of the Polish Press Agency.]

When repatriation began in 1945, the Soviet authorities didn't want to let me go. They made difficulties about my lack of proper documents, on the lines I have described. [When I did eventually get to Warsaw with my family in 1956, we were then not allowed to leave Poland after having left the USSR. It took two years to get an exit visa. We went first to relatives in Australia, then came to the USA.] Australia, America – we've been everywhere. I sometimes feel like the Wandering Jew – or the Flying Dutchman!

50

Hunger

IOSIF EMANUILOVICH DYUK

Iosif Emanuilovich Dyuk was born into a poor Jewish family living in Preluki, a shtetl *near Vinnitsa. His story is one of endurance, and of survival against all odds.*

I was born in 1918 at Vinnitsa in the Ukraine. The town was more than half Jewish. There were many pogroms during the Civil War – the era of men like Petlyura and Makhno.[1] Before the Second World War there were seventy thousand Jews in Vinnitsa. Can you imagine – Hitler killed thirty-five thousand of them. Among those who died were my mother and all my sisters.

With my parents I spoke Yiddish and I went to a Jewish school, where we were taught in Yiddish. People didn't really like it when one spoke Yiddish in public. The Ukrainians recognized Yiddish and made fun of you. I never spoke it on public transport, but some Jews did. They would start arguing saying, 'Why is it that all the other Soviet nationalities have the right to speak their languages and we don't? It's simply a manifestation of anti-Semitism.'

Jewish schools continued until the beginning of the war in 1939. They were closed then because for Jews to get into universities or other places of higher education, they had to take the national exams in Russian. As a result, Jews who were ambitious for their children did not want to send them to schools that taught in Yiddish.

My father was a self-employed cobbler. He was classed as a *kustar-odinochka* – a craftsman with a one-man business. He worked very hard, but he had a family and little money. We were terribly poor. We had absolutely nothing. We could just afford a one-room flat. Four bare walls. There often wasn't enough money for food. We didn't even have any bread – I shall never forget that.

I left school in 1933. There was a terrible famine in the Ukraine then,[2] because many peasants burnt their grain and livestock rather than join the collective farms. I saw people dying of hunger on the streets. My father, too, died of starvation in 1933. I remember it well . . . it was in August, and I was at school. Somebody came rushing into the classroom and told me that my father had died. I ran home and saw him lying on his bed. We had absolutely nothing to eat.

Soon it became very hard for my mother. When my father died she went to work in schools and kindergartens, cooking the children's midday meals. I can remember every detail of those times. We were so poor and life was very hard.

When my father was still alive, there were days when he would sit on his little stool doing nothing. There was no business. We children ran around the place half naked and barefoot. At twelve I'd run home to get something to eat from my mother, but she had nothing to give me. So what do you do? Sometimes other children would give me a bit of their bread and jam when I asked them. Sometimes I would burst out crying when there was no food; I would get quite hysterical and lie down on the floor, bang my feet and shout for food. The Yiddish word for 'nothing' is *nichts* – that's what my mother would repeat all the time. Sometimes she would go to my aunt, her sister, who was better off than we were because her son had emigrated to America and used to send her parcels. We would receive foreign-currency tokens which we could spend at the *Torgsin* foreign-currency shops.[3] Her children were already grown up and lived a better life than we did. She would go to the baker to guarantee my mother some bread. The bakers were all Jews, but even in times of famine they would not give you bread if you couldn't pay for it. The bread was marvellous – big, brown rye loaves. Mother would come home with a piece of this bread in exchange for some work done by my father. Occasionally, when we had 5 or 6 roubles, Mother and I would go to the market with a basket. She would get a bit of meat, some pickled cucumbers, tomatoes, apples or potatoes, and we would be so happy – it was a feast. But that happened very rarely.

Neither my mother nor my father was religious. We had great problems at Passover, but my parents always managed to buy us presents, such as new shoes or a new shirt, which made us very happy. Poor Father had so little money. White flour, for instance, was very expensive in those days; our greatest treat was the white rolls that Mother used to bake in a Russian stove. Of course you're not supposed to eat leavened bread at Passover, but if we happened to have white flour at that time, Mother could not resist baking us some rolls as a treat. We little children didn't know there was anything wrong in eating white bread then; Mother used to lock the door, telling us to eat our rolls at home and not to run out into the street with them. She was so worried that other Jews might see us eating bread during Passover and spoil this rare treat for us.

When I was about fourteen I used to roam all over the place in search of food. I remember seeing dead people around the porch of the church (this is the traditional place for Russian beggars to beg for alms from churchgoers); they had gone there to beg for food and had simply died where they sat on the ground. Nearby there was a market on Verkhnyaya Grazhdanskaya Street. There the wretched, ragged beggars were so filthy that you couldn't even make out the features of their faces and so hungry that they could hardly stand up if the wind was blowing. In the market women would sell home-cooked *pirozhki*, *bliny*, and baked potatoes. Sometimes a desperate, starving beggar would go up to one of these women, grab some food from her stall and start eating. The women would shout for help, whereupon people would rush over and beat up the poor, starving wretch. He would fall over still eating, while the crowd continued beating and kicking him to death. I saw this several times. It was appalling. By the time the police arrived the man would be dead, beaten to death with sticks or whatever people had to hand. And yet all the time he was eating. He was reduced to naked animal instinct: he just wanted to live . . .

I lived through several famines; that is why I have such awful teeth. We had no vitamins. Even though apples grew in and around Vinnitsa, they were terribly expensive. We would sneak into gardens and orchards to gather green apples in our shirt-fronts, then race off and gobble them up. They were usually unripe, and even now I can't look at an apple! If they caught you, you would be beaten to death. But I was difficult to catch. I was very sharp and quick, and could run like the wind. No grown-up could catch up with me.

[Homeless and orphaned children] just wandered about the streets. They were worse off because they had no parents – at least we had my mother. We had an acacia tree where black crows used to perch. They nested there, and the homeless children used to climb up there, steal the baby crows from the nest and beat a hasty retreat from the cawing mother birds. Then they would make a fire, cook the little birds, and eat them; it saved their lives.

[When I left school] I went to a clothing factory to learn sewing and tailoring. They didn't really teach us there; it was more like on-the-job training. It was boys and girls together, and the girls fared much better! I was actually quite dexterous. I used to sew little dresses for girls, blanket-covers, pillow-slips and underwear. But I didn't like it much – I wanted to be a mechanic rather than a sewing-machine operator. When my mother got herself a job, I left the tailoring workshop and became an apprentice at a big garage that repaired cars and lorries. At that time there were no vocational schools. I was about fifteen by then. I didn't stay there for very long. At sixteen I got a job in another clothing factory. The foreman in my section, a Jew named Greenblum with red hair, made the mistake of putting me to work on a vast stamping press that punched out metal popper-fasteners for sewing on to clothes. Greenblum explained what I had to do: it was to twist hemp around a length of wire, then coat it in oil in order to lubricate it before feeding it into the machine. I was very small and reaching up to do this job was very difficult for me. Once I forgot to take my foot off the operating pedal, I bent forward and the machinery started to whir. The stamping-punch came down and injured my hand so badly that I couldn't work for a year afterwards. I could only stay at home and make regular journeys to the hospital to have my bandages changed. This lasted six months, during which I received some minimal sick-pay. When the bandages were finally removed, my hand was practically useless, but after exercises and massage I was able to use it again.

I went back to the same factory and worked there for six years, until 1939; I was conscripted into the Army in November of that year. They didn't want me, however, because I was blind in my left eye. So I was sent home. All my friends had gone off to the Army and I was so unhappy that I cried. I decided to go back to the Army induction centre, in the crazy belief that somehow I would be 'somebody' in the Army. I went and complained to the commissar, who said, 'You're unfit. You can't even see properly – how on earth do you think the Army can use you?' I told him this was ridiculous, that I was prepared to peel potatoes and make *kasha*. He swore at me, insisting that I was unfit, but that if I was really so desperate he would telephone the clinic. He spoke to the doctor who had conducted my medical examination; he was a red-headed Jewish doctor, I remember, called Shklyar. He asked me in a mocking tone, 'Do you really want to join the Army? All right, if you're so keen, it can be arranged. We won't say anything about your blind eye. Since you can see with your right eye, you can at least fire a rifle – as long as you're not left-handed!' I wasn't, so I was able to become a Red Army soldier.

I was in a unit of the Army Supply Service. I was a self-taught artist and painted propaganda posters with pictures of Lenin, Stalin and Karl Marx. I painted and drew very well, and they kept me hard at it. One of my last jobs before demobilization in May 1941 was to take part in digging the foundations of the new Moscow University on the Lenin Hills.

I then got a job as a postman in Moscow. One fine day I was delivering the mail somewhere near the Kremlin. I saw a crowd gathering around one of the radio loudspeakers that used to hang from lamp-posts and went over to listen. Molotov was announcing that the Germans had attacked the Soviet Union and that we were at war. I rushed to re-enlist in the Army and a month later I was drafted to the Byelorussian front. I was employed in the kitchens. I was with a forward unit of the 13th Army, in charge of supplying them with food. It was my job to distribute dry rations like sausage, meat, tinned food, sugar and dried fish to the men in the front line.

It was 12 October when we were surrounded. We were between Orël and Kursk. Our commissar managed to send us a section of soldiers to tell us how to get out and told us to issue each man with as much food as he could carry, plus a hundred grams of vodka – and off we went. Our men deliberately started a huge fire and we were able to escape in the confusion. It was dusk and very cold. Another soldier called Kolyushko and I started running away when it grew dark. We fell into a swamp and were sucked into it. It was awful; we were up to our mouths in mud. We spent the night there until morning, when we could see to find a way out. We looked like drowned rats. We found a way into the woods; there we took off our filthy clothes and washed them in a little river, where we luckily met up with our comrades again. Our commissar collected us together and we slept in the open that night; we gathered pine-needles and lay down on them, huddling together for warmth.

Next day the officer told us to form groups of twos and threes and try to escape through the German lines. We were completely surrounded by Germans. I was with a Jewish friend from Vinnitsa and a

Ukrainian, who began spreading the word that the Jews were responsible for all this. My friend Yasha and I left him, because he was positively dangerous; the Germans were already dropping anti-Jewish leaflets. We found a village and asked for food. We changed into civilian clothes and worked at the mill for the peasants in exchange for food.

Then Yasha let the cat out of the bag and told the peasants we were Jews. This was a big mistake. They went to the German-controlled police (although our landlady, who was very nice, kept quiet about it). We were in the Ukraine – Chernigov *oblast*. One day some children came to us and told us the police wanted us. The landlady said that if we went to the police we would be shot. She gave us some food and told us to go to another village as fast as we could. She warned us not to tell people we were Jewish, so I told Yasha to keep his mouth shut or we would be killed, otherwise I would have to leave him. I told him to say he was an Uzbek, as he was quite dark and had a thick accent. Luckily I spoke good Russian and didn't look Jewish, so they didn't recognize us. We spent the winter in the village of Zagorovka, living in separate houses. There, too, we went to work at the mill and didn't see much of each other any more.

One day in January or February the police came for us. We were told to get a certificate that showed our ethnic nationality. I changed my surname, pretended I was Russian and said I was from the village of Makhachkaly. I got my paper certifying that I couldn't return home because of the occupation; this allowed me to stay and live in Zagorovka, but Yasha didn't go to the police because he was afraid they would discover his true identity. So when the police came to me, I was terrified, thinking they must know who I really was. But they didn't know, and they told me I had to go and report to the Germans, because they were afraid that all the stray Soviet soldiers in the area would join the partisans in the forest. Anyone who didn't report to the Germans would be shot as potential partisans.

Yasha came running to me in a panic. He dared not go to the police, since he had no papers. He cried and asked me what he should do. I could only advise him to hide somewhere. For all I know he was caught by the police and shot, because he never returned home as I eventually did.

Those of us who reported to the Germans were taken off to a place called Bakhmat in Chernogolsk, where there was a train waiting for us. It was by now midwinter and freezing cold. The police handed us over to some Hungarian troops, who were worse than the Germans. I was badly dressed and had nothing to eat. The Hungarians took everything we had and beat us terribly. They wore Hungarian uniform, but were under German command. They put us in a basement where we spent the night half naked and freezing. In the morning they called us out and counted us, lest anyone had escaped during the night or on the journey. They beat us as they counted us. Then we were crammed into freight waggons and sent on to Konotop, where they made us sit on the ground until the Germans arrived. When they eventually arrived, we were counted again; all that concerned them was the correct number of bodies. They kicked us and beat us all the time with rifle-butts. While we were sitting in the station yard, some women came to give us bread. They could only weep bitterly at our plight.

We were marched off to a camp, that had once housed a Soviet Army artillery unit. An Armenian captain asked us, 'Are there any Komsomols here?' No one moved, knowing they would be instantly shot. 'Are there any Communist Party members?' he continued. Again no one moved. He then said, 'Are there any Jews?' One by one a few men stepped forward. I was on the point of moving, when I thought to myself, 'You'll be found out in a couple of weeks or so anyway, so why not live a little longer?' So I stood still. Outside the barbed-wire perimeter fence I saw those poor Jews digging a hole in the ground. German soldiers then shot them dead. The next batch of Jews had to shovel the earth on top of them before being made to dig their own communal grave.

So camp life began . . . We were fed twice a day. The food was awful. Once we were given half a litre of bran, without salt. There were no crockery or utensils, so we ate with our fingers as best we could – from a boot or a cap, or something. I ate like this for three months. Later we got two hundred grams of bread per day. God knows what it was made of, but it was disgusting – it tasted like a mixture of sawdust and chopped straw; we also got potatoes and millet twice a day. We were counted twice a day by the Germans and the Ukrainian police who accompanied them. We Russians (including me, of course) were locked up at night. They were far more scared of the Russians than of any other nationality. The others were allowed to go out at night to a disgusting outdoor latrine, while we had to use a *parasha* – a tank in the hut that held about a hundred litres. It was always overflowing all over the place by morning. When the police opened the hut in the morning, they would order one of us to empty it and clean up. Fortunately I was never chosen! The worst thing about that job was that one had to empty it with a bucket.

One morning I was standing around with three or four men from Leningrad. They were well educated, unlike me. They recognized me as a Jew from my sing-song accent. One of them said to me, 'You're a bloody Yid, aren't you?' Luckily no one heard him, and they didn't give me away, although I took care never to mix with them again. Oddly enough, the one who recognized me as being Jewish looked like a typical Jew himself . . .

The Germans took the Ukrainians and other non-Russians out of the camp to work. While they were outside they would pick up fag-ends and scraps of paper, make them into cigarettes and barter them for bread. We just sat in the hut, playing cards or other games. After a couple of months of inactivity and revolting food, I was so run down and weak that I had no more strength to walk. I felt dizzy and had a high temperature, so that I could only move by holding on to the walls.

Every day they picked prisoners to work in the kitchen. They were so hungry that they would stuff themselves on the leftovers of the dreadful food that was prepared in the kitchens, and they would die during the night. Every day several people would die from this; their guts just burst. They would be taken to the graveyard and buried like dogs in a common pit.

On 1 May they gave us food to celebrate the holiday. We got some bread and cottage cheese that was sour. Two days later a German medical commission came to the camp. I was classified as fit, being far healthier than many of the prisoners who had been in captivity for longer than I had. Those of us who were fit were shoved into freight cars and the train set off for Germany, where we were to be put to work on farms. Those same men from Leningrad happened to be in my waggon, and the senior of them was planning to escape. We decided to escape through the one tiny window at the top of the waggon's wooden side. Two men lay down and we stood on their backs to reach the window and remove the barbed wire. The train was jerking and swaying all the time, but we managed it. At eleven o'clock at night the train was still going at full speed and we decided to jump. I was the sixth man to go. I jumped all right, but hurt my left knee badly when I hit the ground. I was hoping we would all join up, because I was frightened on my own. I watched the train rumble into the distance and tried to find a village.

We were still in the Ukraine. I crawled to a signal-post, not knowing what it was, when it was suddenly switched on and moved with a loud bang. I almost died of fright, thinking it was a gunshot and I had been caught. Then I realized what had happened and crawled on. I lay on my back and looked up at the clear sky, and could tell from the stars that I was going in the wrong direction, as I was aiming for Vinnitsa. So I went back a couple of kilometres in the direction from which I had come and moved towards the sound of barking dogs. Then I saw a light. I thought it might be the police, but went on all the same because even though I was pretty sure they would shoot me, at least I might get a morsel of bread to eat. When you're starving, that's the way you start to think. So I reached the house, peered through the lighted window and saw an old lady, a girl and a young man sitting down together. The girl had come from Vinnitsa and was describing the atrocities committed by the Germans.

When I knocked at the door, they jumped up in terror and rushed to the window. I tried to tell them who I was, but they couldn't hear me. I must have looked like a partisan, because the young man came out and I explained that I was a Russian POW and so on. I begged them for food, which they gave me. I asked them to let me sleep there overnight. The old lady insisted that I use the adjoining room, despite my objections that it was bug-ridden. I woke at 5 a.m. covered in insect bites. The old woman had made some potato soup, which she gave me for my breakfast. Having told her I was a Russian, I tried to look a bit authentic by crossing myself in front of the icon that hangs in the corner of every peasant cottage. She laughed and said, 'You don't have to cross yourself! I know you're a Jew.' I insisted I wasn't. 'You can't fool me,' she said. 'This was a mainly Jewish village. The Germans killed the rabbi and his children.' They told me which way to go and to be careful, Jewish or not. So I set off towards Vinnitsa.

In the next village an awful thing happened. I went to a house to beg for something to eat. The woman looked at me and said, 'Where have you come from? Get out of here as fast as you can! The police will shoot you on sight. Yesterday the Germans brought hundreds of prisoners through here and let them go into the local homes to get food. Many of them hid and ran away, so the Germans took men from the village to make up the numbers of those who had run away. It was a disaster, a tragedy for the village.' As soon as she had explained the way to reach the next village along untrodden paths, I immediately ran on, thanking her, but with my stomach still empty.

I reached the last village before Vinnitsa absolutely exhausted. I chose the poorest-looking hut as usual, because I had found by experience that while the poor would invariably give you food, the richer peasants would give you nothing. There I found an old woman with her granddaughter and asked for some food. They had nothing at all. At the fifth hut along the village street I noticed someone looking at me as though he could kill me. He turned out to be a Pole, a dreadful anti-Semite who had immediately recognized me as a Jew. The old woman said I shouldn't take any notice of him, although he was a horrible man. She directed me to the fourth cottage, where a young woman lived. She was rich and fed all escaped prisoners, and would even let one stay overnight. Her own brother had escaped from a POW camp, but had then turned his coat and become the head of the local German-controlled police.

The Pole who had been staring at me went straight to the police and told them where I was. Meanwhile the young woman listened to my story and offered me food. While I was eating, her brother arrived, began questioning me and wanted to take me to the police station. She refused to let me go – she was very brave – and swore at him. She reminded him of his own experiences as a prisoner and said, 'No matter who he is, he's staying here tonight. He shall have something to eat and tomorrow he'll be on his way. You will not touch him.' The brother then questioned me about Vinnitsa, to check whether I was telling the truth about trying to rejoin my family there. We had a drink and he left. She gave me some more soup and told me that I mustn't worry, but her lover, a German, was coming over to see her. He duly arrived, and she told him I was a relative of hers. Next morning, when the German lover had gone, she gave me more food and I set off to cover the last forty-odd kilometres to Vinnitsa.

At the station I met a man who started to talk to me. He began telling me how the Jews had been rounded up and shot, saying it was a shame there were still some Jews left and they should all be shot. I got away from him as fast as I could.

I reached the river at Vinnitsa, only to find the bridge swarming with Germans and guarded by armed police. I suddenly noticed that one of the guards was an old friend of mine from the clothing factory. He saw me and called out: 'Iosif, where are you going?' I thought it was the end, but he was still my friend and he let me cross the bridge. I set off for my old home; it had been completely destroyed and the building that stood in its place was a public lavatory. I went to some Ukrainians of my acquaintance, who refused to let me stay because they were likely to be shot for sheltering a Jew. So I went on until I came to a place I remembered from my childhood. It had been a swimming pool, but now it was just a concrete-lined hole in the ground, into which people chucked their garbage and slops. I slept there standing up. In the morning a woman came to the edge, didn't see me and threw the contents of her piss-pot all over me. I crawled out and went to the river, about thirty-odd metres away, where I washed myself and my clothes; it was 30 May and already quite hot. Some people recognized me, but said nothing and didn't give me away. I hung around for a few days, sleeping in stables and haylofts. I went to some old friends, who told me that my family had all been killed on 16 April. Twice the Jews of Vinnitsa had suffered at the hands of the Germans; the first time was on Yom Kippur, on 19 September. My family had survived the winter, but at Passover, on 16 April, the Germans had rounded them up and shot them all.

I had nowhere to go. There were, however, some Jews left in Vinnitsa who worked for the Germans. I found them and they sheltered me. The Germans took us to work every morning under armed escort. I spent the winter there. Then one day in spring the Germans started to round us up in order to kill us. Two others and myself escaped before we could be marched off, and we were joined by three more who managed to get away; the rest were all shot. We decided to take refuge in the special ghetto that was set aside for Romanian Jews; they were a tough lot and the Germans didn't venture there. The Romanians took us in, but there was no work and nothing to eat. People were dying of hunger. My clothes were in rags.

Somehow the winter passed and we learned that the Russian tanks had broken through; this was on 17 March. On the 22nd we were liberated, but I was so scared the Germans would return that I went straight to Vinnitsa, which had been liberated on 20 March. Russian and German tanks lay strewn around, bodies littered the streets. After a couple of days posters went up calling for all able-bodied men to report for remobilization. I decided to go, even though I was half blind and physically weak. We were sent to the front on foot, a march of about three weeks. The snow was so heavy that all transport had stopped, no vehicles could move and the only way to move anywhere was on foot. We marched two hundred kilometres, past dead horses, dead men, burnt-out tanks and abandoned machinery. When we reached the front, we were split into two groups – the fit and the unfit. After my medical examination, I was classified as unfit and sent back to Vinnitsa. As we were still under military orders, I was directed to work in Kiev as a builder, reconstructing a bombed-out tank factory. I stayed there until the autumn of 1945, when I was allowed to return home.

I got married in 1946; by 1956 we had four children, three girls and a boy. Life was hard during those post-war years. I worked as a painter and decorator, doing a full day's work and then a lot of moonlighting on the side. Even then it was difficult to make ends meet, though by the mid-1950s things were looking up a bit.

Anti-Semitism [was rife] in the Ukraine. One day I was sitting with some Ukrainian colleagues having a drink during our lunch-break when one of them said to me, 'You damned Yid – we know you're making a fortune at moonlighting.' This wasn't the first time I'd had to put up with that sort of thing, either. Another time, when I was just walking down the street, a drunken Ukrainian lurched up to me and said, 'What the hell are you doing here, you bloody Jew? Why don't you go and live in the country? This is a town – you have no right to work here.' Another incident involved one of my daughters. She had tried to get into a polytechnic and failed twice. Then she applied to be a telephonist at the central exchange. She was studying at evening classes at the time, which prepared students for university entrance, but the telephone exchange wouldn't have her, insisting that she finish her tenth grade although she was already amply qualified for the job.

Eventually things got so bad that I decided to emigrate. I think the following incident was the last straw. My eldest daughter got married, but there was nowhere for them to have a flat of their own. We all had to live together in one room of twenty-two square metres with a little kitchen. My daughter was now pregnant as well. By now our family income was enough for us to buy a much larger 'co-operative' flat, so I applied for one through the art school where I was a part-time student, learning the art of *trompe l'œil* painting. The school offered several of us the opportunity to apply for a co-operative flat. There was one man who had graduated from the school but made no use of his art-school training; he went to work in a warehouse to earn easy money. He applied too; he was accepted and I was refused. I was furious at this injustice.

Then there was a meeting at a factory where I did shift-work, and they held a discussion about Jews leaving for Israel. Everyone thought it was unfair that Jews were allowed to emigrate but Russians and Ukrainians could not. The speaker, a Party propagandist, just sat listening while the audience shouted remarks like, 'None of the bloody Jews fought at the front: they were all sitting safely in cushy jobs in Tashkent!' – 'They should all have been killed!' The Party lecturer said nothing, though there were lots of Jews in the room.

Almost a hundred thousand Jews were slaughtered at Babii Yar in Kiev during the war – all in a few days, mostly by Ukrainians manning machine guns under German orders. All done in cold blood – it was one of the most terrible single atrocities of all time. Well, my daughter was a schoolteacher and she told the children about Babii Yar. The children in her class didn't know she was Jewish; she didn't look Jewish and she didn't have a Jewish name. All of them then shouted in unison: 'Pity they didn't kill *all* the Jews!' Even little children in the Ukraine were hardened anti-Semites.

Then on 9 May, when we lay wreaths on the memorials to those who fell in the war, the staff and pupils of several schools went to visit the monuments to the fallen, about ten kilometres outside Kiev. There, alongside the monument to the Russian soldiers, were memorials to those Jews who had been slaughtered. The grave of the Unknown Soldier was wreathed in beautiful flowers, while the Jewish monument was left bare. My daughter watched her fellow teachers laying wreaths on the Russian graves and purposely leaving the Jewish ones alone. The Jewish teachers took offence and complained, but it had no effect.

In all the really important organizations in the Soviet Union – the Party, the police, the KGB, the armed forces – there is nowadays not a single Jew in a responsible, senior position. I had a childhood friend, a Jew who had fought at the front throughout the war and was twice decorated with one of the highest medals for gallantry – the Order of Glory. After the war he joined the police and seemed headed for the top; but just when he should have got his crucial promotion, he was ordered to apply for 'voluntary' retirement. He now had to leave the police because he was a Jew. And these injustices were happening in a Communist country, the creation of Karl Marx – a Jew.

So I decided to emigrate and thought my family would go too, but after much hesitation they decided to remain.

First I went to Israel, in 1975. I didn't like it there, so in April 1977 I came here to Vienna.

To receive my exit visa I had to divorce my wife and give up my Soviet citizenship, making it impossible for me to return [to the Soviet Union]. I had no wish to renounce my citizenship, but they force you to do so to make sure you never return. I used to write to my family and they wanted me to return home. I love my eldest daughter dearly, and she kept writing, 'Daddy, please come home!' – and I wanted to return. But I couldn't. What sort of a world is it where a father cannot visit his children, or the children can never be reunited with their father? Now I may not even write: my daughter has been forbidden to write to me or to receive my letters, because she is a schoolteacher. She is not allowed to correspond with an 'anti-Soviet person'. I was never anti-Soviet; I wrote equally about what is bad in Israel and Austria, as well as what is good. So do they punish you for telling the truth?

51

A Nuisance to the State

VALERY ANDREYEVICH FEFYOLOV

Valery Andreyevich Fefyolov and his wife together tell the story of their emigration from the Soviet Union to Vienna in 1982.

Valery Andreyevich's father, who was born in 1911, came from a fairly comfortably off peasant family living in the village of Poyelovo in the Yuriev Polsky district.

FEFYOLOV   When Stalin's collectivization drive began in 1929, the process of dispossessing the *kulak*s took place in my father's village. The wealthiest (and most efficient) peasants and their families were deported to Siberia. The Bolsheviks came to my father – who was about eighteen at the time – and said, 'We need to make someone Chairman of this *kolkhoz* [collective farm], someone who knows the people and the land. One of you must accept this post. If you refuse, you'll be sent off to Siberia with the rest of them.' There was no way out, so my father became Chairman of the *kolkhoz*. After serving for about two years, he was suddenly arrested one night and sent for trial. Someone in the collective farm had denounced him. People had come to him for permission to grind some grain in one of the *kolkhoz* mills; he didn't know who the grain belonged to, but out of kindness he let them grind it. It turned out that the grain belonged to someone outside the farm. Then without an investigation or trial he was packed off to the Urals for a stretch of ten years and put in a labour camp along with ordinary criminals. He was arrested in 1932.[1] In fact, with remission for good behaviour he served only two and a half years and was released in 1934.

On his release he went to work as a stevedore on the railway – until one day, out of the blue, he was summoned to the police station. Suspecting nothing, he went along there – and never came out, at least not through the front door. It must have been some kind of round-up. After a while he got fed up with waiting and demanded to see the District Prosecutor. 'Why are you holding me here? I was arrested hours ago and nothing's happened. Either put me on trial or let me go.' The Prosecutor answered him frankly, 'Andrey Mikhailovich, we can't try you because there is nothing to try you for. But we can't let you go either.' Finally he was sentenced to ten years, working on the construction of the White Sea Canal in a labour camp. Again, with remission of sentence, he served only two and a half years, from 1939 to 1941.

[Father served in the Soviet Army during the Second World War, then returned to work on the railway in Yuriev Polsky, where I was born in 1949. I grew up there, left school at fifteen and qualified as an electrician.]

I worked for the Electricity Supply Authority in a power station near Yuriev Polsky. I was one of the team of linesmen and electrical engineers who were called out to help whenever there was a supply failure or an accident. My particular job was to repair the power-lines that distributed current to all the villages in the region. Before long, though, I had an accident at work that crippled me. I was repairing a fault on a line when I received a powerful electric shock (because someone at the power station had failed to switch off the current, as they were supposed to do) and I fell about twelve or fifteen metres to the ground.

I was seventeen or eighteen. We didn't want to emigrate, but a situation arose in which we either had to put in an application to emigrate or face the risk of being arrested and exiled to some distant spot such as Kazakhstan. The KGB made this quite clear to us. I was becoming a serious nuisance to the Soviet regime, thanks to my attempts to obtain the basic rights and benefits due *by law* to any Soviet citizen disabled through an industrial accident. I was supposed to get medical treatment, a wheelchair, etc., and a disability pension. I did receive medical treatment, but could not get a wheelchair. That mattered much less, however, than my failure to be given the State pension, payable by law to someone, like me, who was suffering from a sixty per cent disability.

The reason for this was perfectly obvious: the Director of the power station refused to sign a document admitting that the cause of my accident was ultimately the misbehaviour, negligence and incompetence of several of his subordinates. The man who was supposed to switch off the current was not only missing from his post at the critical moment – he was drunk. His immediate supervisor, the section foreman, should have checked on him, as this was a situation involving potential risk to life, but he didn't, out of sheer laziness. This state of affairs, by the way, was typical of the slack discipline in the whole plant. So the power-station Director refused to admit liability on the part of his staff, asserting that the accident had been entirely my own fault for not observing the safety procedures. If this had been true, no blame would have attached to him or his station staff and I would have been due for only a small, minimal pension. As it was, the Director knew that if the true facts came to light, he and the others would have been not only sacked but prosecuted and almost certainly jailed for criminal negligence. So instead he organized a cover-up.

We were forced to leave. In May of that year, I was charged under Article 91 of the Criminal Code – 'opposition to the State'. This charge was a way to pressurize us. In August an investigator from the Procurator-General's office was put on the case. After several months of questioning, the case was closed: the investigator realized that if it ever came to court, there might be some very uncomfortable revelations; at the same time, I had shown myself to be such a potential nuisance that they couldn't just let me go. So it was suggested that the best way out was for us (my wife, myself and our children) to emigrate. The investigator made it quite clear that all would be well if we voluntarily applied for exit visas; if not, well . . . The local head of the KGB came to see us regularly, and also made it plain in no uncertain terms that we should apply to leave, or else . . . When we did submit our application, it went through very quickly – normally there was a mound of paperwork to be dealt with, always at a snail's pace. And we didn't have to pay a penny, either; the usual procedure is for an emigrant to be made to pay 300 roubles to cover repairs and redecoration of his apartment, plus an undisguised 'emigration tax' of 1400 roubles. We simply said we had no money (which was absolutely true); they replied: 'No problem . . . '

FEFYOLOVA I had been out of work for two years, because no one would employ me. Before that, I had worked for a while as a nurse, but after that I couldn't get another job. Every potential employer in town had been warned against taking me on. All sorts of extraordinary gossip circulated about me, deliberately spread by the KGB. On one occasion, when I was still a nurse, I had to distribute some harmless pills to children at a kindergarten. Their teacher took the pills away from them and sent them to a laboratory to be analysed – as if I was trying to poison the children! The KGB made out that we were spies in the pay of the CIA. Remarks were even made publicly during the weekly political lectures at my place of work. They said terrible things – for example, that when I was working in the maternity ward I used purposely to hold children upside down . . . Some of these lies were so fantastic and so stupid, it is hard to believe that people would give them any credence at all – but they did. Many Russians are terribly gullible. At one point somebody said to me, 'Do you know why the authorities are giving you a flat? It's because a broadcaster on the Voice of America announced that if you weren't given a flat, America would drop a nuclear bomb!' And that woman – and also plenty of others – seriously believed it. Another disgusting slander that was deliberately spread about was that I was a member of some strange religious sect that held secret meetings at which we drank the blood of children.

In the end, the people orchestrating this campaign decided that I should no longer be allowed to work. This was the last straw, because by then I was the family's sole breadwinner. I was dismissed on grounds of 'unsuitability', and this was written in my work-book, the document that every Soviet citizen must have in order to obtain employment. For the last two years I was unable to find any organization whatsoever that would take me on.

FEFYOLOV We knew the KGB intended to force us, if necessary, to leave the USSR, so we decided to make the most of it. Being disabled, I find it hard to travel by train, so we told them we would not leave except by car. The officer said he would have to consult his superiors. Within a week we got a call to say that we could come straight over and pick up a car. The KGB officer said, 'When you get to the West, be sure to tell everyone how I helped you to buy this car.' Well, I am now carrying out his instructions!

We left Moscow on 14 October 1982 and arrived in Vienna on the 20th. We crossed the greater part of Russia in a few days . . .

FEFYOLOVA On our way through Russia we stayed at hotels. Once we had a problem: the hotel refused to let us stay there. They wouldn't take us with our one-way exit visas. Even when I pointed to a sign that read 'Preferential service given to the disabled', pointing out that my husband was disabled, they still refused, on the grounds that since he was now legally a stateless person, he was not eligible for any of the benefits due to a *Soviet* disabled person. We made such a fuss that a plain-clothes policeman appeared and threatened to send us back to where we had come from. Rather than be humiliated any further, we spent the night with some kind people in a private house for a payment of 10 roubles.

Next morning at the frontier we were subjected to a rigorous search at the customs post, which lasted from 9 a.m. to 5 p.m. They searched everything: our luggage, our car and our bodies, forcing us to strip and then bend over with our feet apart while they shone a torch and probed our anuses. In my case I had to submit to a similar examination of my vagina. It was quite horrible, and was done in the most disgusting manner; they said they were looking for drugs, but you could tell from their expressions and their sniggering, obscene remarks that they were simply doing it for their own sick amusement and because they had us at their mercy.

The final irony was when our 'friend' the KGB officer from Yuriev Polsky came to see us off. 'When you have left Soviet soil,' he told us, 'don't slander the Motherland. It may happen that you miss your country and your parents very much and will want to return one day. So say nothing slanderous about the Soviet Union.'

FEFYOLOV They took away some papers, which they claimed were anti-Soviet in content. It was simply a long list of disabled people, like myself, who, on various pretexts (or none at all) had never received the disability benefits, artificial limbs, pensions, invalid cars, etc., that by law they should have had. I was one of a few people who had founded the 'Initiative Group for Support of the Disabled', in an attempt to persuade the authorities to do their legal duty to those who had been crippled in the Army or in industrial accidents.

They have now launched a campaign to liquidate all protest and human-rights movements entirely, and they saw our Initiative Group as one of those. They didn't want to imprison me, though, because I am, after all, a cripple in a wheelchair and I had made my case known to many foreign journalists, who could have made things very awkward for the Soviet regime if the authorities had tried to send me to a prison or a camp. It was far easier for them if I would just quietly leave the country . . .

[We had an 'invitation' to Israel], although neither of us has a drop of Jewish blood and no relatives – not even relatives by marriage – in Israel! But the 'invitation' named us by our names and was signed by someone claiming to be my wife's aunt – although the signature was an illegible scrawl. Yet it *looked* genuine. It was certified by a couple of rubber stamps in Hebrew, and the envelope carried genuine Israeli stamps and postmarks. If you ask me, the KGB has its agents in Israel who supply these 'invitations' to order when the Soviet authorities want to expel someone without causing a fuss.

[My parents] wanted me to compromise and not to leave the Soviet Union, so that they could keep me with them. Naturally I understand this attitude; family ties are often very strong in Russia and it can be very hard for parents to be separated from their children – especially when, as in our case, the separation will probably be for ever. It is interesting that when I emigrated my parents were very worried that my family and I would starve to death in the West; this was the result of ceaseless propaganda from the Soviet media about the horrors of life under capitalism – unemployment, starvation, crime, violence, exploitation. They actually sent us food parcels to help us out, and only stopped doing so when I sent a large parcel to *them*, containing the sort of Western goods that I was able to buy on my Austrian social-security income – fruit juice, instant coffee, canned food, chocolate biscuits and so on, many of which they had never seen in their lives.

52

Escaping the System

VSEVOLOD BORISOVICH LEVENSTEIN

*'Seva' Levenstein's father was born in 1904 and at the age of fifteen
decided to be a sailor; at the same time he cut himself off from his Jewish
family and joined the Komsomol. He eventually became the youngest
captain in the Baltic and in 1939 was made Deputy Chief of the Soviet
Baltic Merchant Fleet – a position he accepted with some trepidation: by
1939 twelve people who held that job had been shot in the Purges.[1] Borya
Levenstein was more fortunate and survived.*

Just as the Purges ended, the war began and my father then went into
civil defence. He was engaged in shipping food into Leningrad and in
evacuating the population. Then came the Siege of Leningrad, and he
practically died from typhus. He fell into a coma and was thrown in a
pile of corpses. His friend, Lyova Katz, turned up, asking for Borya
Levenstein. On being told that he had died, Lyova Katz asked them
to show him the body. He was told to look amongst the typhus corpses,
so he looked there, found Father and could hear his heart still beating.
He took him away, and my father survived . . .

After the war was over, Father returned to work, by now decorated
with several Orders and medals. In 1949 he started secretly seeing
Jewish people. In the same year there was an accident: one of the
Baltic ships ran aground on some rocks, because the navigator made a
mistake; a woman was killed, and the ship was wrecked. The judge
sentenced the captain to death by firing squad, although he had been
asleep at the time and hadn't really had anything to do with it. The
second-in-command was given fifteen years in a labour camp – that was
the equivalent of a death sentence in 1949. My father was also sentenced, because he was the chief of the fleet – it was his responsibility
too, and the Procurator gave him ten years. My father, however, had

a good lawyer; there was some fairness and justice in 1949 – this wasn't 1937. It was proven that he had done everything humanly possible to save this ship, that the rescue operation had been carried out competently and all the right steps had been taken . . . In the end he wasn't sent to prison, but he was removed from his job and expelled from the Party. That was a bad sign in 1949 – expulsion from the Party meant arrest within six to twelve months. Father was under great stress and went into a psychiatric hospital for a month. He had a nervous breakdown and has been a different man ever since. Before that he was happy and energetic, then he became terribly withdrawn.

[That year our family moved from Leningrad to Tallinn, capital of Estonia, and my father began his career all over again, starting as a clerk in a shipping office. Gradually, however, he worked his way up to Deputy Chief of the steamship line. He retired in the late 1960s, received the Order of Lenin, and returned to spend his final years in Leningrad.]

[I was born] in 1940. I was one year old when the war broke out, and Leningrad was besieged from 1941. My mother and I were evacuated to Siberia – to Kurgan, in north-west Siberia. My mother had no means of help or support there; the village was poor. The evacuees lived very poorly. My mother suffered dreadfully and practically starved. She told me how, when I was two or three years old, I forgot how to walk because I was so weak. Then we were sent food parcels and she nursed me back to health. In 1942 she got work at the *sovkhoz* [State farm] as a bookkeeper in the canteen, and we survived the evacuation. But I almost died then. When we returned to Leningrad in 1945 I was such a small, skinny boy!

My first memories as a boy are of standing on Nevsky Prospekt watching the Leningrad troops return home from the front. There was no music, the street was silent and people just stood and watched – no cheering could be heard. If flowers were thrown, then it was a quiet, timid gesture. The troops were all in high-collared tunics of a grey, dusty colour and the civilians were all grey coloured and dusty. And on that day my mother bought a glass of grape juice, and I was sorry to drink it because I couldn't help thinking how many grapes had to be picked to make that juice!

[I received most of my education in Estonia, then in 1957, having resolved to follow my father into the Navy, I returned to Leningrad.]

I went to the best Naval Academy in Leningrad and passed the entrance exams – I got 22 out of 25 and, as my father was a famous sailor, I had an advantage.

We had our heads shaved, were dressed in cotton uniforms, and were sent on a river steamboat up the Neva, Lake Ladoga and some other rivers – to pick potatoes! We arrived at a landing-stage and from there we had to go forty or fifty kilometres by lorry to get to the village. However, it rained, the lorry got stuck and wouldn't budge, and it took us the best part of two days to cover fifty kilometres, pushing this lorry. It would get stuck, we would get out and put some branches under the wheels; it would go again for about another two hundred metres and then get stuck again. When we got to the village, we found somewhere to sleep on the floor of the village hall. In the morning we met the Chairman of the *kolkhoz*, who said to us, 'What on earth am I going to give you to eat? There's nothing in the village.' Then he said, 'Vaska, bring me my lame horse – the three-year-old.' Vaska brought a horse which was lame and couldn't be used for work. The Chairman fetched his double-barrelled shotgun from the village hall and put it to the unfortunate horse's head. Bang! Bang! The horse fell to the ground right in front of our eyes, and he said, 'Right – eat!' Of course I *didn't* eat that horse!

The work consisted of gathering potatoes and loading them into panniers carried by the horses. These poor beasts were also dragging an ancient wooden plough – like in the fourteenth century – to dig up the potatoes. The plough would remove the earth and we had to follow behind and gather the potatoes by hand. It's possible to do this for an hour or so, but if you have to do it for eight hours bending double, your back nearly breaks; all the more so because we weren't used to such work: I was from an 'intelligentsia' family, so to speak. My back couldn't stand it and my knees started to ache because the ground was very cold – it was the end of September. I remember that I ripped the communal towels in half and made two knee-pads out of them, padded with hay, and I worked the whole month on these pillows. The ground was already frozen by the end of the month and you had to dig with your hands. My hands were all cracked, chapped and bleeding. [There were no spades.] Also, it was typical socialism . . . the work wasn't calculated by the number of potatoes, but by the length of the furrows in metres, so in the end you weren't digging them up, but putting them back in the ground!

I used to sleep in a peasant hut [*izba*] – well, not actually inside, but in the barn next to the cow; it had a mattress made of hay and I could lie and hear the cow breathing loudly and passionately all night! [Although] the weather wasn't very warm, there was warmth from the cow!

In 1957 there was at least electricity in the village. Two things were sold in the village shop: crushed sweets called *podushochki*, which didn't have wrappers and so stuck together in one big lump; and one huge tyre – of such a size that it wouldn't fit anything!

Anyway, a month had gone by and my naval career had begun. [I served until 1963 and then] I came to the conclusion that I didn't want to spend my whole life at sea – I wanted to become a musician. But how could I leave the Merchant Navy? It was impossible; normally you can resign only for medical reasons. Then the biggest 'fiddle' of my life occurred . . . I returned to Tallinn and spoke to my father, saying that I had followed in his footsteps, but I didn't want to be a sailor. My real vocation was to be a musician, and I asked him to get me out of the Merchant Navy. My father, as a Party member and a very honest man, said he couldn't make a deal like that. He nevertheless changed his mind and phoned a friend of his, the chief doctor at a polyclinic, and asked him if he would help his son. Georgy, the doctor, gave an order to one of the female doctors – I think she was probably his mistress – and the next day I went to the X-ray department where she was a radiographer. In the dark it wasn't clear what was happening . . . but she placed her finger low down on my body and the outcome of the examination was that there was a dark spot on the X-ray and they came to the conclusion that the X-ray showed I had an ulcer. I went to the personnel department with this result and said that I couldn't go to sea any more. They replied that they would move me to a shore job, to the Commercial Department, as I knew English and would be able to write letters abroad. I moved to the Commercial Department, but within ten days decided that I would die of boredom there . . . I had been moved ashore, so what was I to do? I still had three years to serve and no one would release me.

I went to Leningrad for a couple of days and there met another friend of my father's, who had been a prisoner during Stalin's time. He had almost died, but had somehow miraculously survived. When he returned from exile, he was given the position of head of the Scientific Institute of the River Fleet. I said to this man, Melnikov, that I needed to be released from the Merchant Navy and asked him to get me transferred to his Institute. He didn't say anything, but gave me a letter saying that he wanted to employ a specialist such as me.

I went to see the boss of the shipping company in Tallinn and told him that I had a pregnant girlfriend in Leningrad, that I needed to do the decent thing and marry the girl and move to Leningrad. When he asked, 'What about your job?' I replied that I had a letter of recruitment, but he refused to let me go. The next day he was called to Moscow and his deputy, who didn't know about this, took his place. So I went to him with the same story and he phoned my father and asked him what to do. My father told him to release me, so the deputy signed a document that allowed me to leave.

The trick was that before moving from organization to organization you remain a so-called 'junior specialist', but after the move that title is automatically dropped. Everything was planned. So when I arrived in Leningrad, I was no longer a junior specialist: I was simply a worker. I arrived in the morning to sign the documents, and that evening they made me redundant. The whole operation took eight days.

I started to work in Leningrad and a year later [in 1964] I was invited to join a very good jazz orchestra – Lenstein's – with many famous members. I used to play the saxophone. I stayed with them for about five years, then went to work with some young people in a group, as their leader. We went on tour all over the country for about eight years. Then in 1970 I left.

The higher you go, and the closer you are to the Government and the Party power, the more they demand from you ideologically. I wasn't a Party member, but I had to report to the Soviet authorities before every tour. You're given a list of things you must and mustn't do. On that list, there are the signatures of three responsible people. If you're going to ten towns, you get ten pieces of paper. It's like your driving licence – a vital document.

[My decision to leave] was an evolutionary process. I had tried to get away from the system all my life. I went into music because it's less controlled . . . and for some time it really was. But as you progress and improve, you move up higher and automatically become more involved with the system.

I finished my career in Moscow, under the aegis of *Mosconcert*, and we were very close to the Ministry of Culture and therefore to the world of politics. In 1971 in *Novy Mir*[2] there was a whole page about our ensemble and partially about me, because we would insist on playing Russian songs. It was the result of an internal political battle, because our ensemble used to play old, forgotten Russian songs with a modern orchestra – a type of folk rock. We were very popular on television and we played three concerts a day. We were a great success. Naturally, the 'straight' folk singers didn't like us. Because of us, they were likely to starve! People who had influence would smother anything new.

Some awful things happened to us. In 1971 we stayed in Moscow for seven or eight months without work, and without a kopeck. We were all from other towns and everyone had to find accommodation for themselves. In the end we played in the kitchen at the Hotel Rossiya, without being paid; in return, the management gave us several rooms from their allocation and we lived like this for a month. I had to manage somehow. I used to make my money go a long way. We used to rehearse daily at the Moscow liquor factory's club, and the local girls who worked there lived in a hostel nearby. They used to bring along alcohol from the factory in rubber balls . . . they would make a third breast for themselves . . .

By 1974 I couldn't play professionally any more. In December I started to go on hunger strike – I had problems with my stomach. I starved myself for twenty-one days (it was fashionable for musicians to go on hunger strike at that time). It was considered that starving yourself would cure all other illnesses. After twenty-one days I went home a bag of bones and had a complete rethink, because my body and my mind were both functioning differently. I didn't think about food or women, only about the meaning of life: as a Russian once said, the flesh is dead, but the spirit remains. And then everything appeared to me in a different light and I thought, 'What am I doing? How long can I carry on like this?' So I decided to give it all up, packed my job in, went home and stayed there for several months, doing nothing. It was then that I made the decision to emigrate.

I had 2000 roubles left from what I had earned . . . my wife worked . . . and I stayed at home and didn't spend anything. I had a collection of records and exchanged and sold them on the black market amongst friends and acquaintances. If you don't work in the Soviet Union but you know the people and the system, it's easier than working! In principle, that is. A working man earns 80–100 roubles a month – what kind of money is that? You can't live on it. One Western record costs 60 roubles. So if you have a collection and buy and sell things, you make some kind of arrangement with a student – you get him something he wants and he'll bring you fifteen or twenty records – which provides enough to live on for three months if you sell them gradually. It's a common form of enterprise in Russia. I had a very high-grade collection – no rubbish, so it was an honest business. A normal collector gets fed up with something, sells it and buys what he wants to buy. I know people who have been involved in many such enterprises and have never worked in their whole life. There is a whole section of the population who are 'nightwatchmen' or some kind of non-existent scientific workers . . . people who turn over a lot of money. But they appear to live very modestly on the outside. If you want to clothe yourself on the black market, it's very expensive, so really they just live a normal life. They can go to restaurants, go by taxi, buy trousers, everything.

That's why I wanted to emigrate. I was fed up with living this vague, indeterminate, semi-normal life. As long as I mixed with people who also did this, I found they had an irresponsible way of thinking and this became rather offensive. I had a kind of wishful desire to earn my own money by honest means. Also the system of values in the USSR is disintegrating: honesty, decency, all the best qualities are worth practically nothing. No one needs them. It's good if you have a friend who can value them, but generally these principles hinder you in life instead of helping. They are a luxury. People are naturally weak, hence it's the swindlers, time-serving, dishonest people who all emerge at the top. They have cars and flats but somehow look down on honest people with a 'Well, why can't you make it?' attitude. This is what I find offensive. I've known swindlers in the black market and I deeply despise them, because in human terms they are nothing. Besides that, there is nothing in the future for them, and their whole life is one of extreme anguish. People unconsciously understand that their life is deprived, that they haven't got any friends left, that they haven't got any real free choice, they're not *going anywhere*. Even if they have a favourite profession – for example, I was a musician – they must degrade themselves in the ranks of this profession. I decided to give up music only because I had to degrade myself during the last few years. My honest and uncompromising friends gave up all commercial music . . .

Levenstein emigrated first to Vienna, then spent some time in Rome, where he was baptized as a Christian and helped establish a Baptist mission. He managed to obtain a British work permit and moved to London, where he has lived ever since with his wife and son.

53

Defectors

KATJA KRAUSOVA

Katja Krausova is a Slovak Jewess from Bratislava. Her father, a pre-war member of the Slovak Communist Party, was imprisoned as a Communist by the Tiso Government of Slovakia and thus escaped deportation as a Jew; he was later reincarcerated by the Communist Government as a result of the Slansky trials in 1952. Katja's mother survived the war by a miracle, although her family was not so lucky – many of them, including her mother and sister, perished in Auschwitz.

Katja came to England a week before the Soviet invasion of Czechoslovakia in August 1968 and has remained here ever since. She has a degree from the London School of Economics and did postgraduate work at St Antony's College, Oxford. She has worked in documentary television since 1977, first for the BBC and then for Prime Time, a contracting company producing programmes for Channel 4. Her last work for the BBC was a ninety-minute documentary on the two top-rank Soviet musicians who defected in 1983, the violinist Viktoria Mullova and the conductor Vartan Zhordania.

Herself an émigré from Communist rule, Katja Krausova spent a year living cheek-by-jowl with Viktoria and Vartan. Her own background, together with her immersion in the lives and personalities of her two subjects have meant that she has been able to provide a penetrating yet detached exposition of the psychology, biography, motivation and behaviour of these Soviet defectors that is undoubtedly a more truthful and more balanced account than could have been obtained from the subjects themselves.

When I saw Viktoria's picture in the paper, her story immediately struck me as a variation on the theme that I had been trying to persuade the BBC to do for a number of years. Since 1980 I'd been wanting to do a documentary called 'Welcome to the West'. I wanted to look at the process of coming to the West and to look at what the West is, or seems to be, for the people who make this step, before, during and after their move. Not because I wanted to relive my own experience, but because it has always fascinated me that the West is one thing for people who live here, and a completely different thing for those who live 'over there' and then come 'over here'. For one thing, the propaganda war on both sides is so extraordinary and the image of the West created by both sides is so distorted. I was always struck, for instance, by all the posters you see when you arrive at airports, which say seductively: 'Welcome to American Express' and 'Welcome to Trusthouse Forte' or 'Welcome to Geneva' – and you know how much money you have in your pocket! I had always wanted to tackle this subject, but the BBC objected that the theme was too earnest and complex.

So when I saw the picture of Viktoria Mullova, I thought that all my preconceptions about this topic – the bewilderment, the financial problems, the helplessness and lack of adaptability of Soviet émigrés to the West – would all go out of the window, because she was beautiful, she was already a professional solo violinist and presumably well equipped not only to survive but to prosper. And although it sounds very pat and simple, that is exactly what happened.

I followed her for exactly a year. Although I had far too much material by the end, I needed that length of time. My argument with my bosses was that the effect of a year cannot be telescoped into six months because a year is a year is a year, and not only can a lot of things happen but people develop an ability to see things differently and more clearly within a year.

I suppose my Russian, when I met Viktoria, was worse than rusty, but I ploughed into it because I had no alternative. Her passive English vocabulary was stunning, and certainly far better than my English when I came to the West, but because I wanted to acquire some form of intimacy or because I wanted to get talking with her as soon as possible, I said, 'You talk Russian, I'll talk English.' But as we went along, my Russian started to come back to me. And Vartan, Viktoria's boyfriend and co-defector, speaks no English, so with him I had no option.

In so far as I believe Viktoria – and I think I do believe her in this – Viktoria's mother had no idea what was afoot. One of the most vivid things that Viktoria told me throughout the year was about the kind of terror she lived under during the two years that she and Vartan planned to defect. Keeping a secret for two years is an awfully long time, especially when you're young and it is likely to be the most fateful and exciting thing that will ever happen in your life. To have been able to keep that secret, of course, meant that her relationship with her parents was very bad.

Another reason for these very serious tensions in the family was her relationship with Vartan. She met Vartan as a nineteen-year-old. It was just before she went in for the Sibelius Prize competition in Finland. She was sent on a kind of playing circuit to get practice, in which she was sent to Kharkov. There she played with Vartan, who conducted the Kharkov orchestra, and the story has it that they ended up in bed together that same day and have not been parted since. In her parents' eyes, I suppose, she caused the break-up of Vartan's marriage. [He had two children] – and he was her senior by twenty-one years. To get an idea of what this means, I would extrapolate from my own experience in Bratislava. I had a boyfriend who was five years older than I was, and that was scandal enough. In Central and Eastern Europe it is a fairly rigid convention that you don't mix with people older or younger; you stick to your own age-group, give or take a year up or down.

So you can imagine what her family must have felt about it. Not only was she causing a scandal in the Moscow musical world – certainly at the Conservatoire, because she was already a concert player – but it must have been a terrible shock for her parents.

Moreover, Vartan comes from an extremely anti-Soviet family. He is the grandson of Noah Zhordania [the Menshevik who was Prime Minister of Georgia during its independence in 1918–21], and his father is a famous historian, who is still alive in Tbilisi and who has opposed the Soviet regime all his life. Vartan was therefore brought up in a highly intelligent, politically conscious family that has nothing but contempt for the Soviet system.

My heart went out to Vartan within the first few hours of our meeting. When I arrived in Stockholm, at the 'safe house', I was scarcely aware that there was another person involved besides Viktoria; Vartan had featured solely in a one-line mention at the bottom of the newspaper article about her defection. Literally within seconds of my arrival, he said, 'Will you be making the film about me too?' I replied, 'In so far as you are part of Viktoria's story, I will.' To which he said, 'What do you mean?' And for the next hour he proceeded to tell me everything about the relationship between him and Viktoria and how the defection came about, so by the end of my first hour with them I had a pretty good picture of what had happened and an idea of who and what they both were.

Next morning, when we got on a jumbo jet to go to America, Viktoria was thrilled and terribly impressed by the aircraft – she couldn't get over how spacious it was compared with Aeroflot planes, and was amazed that it had a second floor. She was like a child, chattering excitedly about it to Vartan – while Vartan was reading Voinovich's hilarious satire on Soviet life, *The Life and Extraordinary Adventures of Private Ivan Chonkin*. I think that said so much about him; he wasn't looking at American magazines, but instead he drank endless brandies and read *Chonkin* as a preparation for going to America!

One of the things that interested me enormously was: who had first raised the question of defection? After all, it's one thing to have an affair, and another thing altogether to trust someone so completely that they would go through with all this. In fact, this immediately told me something about their commitment to each other. At that point I didn't know enough about the nature and strength of their psychological interdependence, but they both told me, separately, that it was he who made the suggestion in 1980, as soon as she had won the Sibelius competition, two years before the Tchaikovsky competition. He said, 'You must win the Tchaikovsky, then we will go.'

They planned it in secret. Personally I don't think they were motivated by a desire for artistic freedom. Maybe Vartan was, but not Viktoria; I don't think she knew what artistic freedom means. It is part of Western propaganda to expect everybody to have concise and well-articulated reasons for defecting. [That certainly wasn't true in Viktoria's case.] She was going because she was in love with a man and thought it would be the most wonderful thing for the two of them to travel the world and conquer it – he with an orchestra and she as the soloist – and you can see how the dream was enough to make them want to do it. I doubt that they ever realized how difficult it would be. Partially because (this is something I discovered from Vartan) they were terribly, totally naïve about their venture – I wouldn't say ill-informed, I would say uninformed.

Obviously they thought that you just go to the West and it's going to be Nureyev, Makarova, Rostropovich . . . I don't think it ever occurred to them that they were not going to be classed as artistes of Rostropovich's standing. She is – but on the other hand the previous Russian musicians and dancers have defected more or less at the zenith of their careers, not at the beginning. That is why I think the element of risk in their case was many, many times greater than with their distinguished predecessors. They weren't thinking about that factor; they were just carried away by the spirit of the idea. And like many other East European runaways, so much energy and calculation goes into planning the actual departure that one never thinks about what will happen from the moment the new life in the West begins. Nobody ever seems to think about that; they certainly didn't. The actual business of jumping over the wall is so tricky and stressful that the rest can only be simple, they felt. And they also knew that other Soviet artistes had done very well; they didn't seem to have heard about the ones who hadn't done so well.

For instance, they knew about Makarova, Nureyev, Baryshnikov, Rostropovich, Vishnevskaya. Viktoria, after all, had travelled to the West several times, when she would have heard about these people. She had toured all over Scandinavia, she had been to Poland more than once, which by Eastern European standards is practically the West. She also went to the Philippines, although she probably didn't learn much there; it's rather ironic that she went there as the guest of Imelda Marcos.

So how did the defection come about? He suggested it and they then waited for an opportunity, meanwhile concentrating on her winning the Tchaikovsky Prize and learning English. She decided she must learn the language as well, and this is a great tribute to her incredible strength of character. Any ordinary young girl would be looking at the moon, or something; this girl spent eight hours a day playing the violin and the rest of the day she was learning English – and in secret, incredible as it may seem, from books and from Linguaphone-type tapes. Her pronunciation is excellent. She was not exactly fluent when I was with her, but of course she has a marvellous ear, and in another year or so her English will be extremely good.

She and Vartan thought hard about how to pull it off, and they hit on the extremely intelligent idea of getting into the good books of the people who really run Soviet music. So they decided to become the absolute No. 1 interpreters of the music of Khrennikov, who is Chairman of the Union of Soviet Composers. It was brilliant stroke. Part of the idea was to get Viktoria enough practice, because Vartan was already a very accomplished musician; in the Soviet Union he was undoubtedly in the first rank of conductors – he had conducted in Moscow and Kiev, and then five years previously he was given his own orchestra in Kharkov, which he built up virtually from scratch and toured the whole Soviet Union.

Vartan knew that the only way for Viktoria to win [the Tchaikovsky Prize] – apart from obviously having talent – would be for her to practise unremittingly. He therefore took her all round the Soviet Union while she was still a pupil at the Conservatoire and gave her enormous opportunities to play. Before leaving for the tour, they went to Khrennikov and said, 'We will be touring Novosibirsk, Omsk, Tomsk, Donbass – you name it, we're going there – and we would love to play your symphonies and your violin concertos.' After all, it didn't matter what Viktoria was playing as long as she was practising. By this means they became the great interpreters of Khrennikov's essentially third-rate music, which naturally flattered the influential old composer and made them thoroughly kosher from the authorities' point of view.

Viktoria denies that she was a member of the Party, although she did say, in a conversation with Rostropovich in Washington, that she was the Komsomol rep. of her year at the Conservatoire and for that reason she couldn't understand why she hadn't been given more concerts and recitals while she was a student.

[Vartan, of course, is a committed anti-Communist.] He was very successful as a young conductor and in the late 1960s he was allowed to go to West Berlin as a competitor for some international prize, in which he was placed second – and that was the last time he went abroad before his defection. After that he was invited to become the resident conductor of the Bratislava Opera House, but they wouldn't even let him go to Czechoslovakia; obviously he was not in 'their' good books. It was after Viktoria won the Tchaikovsky Prize that they were given an opportunity to get out. Vartan was invited to be a member of the judges' panel at a competition for young conductors in Montreal, and the Soviet Ministry of Culture said, 'OK, you can go.' He and Viktoria then agreed that he would defect in Montreal; Viktoria would skip on her next foreign trip and they would then join up.

This elaborate plan, however, was never put into effect, because an extraordinary, million-to-one chance came along instead. Viktoria was asked to do a tour in Finland, and she was told that her usual accompanist would not be going; being Jewish and in his fifties, the authorities had a hunch that he might defect. Viktoria was called to the Ministry of Culture and told: 'Find yourself another accompanist.' She went downstairs to where Vartan was waiting for her and told him that she had to find another pianist to accompany her at the recitals in Finland. He at once said, 'Go back upstairs and tell them that I will go with you.'

She told me (very charmingly, I must say), 'I didn't want to go and interrupt those very important people again, but I thought, well, if Vartan thinks it's worth risking it, I'll do it.' The thing about her is that she will do as she's told; this seems to have been part of her training, and at that stage if Vartan said 'Go and do this', she went and did it. (This, incidentally, is why the whole balance of their relationship has now gone wrong: in their present circumstances, *she* has to tell *him* what to do.)

Anyway she went upstairs again and said to the woman who handled foreign concert bookings, 'Why shouldn't Vartan Zhordania come with me?' The woman objected, not unreasonably, 'But he's not a pianist!' Viktoria replied, 'Oh, but he graduated from the Conservatoire as a pianist' (which was quite true) 'and he plays all the time on the piano in his flat.' Apparently the Ministry then agreed to Viktoria's proposal. Personally, I doubt whether that was quite the whole story. From the little I know about Soviet bureaucracy, if this woman official did indeed agree to it, there must also have been a certain greasing of palms, because since everyone knew that Viktoria was living with Vartan I can't believe it wouldn't have occurred to them that these two were up to something. On the other hand, maybe not; maybe it was just a lucky break – and it worked.

Vartan then had to get four KGB permissions in order to go to Finland; these were not forthcoming. He also needed a *nihil obstat* from the Ministry of Culture, and this was not given either. It was forty-eight hours before their departure, and he still didn't have the necessary papers, so at 9 p.m. Viktoria went to Khrennikov and said, 'Comrade Khrennikov, I don't understand this hold-up – can you please help? I know that married couples cannot travel abroad together, but as you know, we are not married.' Khrennikov said, 'I see no reason

why you and your lover shouldn't go together. I'll see what I can do.'
Within twenty-four hours Vartan had permission and they left on time.

On the day of their departure, the KGB man assigned to be their
escort was withdrawn; apparently he, too, was suspected of being a
potential defector. Instead, they were accompanied by the same woman
from the Ministry of Culture who had OK'd Vartan as her accompanist.
She wasn't a KGB officer, but was obviously under KGB orders.
Luckily for them, she wasn't sharp enough to spot their nefarious plan,
and when the crucial moment came they were able to elude her.

They had made their preparations very carefully, which included
purposely leaving behind virtually all their possessions. They were worried that if someone went into Vartan's flat while they were on tour in
Finland and found the place stripped bare, they might smell a rat.
Among other dodges, Vartan 'lent' his extremely expensive Western
hi-fi system to a man at the recording studio at Kiev Radio, so that he
could make for Vartan a professional recording on quarter-inch tape
of his orchestral performances with Viktoria; Vartan would then collect
the recording 'after his return from Finland'!

When they finally defected, all they had with them were two plastic
bags. They left all their luggage in the hotel, in order not to alert their
'nanny'. Viktoria was wearing three layers of clothes, and they also
had two allegedly most valuable antique violin bows, which they had
bought – quite legally – from a dealer in Moscow. [These turned out
not to be genuine, which] came as a tremendous shock to Viktoria
when she tried to sell them in New York – the very reason for bringing
them out with them. This fiasco, in fact, was not only a disappointment
but a tremendous surprise to her because she had really trusted the
man who had sold them to her. She told me that she had paid 20,000
roubles *each* for these bows. To me that sounded like an extraordinary
sum of money for anyone to have in their purse, but apparently in the
Soviet music world it isn't so astronomical; people go abroad, buy gold
with their hard-currency earnings then bring it back and sell it on the
black market at an enormous profit. I checked all this out, and people
from that milieu said the figure wasn't as way out as it might sound.

So they had these two bows; they had a lot of cassettes of their
performances; they had a handful of *Gosconcert* brochures about themselves and their careers, written in English; and they had some money
in dollars.

They were in Kuusamo, where they apparently grabbed a cab and asked the driver to take them to Tornio, which is the point on the frontier opposite the Swedish town of Haparanda. Kuusamo is on the *eastern* side of Finland, only a few miles from the Soviet frontier, and it's four and a half hours' drive westwards to the Swedish frontier over bad country roads. Kuusamo is a tiny little place, and I found it highly unlikely that you could just hail a cab in what is little more than a large village and say, 'Drive me [three hundred miles] to the Swedish frontier for the afternoon.' So I suspect – although I have no evidence – that the drive from Kuusamo to Tornio was pre-arranged in some way. I often questioned Viktoria on this subject; for instance I asked her, 'What did you talk about in the car?' and she replied, 'Nothing.' Her description of the actual crossing of the frontier, too, was somehow lacking in any genuine-sounding impressions and verisimilitude. I cannot believe that, if you are crossing a frontier that represents the most momentous step you will ever take in your life, you remember practically nothing about it.

[They didn't need visas to get into Sweden.] The Scandinavian countries have completely open borders between each other, even for citizens of third countries – at least of most countries. And our pair knew perfectly well, in advance, that at this crossing-point, the main one between Sweden and Finland, there are no passport checks. There is a customs house, but there is no control of travellers' movements. I kept on asking Viktoria, 'How did you know that nobody would stop you at the frontier?' and she would answer, 'We knew it in Moscow.' Her actual words were, 'It's common knowledge in Moscow,' which I found very hard to swallow. On one level these people are incredibly ignorant about the most basic features of life in the West, and on another level a detail like this is 'common knowledge' . . . Common knowledge to whom? Whom do you ask? Who is trustworthy enough to ask such a loaded question: 'Will the Finns and the Swedes check my passport if I cross from Tornio to Haparanda?'

I found all that so dubious that my personal hunch is that they were helped. Viktoria, don't forget, had been to Finland several times before. It is my conjecture that there was somebody in Finland whom she trusted enough to ask, and that this person either took them across or helped them arrange it . . .

They then changed taxis at the border, and took a Swedish taxi to Luleå, which is eighty kilometres, and bought themselves a ticket on a domestic flight to Stockholm, where they arrived late at night and booked into a hotel. Next morning they tried to go to the American Embassy, which was closed because it was Labour Day, so they went to the Swedish police, who immediately removed them from their hotel and locked them up for safety reasons.

The reason why I felt doubtful was that the whole thing seemed too well organized, with too much foreknowledge, know-how and confidence: change taxis, go to Luleå (the nearest town with an airport), take a domestic flight, check into a hotel in Stockholm in the middle of the night. It was Viktoria who spoke English and had to make all these arrangements. And what about their passports, devoid of Swedish visas, when they checked into the hotel? I feel it was all too good to be true, unless they were helped – perhaps not by an organization, but an individual . . .

But after their arrival in Stockholm they gave a press conference at which they got into terrible trouble, because they were so hopelessly uninformed, or they were not briefed on exactly what a defector should say at a press conference. They told much the same story that they later told in Washington: that they were totally apolitical, that they had no political motivation, that they had come because they were not given the opportunities and artistic freedom that they wanted. When asked in what way their artistic freedom was restricted, Viktoria replied that she hadn't been given the flat she was promised for winning the Tchaikovsky competition, that she was sent to play in the provinces instead of being allowed to play in the Great Hall of the Conservatoire, and that as a Tchaikovsky prizewinner she had expected to have a record made, which the record company had failed to do – in short, very, very poor reasons for applying for political asylum.

It was from that first press conference that I got hold of the story. As soon as I had got the project together at the BBC, I got in touch with Swedish security, who said I could come at the weekend. This was on a Wednesday; on Thursday morning they called back and said, 'If you really want to see them, we recommend you to come now, because they have made such a hash of their press conference that the Americans are dubious about giving them political asylum, and they're being shipped off to some American transit camp near Frankfurt. Once they're in that camp you'll never get to see them.'

So I got on the next plane, and in the time it took me to get from Heathrow to their safe house outside Stockholm, Rostropovich had telephoned them to say that he had intervened at the White House and they were being given letters of parole to fly to the USA the following morning. Vartan apparently knew Rostropovich, who had contacted them when he heard the name Zhordania in the report of their press conference. It was Rostropovich who pulled strings to ensure that, first, they got to the United States, and, second, they started off in Washington.

[Viktoria's bad relationship with her parents was basically, as I have said,] all to do with Vartan. They strongly disapproved of the fact that she was living with him. She was still a young girl at school . . . she met him when she was nineteen; she was twenty-three when they defected. Also they probably didn't see eye to eye, because both the parents were real, committed Party members, not just paper Party members. Her father works on some secret engineering project – a missile project, or something of the sort. Furthermore, Viktoria once said that she lived in a suburb of Moscow where most high-ranking Party members have their houses, and the chances of them living there were extremely unlikely unless they were 'super-clean', as it was a very privileged area.

Viktoria's talent was spotted when she was in kindergarten and she was at once sent to a special Suzuki-type school for musically gifted children in the suburb where they lived. You don't find that kind of school in any old Moscow suburb, but only in the areas reserved for high-ranking and privileged people.

In the Suzuki system, a parent has to be present all the time and the parent has to learn with the child. Viktoria and her father played the violin together five hours every day. She told me that although she obviously owed a great debt to her father, who gave up a big slice of his life for her, nevertheless they grew very far apart in their views. I presume she referred to her father having certain ideas about how she should behave, or something of the kind. It was obviously her mother who tried to keep the peace in the family, and she would occasionally come and live with Viktoria and Vartan at his flat.

During the period of two months between the Ministry of Culture accepting Vartan as her accompanist and their departure, they played ten hours a day: Vartan hadn't played the piano for twenty years. Now Viktoria had not told her mother that she wasn't going with the usual accompanist. Nobody, apart from the bureaucrats at the Ministry of Culture, knew that she was going with Vartan. Two days before their departure her mother said, 'Who are you going with?' and she said, 'Vartan,' to which her mother said, 'But Vartan can't play the piano!' and Viktoria replied, 'Why don't you come and listen to us playing?' Her mother was therefore the only person who heard them play together before their public performance in Helsinki.

That performance was quite frankly a disaster, because the critics immediately spotted the fact that, while she played beautifully, he was simply not up to her standard. Although the Helsinki critics picked this up, the rather dumb lady who was their 'nanny' failed to grasp it, so the bad news didn't filter through to the Soviet authorities. In fact, our couple had dinner with the Soviet Ambassador in Helsinki the evening before they left to go north. They apparently behaved themselves very, very well!

According to Viktoria, once their defection plans were well on the way to being realized, she wanted to make peace with her mother; but this was not really possible, because the tension and prevarication imposed by the need to keep their plans secret made any real *rapprochement* between daughter and mother impossible. In fact, she only really began to make peace with her mother during their telephone conversations from New York to Moscow (although it doesn't actually seem to be so in the film). Because she was actually telling her mother what she had done and, to some extent, why she had done it, they started to develop a real relationship again for the first time in many years. The mother was still very emotional and Viktoria was very defensive, but the telephone conversation (much abridged in the film) actually went on for twenty-seven minutes, and the transcript of it is an extraordinary human document.

After seeing and hearing the edited version on film, many people said they thought Viktoria was cold and heartless. I would rather say that she is what Russians call *bezdukhovna* – soulless; she just doesn't seem to have developed what we might call humanity in her character. Throughout the year, directly and through Vartan, I tried to get her to consider the concept of 'vulnerability', and she said she didn't know what I was talking about; so I found the word in an English–Russian dictionary and showed it to her, to which her response was, 'Yes, I recognize the word but I don't quite know what it means.' I may be wrong, but I think that it's not that she's heartless; I believe that because she has been brought up like an Olympic athlete, she has just never developed those perceptions that are needed to take note of other people.

A great part of it, I think, can perhaps be explained by the fact that she had been brought up in a world where she never had to take any notice of anybody else. She was brought up as a child prodigy, therefore she would probably have developed the same character-traits anywhere else in the world, and without that degree of self-absorption she would never be the kind of musician that she is. Now you may say, 'What about Menuhin, Isaac Stern, Pinchas Zuckerman, and so on and so on – they aren't like her.' In that case, she certainly wasn't born with the capacity for their kind of warmth and human responsiveness. Yet she has a tremendous capacity for simple pleasure, and at such moments she is quite touching. It was her great dream, for instance, to go to Disneyland. She came away from there with bags full of soft toys . . . There is in her a child that never had a chance to grow up, and when that emerges she is very sweet . . .

54

Suffocation

MIKHAIL LEONIDOVICH TSYPKIN

Mikhail Leonidovich Tsypkin was born in 1950. He and his wife emigrated in 1977 to the United States, where he received a fellowship to study for a doctorate in political science at Harvard. He now lives and teaches in northern California.

I took my university finals on 20 August 1968 at the time of the invasion of Czechoslovakia . . . I was eighteen, my relations with the Soviet regime had already come to an end because of what was happening. I remember on 21 August – the horror of it – when I came out on to the street I saw a crowd of people who couldn't care less about what had happened. Or if they did care, they were pleased. And I felt such a fish out of water – even my school friends, whom I trusted, all said that it had to be done, that it was dictated by *raison d'état*. The usual Russian nonsense. And I suddenly realized, as Lenin once said, that we would take different paths.

It's difficult to say what the mood of the students was, because I was afraid of most of them. When I started at the university I had a talk with a friend of my father's, a journalist and a cynical fellow who understood things in those days. Later he sold out and lost touch with what was happening – good and evil no longer had any significance for him; but in those days he understood what was what. He said to me, 'Right, so you're going to university. Remember this: you can talk about football and girls, nothing else. You're an intelligent lad. Talk about these things if you don't want to slip up.' And he was completely right, because even then, in the first year, I noticed who were the *provocateurs* who would come up to you and ask questions, like 'What do you think about Czechoslovakia?'

The atmosphere had changed a lot. When I was at school, there was less to be afraid of. We were children, after all. The atmosphere was almost Khrushchevian. At university it was different. On the one hand there was the pressure to keep your mouth shut; on the other they treated you as adults. In Soviet schools, the pupils are insulted and the teachers are rude; [at university] no one was rude to us, everyone was polite. But of course, gradually I found myself a circle of friends who had the same attitudes as myself. They were all Jews, like me. This helped us to trust each other.

But as always, we deceived ourselves. For many years I more or less trusted Denis Dragunsky, the son of the children's writer, Victor Dragunsky. A few years later, after we had finished our studies, I learned from a reliable source that this Denis had been reporting on us all, that he was an informer, and what's more – that he did it out of conviction. It was very interesting – you should always listen to what people say about themselves. One of our teachers was no less a person than the famous literary critic Vladimir Nikolayevich Turbin. (That's another one who isn't what he seems. He was one of the people Andropov's daughter used to hang around.) Turbin once said that he didn't approve of all those *frondeurs* who go around cursing the Soviet authorities. Denis said, 'No, you have to go even further.' He believed in complete subjection to Soviet power, complete identification with it. Turbin said to him, 'If the authorities ordered you to say that Misha Tsypkin was a Portuguese spy, would you do it?' And he said yes, he would, out of conviction. Of course I should have understood then that a man like that had to be an informer. But because he was one of us, an intellectual and half Jewish, it seemed impossible.

So I had my own circle . . . It's hard to say what the mood was because I didn't have anything to do with most people. Basically it was a mood of Brezhnevite conformity. It was interesting to notice how the Languages Faculty changed, because when we came, it was full of all sorts of bearded intellectuals. At the beginning of the 1960s Sinyavsky was lecturing on the special course; then, later in the 1960s Lakshin gave a special course on Bulgakov.[1] But it was getting much worse by the time I arrived, and when we were in our final years we were horrified at what was happening to the younger students. They had started recruiting large numbers from workers' families. And what a sight they were! (Forgive me, Lord!) They were such a shower! Party workers and all sorts. There was among them a certain percentage of intellectuals, young men and women who had parents who could pull strings. I remember I had a friend who was dreadfully anti-Soviet but all the same he was responsible for the ideological sector of the Komsomol bureau. He needed to get a degree, so he had joined the Komsomol, although he didn't believe in it for a second . . .

There were two friends whom I could trust absolutely. The rest – not absolutely. Only two. One of these, a woman, emigrated; the other, a man, stayed there. You can't really know for sure [whether to trust anyone], though I can only speak for intellectuals like myself. I can't speak for an ordinary person, because workers at a factory aren't usually afraid; they blab whatever comes into their head. It's a bit like in Orwell: 'The proles, who cares about them?' They don't do anything outstanding and nobody pays attention to them. An ordinary person doesn't need to be able to trust anyone. He doesn't carry seditious thoughts in his head. I can't speak for different groups of people, how they choose their friends, because for most people there isn't a problem. Politics is not so important for them. At the very worst they might tell a political joke – you don't get sent to prison for that.

My parents more or less shared my views. It ran in the family. They could trust some friends . . . They simply didn't invite home the ones they didn't trust. In our family, during the invasion of Czechoslovakia or the Six Day War, they did not refer to the Soviet regime otherwise than as 'those bandits'.

I couldn't breathe any longer. I walked outdoors and suffocated from hatred. I couldn't stand the country. I hated everything. I realized that to live in a country and to hate it is crazy. And there were practical considerations; I knew that I couldn't make any sort of career because of the discrimination; that I couldn't earn any money; that I had absolutely no future. I sat in an office and worked as a technical translator and I knew that I had thirty years of working life ahead of me and that I would spend them all there; I wouldn't get any other job and I would be grateful to be kept on where I was. And [my wife and I] didn't want to have children there. We didn't want to have Jewish children in the Soviet Union.

I struggled with this decision for a long time, because I'm not a decisive sort of person. After that I became decisive, and once having decided . . . even though it went against my nature I knew that I had to put it into effect.

We applied to leave on 24 February 1977 and we left [for America] on 29 July. It took exactly three months to obtain permission – we got it on 24 May.

In the beginning my parents objected: we had just got married and they were worried about our future; they were afraid, they didn't know what would happen. But as the years passed, they came to realize that there was not much of a life for me there. My mother supported me; my father behaved well, but there was no support at all from him. He suffered a lot and when a man suffers . . . Later, when I had gone, he felt terribly proud and he was extremely pleased. He thought I had done the right thing, and he was worried for me. How would things turn out? Because they had all considered me a simpleton. They'd say of me: 'Our fool, he's not capable of anything, he won't cope.'

There were all these exaggerated myths about the harshness of life in the West, especially in America. There's a general impression that if you're three minutes late for work you immediately get the sack. When we came here, we thought it would be like a giant Swiss clock, everything working, everything on time. But we found the old familiar lack of organization – that encouraged us very much! And when you meet Americans, you discover that their chief characteristic is that they are such kind people. But we had no idea of this. It's a part of Soviet propaganda that we couldn't get rid of. It's all part of Russia's inferiority complex – if life is so affluent and they have such wonderful technology, then it must be achieved at some price, and they think that the price is that Americans are concerned only with money, and their business and so on, and this is, as always, unbelievable rubbish . . .

the radio before either, and so she fell in love with it. Her mother sent to say that they were dying of hunger, so when the spring sowing began, her mother took her back. When she was leaving we made her a present of these overshoes and a dress of mine. She went down the road howling her eyes out. She sobbed loudly all down the street. People asked her, 'Maryusa, what are you crying about?' She answered that she wouldn't be able to listen to the radio any more.

What I saw in Mordovia when I went off to give those lectures was unlike anything you have ever seen, heard or read about, although it was only five hundred kilometres from Moscow. Maybe it was not like that every year, but I was there when there was nothing to eat anywhere. Around February the cattle started to die. I went down roads which were almost unusable, the like of which you've never seen. There were potholes big enough for the car to fall right into. And when we got to the next village – I had with me some woman official – we went to see the cattle pen where the sheep were dying from hunger. When we opened the door these sheep could no longer stand up and they crawled towards us because they hoped someone was going to give them something to eat. In the fields there were the first signs of spring. It was probably April, or maybe March; the snow had only just melted and the grass was starting to grow. They were beginning to put the animals out. There were cows in the field and they were *pink* because their coats had dropped out from hunger – bare-skinned cows with pink skin just like a human being. It really was pink – it wasn't like a white human skin; but absolutely pink like human lips. And there wasn't any meat to be had either. There were just bones covered in this pink skin.

I heard a shout one day in the village Soviet when something or other was under discussion. In Russia you could subscribe to a State loan; they were issuing bonds. A man was signing for 75 roubles. He wept and cried that he had never seen 75 roubles in his life. These people lived terribly – maybe they still do today. They all spoke Russian. They had lost their language and their culture. There were no toilets in the villages. And it wasn't just that there were no toilets, but more than that – they didn't even know what toilets were. If they were indoors, they would just come outside and do what they had to do. And all the animals were in the house. Each house had its own vegetable garden, but these people usually kept their cattle in the house, if they had any, and their chickens, goats and sheep. The houses were built in the following way: one room was heated by a Russian stove which the grandmother slept on. Then there was an enclosed stove in another room where the master and mistress of the house slept, although in actual fact there were very few houses that had a master around – there were very few men there. I don't know what had happened to them. There were a great many children and it wasn't clear where they had all come from. They all slept on the floor amongst the chickens, goats and sheep, amongst whatever animals there were.

After that, with great difficulty my husband got a job in the Scientific Research Institute of Physical and Technical Measurement [in Moscow, so we moved there in 1955]. In Moscow there is the so-called *propiska* [residence permit – an identity document and pass] and since we didn't have one he was first taken on as a research student. Since he had been accepted to do research he was allowed to register for a period of six months. We had nowhere to live and it was impossible to rent anywhere without a *propiska*. We were extremely poor. As we had nowhere to live we spent our nights at the Central Telegraph Office. Then we found somewhere, but we were thrown out of that for not having a *propiska*. Someone must have informed on us. So then we decided that I should try to get into the Institute of Literature. By this time I had started to write poems and to translate poetry from English, which I hardly knew at all then. But that didn't matter. Kornei Chukovsky[2] came to see me and this is where my literary career took off. He said that I had talent and became my patron. He even found me odd bits of paid work. After this I decided to get into the Institute of Literature in the hope of getting a Moscow *propiska*. It is the institute under the aegis of the Union of Writers.

My life was then going very well in Soviet terms in the sense that I was making a career for myself as a translator, because in Russia everything else was closed to me. I knew I couldn't publish what I was writing, except for a few books of poems in Russian for children; I did manage to publish a couple in some journals. Then I started writing plays. The first play I wrote and the second, both for children (that was when I still hadn't really learnt how to write plays) were very well received. I won a prize in the All-Union competition for children's plays.

Getting the plays put on wasn't so easy. One play was put on in the Leningrad region and the other, the play which actually won the prize, was never staged. I translated *The Happy Prince* by Oscar Wilde, which if I'm not mistaken did have a print run of half a million. The first print run was three hundred thousand and then it was reprinted. Then I translated the poems from English fairy tales which I think went up to a million. I translated a lot, primarily from English, although there were interlinear translations as well. And there was a time when I was translating a lot from Persian, when I knew both the language and the literature well. I translated the poems for some novels which were also very profitable because they came out in big editions. But in time I stopped translating because it was a field already occupied by others, and also because I began translating less and writing more. In the beginning I tried to get my poems published but with no success at all.

By then I understood what it was to write plays, and I had already stopped writing them in accordance with Soviet canons, in which everything has to be simple. There has to be the good and positive and the evil and negative, and a struggle is waged between the two. In the end the good always triumphs. I gradually realized that this was a very boring formula and I began writing in another way. Already with the third play I was having problems, because it turned out that it didn't correspond to the outline for which they paid me the advance. Then there began a period of arguing with them, during which time I started writing a play for adults and that attracted me a lot. But even this play wasn't the sort I could offer to anybody, though I did try.

And then came the moment when I started writing my fourth play for children, which was based on material by A. A. Milne. This play was successful in a way, because it provoked great excitement amongst a great many producers, who all tried to put it on. To all intents and purposes it was banned. The authorities asserted that there were critical allusions to the present day in it, and indeed there were; if you try very hard you can always find them. The Soviet Ministry of Culture is unusually shrewd; it will always discover your true intentions under any mask. As a result of all these squabbles and arguments, the woman who was the head of the literary section of the Ministry of Culture, Svetlana Romanovna Terentieva, came to me with her face all covered in red blotches and said, 'My producers will never put on your plays.' And nor did they put them on.

This was around 1970 and by that time I couldn't have cared less. To tell the truth, after 1968 I couldn't care about anything any more. I had already seen that I had no chance of doing anything there. But from that it doesn't follow that I wanted to leave. I can honestly say that I didn't want to go. My husband wanted to go but, however stupid it may seem now, I then felt that I had a blood tie with Russia. I wrote in Russian. I wrote about Russia. I thought I understood everything about Russia. I wrote about Russia so that it should be seen. I knew that I would never understand another country so well. I understood the psychology of the people I came into contact with. I thought that if I left I would die. It didn't turn out like that, but I didn't know that then. It seemed to me that having to emigrate was the most terrible thing that could happen to a Russian poet or dramatist. So I preferred to live there somehow, to be unacknowledged, but not to leave. But then my husband was saying something along the lines that if he didn't leave he would die.

There were several stormy periods in our lives because we were participants in the trial of Daniel and Sinyavsky.[3] We were very close friends of theirs and therefore we were the first people to be called in for questioning. My husband organized the making of the shorthand transcription of the trial and I wrote it up. The book which came out was the end result of my writing. My husband was very much involved with the trial. He went there a lot – he wasn't allowed in court, so he walked up and down the corridor. But everyone passed through our flat – they all came to see us from dawn till dusk. We were living then in Khlebnoy Pereulok, next to the Union of Writers, and Ploshchad Vosstaniya where the court building was. So we sort of had the headquarters at our place. There was always someone on duty and everyone phoned us. We lived in the end flat on the sixth floor, and a couple of days before the trial the KGB came and installed a lot of equipment and put in a microphone so that they could overhear what was going on. We heard the knocking and knew what they were doing. It was a communal flat and on the whole our neighbours were not enthusiastic about it being turned into a headquarters of the pro-Daniel–Sinyavsky group.

Lara [Larisa Bogoraz, Daniel's wife] and Maya [Marya Rozanova, Sinyavsky's wife] would arrive early in the morning and have breakfast with us before setting off for the court with my husband and Dr Luboshitz [a doctor now in Jerusalem] and Luboshitz made the shorthand record and brought it out. My husband brought it home and gave it to me. And I would say that this was a happy time.

A couple of days after the end of the trial we went to a winter school for physicists outside Sverdlovsk. My husband and Professor Razvelli travelled together by train in the same compartment. When they got out at Sverdlovsk they were arrested on some quite ridiculous pretext. I don't even remember now what they were accused of, only that the police were ostensibly looking for drugs. In any event they were arrested, taken off to the police station and held there for a day because the police were trying to find something in their papers. In the end they were released. The authorities were probably worried about why they had caught a train right after the trial had ended. Lara had seen us off at the station. From that moment on my husband started suffering all the unpleasant things which were to go on happening to him right up until our departure.

The [Daniel–Sinyavsky] trial, that whole series of events, had co-incided with my husband being invited to go and work at the atomic energy institute in Dubno. And what's more he was offered very good conditions. They gave us a cottage, which is extremely uncommon in Russia. This was August 1965, a month before the trial. On 8 September Sinyavsky was arrested; Daniel was picked up on the 11th. Our life took a completely different course because they then wouldn't take [my husband] at Dubno. Six months later his contract, which had been for six months, ran out and was not renewed. They started to throw us out of the cottage and an action was brought against us. They chased us out with the help of the court although the Procurator said that the institute had no right to do so: there was no basis whatever for court action, but nevertheless we were evicted by the court. From then on my husband's scientific career was not perhaps absolutely destroyed, but his position was badly weakened. He was openly and obviously followed by the powerful arm of the KGB . . .

We left the Soviet Union in December 1974 after three years of a very tough struggle to be allowed to go. When we gave in our application to emigrate, it was the beginning of 1972; my husband was then, I think, only the second doctor of science to apply. The first was Professor Lerner. No doctors of science had been let out before. And since it was clear they weren't going to let us out right away, we got ready for a long siege.

I helped my husband to set up a *samizdat* magazine called *Jews in the USSR* and the first issue came out in September 1972. We went off to Koktebel to type it up. We hired a flat there – well, not a flat but a room – and we sat there typing it up, terrified of being arrested and of not getting back to Moscow with it. Somehow or other we did it. In the three years before we left, we got out seven issues of the magazine. Nudelman, the editor of our journal '22', became editor-in-chief of *Jews in the USSR* after we left. It carried on until 1982 and there were twenty-one issues. Then Victor Brailovsky, the last editor-in-chief, was arrested.

In addition, the second undertaking which my husband got going, and which exists to this day, was underground seminars for scientists. There had already been several international seminars and scientists from all over the world had come. The first international meeting was in the summer of 1974, and that was the first time 'comprehensive measures' were taken: all the participants were arrested, all the wives were put under house arrest and, since it had gone on in our flat, those living in our flat were arrested and evicted. I was moved into a flat belonging to a friend of mine and was tailed by two cars, each with four men in it. They parked at the entrance to this friend's flat and wouldn't let me go out. If anyone came to see me, a car would follow them afterwards to see where they were going. A friend of mine, Alina Chaplina, stayed there with me so I shouldn't be by myself. She lives here now. At the time she was working in television; when we went to work she was followed to the Television Centre by a car and when she went into the building one of the men from the car came in after her. They had a pass system there, but he was allowed in.

The last six months were really dreadful. They followed us quite openly wherever we went, whether we went on foot or by transport. Over this period my husband was taken off to the KGB; he was arrested for two weeks once, but he was taken off for the day not less than fifteen times. The last time he was arrested was on the eve of our departure – actually in the customs shed. He was taken off to the KGB for the day and so the customs check was stopped, because it had to be done in his presence. Our visa was valid only until the 24th and since this was already the 23rd we wouldn't be able to get our things through and would have to give our tickets back. They told me not to worry as everything would be OK [and] took me off to a cashier. He said that they would transfer the tickets from the 24th to the 27th. But the girl said that the visas were good only for the 24th. He looked at her and said: 'Tell the KGB to —— off!'

By the end of 1974, when we were leaving, all my nostalgia had been exhausted and after that last year it had become very easy for me to bid farewell to my country. Everything seemed to point to the fact that the sooner I left the better, as fast as my legs could carry me. It was those last six months – and I can give the exact date: from 2 May 1974, when there was a press conference here in Jerusalem [at which our friend] Dr Luboshitz opened an international seminar. Before that, if they followed us at all they followed us discreetly; but from that moment onwards two cars were put on us and they never left us. And these people would calmly get out of a train, or get out of a car and come and sit next to us on a bus or the metro.

There was even the time when a friend of ours in Russia, Boris Balter, who was quite a famous writer, died. We went to his funeral. A car followed us. We went by trolleybus and two men from the car came with us, one by the front exit, the other by the rear. Balter had lived in Maleevo and so we had to go by train. We got into the carriage and there were a lot of writers in it who were also off to the funeral. Four men got in behind us; they had left their car somewhere. The other car had gone on. Two stood by the rear door and two by the front. All the writers were shaking with fright, because they didn't know who the men were after. But gradually the word got around that they were after Voronel and not them, and then the same idea came to all of them: how could they get out of this? [They] begged us to leave as soon as possible, because when we left that would mean they would no longer be shadowed. It really was extremely unpleasant. Just imagine a hearse going along with a KGB car slowly coming up behind, at the same pace . . .

56

An Island in the Past

VITALY KOMAR

Vitaly Komar, born in 1943, is an artist who emigrated from the Soviet Union to the United States in 1977. He describes how, after years of repression, in the early 1970s artists were suddenly given greater freedom and were even allowed to exhibit their work in public.

In 1974 the unofficial or 'nonconformist' artists decided to show their work in the open air. We chose a field in the outer suburbs of Moscow, and when we came to this field we had the feeling that we should be careful, that something was going to happen. There was a big apartment block nearby and we decided to go upstairs to the top floor and have a look at the field first, to see what was happening down there. If there was no danger, if people weren't being arrested, we would go on with the exhibition as planned. It was early in the morning. I stayed on the ground floor with the pictures, and Oleg went upstairs . . . After a short while, he suddenly came head over heels downstairs.

'What's wrong?' I said. 'There are people up there', he said, 'with telephoto lenses, and there's a man in charge of them who looks like a typical KGB agent.' As far as he could see, there wasn't anyone in the field yet.

So we thought, 'Come on, let's go and join them.' And the KGB man accompanied us to the field. He followed us a little distance behind. We noticed him, and he stopped and went away. A little while later some *druzhiniki* [part-time civilian 'vigilantes' enrolled by the police] appeared and began to smash the pictures and threw some of them on to a bonfire. They were evidently supposed to be workers, working on that piece of waste ground. [They wore red armbands.] There was a great rowdy scene. Then they set bulldozers and those agricultural machines which spray out powerful jets of water on us . . .

So that was the 'progressive' reception we got! Everyone was very depressed. Some artists were arrested . . . It's one of my most romantic memories.

Two days later they suddenly released those artists, because apparently some American congressmen began asking: 'How can we offer friendship and *détente* to a country which sets bulldozers on artists?' I heard someone make a joke on the BBC, quite a good joke, saying that there were many people in England, too, who would happily use bulldozers on modern art, only the system didn't allow them to! So these artists reappeared, and no one did anything to them. Not even a fine, not even the minimum fifteen days in prison. It was all to do with the fact that some kind of opposition force had come into action.

Oscar Rabin, a very practical man, who knows the Soviet authorities well, made the brilliant suggestion, as if he were completely certain that it would turn out all right: 'Next week, let's go back again to the same place.' No one had expected this! After a little while some representatives of the authorities arrived and began to negotiate with us: 'You can't exhibit here. We'll let you hold an exhibition, but in another park.'

Rumours began to circulate round the town, and the BBC broadcast the news that the Minister for Internal Affairs was against allowing artists this opportunity. Suddenly a miracle happened! A second Union of Artists was formed, a local union, and exhibitions were allowed in people's flats. No one was arrested; all they did was to take people's photos. After that a lot of people believed that the KGB had taken film of that disgraceful affair, and were trying to put pressure on their rivals in the MVD. Many people were saying that Andropov (then head of the KGB) collected pictures.

So things turned out in a rather strange way, rather as they might do in any democracy . . . Every State has its Army, its militia, its police, its bulldozers, but they have different degrees of nervousness, here in America someone would have to drop a bomb before the militia was called out. But there, in the USSR, it's enough for someone just to say something. I think that the reason why this nervousness is not as great here is because here there are many different groups, who, as it were, balance each other. No one group can achieve absolute power. There are ethnic groups, Government departments, the police, the Congress . . . and they don't allow each other to gain too much power. And it's paradoxical that in Russia, what we called our 'one day of freedom' – it was freedom, a lungful of freedom – [came about] because obviously two Government departments were at loggerheads, and at once freedom appeared! They had begun to counter-balance each other at that moment. Of course, there's no firm proof that things really were like that, but at least it is known that the person who was the Party Regional Secretary was removed from office and sent as Ambassador to Vietnam. Evidently there were powerful forces turning events to their own advantage. I don't think they really intended to give artists freedom, but it was a good excuse for an internal struggle.

There was a whole renaissance, a whole period of *détente* in the arts in the 1970s. There were a lot of conceptualists, young artists, exhibitions in people's flats. There were a few men standing photographing everyone who went in, but they didn't interfere. A completely new type of art was being shown – pop art, as it is called here. And people queued – students, members of the intelligentsia, workers, even members of the police – to see the pictures. I remember in two exhibitions there were even pictures with a fairly sharp social content, and still no one forbade it, even though in official exhibitions of the Union of Artists they removed such things. And it was paradoxical – things are always paradoxical in the Soviet Union – they lumped together pornography and religious propaganda, and they removed pictures of these two types. They were the only two types which were forbidden.

I wouldn't say that, apart from those bulldozers, I personally felt any so-called pressure. The problem is whether you want to play the authorities' game, or whether you can stand aside. If you want to have money, a lot of money, and have a beautiful studio – the kind of studio which would cost $1000 or $1500 in the USA can be rented from the Union of Artists for 5 roubles a month; otherwise you must make do with some cellar or thieves' den – you go yourself to the Union of Artists and there you paint, say, Brezhnev. The problem is whether you want to or not. You can stand aside. So, we simply didn't play these games. We didn't go and try to obtain commissions for portraits. We gave private lessons to art students, prepared young people to go to the Art Institute.

Of course in Russia the State often encroaches on people's leisure time too. There are groups, officially organized 'clubs', where they get people together in those 'Red Corners' in their free time. And they often keep them at work too, at meetings and so on. All the same, it does depend to a great extent on yourself. People have worked out a system of getting out of these things. Someone will say that his wife is ill, or that he has stomach-ache, and leave the meeting. And lots of people no longer go to the 'club' or the 'Red Corner' any more at all, because there is no worthwhile incentive. So, despite everything, some sort of private life does exist, particularly since Khrushchev's time, when new flats appeared and fewer people live in communal flats. That may be why many people are turning to religion, members of the intelligentsia, young people: because some sort of alternative has appeared. A great many people emigrated to Israel who had begun to be believers and to go to the synagogue only when the opportunity to emigrate arose. There began, so to speak, a quest for spiritual nourishment, because the State does not interfere so actively in people's private lives and they are left with more free time.

There is a widespread theory that the artist needs pressure and that, as a rule, he sublimates such pressure into art. First of all, I don't think all artists are like that, though in Russia it is probably more inherent. But I would say, too, that there are different types of pressure. For example, my landlord sometimes puts more pressure on me than the Soviet authorities did! [He exhibits] the same strange mixture of illogical and yet very pragmatic actions, in which he reminds me of the Soviet authorities. For example, he will suddenly turn off the heating. He's economizing on fuel or something. Suddenly the house goes cold in the middle of winter. Half the house goes on strike. They pay into a special fund. But I'm a strike-breaker, and that sort of pressure probably also finds an outlet in art!

Another very strong stimulus is the impossibility of returning to Russia. That's also a form of pressure – the pressure of fate. Many émigrés, including myself, sometimes dream that they have gone back to Russia. I remember when I dreamed that for the first time. It was as if I had gone there just for a short time and I was to come back, but there was something wrong with my papers. And the horror of believing that I would have to stay . . . Then, about three years later, the two places merged, probably because I was in a more stable psychological state. I was beginning to speak English better, and had more connections, had begun to make friends and to take an active part in the artistic life here. I dreamed that my old house, where I was born, was simultaneously in America: I felt as if I was in America and Moscow simultaneously.

Sometimes instead of 'New York' I say 'Moscow'. It comes out

automatically; for instance, when you're talking on the phone to someone who has gone to Washington, you say, 'And when are you coming
back to Moscow? – I mean New York!' And that probably also plays
a part in exerting pressure – the harshness of fate . . .

We have an acquaintance here who told us his mother was ill in the
Soviet Union, and he asked permission to visit her. They told him,
'When she dies, we'll let you visit her grave.' That was the official
reply, through the Embassy. By law you have the right to visit a grave,
but there is nothing to say you have the right to visit a living person!

There is indeed a sort of pressure, and perhaps that is why we have
moved away from avant-garde experiments, from Dada, etc., and have
gone over to more traditional, nostalgic realism. For example, we are
now taking for our themes only life in Russia in the Stalinist era, the
era of our childhood. I know it was very similar with Chagall – for
most of his life he portrayed those little Jewish villages of his youth,
although he was living in Paris and elsewhere. The core of our individual
personality is very often formed at that time: our individuality is our
past. And that, in a sense, is a form of pressure – the knowledge that
certain vital experiences took place in another time, another era.
Indeed, it is *time* that is different, not just geographical location. In
Russia we were in a different era. Russia is an island. And the impossibility of reaching that island can be a stimulus for painting. There is
Stalin, the memories of childhood, and so on: we have done a lot of
pictures on that theme.

Some people think it's a parody of Socialist Realist art. There *is* an
element of parody in it, but it's not as simple as that. There is also a
lot of genuine nostalgia. Of course, we don't portray Stalin as he really
was. He was a bloody dictator. But when we were children, we were
inculcated with the image of him as a good man with moustaches who
loved children, and many – no, most – people believed it. So it's a
nostalgia for the child's view of the world. It was a very, very harmoni-
ous, coherent world view. Everyone knew what was bad and what was
good. We had the very best society.

I remember what a shock it was to read a Yugoslav reference book,
which another boy brought into our school, about the relative output
of valuable commodities for different countries. In school we were
taught that Russia had the greatest output of wheat, the greatest output
of coal and so on. Suddenly we read that per head of population it was
nothing of the kind. Serbo-Croat is fairly easy to read; it is close to

Russian, especially the numerals. We were staggered! It was just at the beginning of Khrushchev's thaw and the improvement of relations with Tito. We had believed, many of us, that ours was the first and best country in the world, that we were in Paradise and that the West was Hell. And then when the 'thaw' happened, it turned out that Hell was not in the West but in the East. People began to come back from Siberia. For example, we had a teacher of drawing, who had been an architect. He had spent a large part of his life in prison. He told us these terrible things. So our outlook on *everything* changed, even before Solzhenitsyn published his stories. (I never knew – my parents had concealed it from me – that we too had relatives in prison.)

So this false but comforting model of the world is now very interesting. And this loss, not only of place but of time, and this psychological model of Russia – we are trying to use all that in our work now. It's a kind of myth. Of course, since we are now people with experience of life, there is an element here of ironical playfulness towards our own childhood. So there is an element of irony in these works. But there's a sadness too . . .

[I grew up] in Moscow; that was very important. The whole of Russia is a colony of Moscow. Particular conditions of life pertain in Moscow. It's like ancient Rome – you had to receive citizenship in order to live in Rome. It's the same thing with residence permits. Not just anybody can go and live in Moscow. It's forbidden by law. The police have to put a special stamp on your passport: *civis Moscovitus sum.* In Moscow there are many more commodities, more food, many more privileges and amenities. All the more so since my parents belonged to a relatively privileged group. We didn't know that elsewhere, in some other towns and villages, people had hard lives.

[My mother was a lawyer and] a faithful Communist. I remember she was even a little incapable of believing it when Khrushchev began his public exposure of Stalin. She said, 'It can't be!' It was a shock for many people. Because it was a peculiar, sterile atmosphere. I remember that even though she had been through the war, she hadn't seen life, *real* life, especially in rural Russia. She had never once been to an ordinary village, such as, for instance, Grossman described in the novel of his [*The Devils*] that came out in *samizdat* – where people became cannibals because they were dying of hunger during the famine of 1932–3. Terrible pages! Many people simply didn't know about it. *They simply didn't know*, and my mother was one of them. In the same way I imagine that many Germans didn't know about those bloody concentration camps.

[I studied art at] the Stroganoff Institute in Moscow. It was a peculiar time. It was nearly at the end of the Khrushchev thaw and a great many things were changing. In the first place, the teachers were always changing: there was a constant turnover . . . I realize that it put us in a very good position and helped us, because, willy-nilly, we learned pluralism: today one teacher would come and say such and such, and then another would come in his place and would say, 'Now we're going to draw only as they do in America.' In those days Khrushchev was giving money to institutes of higher education and we had Western journals in our libraries: the Italian *Domus*, American *Design*, English *Apollo*. They disappeared sometime in the 1960s.

The trial of Daniel and Sinyavsky,[1] the invasion of Czechoslovakia [were part of the reaction against Khrushchev]. And it immediately told on artists as well. For example, under Khrushchev a committee was formed to exhibit the work of young artists. But as an immediate reaction to the events in Czechoslovakia, it was disbanded. Obviously they thought that events in Czechoslovakia had also begun with small things like that, and then reached such proportions that anti-Government protests were even shown on television. Censorship became worse in the Soviet Union too . . .

[For artists, not only censorship but also having to conform to the tastes of a small group of officials plays] an important role, but officials are important only for those pictures which are painted on commission for the Ministry of Culture. For exhibitions within the Union of Artists, it is the artists themselves who choose and pay for the paintings. The artists themselves sit on the committees, and they have their favourites, their acquaintances. You can make a good living nowadays in the Union of Artists by painting nothing but still lives all your life, or landscapes, or perhaps even Modernist paintings – relatively Modernist. (Not pure abstract art, although you can do pure abstract art, too, in the decorative arts section, if, for example, you sketch fabric designs.) So the Artists' Union has formed a powerful bureaucracy of its own. It's a kind of mafia. For example, they can even get an artist off a criminal charge. They can do it even if he really has done something wrong, because there are many artists who are members of the Supreme Soviet, or have friends who are.

And within the Union there are favourites. They will say, 'Ivan – he has talent!' He has painted flowers all his life. And they help him to do this. They give him money, they give him a studio, they arrange exhibitions for him and they say, 'Ivan mustn't waste his talent by not drawing. He wouldn't make a soldier! His talent is that he loves flowers and that's all!' And this Ivan makes a very good living. No one puts any pressure on him. But the boss-artists themselves are often more conservative than the bureaucrats – that's the paradox, because the artist imposes his own taste, the style he likes himself. So there are different styles. In the Moscow Union of Artists there is one style, and in the Georgian Union of Artists another.

There's a whole system of pumping money from institutions into the funds of the Union of Artists, by means of setting up fictitious orders. For example, a factory does not need paintings, but the Union will come and say, 'If you pay for one, we will give you twenty per cent of the cost.' And the director orders this picture and puts the twenty per cent in his pocket. But it would never have entered his head that he needed a painting for his factory . . . Artists are some of the richest people in the Soviet Union – and the most important factor is the Artists' Union Council, and not those idiotic bureaucrats who have remained in the Ministry of Culture.

Of course, artists themselves have greater discrimination in art, but on the other hand they do manifest a tendency towards conservatism. The official slogan of Socialist Realism is that art can be national in form but socialist in content. And so, in the Baltic states there is one kind of art, and in Georgia another, on the basis that in Moscow people are of a different nationality. It's a very interesting problem. The problem is that often artists themselves exercise far worse censorship than the bureaucrats. They have taken things so far that not only pictures, but everything that is produced has to go through the censor. In the West many people know about censorship of the newspapers and of literature, but no one knows that the design of *everything*, from buttons to matchboxes and milkbottle tops – everything has to be submitted to a special commission of the Artists' Union. The artists themselves sit on this commission, but they very often do worse than the bureaucrats because they are competing amongst themselves. They may want to harm someone, or to take bribes.

I think a lot of artists from Russia wouldn't emigrate if they could travel [although] I would have emigrated in any case. The thing is that one wants to find stimulus or subject-matter in life, call it what you like. Emigration is a unique opportunity. If you have lived in Russia for a long time and if you know that all around you a quantitatively enormous artistic life is going on and that you are taking no part in it, and that you never will take part in it, you realize that your own culture is extremely individual, that it is an insular culture. It's like Gauguin, who didn't stay on that island. Culture in Russia is an island culture. Life takes on a sort of doomed quality. And not to take advantage of the opportunity of emigrating is somehow impossible.

First of all, my relatives began to emigrate: it was that that made me start thinking about it. Then there were many other different events: there was that exhibition; then my friends started to emigrate. They took our work out with them and in 1966 they organized an exhibition [in America, and it] was a success. They told us that we already had some money put away for us, that the gallery which was exhibiting our work was a very good gallery . . .

My mother said, 'You won't survive there, in the West. You'll die in a ditch.' I showed her the *New York Times Magazine*, where there was a big article with photographs of our pictures. 'Of course it will be difficult,' I said. 'But you see, there's a response to our work. The public understands it. A good gallery is exhibiting my work. It's as good as being in the Union of Artists here.'

And she agreed. 'Yes,' she said, 'You'll probably be unhappy here. You're not suited to life under capitalism.'

57

No Free World

EDUARD LIMONOV

Eduard Limonov was born in 1944 in Kharkov, the son of a Soviet Army officer. He became a novelist and, as his books could not be published in the USSR, emigrated to the West.

I feel great because my name is a kind of punk name. I adopted it in 1964 when no punk movement existed, when I was twenty, and at the end of the 1970s I discovered that it was very fashionable to have a name like that – Sid Vicious, Johnny Rotten . . . ! Eduard Limonov is less frightening, but it's artificial enough. In Russian, it sounds even more artificial than it does in English [it derives from the Russian word for 'lemon']. It indicates acidity. One of the critics at *L'Express*, when my book *It's Me, Eddy* came out in French, wrote that if the name was not invented there must have been some stroke of destiny, as the pages of my novels were so acidic.

Russian émigré writers often refuse to learn the new language. There are many reasons for that. There is the traditional Russian laziness – it's a kind of character trait that gives Russian conservatism an immovable quality. It's very difficult for them to organize themselves – especially for the generation of Sinyavsky or even Maximov.[1] If you come here after the age of forty, I think that to learn the language requires a persistent sacrifice of time. It requires study every day, and reading. I don't think that writers who were already distinguished wanted to bother themselves with it. Yes, it's irrational, but I think that's the reason – they think it's better to write new books than to learn the language. Myself, I'm learning French actively. I spend four hours a day and now read with little difficulty. [If you do not learn the language you cut yourself off.] For example, Maximov has no information at all about the Western world. What information he has is from his secretary, who gives him some descriptions or short translations of what he needs, but it's not possible to cover everything. I heard that he desperately tried to learn the language, but was not successful, and he complained that he was too old. That's not true, because he came here when he was almost the same age as I am, and I have been reading French books for nearly two years.

I have no active contact with Maximov, and just a little with Sinyavsky. I think it's suicidal – if they cannot overcome their weakness. They are rejecting the possibility of existing in the present – they can exist only in the past. You cannot take Maximov's political speeches seriously because he doesn't know what he's talking about. If he doesn't read the *New York Times* or *Le Monde*, he's not an intelligent man. He's not informed.

I don't know him to the extent of talking about his psychological structure and how he behaves. I have met him a few times. I think he's a creation of 'dissident fever'. He's a creation of the Western world, together with some internal conditions in Soviet society. In the USSR he was a typical writer of the Right. He was a writer for the magazine *October*. He's still a writer of the Right. He automatically changed camps, just as the KGB defectors change camps to the CIA. It's natural. He's just a malcontent – because he was dissatisfied with his personal position in the Soviet hierarchy. It has nothing to do with the political structure and it seems to me that most of the dissidents are in the same position. The ageing writer suddenly discovers that he is not satisfied with his achievements. We are not talking about the influence of Soviet internal policies on writers.

I never felt strongly that I belonged to any nation, even to Russia. I never wanted to go to America. Even in Russia I had advised the friend who had invented my name that he should not go to America. I said, 'Go to America only if you have no other possibility. Otherwise stay away from that country.' I remember my image of the United States. I was a bit afraid of the country. I remember Konstantin Leontiev's[2] philippics against the bourgeois of the world, and I thought about the United States as a country where the bourgeois is on top, and I have never had a good relationship with that social class.

I didn't want to go to the United States, but I had no choice. When I was in Vienna, I applied for a visa for England . . . I didn't want to leave Europe. I decided on England because I had some friends there who wanted to give me an invitation, but to get a visa I would have had to wait at least six months. In Vienna I needed to receive some sort of Austrian temporary document. I had no documents; everybody who leaves the USSR has none. I was waiting there with my wife – I had been married in the USSR – and she was very scared of Vienna in November. It was very rainy, cold and empty, and not very friendly, so we decided to go to Rome and to forget the idea of going to England. In Rome we had a choice of only the United States or Canada. We felt it was better to go to New York than the forests of Canada . . .

In Vienna we had been supported by the Tolstoy Foundation, as is usual for émigrés, [and it was through them that we went to New York]. I had a very awkward relationship with them, and I didn't like the personalities of the people, because they were so far away from me. I found them very peculiar and strange; they were all half Russians, never actually very well adapted into American society. Some of them were Americans, Irish and so on – the scum of society, or what one might call losers. They have a circle of interests that are completely strange to me; they have very old-fashioned habits. I read about such people in Soviet books – they belong to the nineteenth century in my opinion. But objectively, they did something for me.

From another point of view, the Tolstoy Foundation was responsible for all the American propaganda taking people out of the Soviet Union. I even think that one day some bright émigré will go and sue, if not the United States, then one of the organizations like Radio Liberty, or Voice of America, or Radio Free Europe, to show the damage they did to his life, because a lot of people would actually be better off in the Soviet Union. All those material losses, like losing their place in Soviet society, and the hardship of finding a place in the new society . . . maybe one day someone will be able to prove it. Anyway, the Tolstoy Foundation paid for that propaganda. If you push the people out of their own country, then you have to pay.

I remember, for example, in 1968 at the time of the invasion of Czechoslovakia, I'd been listening to Western Russian-language broadcasting, and all the time they would be relaying the news of the invasion of Czechoslovakia in every possible detail. At the same time there was the Vietnam War, and there was no information about that. There was some information in the Soviet press, but traditionally we didn't believe it. That is the difference between the United States and the Soviet Union: the people there traditionally don't believe official information, and believe all the nonsense they hear on the foreign radio . . . The picture of the world is completely distorted by Radio Liberty – like the émigré newspapers, for example *Russkaya Mysl'*, which was paid for until 1975 by the CIA and is now funded by the State Department. What can you expect from such newspapers? They are very happy about how Soviet soldiers are killed in Afghanistan, they are happy about every major or small disaster in the Soviet newspapers. They are not only anti-Soviet, but also anti-Russian.

[My first job in America was as] a proofreader on a Russian émigré newspaper – *Novoe Russkoe Slovo*. All Russian émigré newspapers look alike, and sooner or later, no matter how they start, they become stupidly conservative, with not even rightist views, and every dark superstition available. They are newspapers for butchers, or back-woodsmen. I don't know any other nation that is able to produce such a press. [There was a weekly called *Novy Amerikanets*] – even in its best days it was kind of 'hurrah-patriotic' and to the taste of a provincial Jewish émigré who had settled down in Brighton Beach. The strong desire to sell the newspaper made the owners and the journalists look alike; instead of trying to develop higher standards for the paper, they chose to give the people what they want now. It is even worse [than local papers], because the Western newspapers somehow belong to the population; but the émigrés are not a population but a group, and everything is more hermetic, more closed. The pressures of a free society upon journalism are ten times bigger for émigrés. If you look at American patriotism, natural patriotism, that is one thing; they can accept a certain kind of criticism, some ironic views – even the *New York Post* can do it. But the Russian newspapers cannot do it. Everything is stonily serious. I don't read them, and said goodbye a long time ago to that kind of life.

In 1977, I left the hotel where I lived with some Russian friends, and after that I never really went back to them. It happened because it happened – I've no idea of the reason. I was so outraged with that existence. I never wanted to be an émigré – I wanted to be the same as everyone else. The only difference was that I didn't know the language very well. Some of my views were more interesting than other American writers, some were absolutely the same. I didn't see any difference between me and the outside world. I did see great differences between me and the Russian émigré community. In emigration, I found myself surrounded by people to whom in Moscow I would not even talk; I would have nothing to do with people like that. I had belonged to a very closed counter-culture in Moscow – a few thousand people living their special life together, quite different from Soviet society . . .

I feel no desire to return to the Soviet Union. That is my past. My criticism of Western society is absolutely forgivable for the person who lives here – there is nothing special about it. I cannot publish my books in the Soviet Union, and with great difficulty I have published my books in the United States. But that is not the same for 265 million people, because they do not all want to publish books. They go to work every day and spend eight hours a day at work. I do not see that on the level of working-class people there is such a difference between societies; it's only a problem of material difference. I always despise the material things . . .

Americans call their society 'democratic' and 'the free world'. It sounds as vulgar to me as the Soviet society that calls itself 'the dream of mankind' and all that vulgar shit. If it is really a free world, why should you talk about it? It's for stupid people. The unfair election is the same in the Soviet Union as in the United States, except that in the Soviet Union it's one candidate and in the United States, it's two. Look at that Democratic primary, for example, in the United States. All the candidates are not less than senators, except poor Jesse Jackson, and he will never win as everybody knows. That society's more predictable than the Soviet.

I am not desperately anti-American – not at all. I judge the country on a very personal level, and on another level, from my analysis of their society from what I saw. I didn't see it from a good window of the *Hotel Americana* as Solzhenitsyn saw it. I saw it from the point of view of an underprivileged member of that society. From what I remember from my welfare days, from my endless waiting for my turn in welfare centres, and later, when I refused welfare and worked as a painter, as a digger and received $3 an hour where Americans received $10 – I see that society as very hypocritical and nasty in its own way, and very dangerous as well . . .

Limonov came to France in 1980 and now lives and writes in Paris.

58

Censored

ZHORES ALEXANDROVICH MEDVEDEV

Zhores Alexandrovich Medvedev was born in 1925 in Tbilisi and became a senior biochemist and geneticist in the Soviet Union. In the 1960s he fell foul of the Soviet authorities for publishing work critical of the biologist Trofim Lysenko,[1] whose ideas had flourished under Stalin, and he emigrated to England in 1973. He now works at the National Institute of Medical Research in London.

I had published some very critical articles about Lysenko [in the early 1960s], but you realize that you have much more to say, so it slowly develops into a book. One version is circulated, then a second – the *samizdat* process gives you a lot of additional material, because people write you letters, give you documents and so on . . .

For [my brother] Roy, who is a historian, the Khrushchev era was very positive – deStalinization, relaxation – and he was encouraged. For me, it was the other way round, because Khrushchev continued to support Lysenko and did it every time he made a speech – he would tell scientists to support Lysenko, and he continued the repression of biologists who were anti-Lysenko. Khrushchev didn't tolerate people who he considered were against his policies, and his agricultural policy was very closely associated with Lysenko's ideas.

I was against many of Khrushchev's measures, because in agriculture he did a lot of bad things. At the very beginning he did a lot of good things, but in about 1958 he started to change the agricultural institutions in a very radical and negative way, and it was not long, as there were many anti-Lysenko professors who felt able to express their views openly, before a very bitter struggle started between Lysenko and his opponents with Khrushchev on Lysenko's side. Finally, he got so angry that he ordered the Agricultural Academy, where I was senior research scientist, to be closed. He made a personal decision to stop the enrolment of students, and the Academy was dying out from 1960 onwards. When Khrushchev was dismissed, there were only the fifth-year students left there, and scientists and professors were leaving and finding positions elsewhere. So we were quite bitter about Khrushchev because we could see that he was making a lot of errors in agricultural policy, and trouble for agricultural scientists and biologists. Biology was not very well developed, because Khrushchev interfered directly, much more so than Stalin. Stalin didn't consider himself an expert in agricultural science and biology, but Khrushchev did. Stalin's interference was more in political sciences, economy, etc.

For Roy, for example, the Khrushchev era did provide the possibility for an open analysis of Stalin's crimes. He was able to approach everybody with the first version of his book, to work officially, and to send it to the Party Central Committee for someone to read. When Khrushchev was dismissed, it was a setback for Roy because attempts to rehabilitate Stalin started, and his work and analysis of Stalin's crimes had to go underground.

In my case, Khrushchev's fall was Lysenko's fall. Classical genetics became popular and the Government started to make a lot of moves to rehabilitate genetics, to develop its study and to invest a lot of money in the building of new laboratories for genetics, molecular biology and so on. We, as geneticists in the 1960s, felt quite happy.

The problem was that my book on Lysenko was already written, and available, and the new regime was against Lysenko but was not against censorship and it didn't encourage publication abroad of any book critical of Stalin's or Khrushchev's or Lysenko's time. So, in spite of the fact that Lysenko was discredited, and my book did not oppose official policy, it was not yet of the kind that would be acceptable for official publication within the Soviet Union.

[The book's publication was therefore, to a certain extent, a turning-point.] When it had been published, there was a special commission to find out how it had happened and why I had done it. When they found out that I had done it deliberately, they dismissed me.

I had some money from the book [so I was able to live]. To attract foreign currency, Kosygin and Brezhnev had introduced a special system of so-called certificates – relatives, friends and children could send money from abroad, and you would receive currency coupons. The system was open to everybody, so I could ask my translator, who was my trustee as well, to send me, for instance $500, and I could go and get a certificate to shop in *Beryozka*,[2] which quite a lot of people like Solzhenitsyn did as well – though the contradiction was that these shops were created for the relatives of people who had someone abroad, and for privileged people who had some foreign currency. Some dissidents did also use the facilities – it was absolutely legal. This finished only in 1976 – it no longer exists. They introduced a law that possession of foreign currency by a Soviet citizen is illegal. They will not exchange foreign currency unless you produce documents to say that you earned this currency through an official job.

I was able to get some money, and my wife continued to work, so we did manage to live more or less normally. I continued to write – I wrote two more books, about censorship and the interception of correspondence. They were published by Macmillan [here in London] when I was still in the Soviet Union.

I was taken to a mental hospital for a while, and was then released, in 1970. Then they had the problem of whether to give me a job or to let me continue this freelance writing. I think a local official decided it would be better to give me a job. In Russia there is a law that if you refuse a job you are considered a parasite, but they can use this law only if someone deliberately refuses to accept a nomination or appointment which is offered, not on a person who is unemployed. I was threatened several times that if I didn't find a job . . . they probably wanted me to move somewhere. I used to answer that I couldn't move my wife, who was working, and my children who were at school. If they would give me some job, I would be quite happy. By law, they can't give you a job that is not of your professional status. They didn't want to restore me to the same institute and the same position, so they offered me a job at a smaller institute, also as a biochemist, a senior scientist, and I worked for two years before I left for Britain [in 1973].

[I began to gather information on the Urals nuclear disaster] for publication in a *New Scientist* article in 1976. I mentioned this as an episode in the history of Russian nuclear science and, because it was treated as fiction, I started to analyse and to get more material. I got all the necessary information while I was here [in Britain]. I knew that it had happened, I knew certain details, I knew where to find information about it – in quite open sources . . .

59

Speaking the Truth

LEONID VLADIMIROVICH FINKELSTEIN

Leonid Vladimirovich Finkelstein, a writer and journalist, defected in London in 1966.

After the war I got a job teaching at the Aeronautics Institute. One day I happened to mention to someone at the Institute that I found it strange that anti-Semitism, against which we had fought the war, was now growing in the USSR. He went straight off and denounced me. At that time, however (1947), it was necessary to have two witnesses. All the same, I was imprisoned and interrogated about my contacts. They tried to get me to write down that I had tried to organize a small cell of resistance to anti-Semitism at the Institute. I realized it was unwise to put down anything about organized cells, and resisted firmly. When the case came before the judge, he found that there were insufficient grounds for finding me guilty and ordered a new investigation. This gave me hope, but my lawyer said I had little chance of getting off. In fact, they dragged up all sorts of slanderous nonsense and sentenced me to seven years, under Article 58 of the Criminal Code.

The first camp I was sent to was a horrible place. You can't find it on any map. It was called SUBR – an acronym for North Urals Bauxite Mines. It was utterly cut off from the rest of humanity. Every day someone would fail to wake up from their sleep; they died like flies. But I was lucky. I had a marvellous section leader – Ivan. He had a brigade of three hundred or so. We used to be underground, hacking away at the granite with picks while the guards with their dogs and guns would stay above ground – they wouldn't take such risks themselves. Ivan was appointed in the place of a section leader who had been stabbed to death with a pick. He had enormous physical strength, but at the same time was very kind. Because of his strength, he was nicknamed Ivan-the-Forehead. He treated me very well. At the bottom of the cavern he had a small cubby-hole, with a permanently glowing stove; twice a day he used to call me and let me warm myself by the fire. That was living!

I was losing so much weight there that I probably wouldn't have survived had it not happened that, in response to a complaint by me, someone from the Chief Procurator's office decided to suppress my complaint by transferring me to Moscow. There I was confined to an ordinary prison, which – though it was heaven in comparison with that camp – was still pretty awful: people living crammed together, riddled with lice, terrible heat instead of terrible cold.

From there I was transferred to a much better prison – a Work Colony of the MVD of the Moscow Region. It was not a *sharashka*[1] as described by Solzhenitsyn in *The First Circle*, or a camp; it was a colony – a place where the inmates had both their living quarters and their work. It was right in the centre of Moscow, so you can imagine that conditions were unimaginably better than in the other camp. We made leather and rubber gaskets for all sorts of mechanical equipment; we were the only place to produce these in the whole Soviet Union – we had the monopoly. For example, the railways depended on these little leather sleeves. This little factory was crucial to the smooth running of Soviet industry – if it had stopped production, so would the entire USSR. There were six or seven hundred prisoners in this 'hard-labour-regime' prison; the conditions were not bad.

Our beloved Stalin died on 6 March 1953; on 8 April I was released. I reapplied to the same Institute to finish off my higher education, but – even though it was written in plain Russian on my discharge papers that I was 'not found guilty' – they would not accept me. I tried to make a fuss about it with the Minister of Higher Education but that didn't help. Finally I was given a place at the Auto-Mechanical Institute. When I graduated after two years (in 1955), I was sent to work as the foreman at the Innovators' Workshop of Automobile Production, now called the Leninist Komsomol Car Factory, where they manufacture the Moskvich. I did not work there for long, but went and became the deputy manager of a daily newspaper. (Since childhood I had been a freelance journalist; as a child I had been a correspondent for *Pioneer Pravda*.) From there I moved on to various other papers and journals: *Family and School*, *Knowledge is Strength*; I wrote three books – popular science books.

I had no thoughts of leaving the country until one day I saw a newspaper article about Soviet tourists going to Poland. I realized that soon there would be tourism to other countries too. By this stage I realized that I had to get out of the country. I understood the regime too well, and every time I smelt its air I felt as though I were inhaling poison. I could not stand the atmosphere any more, even under Khrushchev. I knew from my father's stories, from newspapers and books, that in the West it was different.

I did not know how to set about it. The one thing I could not do was join the Party. On many occasions they tried to draw me into it; first of all on the first newspaper I worked in – they said it was, after all, Party work and would I like to join? Then later at *Moscow Pravda* the Party organizer Malkov tried to persuade me . . .

In 1965 the Journalists' Union organized a tour of France by car. I applied. I had written on my form 'imprisoned but not guilty'. When my application form was read, I was called to the KGB. I explained myself, but they were dissatisfied. 'OK,' I said, 'so I'll go to the Black Sea. What do I need to go to France for?' I realized that my best tactic was to appear nonchalant, even though inside I was terribly upset. 'Next time', they said, 'write the truth!' 'If there is a next time . . . ' I joked. And, believe it or not, the next time the KGB phoned me up and said, 'There's a trip to England. Come and fill out an application.' My application – filled out properly this time, with all the details of my trial and imprisonment – was passed by everyone and I ended up going to England, leaving behind my wife and son.

It was a delightful group: very nice people, a privileged party travelling around England and Scotland. I decided to bide my time and wait until the penultimate day. It turned out that this day was set aside for shopping on our own; we had each been given the princely sum of £6.11s to spend – that was a lot in those days.

That day (28 June 1966) I waited outside our hotel, the Embassy in Bayswater Road, and observed everyone from the group leaving. The last person to leave was our 'escort' from the KGB. They were all going off to Oxford Street. I realized that I was free. I went to Charing Cross Station and put my suitcase in the Left Luggage, and was suddenly filled with the strangest sensation: my boats were burned.

I took my time, slowly drinking a Coca-Cola in Lyons Corner House, and then walked to the Home Office opposite the Cenotaph and came out with my prepared speech: 'I am a Soviet journalist seeking political asylum in this country.' Nobody reacted. They looked puzzled, and then gave me a card showing me the 76 bus route to Princes House, Holborn. I went out again, got on the bus, found Princes House, tried out my phrase again, and this time it worked.

Then I set about trying to get them to release my wife. Kosygin was about to visit Britain, so I wrote a letter that was published in thirty-eight newspapers all over the world asking for them to let her out. And they did. But the KGB got their own back. In the two months it took to organize her departure, they worked her over to such an extent that she was not herself when she eventually did get to the West. She was unable to settle down, and took advantage of a three-day absence on my part to go with our son to the Soviet Embassy and to be repatriated. Back in Moscow, she published a small interview in which she said she was unable to live in the capitalist world. In 1975 she emigrated to Israel and I managed to remake contact with my son. Now he has graduated from Harvard Business School and works in California.

Perhaps because I had no high hopes or illusions about conquering the world, life here did not let me down. It was easy right from the start. And in fact it turned out that a Russian-speaking journalist was extremely marketable . . . When I arrived I first wrote some articles for the *Sunday Telegraph*, then got a contract for a book. First I was put up in a 'safe house' by the British counter-intelligence; then, when I made my first money, they helped me find a small room near Earls Court. When my wife and son came, I moved into a larger flat; when they went, I left this flat. Finally, after some difficulties and hardships, I began to work for Radio Liberty in the United States on 1 October 1967. For ten years I worked for them, first as London correspondent, then as director of the London office of Radio Liberty. Then I moved to Munich.

Despite my broadcasting on political subjects, I had no great problems from the Soviets. As everyone does, I received a summons from the KGB, but it does not mean anything. I realized I was not the sort of person to be hunted by them; there are many more important people higher up on their list! In fact, speaking out strongly on political matters actually helped me; it is in their nature to respect only strength and plain speaking and to have contempt for the weak. If you speak out, they respect you for it; otherwise, they destroy you. I decided that I was not going to spend my life hiding. One day I was giving a lecture at an Institute of Higher Education; I was being heckled by some members of the Communist Party of Great Britain. Afterwards one of them came up and asked me why I was living so openly – didn't I know that people like me were often killed in the West by Communists? I told him, as I tell everyone, that I did not come here to hide away; that if they're going to kill me, let them. In the meantime, I'm going to speak out.

60

A Gold Medal Student

VLADIMIR VIKTOROVICH GOLDBERG

Vladimir Viktorovich Goldberg, a brilliant mathematician, suffered constant discrimination in the Soviet Union because of his Jewishness. He emigrated with his family to the United States in 1978, where he quickly found a job teaching at Leigh High University in Bethlehem, Pennsylvania.

[I was born in 1936 in Moscow and finished school there] in 1953, a couple of months after the death of Stalin. I was always conscious of the fact that I was Jewish – people are constantly reminding you. Children, primarily children . . . you look different from other people.

On the other hand, I was always the top pupil in the class. It was always I who had the honour certificates. The other children were indebted to me because I had explained something to them or they had cribbed something from me. The teachers were fond of me. On the whole, the teacher never made you aware of whether you were Jewish or not, even if he was a latent anti-Semite . . . in any case in those years I never came across a single teacher who was a Jew-hater.

When I finished school with the gold medal [for mathematics], which exempted you from university entrance exams, in my naïveté I didn't understand that such paths were to all intents and purposes closed for Jews. I naïvely thought that with my gold medal I could go where I wanted to. One had to pass the interview, and I of course applied to Moscow University for maths. My teacher went with me; he stood in the corridor. When I came out he asked me all the questions which had been put to me and what answers I had given. He noted everything down and said that I had answered all the maths questions correctly. There could be no doubts whatsoever. However, I was told that I was rejected because there were insufficient places. To put it bluntly, I was knocked off my feet as I thought that this was the only place worth going to.

I tried to take advantage of the fact that I had this gold medal. I tried to get into this or that institute by interview, but I was rejected, despite the fact that I seemed to have passed the interview. In the end it accidentally ended up all right, because I went to study maths not at the University but at the next best thing – the Teacher Training Institute. And it just so happened that the same professors were working there as at the University.

But this was 1953 and it was no joke. Life was taken seriously and not lightly as it had been at school. I did then feel Jewish, when I couldn't get into the University, or the energy institute, or the institute where I ended up working for fifteen or twenty years because I couldn't get through the interview. I had the gold medal, this little piece of gold, but it didn't help in the least.

Somehow or other it never got to me, although at seventeen or eighteen I did begin to experience it more and more. I saw how my father had to change jobs and go around his acquaintances to find work. He had got to hear that something was going on, the MVD was ready for action – it was the time of the 'Doctors' Plot'.[1] Relatives were coming to see us from Baku and the passport regulations were being very strictly observed. We had two small rooms and they wanted to come and spend the night at our place as they had done before. Father said that at any other time that would have been fine, but not now. They would have to go to the police and register. They were offended, and they couldn't understand what was happening. Only later did I realize just how far-sighted he had been and that he had found sources from whom he had learnt that at that time it would have been dangerous. We could have been arrested and the whole flat, all the relatives, sent out of town, because Stalin was preparing to deport *all* the Jews to the east. Everyone was getting ready to be deported to Birobijan or somewhere.

You had to go where you were sent for three years, and then you could work where you wanted to. And when those three years were up we came to the time of the so-called Khrushchev 'thaw'. I managed to get work at one of the technical institutes in Moscow. With all that had been happening, in so far as Jews were concerned, we then had what we call the status quo – that is to say that if you were working anywhere, then you carried on working, generally without any chance of significant improvement. There was a definite ceiling which could stop you getting higher than an assistant professor. There were distinct limits beyond which you couldn't go.

So I became an assistant professor, and as well as that I started getting ready to submit my doctorate, which is the second dissertation in the Soviet Union. I presented it to the department and they accepted it, but I was unable to submit.

So that was just one incident. Later on there was another. This was in the beginning of 1972, my last year at work. There was a sense in which you constantly felt exposed. Many had left, gone to Israel. Many of my friends emigrated in 1971 and 1972, when people had only just started to emigrate. And we got news from them – how they were, how their families were, how they were using their freedom, how they were extending themselves – and I saw that not only would it not get any better for my sons [in the Soviet Union], but that it would probably be worse. I kept on trying to get my wife to see that it was time for us to make a move, while there was still some movement, while the gates, if not actually wide open, were still open, while there was still a stream of people going. And this was at a time when the international situation was such that there was still trade and it was still possible to leave. At the outset [my wife was against it and] I myself didn't know how to do it. I saw how other people were doing it and that it really was the most enormous risk, [but] in 1978 we finally decided we were leaving.

[Our standard of living was better than that of most people around us.] My wife was also a mathematician and held the degree of Candidate of Science – the equivalent of a Master's degree. We both earned 320 roubles per month and so had a joint income of 640 and that was just our salary. In addition to that, if I had time I did consultation work at the Institute which would give me another 20 roubles. Also there was a very large number of schoolchildren preparing to get into the Institute; I was considered one of the best tutors or coaches in Moscow and parents begged me. But I didn't like coaching, though when I had to I did it a bit during my postgraduate years. In particular it enabled me to buy a co-operative flat. By Moscow standards we had a beautiful flat, on Vernadsky Prospekt. A house Nixon was to visit. A model house. And when I tell Moscow people that we had two toilets they can hardly believe me. One bathroom, but two toilets; the second toilet just had a washbasin in it. Four rooms and a balcony. We had all this through our acquaintances and because we had money.

[My elder son] went to Moscow University. He was very bright. He went to the special maths school where I had started teaching and others were teaching. He had had the best tutors in Moscow who had coached him specially for the so-called Jewish tasks: special tests given to those Jews who are trying to get into university so that they fail. Harder than the other tests, much harder. Sakharov has written about this; he himself tried to solve several of them. Normally an answer would be expected to take about ten to fifteen minutes, but he would have to go on for hours.

We had made our decision and we wanted to do it in such a way that nobody, and in particular none of our colleagues, would be harmed because we had decided to emigrate. We gave up our jobs – the phrase is: 'At our own request'. It looks like you are doing it because you want to if you say you are looking for another job. I could make it look as if I was offended because I was not getting on, that I was wanting another job which would give me more space. I even got a good reference when I left work. And then we made our application and we tried to enable our son to continue his studies. But despite all our efforts this proved to be impossible, and he had to leave university. They wouldn't give us the certificate which we needed for our application, the certificate which said there were no material claims on him. No matter where we turned we could not do anything about this. In the end, after about a month of struggle, we had to get a move on, because our son was already seventeen and in three months would be eighteen and then it would be the Army. There was about a three- or four-month period of waiting and we thought we could still manage it, we would do it within the limits. But the process we were waiting for then took six months.

I began getting enquiries from the Draft Board and then from the Procurator's office. Our son went off to live in other towns and we said we didn't know where he was. Police came and people from the Draft Board phoned and I went there myself. In the end we were told that we were going to be left in peace, because apparently the Draft Board had recruited the number of people they needed. By that time I had already phoned the person in the Central Committee of the Party responsible for these things, but nothing was done and I felt as if I had been shouting down the drains. At the last moment, when we had already received several calls from the police and were already making plans for my son's military service, we were told by the Draft Board that my [wife and younger son and I] could go but that my elder son had to remain behind as a punishment for evading military service on the pretext of going to Israel. Then we found in our post box at the very last moment the letter giving us permission to go and we got our visas. At the same time we got news through the Procurator's office that they would close the case the moment we left. Even so, there were difficult moments when our son came to the airport.

Probably just as the Abwehr and the Gestapo in Germany became so badly co-ordinated, so in the Soviet Union the MVD and KGB were badly co-ordinated and even quarrelling amongst themselves. Perhaps they are better co-ordinated now, perhaps they act collectively . . .

61

Revaluations

KIRILL USPENSKY

Kirill Uspensky was born in 1915 in Petrograd. His parents were loyal Party members, who in their lives and careers were models of Soviet citizenship. In his early years Uspensky himself accepted Party ideology, but his experience of life brought many questions.

My father was a second-generation member of the intelligentsia; his grandfather, my great-grandfather was a village sexton, which is evident from my surname, Uspensky – it is extremely characteristic of the Russian clergy. My great-grandfather was, it seems, only a sexton in the north of Russia, somewhere in the Vologodskaya province, to the north-east of Moscow. Among my more distant relatives was an archbishop: he was Archbishop of Alaska. It seems there is a long line of clergy, of priests, on my father's side. My grandfather – the first member of the intelligentsia, in point of fact – was a doctor, principally an army doctor.

My father [was born in 1884 and] was a graduate of the Law Faculty of Moscow University. During the Moscow Uprising of 1905 he joined the local Bolshevik organization, the RSDRP [and took part in the fighting]. Then in 1907 he left the Party and joined it again after the February Revolution of 1917.

From the beginning of the February Revolution he immediately took a very active part in the trade-union movement; he was one of the organizers of a trade union for office workers . . . After the Revolution he became the head, or one of the main leaders of Vsevobuch, which stands for Universal Military Training. At the beginning of the Polish campaign in 1920 he went to the front as a volunteer and gained quite rapid promotion there. At first he was Commander of the political section of the division, Commissar of the division, then Commander of the political section of the Army; he had that rank when the war ended and he was demobilized and returned to Petrograd.

There he did administrative and managerial work in leading capacities. He was a member of the Board of the Petrograd Chamber of Commerce, then of 'Petrotorg', a kind of wholesale trade organization. Then in 1927 or 1928 he became Director of the Leningrad branch of the Rubber Trust and was sent abroad. I remember that he had many projects to manage; he went first to Paris, then to Stockholm, and finally to Prague as representative of the Rubber Trust for Central Europe. In 1930 the whole family went to join him, and we spent about two years abroad.

He came back from abroad rather unexpectedly, because of some mistake he'd made – not of a criminal nature, but rather some commercial transactions he'd carried out on behalf of the Rubber Trust which weren't approved of in Moscow. He was recalled and as a reprimand was forbidden by the Central Committee to work abroad, and then he was suddenly transferred. Legal specialists were needed at that time – the wave of arrests was beginning; they remembered that he had been trained as a lawyer and there were, as now, not many trained lawyers in the Soviet Union. He became a member of the Leningrad City Court, transferred according to Party policy. Then he became a member of the Special Board of that Court, which dealt with the most serious cases, mainly to do with the notorious Article 58 of the Criminal Code and subsequently was Chairman of this Special Board. Then very soon afterwards, sometime around 1938, he was dismissed, without any reprimands; officially he was dismissed partly due to ill-health, but in fact he was required to leave because the sentences he gave out were too soft. So he became a barrister, one of the most outstanding barristers specializing in cases under Article 58, and he was a barrister practically right up until his death, although during the war he rejoined the Army as a volunteer and was in Leningrad for the first year and a half [of the siege]; then he left, taking my mother with him, and thanks to that they survived.

My mother, whose maiden name was Kostrinskaya, was half Polish, and that is where my literary pseudonym, Kostrinsky, comes from. I have written under this pseudonym right from the beginning of my literary career. She became an actress, a very talented one, and worked in such famous theatres as the Izlobin company in St Petersburg and

Moscow, but when she had her first child, my elder brother, she gave up the stage.

She joined the Party at the beginning of the Revolution, and then did administrative work, mainly in the Theatre Department. For a number of years she was the Deputy Director of the Leningrad Choreographic School, which has produced the best dancers in Russia and the Soviet Union. She was practically the only Party member there, and effectively the Commissar of the School. She then left, not entirely of her own free will – partly as the consequence of some kind of Party purge; as she was a former member of the gentry, someone thought this was inappropriate, and consequently after that she worked on trade-union affairs, mainly in theatres. She was President of the local trade-union committee of the Kirov Theatre.

My parents both had positions of responsibility, so neither of them had any time to devote to my brother and me. I grew up a hooligan – a fully fledged street gangster. But I was attracted by the Army, like all ne'er-do-wells, by the romance of the uniform, the thunder of battle, the military bands and so on, and this fact saved me from a life as a professional criminal.

I don't know how the Army affects other people, but on me it had an extremely beneficial effect. I graduated from the Military College; at the same time I had been studying at evening classes at Leningrad University, in the Department of Philology. I became an officer, somewhere in Kherson, commander of a platoon and of a half-company. My first baptism of fire was the 'liberation' campaign in Poland. I wasn't aware of it then at first, but I was present at the so-called dispossession of the kulaks. Moreover the Soviet authorities dispossessed them immediately, as soon as they had marched into eastern Poland – and not even the kulaks as such, not the prosperous peasants, but small landowners in the southern part of central Poland, in the region of Krasny, to the south-east of Lvov. Without being aware at the time of what was going on I saw how the participants, mainly Soviet officers and political workers, accompanied by timid local peasants who were present but didn't want to take part in this, filled their pockets with everything they saw which had any value; how we were all stunned by the abundance in this already devastated part of Poland; how we crowded into the shops and stocked up with suits and lengths of lousy material; how it all seemed to us to be a land of unheard-of luxury.

Then I returned with the regiment to Vinnitsa in southern Russia, in the Ukraine.

When I came across ideological dogma, Party policy or Party propaganda, I always asked myself, and very often other people, a lot of questions. In particular, I was extremely troubled by the 'Great Trials', the Purges, and I was perplexed about how they could have come about . . .

A friendship had formed between Bukharin[1] and my father which gradually became less and less close, but every time he came to Leningrad up to 1934 Bukharin paid us a visit and he once stayed the night. The last time I saw him I was already at the Military School; I came home on leave and found Bukharin there. And it is interesting that the next time I came home on leave, a week later, my mother was talking to my father about some general political events, and said a memorable sentence about Bukharin which has been engraved on my memory all my life, and which strengthened to a considerable extent what was, if not yet scepticism, at any rate my desire to seek answers to some complex questions. Her sentence went something like: 'If Nikolay Ivanovich is correct then *he* really is mentally abnormal – he is obviously paranoid.' And it was obvious from the context that she meant Stalin.

A few years later, in 1938, I recalled [her words] when I was arrested for the first time and accused of some utterly inconceivable crimes. I was accused of working for the Polish intelligence service and for the Romanian intelligence service – the Siguranţa – and, of course, for the Gestapo. I was in the Komsomol [at the time. I spent a month and a half in prison, then] I was released on the grounds of having been wrongly arrested, and due to a lack of sufficiently well-founded charges. But while I was there, I saw how they beat people up; they also beat me up and knocked out some of my teeth and broke some ribs. I started to write letters to Stalin. The correspondence was of a rather one-sided nature: I wrote to him, but he didn't reply to me!

While this was going on I entered the Frunze Military Academy, from which I graduated in an accelerated course lasting two and a half years in 1942, and went to the front near Stalingrad. Incidentally, when I graduated I could already speak English fairly well, and since I had passed out with distinction I was selected as a kind of official in the Soviet Embassy in the United States. But at that time I was burning with the desire to give to the Motherland everything I could as a soldier, officer, or intelligence officer, and after a rather long struggle lasting a month I managed to get them to send me to the front and I didn't go abroad. I probably did the right thing, because all my colleagues at the Academy who went abroad came to a bad end; they either died in the camps or they were shot. I spent the whole of the rest of the war at the front.

I became a candidate member of the Party during the war, in 1941, a member in 1942 and was expelled in 1943. I joined the Party fully consciously and for ideological reasons; at that time it was for me the only acceptable and just way.

Until my expulsion from the Party, I served in the Army intelligence departments. After my expulsion, I was expecting to be arrested, because I was accused of professing anti-Party, pro-Fascist opinions – but I was not arrested. The only explanation I can find for this is that Army Intelligence in general worked in close collaboration with the organs of *Smersh*, the counter-espionage organization. We constantly exchanged information; if I got hold of information that was of interest to counter-espionage I quickly passed it on to them, and if they got information which was of military operational interest they passed it on to me. I was commander of the Information Department, which dealt with the gathering, processing and analysis of all intelligence about the enemy; consequently all operational intelligence from any source came to me. So I was on personal terms with the *Smersh* officers, and I was told later, when I met one of them, that the Political Department of the Army had insisted that I be arrested but that the head of the Army *Smersh*, when he received the document containing the recommendation that I be arrested, looked carefully at it and said, 'Not only do I think that there are no grounds for arresting him, there was also no reason for expelling him from the Party.'

The pretext and, incidentally, the subject of my anti-Party opinions was threefold. It had been suggested to me that I give a political paper. I refused to do so, since I was snowed under with routine work and I replied that my duty was to the Army, that it was to gather and process intelligence about the enemy and give a report on it in due course to my commander. In the end they put more and more pressure on me and I agreed to give a supplementary paper. I expressed the opinion that the standpoint of the Communist Parties of France and Britain was deeply misguided, as the result of the mechanical application of Lenin's directives to the Bolsheviks during the First World War. I then expressed the opinion that, as we moved towards victory together with our Allies, we should not forget about American expansionism, nor about British imperialism, and that after the war conflict was inevitable between us and our Allies; which was absolutely correct, and would be correct today if it hadn't been for nuclear weapons. And the third opinion I expressed was the idea that the disbandment of the Comintern did not at all seem, as was said, to be a sign of the maturity of the Communist Party, but was a concession to the Western powers; that in fact, when the war ended, the Comintern would be quickly reformed, which indeed took place under the name of Cominform. All these opinions were considered to be heretical.

[After the war] I went back home to Leningrad, and started to do what I had been striving towards for many years, namely literary work. I published a number of books. I began to write mainly about the war, about the subject that I knew best, and the appraisal of which – or, more precisely, my standpoint – sharply differed from the official directives; consequently I had more and more difficulties with each book. This again provoked in me a whole series of reactions, evaluations and re-valuations of what had happened in the country and in particular on the so-called ideological front. Gradually this led to my being compelled to start to write, around the middle of the 1950s, a big war novel. Due to the moderate liberalization that occurred after the Twentieth Party Congress in 1956,[2] I had some hope that in time my novel would be published, that in time the conditions of suppression which had always existed up to then would become easier. Meanwhile, in order to main-tain myself and my family on a decent level, I started to do translations, and my most active and, from a financial point of view, productive, work was translations from Azerbaydzhani, which I didn't know; I worked from crude literal translations. From time to time I also trans-lated a certain number of stories by Hemingway, Saroyan, Robert Penn Warren.

But it somehow came about, with my open attitude of opposition, in particular in the literary and ideological sphere, and with my sharply negative and unconcealed attitude of indignation towards Soviet con-duct in Budapest, and my sympathy towards Imre Nagy[3] and that Hungarian liberal grouping, that young literary and artistic people started to group around me. As a result a sort of literary salon formed in my home, where young writers and artists constantly met – and evidently informers now and again. Finally, in the summer of 1960, I returned from Moscow and discovered that a search had been made of my home. A few days after this, after being interrogated almost every day, I was arrested. From the nature of the questioning, I established that for three years I had already been followed intensively, my telephone had been bugged, my mail had been read, so that in the terminology of the KGB I had been 'under a bell-glass' – under constant observation.

I was kept in prison for a long time awaiting trial. When my defence counsel went to Moscow with my appeal, for a long while she was unable to obtain the file, which was in the Central Executive Committee, so for me the Party's involvement in my case was absolutely obvious.

I was tried for claiming that freedom of speech does not exist in the Soviet Union! The situation itself, at least the humorous side of it, did not occur to the judges, nor to the Procurator. The Procurator said: 'What would you, the defendant, have been if it hadn't been for the victory of the October Revolution or Soviet power?'

'What would I have been? Most likely a more successful writer, or, perhaps, an officer, than I have been under the Soviet regime. There could scarcely have been anything worse for me than what has in fact happened in my life.'

I was given five years in a prison camp. I served the time in Mordovia, and there, almost immediately after my arrival in the camp, I started to collect material for the *Dictionary of Non-Standard Russian* that I am now compiling. At the time I didn't think that it would turn into such a gigantic work; I collected at first only thieves' and prison slang out of curiosity, but then I realized that a work of this kind is limitless, that I could also use it as a dictionary of terms used by the KGB, or the Criminal Investigation Department, or the police; but I didn't want to collaborate with them in any way at all. I gradually came to the conclusion that the wider my collection of material was, the more interesting it would be, because it represents a stage in the evolution of a branch of the Russian language, and it is a branch which has an enormous influence on the literary language.

[I compiled entries on cards, which my wife sent to me or which I cut out of paper. It was still quite a liberal time, so when I left the camp in 1964 I brought out, completely legally, fourteen thousand cards.] During my last two years in the camp, thanks to the fact that friendly doctors certified me as an invalid (which was not true) I worked for a time in the library, as assistant to the librarian, and this gave me both time and space [to work on my dictionary]. Then for the last year I taught German and English in the prison school, and there almost all my time was my own because I had only two hours of English per week and two hours of German, which meant that I could quietly get on with this.

I was lucky, in that I didn't serve out the entire five years. Thanks to the intervention of a great many writers, in the first instance Ilya Ehrenburg, and also Yury Dombrovskiy, I came out of prison almost a year early.

From about the beginning of the 1970s, I managed to get an official job. This was periodic work dubbing films, both foreign and films from non-Russian Soviet republics: Estonian, Azerbaydzhani, Turkmen. But at that time, whereas before I was arrested I had taken part in discussions, in a circle of mainly close friends, after my release I was not afraid of being arrested: of course I didn't want to be arrested and imprisoned – I didn't want to go back there at all – but nevertheless I started to take some part in the Human Rights Movement, probably because I had been arrested at the same time as Alex Ginzburg,[4] and Ginzburg had refused to give any evidence against me. So I gave evidence which characterized him as a completely loyal Soviet citizen; he had been arrested and charged with the publication of *Sintaksis*, an uncensored poetry magazine: what is criminal in that? Later we became good friends. Thanks to him and to my acquaintance with him I somehow immediately became part of the dissident movement at a very high level. I am closely acquainted with Grigorenko. I have visited Sakharov's home several times; I know Yury Orlov very well, Tolya Shcharansky less well; I know Sasha Podrabinek well, and Father Gleb Yakunin. I took part in the movement in minor roles: I signed some protest letters, I translated from Russian into English several times at press conferences. I collected money for people in prison and for the Solzhenitsyn Fund. On several occasions during these years the KGB called me in, and each time I refused to make any statement, or gave statements which clearly didn't suit them, then gradually refused to make any kind of statement.

I thought about emigration for a long time, usually deciding against it, because Russia was my country: I loved it, I had fought for it, and even now, several years after my emigration, I consider it to be my beloved homeland. But despite this, the cause of my emigration was twofold. Firstly, and mainly, I was involved in the very hard and, from my point of view, very important, work on my dictionary, which had somehow become the goal of my life. And it was in danger, because twice during the last year and a half that I was living in the Soviet Union my apartment was searched, and just by sheer luck they looked into my card files and didn't find anything which might have caught their attention. They considered it to be craziness, stupidity; they didn't come across cards containing what they would have considered obviously anti-Soviet words and expressions, showing the hostile or at any rate ironical attitudes of the speakers. Secondly, during these last years I was harassed by the KGB. Several times during my last interviews and talks with them they hinted that if I continued to behave in this way I would end up in prison and somewhere in the east. 'The east' is a euphemism for exile or a camp. About two and a half months before my actual emigration I was all of a sudden attacked on the street by three hoodlums pretending to be drunk and smelling of alcohol; it was evidently only a pretence, [but] these guys were KGB-instigated provocateurs. I took it seriously and I decided that I had to get out of the country.

The difficulty was that I wasn't a Jew; nevertheless, I decided to try my luck pretending that I was. I had a so-called invitation from Israel, through some Jewish activists in Moscow; it was signed, or forged, in the name of my presumed relative, and I used it pretending that my mother was a Jew. But then they demanded some kind of confirmation that she was a Jew, and I managed to play a trick. My mother was born in Kharkov, but when she was two years old her family had moved to Sevastopol, so I asked the local Sevastopol register office to send me her birth certificate; I did it because Sevastopol had been completely ruined and all the archives had disappeared in the war. I received a paper stating that no records about the year 1884 were available. When I went to the Visa and Registration Department (OVIR) with these documents they said, 'But there is nothing stating that your mother was a Jew.' – 'But at the same time it doesn't say that she wasn't.' For some time they refused to accept my application, but after some insistence they evidently decided to ask the opinion of the local KGB. And all of a sudden, after several days or maybe a week, I got a phone call from some lady at OVIR saying that I could surrender my documents. So I did, and in ten days I received permission to leave the country. In June 1978, to the delight of the KGB, no doubt, and to my own, I happily left.

[I spent a year in Vienna.] There, for the first time I was able to get a lot of my work published, about the Revolution and the war, and I was able to get hundreds and hundreds of new words and expressions to add to my card file. I received some very modest, but still sufficient, help from the Tolstoy Foundation. [I also lectured in Austrian and West German universities. Then I got an invitation to come to Harvard, where I have a grant for my work on my dictionary. So, because I have been able to continue my work, in a way there hasn't been so much of a break in my life as there has been for some émigrés, for whom the change from the Soviet Union to the West is rather traumatic.]

I hope that when I have finished my dictionary I will be able to return to my literary work. I will hardly be able to finish any big, serious work, but I think that I will write my memoirs, which should be of some interest, because I have lived a long life and had a lot of very interesting encounters . . .

Afterword

Emigration from Russia under Gorbachev is now far easier than it was in the past. The problem now is whether the West *can* take in the hundreds of thousands of Russians who wish to leave. At the moment of writing – October 1989 – there is a rush. Steadily, by arrangement with the German and American Governments, virtually anyone who can claim asylum in Germany, the United States or Israel can go, and at Sheremetyevo airport you can see them: people brought up from the far depths of the Soviet Union by train, on endless, exhausting journeys, with their rather pathetic belongings, able now to join large communities abroad – Germans, Armenians, Jews. After these journeys, the men lie, stretched out, exhausted, on huge kit-bags which they have lugged. The women and children are exhausted, too, though less dramatically. The ones guarding everything are the old women: hunched, dressed in black, their heads in their hands, wondering what happens next. After a wait, they are all safely in the West or in Israel, where they settle down, armed with sufficient funds for a new life, and with the social-security arrangements of the non-Communist world to take care of them in case of misfortune.

In other words, no story. These emigrants from Russia simply join the enormous flood of emigrants into Western Europe since 1945. They buckle to, and settle down, the only memory of the past being occasional meetings of emigrants who have in common only the experience of emigration. There are virtually none of the great dramas of the past – those escapes through Bolshevik guards, across snow, to a hostile world in which they have to find their friends, sell their diamonds at a good price, and work out whether they want their children to be Russian or foreign. It was noticeable, in our interviews, that the emigrants of the 1920s went through a tremendous and testing drama, whereas, with the emigrants of the later 1970s, experiences were much more prosaic, even if nasty.

Efforts have been made to record the memories of Russia of these recent emigrants, and they should, some day, be recorded in a book of this kind. It is difficult. The technical problems of interview, transcription of interview, and editing of transcript are formidable, and we are not surprised that ours is the first such book to appear. The difficulties of 'oral history' are immense, especially when you concern yourself with checking – which, in so many cases, it is impossible to do. People tell their stories, some interesting, some not. Can you tell what is true or not? Here, we have made no effort to do so, and have treated these stories as a source – to be criticized as required. We have selected and severely edited sources as they strike us as likely to be accurate. The sample of records that appears here is only a tiny proportion of what might be done, but we know that it is a representative sample, and wish our successors well.

Will there be another Russian emigration – as it were, a fourth wave? The first three waves have nothing in common, beyond hatred of Communism. The first wave consisted of those people who knew that Communism would be the end of the great promise that Tsarist Russia represented in its last days. There is a haunting presence to the world of St Petersburg in 1914, and if ever you go to the Russian Museum in Leningrad you will see it – here a portrait of Prince Yusupov, fondling a pussy, László- or Sargent-style, next to his father, all military, bemedalled, on a horse; and there a wonderful portrait of the poetess Akhmatova, done to demonstrate that 1920s Russia was, after all, Europe. (A recent book, Michael Ignatieff's *Russian Album*, showed this brilliantly.) St Petersburg is nowadays in poor shape – falling to bits. It threatens to be the ghost-town of modern Europe. Those old palaces are in bad condition, and so are the vast nineteenth-century tenements that followed them. Foreigners who go to the city have to live in ghastly concrete piles, with disagreeable food and silly restrictions. The place is now in deep crisis, with one explosion after another. The arrival of Mr Gorbachev means that these things are recognized, and the Russian press is now the most interesting in Europe.

The memoirs that we record here show another Russia. What *would* have happened if there had not been a First World War? That question haunts Solzhenitsyn, whose father died, in dreadful circumstances, before his birth in 1918. The fact is that the very advance of Russia before 1914 virtually caused Germany to attack her in that year. If Russia had continued to advance at the same rate as in the years from 1908 to 1914, then Germany would not have won the war that everyone foresaw. The Russian Prime Minister Stolypin, whose assassination is recorded in the second chapter of this book, said: 'Give the State twenty years of internal and external peace, and you will not recognize Russia.' She did not have these twenty years, but in 1914 she was very nearly there. By 1917 she would have become a European super-power, capable of taking on the Germans on equal terms. The German Chancellor, Bethmann-Hollweg, said as much to his private secretary on 8 July 1914: 'Russia grows and grows, and weighs upon us like a nightmare.' Therefore, in 1914, Germany attacked, and the promise of Tsarist Russia was destroyed.

The emigrants who talk in this volume are the victims of that. Why did defeat by the Germans mean Bolshevism, Stalinism, and the rest of the story? Therewith you are into the deepest problems of the history of Russia. What is the relationship of Russian past and Soviet present? Our informants are, all of them, victims of that relationship – from Countess Kleinmichel, observing the motions of the Tsarist court, to Nina Voronel, wondering why internationalism went so badly wrong. It is the greatest problem of the modern world. In this collection, we can only lift a corner of the curtain of this immense stage.

Notes

2. The Death of Stolypin

1. A great many people of German origin became established in Russian service in the eighteenth and nineteenth centuries – most, though not all, from the Baltic provinces and many of them related to Prussian *Junker* families (hence 'von'). They were known in Russian, often enough, as *Ostzeyskiye barony*, from the German word for 'Baltic', *Ostsee*. By 1900 there was a strong tendency towards assimilation with Russia and with the Orthodox (as distinct from Lutheran) religion, but it was far from universal. See also Chapter 16, note 1.

2. The use of electricity for domestic lighting spread from the United States to Europe in the late 1880s. The light was very hot.

3. In Russia, as in continental Europe, the usual training for State service was a law degree, requiring several years' arduous study.

4. Russian railways were under State control from the beginning, but there was scope for private lines until 1917.

5. The Davydov family (one branch of which became hyphenated with a branch of the Orlovs) supplied several well-known figures: Denis, leader of the partisans in 1812 against Napoleon (he appears in *War and Peace*) and also a poet; some of the 'Decembrist' officers of 1825, arrested for conspiring towards constitutional monarchy and exiled to Siberia for decades. The estate Kamenka had originally belonged to Potemkin, Catherine the Great's favourite, whose niece married a Davydov.

6. In the Bolshevik period, Madame von Meck's father, out of patriotism, continued to administer railways and so to promote economic advance. His past, under the Tsars, made him (quite without reason) suspect.

7. The Arbat was a very old district of Moscow, which in the sixteenth century was the foreigners' quarter (the name comes from the German *Arbeit*, meaning work). It became a rather fashionable part of town, although with a bohemian fringe; it is nowadays just about the only part of central Moscow which has been preserved and is something of a showcase.

8. Although the von Mecks were related to many of the nobles by marriage – Shirinsky-Shikhmatov, Bennigsen, etc., they never accepted an hereditary title. The Moscow industrialists were often self-consciously progressive in the Edwardian sense. Their money came mainly from textiles.

9. In fact, Madame von Meck means S. I. Shchukin. Shchusev was an architect, of, among many other things, the Kazan Station (1913) in Moscow.

10. *When Miss Emmy Was In Russia*, by Harvey Pitcher (London, 1977).

11. Presnya was a mainly working-class quarter, where the Bolshevik Revolt of 1906 occurred. It was characteristic of Russian cities in this era that class-differentiation of quarters – a product of the modern age of transport – developed a generation later than in the West, so that, apart from the Government area in the centre, rich, middle and poor lived quite close to each other.

12. Pyotr Arkadyevich Stolypin (b. 1860) was President of the Council of Ministers (i.e. Prime Minister) from 1906 to 1911. He had previously been Governor of Saratov, where his repressive measures against rebellious peasants earned him a reputation for strength. However, he was committed to a programme of modernization, where possible, in collaboration with the *Duma*, Russia's first parliamentary body. Agriculture, education, the military and naval machines were all subjected to reforms and Russian industry developed at remarkable speed. Stolypin himself remarked to a French journalist, 'Give the State twenty years of internal and external peace and you will not recognize Russia.' See also Chapter 3, note 3, and Chapter 4, note 3.

3. On the Estate

1. The *sov(yetskoye) khoz(yaystvo)* was an early form of collective farm, based, initially, on principles of co-operation.

2. The *Duma* was Tsarist Russia's Parliament. It was based, after a difficult start, on restricted voting, which was open to 'influence' by the Government. This did not prevent a lively Opposition from developing, but its power was limited. The Fourth *Duma* was elected in 1912 and sat (with interruptions) until March 1917.

3. See Chapter 2, note 12, and Chapter 4, note 3. Stolypin, as the Tsar's 'strong man', made a name for himself as a reforming conservative. The most notable reforms were of agriculture, but local government (*zemstvo* was a county council) was also affected. In the west of the country, where there were heavy concentrations of non-Russian property-owners and Jews, voluntary and elected local councils had not been permitted because they might have led to agitation against the Empire, especially among Poles. To improve the administration of the region, parallel with its considerable economic development, Stolypin proposed to allow local property-owners to have a voice in it, as well as contributing via the rates. This proposal incurred severe Russian-nationalist opposition in the *Duma*, and was eventually carried only with great difficulty and unconstitutional action.

4. The most famous pogrom against the Jews in Tsarist times occurred in 1903 in the town of Kishinev, capital of Bessarabia (a province widely inhabited by Romanians rather than Russians, and where, virtually uniquely in the Tsarist Empire, Jews could own land – see Chapter 7, note 2).

5. See Chapter 5, note 2.

6. Grigory Alexeyevich Alexinsky (b. 1879) was not in fact a Socialist Revolutionary, but originally in the Bolshevik wing of Social Democracy as a member of the *Duma* from 1907. But he broke with Lenin over matters of parliamentary tactics (he was a 'recaller' or *otzovist*) and became a supporter of the First World War. He emigrated in 1918.

The Socialist Revolutionary Party (SRs) was a non-Marxist one, founded clandestinely in 1901. It rejected the discipline upon which Lenin and other Social Democrats insisted, in the Prussian style, and its sympathies lay more with the peasantry than with the proletariat in the factories. However, it failed to agree on a programme or tactics and, although easily the most popular party, its effectiveness was limited. In the Constituent Assembly of January 1918, the outcome of Russia's only free election since the Revolution, the SRs took almost two-thirds of the vote, but their division, and the establishment of 'Left SRs' who sympathized with the Bolsheviks, meant that the Constituent Assembly could be forcibly disbanded by the Bolsheviks after a day and a half, without resistance.

7. See Chapter 18, note 2.

8. Denikin: see Chapter 19, note 6; Kolchak: see Chapter 18, note 1.

9. Pavlo (Pavel) Petrovich Skoropadsky (1873–1945) was a Russian landowner in the Ukraine, and a general of the Tsarist Army. His family had sympathies with the Ukrainian movement earlier on, and when the German occupants needed to have a collaborationist government in the Ukraine they installed Skoropadsky as Governor, or *Hetman* (29 April–14 December 1918). His regime depended on German bayonets, and it collapsed when these were withdrawn after the Armistice of November 1918. Skoropadsky himself emigrated to Germany, and was heavily involved with nationalist politics until his death in 1945. Mikhail Bulgakov's celebrated book *The White Guard* (1924), first published in the Soviet Union in 1986, describes these events.

4. A Russian Moderate

1. The Lycée of Tsarskoye Selo was a college of secondary and higher education which catered for upper-class pupils from the early nineteenth century until 1917.

2. If you had higher education, you were not liable to conscription but you might nevertheless expect to serve as reserve officer. Young men, paying their own way, entered military service as 'one-year volunteers', following a German model, though they might sometimes serve for only a few months. Failure to conscript the educated classes meant a shortage of officers in the First World War.

3. See Chapter 2, note 12, and Chapter 3, note 3. The Stolypin reforms of 1906–11 were designed to create a class of private farmers out of villagers who generally held their land in common. As a result of the reforms, roughly one-quarter of the peasantry acquired individual title to their land-holdings, and approximately half of them sold their land to the other half, who were thereby expected to become independent farmers of the Western European kind. These new farmers might have developed such a stake in property that they would have greatly strengthened the conservative cause; to the Bolsheviks, they were therefore a great menace, and the term *kulak* was applied to them. It was a misnomer: it did not mean 'rich farmer' but 'usurer'. The misnomer has stuck.

4. Alexander Fyodorovich Kerensky (1881–1970) was the chief figure of the pre-Bolshevik Provisional Government of March–November 1917.

5. The Progressive Bloc was a semi-Opposition in the Fourth *Duma* during the First World War, uniting liberals and moderate conservatives.

6. Vasily Vitalyevich Shulgin (1878–1976) was perhaps the strangest survivor of the revolutionary period in the Soviet Union. He was born into a family of Volhynian gentry in Kiev, and became a *Duma* politician of the Right, as 'Nationalist'. This would normally have involved anti-Semitic causes, but Shulgin supported a Jew, Mendel Beylis, who, in 1912–13, was accused on trumped-up charges and imprisoned in Kiev, to great scandal in the West and among liberals (see Chapter 10, note 1). Shulgin, defending him, was himself imprisoned for three months. Later, as *Duma* deputy, he supported the Progressive Bloc (see note 5 above) which challenged the corruption and incompetence of the autocratic Government, and in March 1917 was among the men who persuaded the Tsar

to abdicate. He himself emigrated to Yugoslavia (and wrote a book, *Dni*, in 1920), but returned to the Soviet Union in 1925–6 on a mission that turned out to have been staged by the secret police as a 'provocation'. Shulgin went 'clandestinely' across the border with Poland and met people who were thereby provoked into plotting against the Communists, so that they could be arrested. He himself went back to Yugoslavia and was arrested there in 1944 when the Soviet armed forces entered the country. He was carried back to a camp in the USSR, from which he was released only in 1956. He continued to live in the Soviet Union, however, and died in 1976, in Vladimir.

Mikhail Vladimirovich Rodzyanko (1859–1924), a well-off landowner, became Speaker of the Third and Fourth *Dumy* (1913–17) having been a right-wing liberal deputy. He defended the constitutional role of the *Duma* and therefore clashed with the Tsar. In 1919 he emigrated to Yugoslavia, leaving memoirs (*The Reign of Rasputin*, 1927).

5. Things Fall Apart

1. Pavel Nikolayevich Milyukov (1859–1943) taught history at the University of Moscow but fell foul of the Tsarist Government because of his belief in liberalism. After being exiled to Ryazan, he taught at the Universities of Sofia and Chicago, returning to Russia as one of the leading figures in the Constitutional Democratic (*Cadet*) Party. After the March Revolution he became Foreign Minister, but shortly afterwards was forced to retire because he unguardedly promised the Western Allies that Russia would prosecute the First World War to a victorious conclusion. After a brief flirtation with the Germans in the Ukraine, he emigrated to France, where he wrote several (good) books on the Revolution and edited the leading Russian-language daily newspaper, *Posledniye Novosti*. During the Second World War he supported the cause of the Soviet Union.

2. The famous ballerina Kseshinskaya, reputed to be the Tsar's mistress, had a prominent house, which Lenin took over as headquarters. He addressed crowds from the balcony.

3. Soviets, a form of strike committee, became mass bodies which at various levels represented 'the people' – soldiers, workers, etc. – as against the 'bosses' in the *Duma* Government and civil service. Soviets ('councils') arose spontaneously in the first days of the Revolution, and to begin with the chief one, in Petrograd, which united workers and soldiers, tended to follow the lead of the Provisional Government. However, after July these bodies became more radical, becoming in majority Bolshevik in September. It was with the cry 'All Power to the Soviets' that Lenin led the Revolution of November 1917 against Kerensky's Government. Locally, the smaller Soviets were also radical, often subjecting landlords to harsh measures. The name still figures prominently in the constitutional arrangements of the Soviet Union, though quite soon after the November Revolution Communist control of the Soviets became absolute.

4. See Chapter 4, note 4.

5. General P. A. Polovtsev, *Glory and Downfall*, 1935. Polovtsev was a very rich high aristocrat with a palace in St Petersburg and great estates elsewhere. He was a prominent figure in the last years of the old order.

6. Lenin, with more conviction than other Bolsheviks, pledged to end the war, promising that, if Russian soldiers gave up the massacring, then German ones would do so as well. The policy of virtually every other party, though with reservations, was at least to support national defence; but they disagreed over the shape of the Army and the war-effort, and

by summer 1917 the national breakdown had gone so far that it ruled out an energetic war-effort.

7. Prince Georgy Yevgenievich Lvov (1861–1925), a member of a very old, princely family, was a prominent figure in Russian local government before 1917 and briefly became Prime Minister in the first Provisional Government of March–April 1917.

8. Kronstadt was the naval base protecting St Petersburg, on the Gulf of Finland. Its sailors became one of the best-known revolutionary elements and took a prominent part in the November Uprising. In 1921, they rebelled again – this time against the Bolsheviks, whom they saw as cruel and dictatorial. They were crushed.

9. The *Aurora* (sometimes called *Avrora*) was a cruiser of the Russian Baltic Fleet. It was sailed by Bolshevik sailors along the River Neva to overawe the anti-Bolshevik defence based on the Winter Palace, itself on the Neva. To avoid harming that very historic monument, it was supposed to fire only blank shot, and did so, though in faulty timing as far as the rest of the Uprising was concerned.

6. The Kiev Pogrom

1. The *Gradonachalnik* was a sort of administrator-cum-police chief.

2. The main liberal newspaper of Berlin, known familiarly as *Tante Voss* ('Auntie Vossie').

3. The Karaites were a non-Semitic Jewish sect.

7. The Coming of Chaos

1. At that time the name de Gunzburg was normally spelt 'von Ginzburg'.

2. The Bessarabian anomaly occurred because that province had been attached to the Romanian principality of Moldavia (with which most of its people shared their language) while Moldavia was theoretically subject to the Ottoman Sultan. In 1878, with the Treaty of Berlin, Bessarabia was returned to Russia as a reward for her part in the liberation of Balkan states. However, as a precondition for recognition of the independence of Romania, the European powers tried to limit the anti-Semitism which they feared might result; therefore the right of Jews to own land in the Romanian territories was guaranteed by the great powers, including Russia, and had to be maintained in Bessarabia. Curiously enough, the Romanian Government got round this by a law in 1903 which forbade foreigners to own land, but Jewish estate-owners nevertheless continued in Bessarabia. In any case, since Jews could lease land the formal prohibition was often ineffective and in some areas – as happened with Trotsky's father – it was just ignored.

3. Father Gapon was an Orthodox priest who in the West would have been called a Christian Socialist. He was popular with the working classes of St Petersburg, but at the same time led them away from the socialists; in this capacity he operated with elements within the police, who tried to oppose the socialists by establishing trade unions controlled by enlightened policemen, particularly one Zubatov. In January 1905 Father Gapon led a great crowd of workmen and their families towards the Winter Palace to petition the Tsar for better economic and political conditions. The local military responded cruelly and stupidly, causing hundreds of casualties on 'Bloody Sunday', 9 January 1905. Gapon fled to France, where he died in unknown circumstances.

8. Terror Comes to Smela

1. Maurice Baring (1874–1945), English man of letters, wrote extensively about Russia (cf. Arthur Ransome). His autobiography, *The Puppet Show of Memory*, was published in 1922.

9. Prisoner of the Tsar

1. The People's Will (*Narodnaya Volya*) was a revolutionary political movement founded in 1880 and pledged to assassinate the Tsar and his officials. It claimed the life of Alexander II in 1881, but was soon put down.

Khalturin was a joiner who organized the explosion at the Winter Palace in St Petersburg in 1880 and then shot the Military Prosecutor, Strelnikov. He was hanged.

10. In the Shtetl

1. Mendel Beylis, a Jewish bookseller, was charged in Kiev in 1913 with the ritual murder of a Christian child. There was no foundation for the accusation, which was fabricated, in part by the police, in order to provide a pretext for anti-Semitic activity. Beylis was eventually acquitted, after worldwide outcry, but the trial was dragged out – to the Government's great discredit, even in conservative political groups attached to the *Duma*.

2. V. I. Purishkevich (1870–1920) was a right-wing member of the *Duma* and a prominent nationalist politician, given to outbursts of anti-Semitism. However, he was not a rabble-rouser, and he disapproved of the Tsar's rule during the First World War – in particular of his association with Rasputin, the *starets*, or 'holy man', who achieved spiritual ascendancy over the Tsar and Tsaritsa. Purishkevich was involved, with Prince Yusupov, in the successful plot to assassinate Rasputin in January 1917.

3. The (Jewish) Pale of Settlement was the area designed by Catherine the Great when she took over large tracts of Polish–Lithuanian territory in the Partitions of 1772, 1792 and 1795. Medieval Poland (to which Lithuania was attached) contained a great number of Jews, and under Russian rule they were compelled to live in a precise area (a large one, however) of western Russia, the Ukraine, Lithuania, etc. They were forbidden to reside elsewhere, particularly in the cities, and their expulsion from Moscow was decreed as late as 1892. There were various ways of circumventing the prohibition – conversion to Orthodoxy, bribery of the police, or imaginative use of a trading permit; a Jewess might reside in St Petersburg, for instance, and study there provided that she registered as a prostitute; the families of musically gifted children studying at the Conservatoire might also live in Moscow or St Petersburg.

4. Prince Peter Kropotkin (1842–1921) from an old, noble family, became a revolutionary and an anarchist of generous and voluble disposition. After spending some time in prison, he lived in exile, returning only after the Revolution, of which he did not greatly approve.

5. *Russkoe Slovo* was a well-known nationalist anti-Semitic newspaper.

11. 'Long Live the Provisional Government!'

1. The Russian Empire did not modernize the early medieval Julian calendar which continental Europe altered with the sixteenth-century Gregorian calendar, more accurately taking account of the fraction of the day which the earlier calendar had omitted. The British themselves went on with the old calendar until the mid-eighteenth century. The Russians took a characteristic view that anything existing was a manifestation of Heaven and not to be altered on pain of sacrilege, even when the accumulation of fraction-days meant that it was nearly a fortnight out. It was altered only when the Bolsheviks came to power, when, similarly, redundant letters were dropped from the alphabet and ancient weights and measures were altered to the metric system.

2. Nikolai Semyonovich Chkheidze (1864–1956) was a leader of the Menshevik wing of the Russian Social Democratic Workers' Party in the Third and Fourth *Dumy*. He became Chairman of the Petrograd Soviet upon the Revolution of March 1917 but went to Georgia – then independent – in 1918 and emigrated in 1921, when her independence was suppressed. He died by suicide.

3. Rodzyanko: see Chapter 4, note 6.

4. Alexander Ivanovich Guchkov was a rich Moscow industrialist who emerged in the *Duma* as leader of the Octobrist, or conservative, Party. In 1917 he briefly became War Minister, subsequently emigrating to Paris, where he eventually supported the Nazi invasion of Russia. He died in 1943. His daughter, Vera Trapp, married an Englishman and lived to a great age in Cambridge, having been involved with the anarchist movement.

5. Shulgin: see Chapter 4, note 6.

6. Maxim Litvinov lived for years in exile in London, marrying an Englishwoman, Ivy Lowe (who wrote her memoirs: *Ivy*), and was used to represent the Bolsheviks in London. He became Stalin's Foreign Minister until May 1939, and was then Ambassador to the USA. His grandson, Pavel, became one of the main dissidents in the 1960s and 1970s, and now lives in exile.

Georgy Vasilievich Chicherin, of an aristocratic family, was archivist in the Imperial Foreign Ministry, but was also a Bolshevik. He became Commissar for Foreign Affairs, being particularly useful in the early stages of *rapprochement* with the West, especially Germany. He retired to Berlin to be looked after by doctors there: he was a neurotic homosexual, and a brilliant pianist with an encyclopaedic knowledge of Mozart's music.

7. This was the so-called 'Kerensky Offensive', designed to show that the Army still had heart. It was prepared, at least from the viewpoint of morale, by Kerensky's own remarkable oratory at the front (see p. 37), but after some success against demoralized troops in the Austro-Hungarian sector, it broke down.

12. Crossing the Frontier

1. '*Duma*' roubles co-existed with all kinds of currency. By late summer 1917 notes were not provided with numbers because the printing presses were too busy churning out money; you had to ink in your own.

14. A Sudden Flight

1. The Decembrists were so called because of their brief uprising on Senate Square in St Petersburg in December 1825, when they attempted to prevent the accession of the reactionary Tsar Nicholas I by promoting the cause of his brother, Konstantin, Viceroy

of Poland. They were a group of officers generally of good lineage who had absorbed doctrines of European liberalism, partly when the Russian Army crossed Europe in 1813–15. Their leader, Colonel Pestel, set up a conspiracy within the Army, which, after years of talk, finally led to the mutiny of December 1825. It collapsed and leading Decembrists were in a few cases executed, but in most others exiled to Siberia, where many of them – and particularly their wives – behaved heroically. They were finally amnestied only in 1858, after the accession of Nicholas I's son Alexander II.

15. Exiles in Finland

1. The Finnish Civil War broke out soon after the Bolshevik Revolution. Nationalists, led by Baron Mannerheim, sought to establish an independent state, and used German protection: a German prince (of Hessen-Darmstadt) was proposed as Grand Duke and a German force landed, under Generals von der Goltz and Wolff. After severe fighting in 1918, the Reds, who wished to have Finland attached to Bolshevik Russia, were defeated.

16. Through Latvian Eyes

1. In Latvia, as in the other Baltic provinces (Estonia, Kurland, Livland, Samogitia or Samland, etc.) there was a caste of German landowners, 'the Baltic Barons', often related to the Prussian *Junkers*. They were strongly conservative, supplying far more than their due share of Tsarist functionaries; when the Army went to war in 1914, half of its commanders had German names. The Baltic Barons descended, often enough, from knights of the Teutonic Order, the best-known names ('the Four of the Fist') being Keyserling, Manteuffel, Ungern-Sternberg and Üxküll-Gyllenband. In 1918, most of this class welcomed the German Army and many looked forward to annexation by Prussia, a step that was under consideration until November 1918.

2. See Chapter 5, note 9.

3. Alexander II in 1881.

17. Escape Through Poland

1. Poland was re-established as an independent state in November 1918 (although the Central Powers promised to restore a much smaller kingdom two years before). The Polish forces tried to recover the western Ukraine, which had once belonged to Poland, including the capital, Kiev. They were forced to evacuate it in May 1920, and an onslaught by the Red Army followed, leading to the Battle of Warsaw in August 1920, where Polish forces won.

2. Simon Petlyura was a Ukrainian nationalist leader who managed briefly to assert his authority over the Ukraine between the German evacuation in November 1918 and the Bolsheviks' return in July. His relations with potential allies, such as the Russian Whites and the Poles, were tense, but belated recognition of his regime was given by the Poles (until 1921). Petlyura (b. 1879) was murdered in Paris in 1926 by a Jew seeking revenge for the anti-Semitic activity which was promoted by some of the Ukrainian nationalists.

18. Destination America . . .

1. Admiral Alexander Vasilievich Kolchak (b. 1874) led the White forces in Siberia, with British protection and the help of a Czechoslovak legion. In summer 1918 he reached the Urals, almost in time to save the Tsar and his family from being murdered (at Ekaterinburg on 18 July), but his force disintegrated through pestilence and desertion. In 1920 Kolchak was shot at Irkutsk.

2. After a successful career on the Turkish front during the First World War, Nikolai Nikolaevich Yudenich (1862–1933) became commander of a White force in the Civil War – the North-Western Army, which was based in Estonia and which almost succeeded in capturing Petrograd from the Reds, who, however, managed to beat back Yudenich's forces in autumn 1919.

19. In the Crimea

1. See Chapter 21.

2. Nestor Ivanovich Makhno was a famous anarchist – or bandit – leader during the Civil War. He fought indiscriminately against Whites and Reds, eventually fleeing into Romania, and dying in Paris in 1935. See also Chapter 22.

3. Latvian soldiery ('Riflemen') had had a disproportionate role in the Bolshevik Revolution.

4. A radical liberal party, led, in the main, by the professional classes, and known as 'Cadets'. They were important in the *Duma* before 1917, but were badly weakened by the two Revolutions of 1917.

5. Time tended to change with regime. There was Moscow time; but there was also Constantinople time (for the foreign intervention troops) and local time.

6. Admiral Kolchak: see Chapter 18, note 1. In southern Russia, however, the White leader was General Anton Ivanovich Denikin (1872–1947), replaced, after defeats in the latter months of 1919, by Baron Pyotr Nikolayevich Wrangel (1878–1928), who was supported mainly by the French.

7. Under Bolshevik rule, elections were held for this body, but Bolsheviks were in a minority (of roughly one-third) and it was speedily closed down.

8. See Chapter 12, note 1.

9. Turkey was then under Allied occupation, having lost her Empire in 1918.

20. The War in the Caucasus

1. The Counts Vorontsov-Dashkov were a family distinguished since the eighteenth century. Woronzow Road, in London NW8, is named after one ancestor who promoted Anglo-Russian alliance in the Napoleonic Wars. The Vorontsov-Dashkov mentioned here was Viceroy of the Caucasus in the reign of Nicholas II. He was known for discrimination against the Armenians.

2. See Chapter 19, note 6.

3. After the Revolution of March 1917, there was great ferment among the peoples of the Caucasus: Georgia, Armenia and Azerbaydzhan achieved independence, although the boundaries were a subject of dispute (and in 1918, when there was a German presence, of open fighting between Germans and their Turkish allies). There were innumerable complications, since the area contained several widely different nationalities, some

Muslim (the Ossetes and Chechens) and others Christian, though belonging to different rites.

21. The Departure of an Empress

1. General Lavrentia Georgievich Kornilov (1870–1918), the Commander-in-Chief, attempted to set up a military dictatorship, and to suppress the extreme Left, in September 1917 (late August, by the old-style calendar). He marched troops on St Petersburg, but they disintegrated and he was imprisoned (though later released).

2. The Kaiser did send a war hero, the one-armed Count Stolzenberg, to offer sanctuary to the Dowager Empress. He was told to go away: she would have nothing to do with Germans, whom she thought responsible for the Revolution.

22. An Unexpected Rescue

1. Makhno: see Chapter 19, note 2.
2. Petlyura: see Chapter 17, note 2.

24. The Russian Church Abroad

1. Vyacheslav Mikhailovich Molotov (1890–1987) was Stalin's Foreign Minister (retired by Khrushchev in 1957). His real name was Skryabin.

2. A Russian Orthodox youth movement similar to scouts.

3. NTS and *Mladorossi* were émigré political movements.

4. There are two separate Russian Orthodox Churches – one (Metropolitan Bloom's own) being 'Patriarchal' in that it accepts the authority of the Patriarch in Moscow, whereas the other, seeing the Moscow Patriarch as a collaborator, owes allegiance to the Patriarch of Constantinople. The latter owns the best-known Russian church-in-exile, the Cathédrale Alexandre Nevsky on the rue Daru, Paris XVII.

5. In the Orthodox Church, Exarch is a bishop ranking between Metropolitan and Patriarch.

6. Nadezhda Yakovlevna Mandelstam (1899–1980; née Khazina) was the wife of the poet Osip Emilievich Mandelstam (1891–1938), who spent much of his life in exile and eventually died in a labour camp. His wife memorized nearly all his poetry, keeping it in her head for almost thirty years until it could be published during the Khrushchev thaw. She wrote two volumes of autobiography: *Hope Against Hope* (1970) and *Hope Abandoned* (1972).

25. From the New World

1. General Lucius DuBignon Clay (1897–1978) was Commander of US forces in Europe and Military Governor of the US zone in Germany, 1947–9. He successfully organized the Berlin Airlift.

26. A Refuge in Manchuria

1. See Chapter 18, note 1.

28. Disaster in Harbin

1. Various currencies still co-existed – some valueless – and there was a vast inflation, which ended only in 1922.

2. See Chapter 27, pp. 217–18.

29. Turning-Points

1. The Russian legal system before 1905 depended to a very large extent on custom, there being little defined property law, etc., while many legal institutions were created only after the wide-ranging legal reforms introduced by Tsar Alexander II in 1864.

2. Mussolini was overthrown on 15 July 1943, and the successor-regime, Marshal Badoglio's, set about switching sides. Relations between Italian and German troops in the Balkans then became very bad (the Austrian President Waldheim's own military career containing episodes in this respect which have been held against him) and there were large-scale shootings and deportations of Italians by Germans. Some Italians, however, continued to collaborate with the Germans, who restored Mussolini to a sort of shadowy power in the 'Italian Social Republic' in north Italy; its base was at Salò, on Lake Garda.

3. Austria, whose restoration was promised by the Allies in 1943, was none the less divided into zones of occupation, of which the Soviet one extended to Linz in the west and just north of (British) Graz in the south. Vienna was subject to four-power control.

4. See Michael Scammell, *Solzhenitsyn* (1982).

5. Money earned by Solzhenitsyn's books was put into a fund to help the families of political prisoners. Alexander Ginzburg administered the fund in the USSR.

30. With the Russian Corps

1. The Drozdovsky, Kornilovsky, Markovsky Regiments (and others) in the Civil War were named after their commanders, many of whom had commanded far larger units in the First World War. The regiments themselves were composed, early on, of officers only.

2. The Russian Corps was established in Yugoslavia under German occupation. It fought the Communist partisans.

3. The *Ustaša* was the Croat Fascist movement, responsible for terrorist activity before and during the Second World War, when its leader, Ante Pavelić, was leader of an independent Croat state allied with Germany.

4. Andrey Vlasov was a general in the Soviet Army, captured by the Germans after being surrounded in April 1942. With great reluctance and clumsiness on the German side, he was eventually allowed to recruit POWs (and some émigrés) in his Russian Liberation Army but it became involved in serious fighting only towards the end of the war and ended up in Prague, fighting side by side with the Czech Resistance. Vlasov's hope was that there might be a Pan-Slav movement of liberation, independent of Stalin and Hitler. He and his chief lieutenants were taken back to the Soviet Union and hanged.

5. The Četnik forces were anti-Communist and also anti-Fascist/Nazi in Yugoslavia. Their leader, Draža Mihailović, was a royalist patriot, and the forces were mainly recruited in Serbia. He was dropped by the British in favour of Tito's Communists, and Mihailović was eventually tracked down and executed.

6. Claus Schenk von Stauffenberg was a chief German liaison officer with the anti-

Communist Russian forces. He staged the bomb plot against Hitler of 20 July 1944, committing suicide after its failure.

7. In May 1945 the British occupying forces handed over to the Red Army some fifty thousand Soviet citizens (and, by mistake, several dozen non-Soviet citizens of Russian origin) whom they found fighting on the German side. This episode has been extensively studied – e.g. Nicholas Bethell, *The Last Secret* (1973), Nikolay Tolstoy, *Victims of Yalta* (London, 1977) and *The Minister and the Massacres* (1986), and Mark Elliott, *Pawns of Yalta* (Urbana, Il., 1982). But by agreement with Tito, the British also refused to accept the surrender of hundreds of thousands of Yugoslavs, of several political affiliations (including liberal, social democrat, etc.), who were butchered after their return to Yugoslavia.

8. See Chapter 49, note 3.

31. 'Your Motherland Awaits You'

1. See Chapter 30, note 4.

32. Masaryk's Guests

1. The German University in Prague emerged from the medieval Charles University as a foundation separate from the Czech University in 1882 when division on linguistic lines was imposed, partly for reasons of practicality in teaching language, and partly because of tension between Czechs and Germans. The German University, which took its students to a large extent from the Prague Jewish community (though it also took in Czechs who saw attendance at a German-language university as a step forward: they made up one-third of its attendance), was a distinguished institution.

2. Christian Freiherr von Ehrenfels (1859–1932) was a philosopher interested in psychology, who taught at Prague in 1900–29. He also wrote on Wagner, and much else. Oskar Krauss (1872–1942) was a philosopher of Value, associated with the Austrian School of economists.

3. Thomas Garrigue Masaryk (1850–1937), Czech statesman and independence leader. He was the first President of Czechoslovakia (1918–35).

34. A Russian Life Abroad

1. *Tumba*: the circular advertisement hoarding of many continental European cities.

36. The Russian Dustmen of Cannes

1. Prittwitz, though a German name, figured in Russian history through the Baltic-German involvement with Tsarist service. A German Prittwitz served, briefly, as Commander of the 8th Army in East Prussia in 1914, before being replaced by the team of Hindenburg and Ludendorff.

2. Rex Ingram (1892–1950), Irish film director.

3. The Russian original is: '*Amursky Kazak razvodit kur*', *kur(a)* being hen, hence *poule* in French, which also means a superior form of whore, and *razvodit* being either to rear or to divorce.

37. A Second Flight

1. General Nikolay Nikolayevich Golovin was the main historian of the Russian emigration. He had been a Tsarist general, and emigrated via southern Russia to Prague and Paris, where he wrote extensively for the Carnegie series on the First World War. He ended up as a supporter of the Nazi invasion.

2. General Ye. K. Miller (1867–1937?) was prominent in the military side of the Russian emigration in Paris. He was kidnapped in 1937, presumably by the Soviet NKVD, and never seen again. In 1919, he had been Commander-in-Chief of the White Army in northern Russia, and before that Chief of Staff, 5th Army.

3. Vichy legislation provided for the deportation to Auschwitz, etc., of foreign-born, though not French-born, Jews.

38. Surviving

1. André Citroën (1878–1935) was a French industrialist, imitating American methods for the mass-production of motor cars, and responsible for the extraordinary growth of French tank-production in the First World War.

2. Paul Doumer, thirteenth President of the Third Republic (1931–2) was assassinated by a Russian anarchist, Pavel Gorgulov.

3. In 1936 the French left-wing Popular Front Government introduced paid holidays into France, several years after similar reforms elsewhere. In many business circles this and similar changes were held responsible for the deepening of the Depression in France, since costs were raised.

4. The Franco-German armistice of June 1940, and subsequent arrangements, laid down the main lines for the German Occupation and exploitation of defeated France. Marshal Pétain, the French Head of State, drastically revised the constitution, acquired semi-autocratic authority, and met Hitler at Montoire in October. Foreign-born Jews were deported.

5. See Chapter 24.

39. 'Ces Sales Russes'

1. See Chapter 5, note 8.

2. The wife of the founder of Shell Oil, later amalgamated with Royal Dutch.

3. 'Teffi' (Nadezhda Buchinskaya, 1872–1952) was a writer and poetess, known before 1914 in St Petersburg, where she worked with the poetess Zinaida Gippius, and equally well known in emigration in Paris.

40. Exiles in America

1. Vladimir Nabokov (1899–1977) came from a prominent professional (legal) family in St Petersburg and emigrated in 1919, first to Berlin (until 1937) and then to Paris and the United States. His early work was in Russian, but he is best known as a writer in English.

2. See Chapter 4, note 1.

3. See Chapter 5, p. 62.

4. Georgy Dmitrievich Adamovich (1884–1972) left Russia in 1922 to settle in France

as a journalist (on the newspaper *Posledniye Novosti*, 1928–39) and as an influential critic. He was also a poet, associated with 'the Paris Note' in émigré literature.

41. 'Here Is Imperial Russia . . .'

1. Sir Peter Bark was a banker, who became Minister of Finance 1914–16, and was much trusted by the British, with whom he negotiated wartime loans.

2. Admiral Volkov and his daughter were involved in a case of clumsy spying for the Germans in 1940.

3. Mr and Mrs Kirill Fitzlyon, who have done a great deal for the Russian émigrés in London, changed their name from Zinoviev. There is a hostel for émigrés in Chiswick, west London.

42. Getting By in England

1. Vickers-Armstrong was the greatest British armaments firm (and had much business with Russia during the First World War).

2. See Chapter 24.

44. Pride Among the Packing Cases

1. The Tsar and his family were murdered at Ekaterinburg (now Sverdlovsk) in the Urals on 18 July 1918. There were persistent rumours that not all the family had been killed. There was 'Anastasia', who claimed to be a surviving Grand Duchess; while A. Summers and T. Mangold, *The File on the Tsar*, have collected stories, some of them plausible, about the family's real fate.

2. See Chapter 41, p. 296.

3. See Chapter 41, pp. 290 and 297.

45. Living with the English

1. See Chapter 11, note 6.

2. See Chapter 48, note 3.

3. Dr Lunts's hospital was used during the 1970s as a centre for 'brain-washing' dissidents by the unethical use of psychotropic drugs.

4. See Chapter 51. The letter was written by Valery Fefyolov.

46. The Peasant's Tale

1. See Chapter 50, note 2.

48. Following Alien Paths

1. See Chapter 10, note 1.

2. See Chapter 10, note 3.

3. *Poale Zion* was one (a large one) of a great number of specifically Jewish political parties that emerged around 1900. The *Bund* was socialist, but not Zionist: in fact, rather

anti-Zionist. Zionists were not very socialist: *Poale Zion*, with links all over the Jewish regions of the former Pale of Settlement, marked an effort to link Zionism and socialism.
4. See Chapter 17, note 2.

49. Polish Affairs

1. Wanda Wasilewska (1905–64) was the daughter of a prominent Polish socialist, and was herself a writer, based mainly in Lvov, in south-eastern Poland. In 1939 she became associated with the Soviet Communist Party and married a Ukrainian writer (Alexander Korneichuk). She is chiefly known as go-between with the Polish Communists, since Stalin, mysteriously, trusted her as he trusted very few other people. The result was that the Polish Communist Party was reconstituted and given a vital role in the Soviet take-over in 1944–8. After 1956 she herself became a member of the World Council for Peace, a front organization.

2. General Wladislaw Sikorski (1881–1943) had been a liberal-minded associate of the Polish military semi-dictator Marshal Pilsudski. He broke with Pilsudski's non-liberal successors and emigrated; but in 1939, in the country's crisis, he became head of the Polish Government-in-Exile (in London) and was both liked and admired by many Western leaders. Stalin signed a treaty with him in 1941. His death, in an aircraft accident in 1943 in Gibraltar, deprived Poland of her most influential statesman.

3. The Polish General Anders, captured by the Red Army in 1939, was released in 1941 following the German attack on the USSR, and allowed to form an army of Poles, recruited from among prisoners-of-war and others in Soviet hands. Relations between Poles and Soviets nevertheless proved to be very poor: the Soviet Government refused to arm Anders' Polish Army Corps and Anders refused to fight in the Soviet Army on the Russian front. He evacuated his men (about two hundred thousand, with wives and children in many cases) through Persia to Palestine, North Africa, Italy and France, where they fought for the Allied cause in the great campaigns.

50. Hunger

1. Petlyura: see Chapter 17, note 2; Makhno: see Chapter 19, note 2.

2. The collectivization of agriculture was proclaimed in November 1929 and carried out, with stops and starts, by 1933. Land of private farmers and village co-operatives was expropriated, the owners being turned into hired labourers. Many resisted this 'socialist offensive' and there were millions of deportations and deaths. Animals were then slaugh-tered, since there was no fodder for them, and this caused further decline, for want of natural manure, in the harvest. Meanwhile, the authorities requisitioned grain for export. In 1933 came a great famine, in which at least ten million people, including a great many children, starved to death – particularly, though not entirely, in the Ukraine. Soviet agriculture has never really recovered from the demoralization that ensued.

3. *Torgsin* shops were set up in the 1930s to exact foreign currency for goods otherwise unobtainable in the USSR, such as French cheese, brandy, etc. The word is an abbrevi-ation of 'Trade with Foreigners' (*Torgovlya s inostrantsmi*). The practice continues in today's USSR with more prettily named counterparts – *Beryozka* (birch tree) in Russia and *Kashtan* (chestnut tree) in the Ukraine: see Chapter 58, note 2.

51. A Nuisance to the State

1. In the years 1934–9, the 'Great Terror' descended upon the land, with imprisonments and deaths that amount, by recent Soviet estimates, to twenty-five million. For years these atrocities were either denied or minimized, in the USSR and by Western apologists. An attempt, now widely seen as entertaining, in a grim way, was made by J. Arch Getty (*The Origins of the Great Purge*, Cambridge University Press, 1986) to explain this business as a rational, indeed popularly demanded, method of making Party rule more efficient. Details that emerge, however, show that the version of Robert Conquest, *The Great Terror* (1968) is much to be preferred.

52. Escaping the System

1. The Baltic Fleet was also subjected to a Purge, which carried off many officers. One admiral confessed, bizarrely, to throwing rocks into the harbour at the base of Kronstadt, in the hope that the water-level would rise and thereby beach his battleships.

2. *Novy Mir* literary magazine, which in the later 1950s and 1960s was known for its outspokenness. Its editor, Alexander Tvardovsky, courageously published Solzhenitsyn.

54. Suffocation

1. Sinyavsky: see Chapter 55, note 3. Vladimir Yakovlevich Lakshin (b. 1931), distinguished Soviet literary critic, formerly chief critic of *Novy Mir* under the liberal editorship of Alexander Tvardovsky. In 1986 Lakshin became deputy editor of the literary journal *Znamya*.

55. Writers on Trial

1. In the Revolutionary period, 'revolutionary' first names, to replace saints, were common. There are currently at Oxford two Bulgarian *au pairs* named Pravda and Izvestiya. Parallel developments can be found in the French Revolution and the English Civil War, when Old Testament references were introduced.

2. Kornei Ivanovich Chukovsky (1882–1969), writer, children's poet, literary scholar and editor.

3. The writers Yury Daniel (pseudonym: Nikolay Arzhak) and Andrey Sinyavsky (pseudonym: Abram Terts) were put on trial, to condemnation throughout the world, for 'anti-Soviet activities' – i.e. publishing abroad. They were sentenced to five and seven years respectively. Sinyavsky emigrated to France in 1973; Daniel remained in the USSR.

56. An Island in the Past

1. See Chapter 55, note 3.

57. No Free World

1. Sinyavsky: see Chapter 55, note 3. Vladimir Maximov, a writer of Dostoyevskian tendency.

2. Konstantin Leontiev (1831–91) was a famous anti-liberal and religious philosopher, with early training as an archaeologist.

58. Censored

1. Trofim Lysenko (1898–1976), the Russian biologist, maintained that environmental experiences can change heredity. After Stalin's death his theories were widely criticized.

2. *Beryozka* shops (the name means birch tree) in Russia, like *Kashtan* (chestnut tree) shops in the Ukraine, exist to sell Western goods for hard currency, the goods not being available in ordinary Soviet shops. Soviet citizens are normally prevented from entering these establishments, just as they are prevented from entering many hotels used by foreigners. See also Chapter 50, note 3.

59. Speaking the Truth

1. A *sharashka* is a top-secret research and development institution, worked by high-level political prisoners. See Alexander Solzhenitsyn's *The First Circle*.

60. A Gold Medal Student

1. The notorious Doctors' Plot of 1949 was part of Stalin's campaign to discredit Soviet Jews. A number of leading Jewish doctors were imprisoned and tried on trumped-up charges of having poisoned Soviet leaders while treating them. The affair was the climax of the Government-inspired anti-Semitic campaign which aimed to deport *all* Soviet Jews to the Far East. It was mercifully terminated by Stalin's death in March 1953.

61. Revaluations

1. Nikolai Ivanovich Bukharin (1888–1938), a leading Bolshevik and friend of Lenin. In 1924 he became a member of the Politburo. He opposed collectivization and became one of Stalin's chief victims in the Purges of the 1930s. He was convicted of treason and shot.

2. At the Twentieth Party Congress of 1956, Khrushchev denounced Stalin, beginning a 'thaw' in foreign affairs as well as a considerable improvement in conditions inside the Soviet Union.

3. Imre Nagy (1896–1958), Hungarian Prime Minister and one of the leaders of the anti-Soviet Uprising of 1956. He was imprisoned and shot, on orders from Moscow. He and his fellow insurgents were officially pardoned and re-interred with honour in 1989.

4. See Chapter 29, note 5.

Index